TECHNICAL ANALYSIS
AND
STOCK MARKET
PROFITS

Every owner of a physical copy of this edition of

TECHNICAL ANALYSIS AND STOCK MARKET PROFITS

can download the eBook for free direct from us at Harriman House, in a DRM-free format that can be read on any eReader, tablet or smartphone. Simply head to:

ebooks.harriman-house.com/technicalanalysisdefinitive

to get your copy now.

TECHNICAL ANALYSIS

AND

STOCK MARKET

PROFITS

The original bible of technical analysis

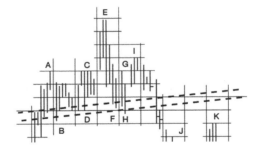

RICHARD W. SCHABACKER

FOREWORD BY **PETER L. BRANDT**

Author of *Diary of a Professional Commodity Trader*

HARRIMAN
DEFINITIVE EDITION

HARRIMAN HOUSE LTD
3 Viceroy Court
Bedford Road
Petersfield
Hampshire
GU32 3LJ
GREAT BRITAIN
Tel: +44 (0)1730 233870

Email: enquiries@harriman-house.com
Website: harriman.house

First published in the United States in 1932 and in Great Britain in 1997. First published by Harriman House in 2005. This new edition published in 2021.

Hardcover ISBN: 978-0-85719-916-4
eBook ISBN: 978-0-85719-917-1

British Library Cataloguing in Publication Data
A CIP catalogue record for this book can be obtained from the British Library.

ABOUT THE AUTHOR

Richard W. Schabacker

Richard W. Schabacker achieved his financial fame in the 1920s and 1930s first as Financial Editor of *Forbes* and later as editor of the *Annalist*, a weekend section of the *New York Times*. During this time he also authored three books: *Stock Market Theory and Practice*, 1930; *Technical Analysis and Stock Market Profits*, 1932; and *Stock Market Profits*, 1934.

ABOUT THE SERIES EDITOR

Donald Mack

If any phrase describes the editor of the Traders' Masterclass series, which is dedicated solely to bringing back to traders and investors everywhere many of the great and rare Technical Analysis classics from the past, that phrase would be "a perpetual student of the market". Students in high school or college eventually graduate. Not so students of speculative markets. The study and the work is never finished, especially when there is an enduring interest in Technical Analysis. The editor's interest grew by leaps and bounds when in the late 1970s and the 1980s he established in Los Angeles the only bookstore in the USA that dealt exclusively in stock and commodity books; those that were in print at the time and those that were out of print. Current books were generally unchallenging and of various degrees of quality. Many out-of-print books were also of varying degrees of quality, but so many fascinating rare works from the 1920s to the 1950s, of great creativity and marvelous technical analytics and application came his way, that a life long appreciation of their quality grew.

Almost needless to say, more attention was focused on the old books than on the new, for he found those old books that made up the great classics were superior to the new in so many ways. While operating the bookstore, there was a natural inflow and outflow of many thousands of books and from those thousands of books a personal library and collection numbering a good 5,500 plus individual titles was put together. A little of the knowledge contained in these great market classics rubbed off on the editor (actually more than a little) and he trusts that it will also rub off on the many market students of today and tomorrow as they also come in contact with the superb Technical Analysis classics that will come their way through this Series.

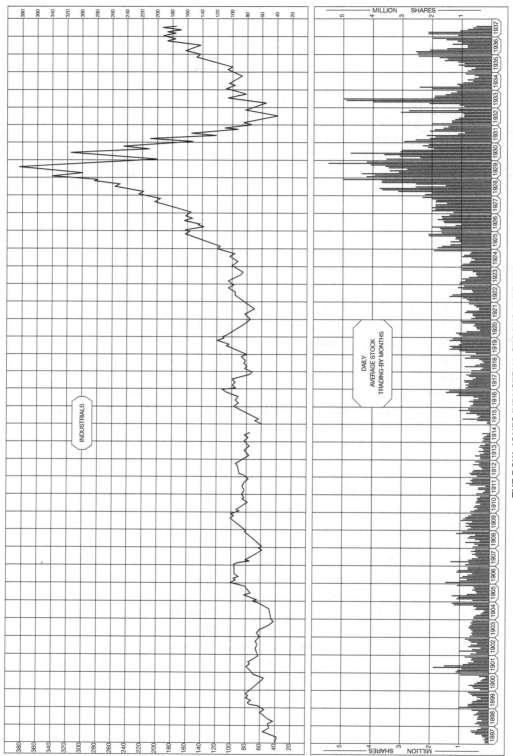

THE DOW-JONES INDUSTRIAL STOCKS AVERAGE

Monthly High and Low of Closing Prices -- 1897 Through August, 1937.

TABLE OF CONTENTS

Volume as an Indication of Continuation · Relation of Volume to Price Movement · Relation of Volume Action to Basic Trends

THE DOW THEORY: Its Major Tenets · Limitations of Dow Theory in Practical Trading

Editor's note

Because of the poor quality reproduction of the original charts it was found necessary to re-draw each one. The vertical price bars on each chart were faithfully reproduced as closely as possible to the original bars, in terms of size and date. The horizontal bars (the Closing Price bars) proved troublesome and the decision was made to insert them only when the author made specific reference to their position. With there being no other references in the text concerning the other horizontal bars on the charts, the closing price indications were superfluous and could be, and were, safely omitted.

EDITOR'S INTRODUCTION

"Part One is based in large part on the pioneer researches and writings of the late Richard W. Schabacker. Students of his *Technical Analysis and Stock Market Profits* (the latest revision of which – now out of print – was made in 1937 by the present writer and Albert L. Kimball) will find in the pages of this section much that is familiar and except for the illustrations, only a little that is really novel"

From the Foreword to *Technical Analysis of Stock Trends*
by Robert D. Edwards and John Magee, 1948

To American technical analysts past, present, and future, the year 1948 stands out as one of the brightest of beacons, bringing the solid foundations of modern Technical Analysis. For it was this year that saw the publication of *Technical Analysis of Stock Trends*, written by Messrs Edwards and Magee, which was the pivotal work in launching Technical Analysis at a time that was to prove ready for it. Without a doubt a great debt of gratitude has to be bestowed on the two authors and their timely book which has sold some 800,000 plus copies and in later years has earned for itself the accolade of "the bible of Technical Analysis." A check with most dedicated technical analysts who have learned their craft since 1948 would confirm their personal debt to this work, which was responsible for introducing them to Technical Analysis or expanding their technical education.

But how did all of this come about? Technical Analysis certainly did not have a long history of acceptance in the 1940s and before by the established investment fraternity in New York, London, Paris and elsewhere. Without a doubt it was easier to keep to long held beliefs that this form of analysis, utilizing charts of share price action, was more akin to mumbo-jumbo than to the accepted seemingly logical approach built around the respectable tools of Fundamental Analysis. To value a company it was enough to analyze its accounts, work out its p/e ratio, be aware of its research developments, weigh up its reported sales figures, estimate future prospects, etc., thus arriving at a basis to value the company in terms of its share price. Comparing that with the technical analyst's toolbox containing charts, horizontal, vertical, angular and squiggly lines, fanciful looking patterns, pictured formations, plus indicators, oscillators and the like, logical investment thinking easily came to the conclusion that Technical Analysis was a pseudo-scientific approach that basically relied on price, time, and volume numbers, and paid little or no attention to the company itself. In comparison, accepted serious investment analysis concentrated on the company's important fundamentals, for it was considered that in these lay the only real basis for valuing a company's share price in the trading markets, which to fundamental analysts is what investing is about.

Looking back now, it is easy to see that the post-World War II period investment scene was ripe for new thinking not contrary to, but in addition to, the established fundamental approach that relied heavily on the work that flowed out of the large brokerage firms' research departments to their customers. Filling that vacuum knowingly or unknowingly, Messrs Edwards and Magee produced their timely and technically definitive book which not only gave organized form and shape to the field of Technical Analysis, but also gave rise to new analytical thought that the post-war age could substantially make use of as an efficient methodology for investment timing and selection. In the years prior to the publication of their influential *Technical Analysis of Stock Trends*, it should not go unnoticed, however, that many books were published that can certainly be described as outstanding technical works encompassing many phases of this analytical technology and thinking. A good number of these books and courses were as original and as technically advanced as anything on the subject of Technical Analysis that has been published since; great technical thinking is just that whether it is expressed in 1920, 1940, 1997 or at any other time. Such is the case with this book by Schabacker, for it, like many of the great works of the past, is a worthy addition to any technical analyst's personal library or any market library. It is our belief that such great classics with their timeless analytical knowledge should never be allowed to disappear from the technical scene, if possible. It is to this end that Pitman Publishing, publishers of this Master Class Series, will be making many of these very rare works available again with an increasing number of additions to this series of great classical writings from the "Golden Age of Technical Analysis," that very productive period between 1922 and 1957.

Returning to the post-World War II period, it would appear the investment world was open to that one vital analytical work turning up to give this recovery period a boost. History has shown that Edwards and Magee were the boost-givers. Delving into their book we find it is divided into two main parts; Part One forms the bulk of the book and contains the main subject matter which is the descriptions contributed by Mr Edwards in his coverage on reversal, consolidation, and continuation patterns, trends, trend line action, support and resistance levels, and other areas of technical price action. The shorter Part Two by Mr Magee concentrates on the practical applications of what to do in the markets and when. While Part Two includes much in the way of general investment and trading knowledge that has been covered in many books before and since, it is Part One that made the difference in 1948. In Part One both private investors and professional analysts were presented with a compendium of chart patterns, formations, and technical action. If they had studied conscientiously and applied the knowledge extensively, they would have had some excellent tools at hand to analyze skillfully any chart that they scrutinized in the light of the tenets of Technical Analysis.

As fine and comprehensive as the Edwards and Magee work is, a careful reading of the introduction and similar statements on the book's cover reveals their debt to Mr Schabacker. Their candor and honesty is to be admired for they freely state that they did not develop or create the many facets of Technical Analysis which they were passing on to a new generation. What their excellent work did accomplish was to save for posterity the vital creative and developmental work of their guiding light who had passed away some ten years earlier, and in so doing they educated many thousands in this new-to-them art of chart analysis. This takes us to a name now unknown to almost all Technical Analysis devotees and cognoscenti around the globe, the mentor of Edwards and Magee, Richard W. Schabacker. For it was from Schabacker's "pioneering research," as pointed out by Edwards, that the monumental concepts and ideas which emerged in this book *Technical Analysis and Stock Market Profits: A Course in Forecasting* came, and have proven to be the foundation of modern Technical Analysis. It is certainly this writer's opinion that this Course by Schabacker represents the finest work ever produced on conventional Technical Analysis. The qualifying word "conventional" is inserted because it must be used in comparison to the work of William D. Gann who was equally as great, but more in terms of the "unconventional" technical approach with which he is associated.

It seems almost unbelievable that such remarkable writings could have remained unknown to the investment public for so long. Other than Edwards in his introduction to *Technical Analysis of Stock Trends*, we know of no other reference to it. Market students should be aware of how this happened, as it is a too familiar story that equally applies to a great number of other superb technical works that also remain almost unknown today; an unwelcome fate that leaves the Technical Analysis fraternity much the poorer. However, before going into the historical reasons and developments that resulted in the dearth of classical Technical Analysis writings that has haunted the field for many years, it would be well to take a closer look at this classical work by Schabacker which remains an example of the highest order of analytical quality and incisive technical thought, and should serve as an ideal to technical students everywhere.

The Schabacker stock market story centers around the time of his financial editorship activities with *Forbes Magazine* and later as editor for the *Annalist* weekly publication that accompanied the *New York Times*. In 1930 Mr Schabacker wrote his first book *Stock Market Theory and Practice*, a task that then firmly established his investment literary credentials. It was an odd book in its own way. For a start it was quite a thick book, some 800 plus pages long. Two-thirds of these pages were involved with describing such pedantic subjects as to the functions of stockbrokers in the market place, the paths the buy and sells orders take to reach the various exchanges, details about these many exchanges, how orders are handled when they come in and so on. Certainly these are not very exciting subjects, and for us today, even less exciting, as the computer has changed many of the mechanical aspects of buying and selling that the brokerage offices and exchanges used to rely on to accomplish their tasks. It is the remaining third of the book that was destined to greatly heighten our interest. For it is here that the author for the first time in memory presented Technical Analysis as a totally organized subject wherein he comprehensively laid out the various important patterns, formations, trends, support and resistance areas, and associated supporting technical detail.

Just two years later, in 1932, came the publication of the first edition of this work. We can only surmise why the author felt he had to publish a second work of a similar nature to the one he had written two years earlier. We have to think that while he must have felt the earlier book with its 250-plus pages devoted to technical subjects gave good coverage of what he wanted to say, he had come to the conclusion that there was a great deal more he could expound on to advance Technical Analysis as a serious analytical approach in investment thinking, a more comprehensive presentation worthy of the subject. The end result was this Course and masterpiece that we now can say was well in keeping with his later recognition as "the father of modern Technical Analysis." Nevertheless, most technical analysts today still remain unaware of Mr Schabacker's place in the order of things or his contributions to what is now the most popular form of investment analysis, Technical Analysis. However, with this re-publishing of Schabacker's finest writings, it is hoped an awakening appreciation will sweep the cobwebs of anonymity away from this extremely important contributor to our world of analytical thought and application.

For any trader or investor, from the rankest beginner to the most experienced institutional fund manager, the most critical point that lies at the heart of any investment position they hold is when they find they have to ask themselves as the trend evolves whether that position is at a peak with a possible reversal in the offing or, as the case may be, at a bottom and a possible reversal in that price movement. Depending on whether they are taking a long-term, a more intermediate-term, or a short-term view (and they are all relative in respect to time), that change of trend could make a vital difference to a profit gained or a loss sustained for that position. This would also hold true for any buying decision or short sale decision being considered as the price action goes through its upside/downside contortions. For this reason Mr Schabacker chose to make Reversal Patterns the area he would give the greatest emphasis and attention to in the Course, and in so doing stressed the importance of this knowledge in the education of technical students, who see themselves as intertwined in the dynamics of the marketplace. (In truth we who see ourselves as students of the market know we are destined to attend Analysis University for as long we are market-oriented. With the potential pool of knowledge that is there to be explored, and our time on this planet so relatively limited, there can never be an end to our learning experience. The only possible graduation ceremony we can expect from our University has to be when we graduate to those Great Stock and Commodity Markets in the Sky.)

In surveying the broad range of Reversal Patterns to be covered in the Course, the initial formation the Author chose and the obvious one to feature was the one that most exemplified reversal indications, the Head and Shoulders Formation and the many variations of its basic construction. His first description centers on its idealized construction (as is the case when initially describing patterns and formations to be seen on the charts. That they have to be "generally" described can be taken for granted, as any description is normally started with an idealized version first. However, this must of necessity be tempered with the student's realization that as in nature, so is it in the reality of any patterned price movement, nothing repeats itself "exactly.") Following this introduction to the price formation or action that he is presenting as he typically does throughout the Course, he presents those factors that can be confidently relied on, and gives equal attention to the blemishes, the weaknesses, and numerous things that can upset the best of analytical forecasts. Certainly the thinking here was not to make analysis difficult (it always is anyway), but really to prepare the student's analytical thinking to see that price is always moving into the unknown as is its nature, challenging the student's mind to be more acutely tuned into looking at other important things that can also give clues to the resultant move out of the pattern that has been noted. One of the most important things that the author especially stresses is the paying of close attention to the Volume factor (too often ignored even by experienced technical analysts, as it is admittedly very difficult to get a handle on) as to whether it is increasing, decreasing, or standing still in relation to the rising and falling price movements at the time. In keeping with his instructive pattern descriptions of the Head and Shoulders, Schabacker similarly covers the other Reversal Formations to be found described in the text, the Rounding Turn, the Symmetrical, Right-angle, Descending, Ascending, and Inverted Triangles, Broadening Tops, Diamond Formations, Rectangles, Island Reversals, and the others. Lest it might be thought that all these pattern descriptions are straightforward there is no lack of attention paid to the possibly troublesome deviation details in the appearance of each formation's structure.

Following the descriptive details in the chapters on the Reversal Formations, the next series of patterns demanding attention are the Continuation Formations. When they live up to their name, which is fairly often, these portray resting places along the trend where they gather strength to continue upwards or downwards as the prior trend dictates if it remains intact. They are generally also very recognizable, for in the patterns found in this group their names are closely related to their shapes like the Flag, the Pennant, the Rectangle, and again various shapes of Triangles. Since

Continuation Formations occasionally turn into Reversal Formations, they can at times be the bane of the chart analyst; however, in any action in the marketplace at any time, the market is going to do what the market is going to do and it does not pay to fight it. Or as has been wisely said before, markets will do whatever they have to do to prove the majority of participants wrong most of the time. Again, the author puts in all his descriptions those fine points that the trader/investor would do well to absorb and apply for the kind of help he or she needs when undertaking the fascinating game of price, time and volume analysis.

With the same thorough attention given to the many facets of the Reversal and Continuation Formations, the following chapters are replete with descriptions of other technical action on the Break-away, Continuation, Common, and Exhaustion Gaps, the Horn Formation, the Zig-zag Movement, the Trend, Trendlines, Channels, Support and Resistance Lines and Levels, and several others. Additionally in Mr Schabacker's eyes Volume of sales was vitally associated with much of the action on the charts (something that many modern technical writers treat much too broadly, and even more importantly, too lightly.) Adding to his many references throughout the book to Volume, to give this subject the attention the marketplace demands he devotes a separate section solely to it, to emphasize its importance in price action analysis. Another tool that technical analysts have in their armory is the means, at times, to apply measuring rules to estimate the next probable move in price terms, definitely rules that should not go unlearned. One problem that seems to plague technicians over and over again is False Moves and Shake-outs, where it becomes very difficult at times to distinguish what appears to be from what actually is, actions guaranteed to see capital lost time after time. Again, Mr Schabacker's coverage of what can be very scary moves when they turn up is masterly and worthy of the great technical mind as he explores the subject; even to the extent that he points out the "bright side of False Moves."

But should this work really be ranked among the greatest stock and commodity market technical literature ever, especially as it was written 70 years ago? Have we not made tremendous advancements in Technical Analysis, especially with computer technology, that surely dwarfs the knowledge of these so-called "great market minds" of the past? The answer is a resounding "No" in this writer's opinion and in the minds of many other students of the market too. Basically markets have not changed and the people who make up these markets have not changed one iota either. Share and commodity prices still move either up, down or sideways in their own ways. Charts from today could be mixed with charts from any time in the past, and were all name and time indications removed, no one would be able to say which were which. People today are no different from people of yesterday in their hopes, their fears, their aspirations, their psychological make-ups and any other way one wishes to look at them. For this series editor William D. Gann, on the basis of the knowledge he has passed down to us, was and still is the finest analytical mind that has ever been produced in speculative markets anywhere. Ever since his passing in 1955 efforts have been made to denigrate his name and his accomplishments (certainly an easy thing to do when his detractors only have the ability to take in the surface meanings of his writings, totally lacking the realization of the depth of meaning underneath these same writings). He did not make it easy for those who choose to delve into his work, something he could not do and would not do.

There can be no running away from the realization that the primary purpose of stock and commodity markets, whether they are those of yesterday, today or tomorrow, is solely buying and selling. Anyone who excelled in their analytics and their trading in markets past with whatever tools and approaches they successfully used in their time, they would be equally at home trading and investing today; buying and selling in speculative markets hasn't changed one bit making time immaterial. So it is with the Schabacker Course here. It is as alive, vital, and instructional today as the day it was written and will be for the foreseeable future. Yet, for practically all this time it has remained almost totally unknown, except for the short reference to it in Edwards and Magee. And, this reference was easily passed over, since copies of the Schabacker work were so rare. The question that always arises is how could such an important and exceptional work as this one remain so unknown in a field that attracts a great deal of studying and experimenting, where self-education is basically the only learning process. A field where those who are serious students are aware that they have only to look at the works of W. D. Gann, R. N. Elliott, R. D. Wyckoff, and others from the past for technique and application that is as current as anything available in the Technical Analysis field. The answer to this particular question lies in the physical printing methods available at the time of publication.

For an explanation we have to look at the tough times of the 1930s in the USA when financial conditions were difficult. Market books were still printed and bought, even if in smaller numbers than in the preceding "Roaring Twenties," and at prices that reflected the troubled business climate of the time. In the investment publishing field there was a relatively small market with lucrative prospects that could be tapped, and where opportunity arose, many authors were prepared to offer material that a number of traders and investors would buy. This area of opportunity lay in producing worthy works that promised finer trading systems, methodologies, analytical thought, and increased forecasting potential, the study of which would help the reader to reap larger profits in the trading and investment markets. To attract this business, authors produced large technical courses which they sold directly to the ultimate purchaser at a premium price, sending one chapter at a fixed price for a specified time period, say one chapter a month for $25 per chapter, until the whole course had been received. An embossed cover was usually sent with the last chapter, and the course was complete. The recipient usually had the opportunity to direct questions later to the author on the course material.

The full title of this book by Mr Schabacker is *Technical Analysis and Stock Market Profits: A Course in Forecasting*. We can be certain from the title that it was a course, and that the author intended to publish and distribute it as mentioned previously. Obviously, the number of courses that would be sold, especially in the light of the high premium charged, was going to be relatively small. There was also a physical reason that limited the numbers printed and sold; the printing method that had to be used. Before the photocopier became a reality, the normal method of reproducing text on paper, where printing press production was not economical, was by means of the mimeograph process (known by other names in countries outside the USA.) Here a specially treated plate containing the typewritten text was placed around a large metal cylinder which in turn was rotated by hand or motor to produce a printed page. The printed pages would then be collated into chapters and the chapters sent out to the purchasing students. The one problem that arose in the printing process was with the plate containing the typewritten text because the pressure on this plate eventually broke down the letters of the text. This meant that rarely could more than about 1,000 copies be printed from any plate and still be legible.

We know that there were two editions of this Schabacker Course, one in 1932 and the other in 1937 (which is this book); and at approximately 1,000 copies each, it is not hard to see that, with time taking its toll on these original editions over the past years, only a relative handful have survived. Even in 1948 when Edwards and Magee produced their fine book, knowledge of the original Schabacker Course must have been fading. That there were special reasons and conditions which limited its numbers can be appreciated, and, in turn, it is easy to see why, in the light of a knowledge of the times and the special market this Course was distributed to, it was almost inevitable that the odds were not good that it would survive the years. While the survival of this Technical Analysis masterpiece could have been in doubt, with this publication we have to feel that its depth of knowledge on its chosen subject, its clarity of expression in describing random, undulating price movements, and its evident excellence of intricate technical evolutionary revelation make the effort to bring it back to the analytical community worth it. If the coming years lead to a universal acceptance of just how superb this Course is in its field of specialization, then we will truly be able to say that there is a new "bible of Technical Analysis" – Richard W. Schabacker's *Technical Analysis and Stock Market Profits*.

DONALD MACK
Series Editor
2005

PREFACE TO FIRST EDITION

The preparation of this Course in twelve lessons, or studies, on the technical approach to successful trading in stocks, comes in answer to a definite and insistent demand from many students for assistance in stock chart work and market analysis.

Some of these students are new to the game, beginners who wish seriously to prepare themselves for an active market career, or who want to study it thoroughly before deciding to enter it actively. Another large group is made up of those who have had more or less experience in the market, trading on either their own "hunches" or the advice and tips of others, and have come to realize that a great deal of money can be made in the market but not by hit-or-miss methods, and certainly not by following blindly the lead of others.

A third group consists of experienced and often very successful traders and investors who know the importance of correctly evaluating the technical side of the market in order to time their operations for maximum profits.

And, finally, there are always those individuals who are seeking an easy key, a magic formula that will take them to riches without effort.

For the class last named this Course is definitely not intended. There is no "magic key" to stock market profits. The founder of the Schabacker methods of technical forecasting in his many years of research, with the facilities of large financial and investigative organizations, tested literally hundreds of "systems" and formulas – not only on paper but in actual market operations – and found no dependable short cuts, no systems that can take the place of careful, constant application of the principles of technical analysis.

(It may well be said at this point, however, that research along promising lines has never stopped and never will. This science is not static, though the fundamental law of supply and demand which it seeks to interpret can never be repealed. This Course today incorporates several amplifications and refinements which have come through the "acid test" since it was first organized.)

So, to the hopeful seeker for an easy answer, we can say only this: You will get out of this study only what you are willing to put into it and continue to put into it for as long as you trade in the security markets.

But the earnest student of the science need have no misgivings. Every effort has been made – with reasonable success, we believe – to make each point and each method taught herein clear to understand and thoroughly practicable. Complicating and, in some cases, highly publicized theories which exhaustive tests have shown to offer results not commensurate with the time and expense their practice entails, have been avoided. Instead, the effort has been to explore and to teach the basic principles and the methods which any man can apply in his spare time, and without the necessity of paying to others a continuing toll for statistical or advisory services.

In brief, this Course is organized to serve the average man who can devote only an hour or so a day, and perhaps only a few hundred dollars, to his market operations, as well as the professional full-time trader.

Also, it has been our endeavor to make the student independent in thought. For it is unquestionably true that no man has ever, over any period of time, made and kept stock market profits unless he has developed the qualities of independent judgment and action. This course of study is designed to enable you to see the opportunities for yourself, to decide the questions of "what" and "when" for yourself, and then to act with confidence.

The average man of intelligence who brings sober study and application to his market analyses can – as we have ample proof – find dependable profits in the stock market, year in and year out, through bear markets as well as bull. He will not suffer the crippling losses that came to thousands, incredibly enough, even in the wild bull market of 1928–29. And he will discover the interesting truth that trading in stocks is the one and only business activity in which money can be made just as well in times of general business decline as during boom periods.

FOREWORD BY PETER BRANDT

To put it bluntly, I owe the success of my career as a market speculator to Richard W. Schabacker and the book you are now reading. Without the principles of classical charting codified by Schabacker in this manuscript, I would have most likely landed back in the advertising business, my career path before venturing into the commodity trading field at the Chicago Board of Trade (CBOT) in 1975.

After graduating from the University of Minnesota, I moved to Chicago to begin a career with one of the world's largest advertising agencies. Through the activities of my children I became acquainted with a man who was a soybean trader at the Chicago Board of Trade. He would invite me to lunch with him on the 5th floor of the CBOT, overlooking the grain pits. I was absolutely hypnotized.

The more he told me about his profession, the more I became enthralled with the idea of becoming a market speculator. At the time, as now, there is no shortcut to trading – everyone begins at the same place, the bottom. In my mid-20s, I secured an entry-level position at one-third the salary I was making in advertising with Continental Grain Co., then the world's second largest grain exporting firm.

My job was to learn the business, then bring commodity-consuming corporate customers into the firm, for which I would earn a commission of slightly less than one-tenth of a cent per bushel of grain. Yet, my goal was singular – to build up an account of my own and trade it for a living.

Zero – this was the composite knowledge I had to start with in the commodity futures world. All I knew was the traders in the pits at the CBOT and its counterpart the Chicago Mercantile Exchange seemed to be making a small fortune, drove German automobiles, only answered to themselves and knew exactly how they did each day. How much better could it get?

There were three major hurdles to my starry-eyed aspirations. First, the commodity business was far more complicated than I gave it credit for at the beginning. Second, commercial customers needed to be secured, not only to pay the living expenses of a young family, but to accumulate trading capital. At the start I did not have enough spare capital to margin a single contract of oats, the least expensive CBOT market to trade. Finally, I didn't have the first clue what it meant to be a proprietary (self-funded) trader.

The face of fortune was smiling upon me. A couple of talented traders took me under their wings and guided me in the learning process. To this day I feel a sense of obligation to help others avoid pitfalls to pay back the graciousness of these men. Within a year I acquired a good working knowledge of the ins and outs of grain merchandising and exchange-traded futures contracts.

The next gap was filled because of some wonderful contacts I developed during my advertising years with senior-level management at major commodity-related corporations. The massive bull market of the early 1970s caught most corporate commodity processors with their pants down and there was great eagerness by corporate management to hedge against more surprise spikes in prices. A couple of years into the business I was making far more than I would have been making in advertising, and I had accumulated my first grub steak for trading (Continental Grain allowed its employees to hold personal accounts).

Over the next couple of years, I funded and blew-up several accounts, each time taking a different approach to trading, ranging from fundamental analysis to seasonal cycles to spread trading to cycles to day-trading – and others. Learning the commodity business was one thing, trading was in an entirely different orbit. Trading was serious business, and I was becoming desperate.

By 1979, I was sincerely wondering whether becoming a commodity speculator was in the cards. This is when I met Richard W. Schabacker. Not the man, of course – he had been dead since 1935 – but his principles of classical charting as codified in this book, *Technical Analysis and Stock Market Profits: A Course in Forecasting*, first published in 1932.

My initial exposure to classical charting was through the book *Technical Analysis of Stock Trends*, co-written by Robert Edwards, Schabacker's brother-in-law, who had formed an educational institute to further the work of Schabacker, who had died an untimely death at the young age of 36. I owe a huge debt of gratitude to a dear friend who first introduced me to the book by Edwards (and John Magee). After a brief introduction to the Edwards and Magee book, I was compelled to return to the origins of classical charting. I was driven to understand charting as originally laid out by Schabacker.

Unfortunately, at the time, *Technical Analysis and Stock Market Profits* was not in print. These were pre-internet years when access to information required some footwork and perseverance. I secured a photocopy version from a rare book seller in Los Angeles. And the rest is history. I consumed the manuscript in a weekend. Instinctively I sensed I had found my way forward as a trader. I was to be a classical chartist.

Viewing the markets (and trading) through the lens of classical charting principles resonated with me in a deep way and offered a unified perspective for trading I had not found in other approaches. Classical charting provided a series of attributes that combined to become the foundation of my trading:

1. A graphic perspective of larger price trends.
2. A means to imagine the buying and selling forces acting upon price discovery.
3. Timing for entering trades.
4. A method for establishing the initial risk of a trade.
5. A process for managing ongoing trades.
6. An indication of the magnitude of a pending trend.

The trading program I began in 1979—using classical charting principles to trade commodity and foreign exchange markets—exists to this day. It has provided a wonderfully comfortable lifestyle for my family for more than 40 years and is the source of accumulated wealth.

Throughout my career I have remained a strict classical chartist, routinely re-reading the Schabacker book (I have worn through several copies). Regularly, I reference the book on specific points, and am often surprised when an important, but nuanced, clarification on a specific chart pattern pops out. Schabacker's brilliance impresses me more each year.

Over time I have adapted Schabacker's classical charting principles, emphasizing some patterns over others, fine-tuning my time frame, adopting customized risk and trade management rules, and even adding a couple of my own patterns to the list. But I am always conscious of the rules for interpreting classical chart patterns set forth in this book and seldom go against Schabacker's guidance.

Even after all these years and repeat readings of *Technical Analysis and Stock Market Profits*, the book might clobber me over the head with a nuanced understanding of chart construction that I previously skimmed over. It is quite common for me to wonder if Schabacker would agree with me on a certain analysis of a price graph.

Classical charting principles are not for all traders. But, if you have a fascination with geometry and a love of maps, as I do, this may become the most valuable book you ever buy.

Peter Brandt
Arizona, 2021

Study I

TECHNICAL APPROACH TO STOCK TRADING

Definition of a Stock Chart

There is perhaps no better way to begin a discussion of stock charts than to agree on a definition for them. A stock chart is a pictorial record of the trading history of any stock or group of stocks. This is a perfectly simple definition of our subject yet it is general enough to cover all of the many charts, pictures and formations which we shall discuss in subsequent pages.

A stock chart may conceivably be so simple a thing as the picture of the closing price of one stock issue on the last trading day of each year for only five or ten years. The picture would not mean a great deal, yet technically it would fit into our definition. It would be a pictorial record of the trading history of this stock. It would be a stock chart. It would differ only in degree from the most complete, most detailed and painstaking stock chart that we might construct.

An "Advanced Course"

For the purposes of this study it will be necessary to assume that the reader is quite familiar with stocks, with securities in general, with the theory and practice of open-market trading and with all of the myriad technical details covered by our term "trading history." To this extent our present study is somewhat of an "advanced course" in stock market operation, and it is only fair to suggest that fundamentals of the market be studied and mastered before undertaking to benefit from this course.[1]

Beyond this introductory generalization, however, it shall be our constant and continued aim to be as certain as possible that our thought is made clear by simplicity of language, by constant stressing of important points, by myriad examples and even by possibly tiresome repetition. And it will perhaps be necessary to request the forbearance and indulgence of our "brighter pupils" or more experienced readers if they find us apparently verging on "complete recall" in order to be certain of full understanding.

As an example of this possible fault we are constrained to return for a few moments to a more detailed examination of our introductory definition of stock charts. The stock chart is a pictorial representation of any stock's trading history. In the study of stock charts we are not primarily interested in anything but actual trad-

---

[1] Refer to *Stock Market Theory and Practice* by R. W. Schabacker, Forbes Publishing Company, New York, NY. (Referring to this particular work is not possible, as it has long been out of print. With the passage of time many market fundamentals have totally changed. Any reader needing information on the operations and fundamentals of current markets will certainly find this available in the many books that cover these subjects today.)

ing – that is, the record or result of the orderly buying and selling of any issue in the course of actual trading on any open market.

Pure Technical Action

We are not interested, for example, in the company behind the stock which we are studying. We do not care, for our immediate purpose, whether the corporation manufactures mousetraps, tin cans, locomotives or aluminum toothpicks. We are not particular as to whether it is an industrial, a railroad, a utility or a what-not. Technically the company behind the stock might even be in receivership, with its plant shut down entirely and making nothing at all. For our primary purpose of charting that stock it would make no difference, so long as the stock itself continued to enjoy fairly active trading in some orderly and well regulated open market security exchange.

The reader must not get the impression that such fundamental factors are unimportant in trading, in analysis, in forecasting. They most decidedly are and they most decidedly should be taken into serious consideration when studying any stock or any stock chart for practical purposes. We merely assert that the stock chart itself has nothing to do with such fundamental factors. It concerns itself solely with the stock's actual record in open-market trading.

Fundamentals Reflected in Technical Action

In the record of such trading all of these many and varied fundamental factors are brought to bear, are evaluated and automatically weighted and recorded in net balance on the stock chart.

The trading in any stock is largely the result of the influence these fundamental factors have had on each buyer and seller of each share of stock. The stock chart is a pictorial record of such trading, so that it, in itself, is a reflection of all those other factors and, from a purely technical standpoint, need therefore concern itself no further with such fundamental considerations.

Stocks Eligible for Charting

And, incidentally, since a stock chart is merely a record of trading, it follows that any stock is eligible for charting which enjoys a trading market. Any stock, and for that matter any article or service, which is bought and sold for a publicly listed price, can be charted. For practical purposes, we shall see later that in order to be a valuable subject for study a stock should have a free and open market, and an active market, but the fact remains that any traded stock can be pictorialized in a stock chart.

And in like manner, according to our definition, a stock chart may be constructed for more-than one stock at a time. Any number of stocks may be included in a single stock chart though the clearest results are obtained by averaging all of the component stocks or figures into one series and thus making the chart into a composite picture which looks like the record of trading in merely one stock, but, in reality, is the composite result of trading in a great many stocks combined. Such composite charts on groups of stocks are called "averages."

Proceeding further with our definition of a stock chart we note that it is primarily a pictorial record. A stock chart then is a picture. One of the most simple and easily understandable advantages of a stock chart is that it presents a picture at any desired instant of stock history which has covered many months or years and which, in the absence of the chart, it would take many hours, or even weeks, of diligent research to produce.

The Pictorial Aspect of Charts

Since the stock chart is a history of trading it finds its primary basis of construction in actual trading, and in the units of such trading. The most common and accepted trading place in stocks is the New York Stock Exchange. The results of trading on that exchange are primarily recorded in brokerage offices throughout the country through the medium of the stock ticker. But for many apparent and practical reasons the majority of people interested in such trading are not able to be in personal attendance to watch the trading record unfold itself in a brokerage office from 10 to 3 o'clock each day.[2] The newspapers and other periodicals and services bridge this gap by reporting daily the results of such trading. Any person interested in the stock market, therefore, may save approximately five hours a day by examining merely the total results of the day's trading.

Just as the newspapers save time and energy by summarizing stock trading each day, so the stock chart goes further in its service by saving days, weeks, months and years for the interested student. If he wishes to review the past year of trading history for any stock without reference to a chart, he must go back over the newspapers for more than 300 days or, at best, his own records summarizing those 300 days of trading. But if he takes advantage of the services offered by the stock chart he may save all this time and effort. At a glance he may have before him the complete record of the past year's daily trading in any particular stock.

Charts as the "Complete Memory"

Even if there were no saving of time and effort, stock charts still retain their greatest

---

[2] Today the New York Stock Exchange is open from 9.30am to 4.00pm, New York time.

advantage, however, which is one of complete memory. If the individual were satisfied to spend his precious hours poring over the written or printed record of the past year's trading in any stock, as presumed above, he would still be under a terrific handicap of trying to remember the characteristics of February trading while looking at the record for October. Unless he had an almost supernatural memory he would have to be constantly referring from one period of time to another in order to make any complete order or analysis out of his research.

But if he uses a chart of this stock, how much simpler is his task. Here is the picture, before his eyes in black and white, permanent, accurate, compact – the very picture which, without the chart, he would be trying hazily to recollect or construct in mental imagery.

The stock chart's chief value, therefore, grows out of its being a pictorial record of trading history. Because it is a picture the stock chart makes the past history of any issue an open book, simple, easy to read, easy to study. Its use brings advantages similar in practical result to the telescope, the X-ray, the electric eye and other modern devices which save so much time and energy in fundamentals and details that they make possible the transference of such energy into the more productive channels of study and research.

Technical Chart Action – the New Science

And this thought brings us naturally to by far the greatest practical advantage of the stock chart. Because it makes the groundwork of fundamental co-ordination of facts so easy, so simple, so readily grasped, it leads naturally into a more detailed study of the phenomena which it pictorializes; the actual results of the trading history presented, the patterns, the rules, the characteristics of behavior. In short, it leads to a new science, the science of technical chart action.

Technical market action is that aspect of analysis which is based upon phenomena arising out of the market itself, to the exclusion of fundamental and all other factors. In fact, technical action may also be explained as merely the antithesis of the fundamental considerations. The fundamental aspect of market analysis lays special stress upon such factors as the corporation behind the stock, its business, its prospects, its past, present and future earnings, its balance sheet, its financial strength, the quality of its management and so on. Fundamental factors include the dividend rate of the stock in question, its capitalization, its yield, its distribution and countless other factors which may have direct or indirect bearing upon the intrinsic worth of the stock, upon its theoretical price, upon what the individual may think it should sell for, or upon the true value of the issue in question.

Such fundamental factors are highly important and must be taken into careful consideration by the investor or trader. But they are not the technical factors which we are about to study. The technical factors are what might be termed the residuum of the total sum of all aspects bearing upon the probable market value of the stock, after the more apparent and fundamental factors are eliminated.

Technical vs. Fundamental Factors

When we have finished our fundamental analysis of earnings, financial strength and all the rest, there is still something left to be considered with regard to the future price at which any particular stock may sell. That final consideration has to do with technical market action.

Realizing the presence and the importance of this "other factor" makes it more simple to analyze it. We have defined technical action as the phenomena arising out of the market itself. That market is nothing more than a group of buyers pitted against a group of sellers. And it stands clearly to reason that in any open market if there were more sellers than buyers, or more shares of stock for sale than for purchase, then the quotations or prices for that stock would decline.

Ours not to reason why there was more stock offered than the demand could sustain. Ours merely to detect the technical fact that there were more sellers than buyers. That was the important point, for it meant the stock was going down, all fundamental factors to the contrary notwithstanding.

Such considerations form the basis for our statement at the beginning of this chapter that stock charts, and thus also technical action, take no consideration of fundamental factors like earnings, management, balance sheets and so forth, in their primary analysis. We shall see later that fundamentals are highly important adjuncts to the study of technical action and are, in many cases, more important for the long pull than are the temporary technical aspects. But in our introduction to the subject and for our basic understanding of stock charts we must realize that in themselves they completely ignore fundamentals. In fact they completely ignore everything except technical market action, the balance between buyers and sellers, the balance between supply and demand for any stock or group of stocks; in short the phenomena arising out of actual trading, per se, in a free and open market.

Reasons for Contrary Technical Action

Perhaps it is too mysterious and suggestive of legerdemain to intimate that we need not question why a stock suddenly declines on weak technical action just when its fundamental aspects appear the strongest. There are many possible reasons, but they arise, like the technical action itself, primarily out of the market.

Speculators may have bought the stock months ago in anticipation of the development of these favorable fundamentals, and as they appear the speculators sell out and take their profits. Perhaps a group of powerful insiders, or officials of the company, have loaded up too heavily with the stock. Perhaps they realize that the fundamental situation is not as strong as the news makes it appear. There are any number of reasons why the technical position may be the opposite of the fundamental position.

The important point is that when they are at variance, the technical position wins out, since it is closer to the market, and the open market is what makes stock prices move. At least the technical position wins out immediately, even if only temporarily, and the technical position is therefore more important than the fundamental position for the short-swing trader or speculator who is looking for his profit from the current price movement of the stock and is not, like the investor, buying to put away for the "long pull."

> *The technical position is the factor which is going to influence prices up or down in the future*

Although through the medium of stock charts we can get a better judgment on the technical position of the market at the moment, that technical position is constantly changing and is subject to very rapid and substantial swings from very strong to very weak in a few days or even, at rare intervals, in a few hours. It takes practically no time at all for a huge lot of buying or selling to come into the market and such events are reflected in technical action and lend themselves to chart analysis.

The fact is, however, that technical action does not generally change so rapidly and, having determined whether the technical position is strong or weak, we are a little ahead of the game already, because the technical position is the factor which is going to influence prices either up or down not yesterday, or even now, but in the future, even though it be only the immediate future.

Technical positions do not generally change rapidly unless fundamentals receive a terrific impulse which is so strong as to overcome the "status quo" between supply and demand. In the general run of affairs a strong technical position will take days, weeks or months to build itself up, will have its strong effect for months, and then will take additional days, weeks or months finally to exhaust itself and switch to the opposite state of weak technical position. During all this gradual change, market profits are available through proper analysis of the technical situation.

Summary of the Technical Approach

To summarize our introductory discussion, it is not enough to know the fundamental position of stocks. We must also know their technical position. For the short range, technical considerations are even more important than fundamental statistics, but "the compleat angler" will know both. Fundamental considerations are easy for the average student. Technical aspects are not so easy or so certain but they are reduced to somewhat of a science by the study of stock charts.

Through the medium of stock charts we may arrive at a better understanding of the phenomena which attend the gradual but constantly shifting balance of power between supply and demand in the stock market.

The Introductory Warning

The following lessons are devoted to such a study but in a spirit of broadminded-ness and conservatism which it is highly important that the reader should share. If there is one generalization about the whole subject of stock charts which we may suggest at the very introduction of our study, it is the definite caution that the reader be skeptical of any apparently sure thing. This may sound like a poor anticlimax with which to open such a study but we do so with well-weighed forethought.

We are most definitely a firm believer in the usefulness of stock charts and their high value in delineating the technical position of individual stocks and the general market. Stock charts are, in our opinion, the most important single aid in forecasting future price movements and we constantly stand on the reiterated premise that they are an absolute necessity for successful stock trading.

Beware of Early Presumption

But it is this very faith in the efficiency of stock charts that leads to an introductory warning against over confidence and mistrust. There is nothing like the thrill that comes to the beginner when he once commences to master the rudimentary principles of chart reading and sees his first few forecast analyses turn out cor-rectly.

Stock charts are most important in forecasting future price movements and are an absolute necessity for successful stock trading.

The greatest danger for the beginner lies in just this primary awakening to the value of his study. With his first few successes he is likely to mistake a probable forecast for a certain one, to become over-confident, to overtrade, and suddenly find himself involved in a disastrous quagmire of heavy losses and, what is perhaps more important, in a hopeless state of indecision, mistrust, skepticism, and bitter disappointment.

No Easy Road to Profits

There are literally thousands of unfortunate examples in our files and in our acquaintance with students who became know-it-alls in the first blush of their maiden success – whose cupidity was so sharpened by the early realization of the basic value in technical analysis that they rushed headlong into the pitfalls of chart reading and chart trading without displaying enough patience and forbearance to complete their study and perfect their knowledge of basic principles.

The reader may be certain that all of the principles educed in the following study of stock charts and technical action are considered valuable or important, or they would not have been included. But the reader may also be just as certain that none of those principles are guaranteed to be 100 per cent infallible. We have been able to find, though sometimes with difficulty, exceptions to practically every formation, to practically every rule. Furthermore, we know of no practical rule of stock charts or stock trading which may not, under certain conditions and at certain times, have such exceptions.

By no means the least important aspect of successful chart reading and chart trading, therefore, is the early detection of such exceptional cases, the almost intuitive, subconscious suspicion of certain formations and, above all, the ability to avoid or limit loss on such exceptional situations.

We have endeavored to suggest methods for attaining this happy state but, in the last analysis, it comes generally from long study, from long experience and from long foresight; and the greatest of these is the attitude which we are attempting to foster in these paragraphs, that of a healthy skepticism toward all rules, a scholarly spirit of conservatism and humility in the face of a great and valuable science and a conservative habit of action in all practical market trading.

Newspapers which Publish Charts

Public and professional interest in stock charts has increased so rapidly in recent years that the demand has led to a growing supply of sources from which stock charts may be purchased ready made. Even some of the newspapers have begun to publish individual stock charts, either in continuous series or merely from time to time. Regular publication of stock charts in the newspapers is still confined generally, however, to the printing of "average charts," or charts showing the pictorial history of leading stock groups, rather than individual issues.

Among the New York daily newspapers which publish average charts regularly are the *New York Daily Investment News* and the *Wall Street Journal*.[3] The *Wall Street Journal* publishes daily an up-to-date record of its own averages of 30 railroad issues,

---

[3] The information given here and in the following paragraphs regarding several newspapers, magazines and chart services is mostly obsolete. Today's readily available computer services with their rapid transmission of market data and chart representations make the type of information referred to in the text easy to gather. Special note should be made that a number of organizations provide excellent weekly chart books for stocks and commodities that many technical analysts find as essential today as in the 1930s.

30 industrials, 20 utilities and 40 bonds, in separate charts, and is the most valuable daily publication for the perusal of charts already made.

The *New York Daily Investment News* publishes the long-range daily chart record of a well-known average of 90 stocks. Most of these average charts also carry the daily volume of sales on the New York Stock Exchange.

The *New York Herald Tribune* publishes every morning the picture up to the previous day's closing of its own highly respected average of 100 stocks. The *New York Times* also prints every morning a chart of the *Times* average of 50 stocks. The *New York Sun*, among the evening papers, carries in its final editions a chart of its own average of 50 stocks. And most of the other metropolitan newspapers of conservative appeal publish from time to time charts on a variety of financial and business trends as well as stocks.

Magazines which Publish Charts

Magazines have been a little slower in keeping abreast of public interest in stock charts but there are a number which carry regular charts on market averages. The *Magazine of Wall Street*, published bi-weekly, is perhaps the best-known and carries not only its own average chart, in which the prices of 295 common stocks are averaged, but a variety of other financial charts as well. *Forbes Magazine* publishes regularly a long-term chart of weekly ranges on the *New York Times*, or *Annalist*, average, showing for the past four or five years the course of the three *Times* series, the groups including 25 industrials, 25 rails and the 50 industrials and rails combined in a single index.

The *Annalist*, published weekly by the *New York Times*, shows these same averages for a shorter space of time and also carries a very interesting series of comparative charts showing averages of groups of the leading stocks in practically every important field of industry. *Barron's*, published weekly by Dow, Jones & Company, offers approximately the same charts which the *Wall Street Journal*, published by the same company, gives daily.

The New York Stock Exchange Bulletin, published monthly and sent free on application, contains a great valuable fund of statistical information as well as many charts on a great variety of financial and stock trends.

Services Selling Daily Charts

Such average charts are useful in gauging the trend of the general market but for the sincere student who wants to make real progress in chart analysis for himself it is mandatory to have at hand charts on individual stock issues, for they are the fundamental basis of all stock chart science.

The pioneer and probably best known publisher of ready-made stock charts is Graphic Market Statistics, Inc., 11 Stone Street, New York City (estab. 1919). This firm offers up-to-date daily or weekly (8½" × 11") charts of all stocks listed on the New York Curb or Stock Exchanges – daily back history being available from 1926, or date of listing, and weekly from 1929.

This concern also publishes at regular intervals, in loose-leaf book form, a "Master Unit" of over 500 daily, weekly and monthly charts (1924 to date) on 100 active individual stocks and the better known market averages. For the student who wishes to follow a fewer number of stocks, a similar record ("set") is also available in either of two groups of 50 active stocks each.

Although daily, weekly and monthly charts are, when considered together, very valuable tools in the study of technical action, those who prefer may obtain separate single books of daily, weekly or monthly charts on either of two standard lists of 50 stocks each.

Graphic Market Statistics, Inc. also designs and constructs to order security and commodity charts of any size, type or period.

Ready-made Charts

Such services offering ready-made charts probably find their greatest subscription demand from banks, brokerage houses and other financial organizations, though the demand from individual subscribers has increased in recent years. There is no objection to the student of stock charts subscribing to such services; in fact, we advise it as the easiest and quickest way to get a group of one's own stock charts started.

A supply of these ready-made charts can get the student off to a running start for they give him immediately the background of past action necessary for the proper analysis of the current picture as it develops. From then on, however, we advise the student to construct his own charts. He may continue to purchase ready-made charts if he chooses, perhaps as a means of keeping in touch with the weekly or monthly picture on a larger number of stocks than he can conveniently chart for himself each day, but to rely entirely on ready-made charts encourages a superficial attitude toward the entire subject. The method is too easy. This may sound like the philosophy of an enemy of progress but the statement is true, nevertheless.

Advantages of Making Your Own Charts

Purely from a psychological standpoint, the student who gets a new set of charts already made up for him periodically is almost certain to view them from a less important angle than the man who is under absolute necessity of making them up for himself every day. Unless he is unusually gifted with determination and single-ness of purpose the former is going to find himself pressed for time some morning or some evening and either skim over them without study, or put them away without looking at them at all. He may return to his conscientious study tomorrow but then again he may not, and the first day of flagging interest makes the next one that much easier.

But the man who makes up his own charts is in an entirely different psychological position. He may be tempted to neglect his work on them for one day but he will soon find that it is too difficult to "catch up" and he will make it a regular rule and habit of his life to post up his (possibly "cursed") stock charts every single day.

Closer Personal Contact

Beside this psychological aspect, however, there is a much more practical advantage to keeping up one's own charts. That advantage emanates from keeping in constant touch with each one of them every day. The man who has his charts before him ready-made is quite likely to skip over all but a few of his temporary favorites and thus fail to notice the development of important profitable signals in the remainder of his series.

Not so with the student who keeps his own charts. He is forced by the rigor of his undertaking to bestow a certain amount of time on each individual chart of his series each day whether he happens to be especially interested in them all or not. Through this forced, but none the less certain, closeness of contact with each single chart the student who makes his own is much more likely to shift his study and watchful attention to different charts in his series as each in turn develops more definite and profitable pictures through the course of time.

Number of Charts Necessary

The first step for the student who is going to keep his own charts is to decide on the number he wants to keep and the individual issues which will compose his port-folio. For the average beginner who is not yet certain that he wants to give much time and effort to his study, a group of perhaps 15 or 20 individual charts should be sufficient for temporary trial. For the average trader who knows he is deeply inter-ested in chart study and technical action a list of 50 to 100 individual charts is not too many.

After a few months of experience, when the matter of keeping the series up to date has become something of a routine matter, the student will be surprised with the rapid progress he can make. Once in full swing he should not need much over 45 seconds per chart. He should be able to fill in a day's trading history on 10 charts in say 8 minutes, 50 charts in 40 minutes, 100 charts in 80 minutes and so on. If he is blessed with either a wife, a secretary or a devoted what-not who can read the necessary figures off to him from the daily papers, the time required can be more than cut in half.

Selecting the Stocks

In selecting the individual issues to be charted, personal interest will naturally play some part and the student's "favorites" may be included. Other things being equal, however, the most active and important stocks, like the "market leaders" lend themselves more suitably to chart study because they are most active, generally fluctuate in more normal patterns, are more likely to be under almost constant "street" interest, and usually show more clearly the trend of the general market.

It is also well to select stocks which have at least a fair-sized number of shares outstanding. This makes for greater public interest, a more ready market, higher activity and generally clearer technical pictures.

The best results are gained in every way by setting aside one particular period of time each day to make up one's charts, preferably either before the market opens in the morning or after it closes in the evening. The evening is better as a rule because more time can then be given to leisurely study of the formations, the proper program decided upon and, if actively trading, the brokerage orders may be sent in that evening by mail.

Whatever the time decided upon, however, it is important for ultimate success that the same time be adhered to steadfastly and by rule. There are so many reasons, so many alibis, that can insinuate themselves into the time set apart for making up charts that the program is almost hopeless unless it be made a matter of ironclad rule.

Chart Paper

The next step in starting one's own portfolio of charts is to secure the proper and necessary paper. There is room for a good deal of latitude in personal taste with regard to this subject. Many chart students have their own pet types and makes of chart paper and swear by none other. Most of the professional, services and chart makers use a loose-leaf binder with paper measuring about 24" × 12", but the average individual should find smaller sizes quite satisfactory, say the standard 8½" × 11".

The smaller size has certain important advantages over the larger size because it takes up less room, leaves less unused white space, can more easily be carried about in a briefcase and can be more easily removed from the portfolio for individual handling and study.

The chief advantage claimed for the larger size paper is that new sheets are not needed so often but, while this is true, there is also some advantage to the shorter sheets which run out more quickly. When this happens the price scale can be moved up or down on the new sheet so that the stock price range is not so likely to run off the sheet before its completion with respect to time. And, for that reason also, it is practicable to use on the smaller sheets a larger price scale which renders more conspicuous the technical patterns as they develop.

In any case, it is possible to put too much stress upon the correct type of paper. This is a minor matter for just about any kind of paper will give satisfactory results once the student becomes accustomed to using it and reading his own charts.

Co-ordinate Scales

About the only requisite for chart paper is that it must be ruled both horizontally and vertically; i.e., what is generally termed co-ordinate paper. Up to the point of confusion, the more lines in each direction the better. Some styles of co-ordinate paper have a dated vertical line for each day of the year. This simplifies keeping track of dates but it also distorts the picture at times, for it means that a space must be left for regular and special holidays when there is no trading in the stock market.

Plain, standard, unlettered co-ordinate paper with rulings or "screen" of about 20 lines to the inch, both vertical and horizontal, is obtainable in most large stationery stores and will serve perfectly well for all ordinary purposes. In our own work we have found Keuffel & Esser's No. 358-17 most practical of the special sheets prepared for charting security prices; this comes in the standard 8½" × 11" size, punched for insertion in a ring binder, and has its horizontal scale divided in sixths to represent the six days of the normal business week, and the vertical scale in eighths to conform with the standard eighth of a point price differential in trading. Their No. 358-17L has the same scaling but measures 11" × 16½". The Keuffel & Esser Company publishes a variety of other styles of chart paper and binders to fit which the student may buy from them direct if he wishes, and which are described in their catalog of co-ordinate papers obtainable on request from their own stores in New York or Chicago, or from their general office at Hoboken, New Jersey.

The Codex Book Company, Inc. of Norwood, Mass. also prints a large variety of types and sizes of co-ordinate paper, making a specialty of stock chart sheets.

Constructing the Scale

Having obtained the proper co-ordinate paper and decided upon the individual stocks which it is desired to chart, the next step is to construct, the scale. The horizontal lines on the paper are used to measure the price and volume, so that the actual scales for these factors will be on the vertical lines, preferably at the left hand margin.

The price scale may be altered in many ways and will depend chiefly on the size and ruling of the paper and on the extent of the stock's normal range. If, for example, we are using a sheet of ordinary co-ordinate paper with 20 lines each way to the inch, and 10 inches high vertically, every inch, or every twentieth line, will generally be found printed in heavier ink to serve as a guide. For the average stock selling under 100 every heavy, inch, or twentieth, line on the vertical scale may be a unit of five full points in the price of the stock. Thus each single line will be one-quarter of a full point and the smaller fractional eighths of a point, will fall half way between two lines.

When commencing a new chart it is well to glance back over the price range for the past year and take the average price, say 65, as the price-mark for a heavy horizontal line near the middle of the page on the vertical scale. The next heavy, twentieth, or inch, line above will be 70, and the one below the first entry of 65 will be 60 and so on, as the vertical price scale is filled on the left-hand margin.

If the stock's average range has been very large and its normal fluctuations are wide then a larger price scale is in order. Each heavy, twentieth, or inch, line may be marked to represent 10 points or even 20 points, making each horizontal line across the sheet count for either a half point, or a full point, respectively. In such case it will be more difficult to plot the fractions of a point but this detail of exactitude is not so necessary for a satisfactory picture when the price swings are so large.

The same general principles apply if you are using a special stock chart paper such as the K. & E. 358-17. For most stocks of average price range each heavy (eighth) line on the vertical scale may be marked to represent a full point in the price and each light line will then represent one-eighth of a point. For stocks with a wider swing or higher price, such as American Can, AT & T. etc., each heavy line may represent two points, and the fine lines one-quarter of a point; and for very low-priced stocks with small swings, each heavy line may be marked to represent only half a point.

Plotting the Price Data

Having established the suitable price scale in the left-hand margin, the price-plotting is simple. The daily paper furnishes the necessary data – high, low, close and volume of sales. Plot the high, plot the low, and join the two points with a vertical line to give the day's range. The closing price is an important part of any complete daily stock chart; it is noted by a short, fine, horizontal line, extending across the vertical range line, just far enough to be noted.

Both opening and closing prices may, of course, be plotted if desired but we consider practical only the plotting of closing prices. It is seldom that opening prices show material change from the previous close and they are not nearly so important as the closing or "last" price.

Moreover, we feel that what advantage is gained by including the first or opening price is more than lost by the tendency toward confusion in trying to include too much and thus impairing the basic picture. If both the opening and closing are plotted then the opening price is noted by a horizontal mark to the left of the day's range and the closing price by a similar mark to the right of the range line.

Volume of Sales

Volume of sales is another important detail of the complete daily stock chart, and is plotted by a vertical line somewhat similar to the price range from a fixed base line. Take any horizontal, heavy line near the top or the bottom of the chart and let it represent zero, marking it on the vertical scale line at the left-hand margin, low enough or high enough not to interfere, for the present, with the price picture.

If volume of sales is normally low for the stock let each heavy line above the zero line represent 20,000 shares traded per day in that particular issue. If volume is normally heavy, or likely to become so, let each heavy line represent 100,000 shares of volume. Plot the volume line by a vertical line, on the same vertical co-ordinate line as the price range for the same day, extending the volume line upward from the zero mark to the point on the volume scale representing the total volume of trading for that day.

It is more satisfactory to try to keep the volume scale at the bottom of the chart. This entails placing the price scale high enough so that the days of high volume will not run up into the price range. If they threaten to do so, on abnormally heavy trading days, the chartist runs them up as high as practical and then simply breaks the vertical line with small dots at its top, to show that the exact volume scale is being temporarily disregarded, and then writes the actual volume of total sales above the dotted line in small figures. This may conceivably become confusing if continued for several days so only the figure for whole thousands of shares is written in, and noted as small as possible.

Shifting the Volume Chart

If, however, the price range of the stock has declined for several months and has dropped so low on the chart that it interferes with even only normal volume at the bottom of the sheet, then the logical procedure is to take the liberty of lifting the entire volume scale and moving it from the bottom of the chart to the top, so that it now appears far above the price range instead of below it.

This, of course, breaks the continuity of the volume portion of the chart but it is a liberty which the student may take when he is keeping his own charts, rather than cutting off the sheet at the difficult point and starting a new one with the price scale high enough not to conflict with the volume. It is a sort of emergency move for use only in special periods of abnormal activity or rapid price movement.

In any case, such a move does not seriously impair the efficacy of the picture, since it is an easy matter to compare the two portions of the volume chart, with the base line at the bottom of the sheet for the first period of time covered, and the later portion at the top of the sheet. When moving the volume chart to the upper portion of the chart it is advisable, of course, still to place the zero, or base, line for volume low enough so that it will not habitually tend to run off the top of the sheet.

The Time Scale

The scale at the bottom of the chart is the date scale and marks, for future reference, the continuous passage of time over which the chart extends. It is a simple affair, for each vertical line counts as one day of trading. In commencing the chart on a new stock the first day of price range and volume is properly dated. The practical type of chart paper will have its vertical lines so close together that it would be confusing to try to enter the date of each successive day. The student may decide upon his own system. He may enter the date only on Saturdays, or Mondays, or at any interval so long as he maintains the regularity of that interval throughout the time duration of the entire chart.

Holidays on the Time Scale

Many stock charts skip one day's vertical line for holidays on the New York Stock Exchange, or even for Sundays, but we do not approve of such practice. From a theoretical, as well as a practical standpoint, it seems highly logical to completely ignore days on which the New York Stock Exchange is closed, no matter for what reason, unless, of course, the closing should be extended over a long period of time, as at the opening of the World War in 1914, or the bank holidays in March, 1933.

So long as there is no opportunity for free and open trading in any stock or in the general market it appears illogical to leave a blank vertical line where the range and volume record should naturally appear. If such blanks are left it tends to distort the true pictorial record of trading which is the basis for chart reading and analysis of technical action.

To make our meaning perfectly clear let us assume, that, for any reason whatever, the New York Stock Exchange decided to suspend trading on Tuesday and Wednesday of a certain week. In such case, no empty spaces on the vertical lines would be left on the chart. The range for Thursday would follow on the very next vertical line after Monday.

Monday's trading picture, in the normal sequence, always follows immediately after Saturday's, without any space left for the Sunday holiday. This theory is the chief objection to yearly co-ordinate paper on which there is a line, dated, for each day of the entire year. Of course, this objection applies to some extent also to special stock chart papers which provide a time scale divided in sixths, but these sheets at least omit Sundays.

On the other hand, however, it seems quite logical to leave vacant vertical lines on days when the stock exchange is open as usual but when no transactions are recorded in the individual stock being charted. This is an entirely different matter, for in such a case there was ample opportunity to trade, and the fact that no trades were made is an integral part of the trading history and should thus be included in the chart picture.

In such cases we may adopt the simple expedient of leaving the vertical range line blank but inserting a small x, or zero, slightly below the base line on the volume scale to show that that day has been recorded but the volume of sales was zero.

Some chartists include a dotted vertical line on the price range scale in such a case, showing the closing bid and asked price, but, in our opinion, this merely clouds the chart picture and serves no very adequate purpose.

Charting Ex-Dividend and Other Information

There are a few other devices which are used to denote special change which seems logically a part of the trading history of any stock. When an issue goes ex-dividend it would be manifestly unfair and confusing not to note that fact. In such case a small x is placed just above the high of the price range for the ex-dividend day. When a stock goes ex-rights or ex-stock dividend a similar device (XR or XS) is used.

Helpful Notes on "Fundamentals" May Be Added

Many students find it helpful also to note in the margins of each chart certain significant fundamental facts that relate to the particular stock charted. By including up-to-date factual comment right on the face of each chart this data automatically comes before the student daily and the need is obviated for reassembling this information every time that technical implications become critical.

Probably the facts most frequently found useful when entered on chart margins include comparative period earnings, dividend rate, dividend meeting date, capitalization, number of shares outstanding, funded debt, large bank or RFC loans, dividend arrears, ratio of quick assets to liabilities, etc.

Anticipated levels of resistance to advance or decline (the subject of resistance levels is taken up later on in the Course), once ascertained from a study of back history, may be checked against the price scale, and your own symbols may be used to represent their varying degrees of importance. Also brief notes on news items of interest may be added – but, of course, in such a manner as not to obscure the present or future technical pattern.

Starting a New Sheet

When the chart reaches the end of one sheet of paper a new sheet is prepared with the proper scale. It is important not to change the scale when starting a new sheet, unless the old one has become utterly impractical, for changing the scale changes all aspects of the picture and infinitely reduces the pictorial value of the new sheet in relation to the old one.

Shifting the price scale up or down on the left-hand vertical margin, without changing the scale itself, however, is not only allowable but advisable. For instance, if the lowest horizontal line on the old sheet was a price of 40 and the price of the charted stock has declined to 46 at the end of the first sheet then the price scale on the next sheet should be lowered so that the lowest horizontal line would be perhaps 20 instead of 40. This automatically raises the position of the price range on the new sheet and places it nearer the middle of the paper where it is not only more easily read but is not so likely to drop off the sheet in charting of the subsequent movement. And vice-versa in the case of a rapid upward movement which has brought the price range too close to the top of the sheet.

In what the chart maker always hopes will be very rare cases the price range may go up or down so rapidly that it runs off the current chart paper before it has consumed the time capacity of the entire sheet. In such cases start a new sheet with the price scale raised or lowered to bring the range again near the middle of the new sheet. The old sheet may then be cut off on the last vertical range line so that it can be moved over to join onto the next sheet of the chart whenever reference is desired with the preceding movement.

In some cases you may discover that your stock moves off the sheet, either up or down, too rapidly because you have made your price scale too large. When this error becomes apparent there is nothing to do but start a new chart with a smaller price scale; that is, allowing less vertical space to a full point of price change. Moreover, since it is difficult to compare two charts on which the price scale differs, you will find it advisable as a rule to re-draw your first chart to the revised scale. This should not happen very often, and you will soon learn to set your price scale to accord with the normal price range or "swing" habits of any stock you start to chart.

All sheets of a chart series on the same stock should be carefully numbered at the top of each sheet. The name of the stock, or its ticker symbol, may be placed in any convenient available position, being careful, for later reference, that it appears on each sheet of the series.

Chart work may be done with pen and ink, but we have found it easier, quicker and fully as satisfactory to use pencil – preferably a No. 2 or medium soft lead to give a fairly heavy black line. Trend lines, patterns, and other notes which are not an integral portion of the chart itself, are subject to revision and should be easily erasable in light pencil marks; for this we suggest a No. 3 pencil, sharply pointed.

Time Range Necessary

In order to be of practical service in studying formations and technical action a daily stock chart must cover at least several weeks, and preferably several months. The longer the period of time covered the more complete is the pictorial record and the more satisfactory and valuable the chart in practical study and analysis.

Even though daily charts are necessary for gauging the very nearby minor trend, from recent price action formations, we can construct charts covering practically any period of time that we may choose, such as weekly, monthly or even yearly. Note the daily, weekly and monthly charts of American Can that clarify this lesson (Figs. I.1, I.2, I.3).

Although weekly charts require less frequent entry and provide a more compact record they do not give as close a picture of immediate nearby movements as do daily charts. The principle value of weekly charts lies in the student's ability to more readily judge the longer range trends and formations and assist greatly in determining the approximate limits of important trading areas where strong buying or selling may be anticipated.

Monthly charts afford a condensed picture of the long Bull or Bear market swings, of years' duration, and show the important reversals of these same major trends. These monthly charts, although by themselves of limited aid in short term trading, do afford helpful long term perspective. Of all these types we believe the daily and weekly charts to be the most profitable tools for technical students.

Thus far we have been speaking almost entirely of charts on individual issues but we have previously seen that charts may be constructed on groups of issues as well or even on the entire market – in fact on almost any conceivable object which is traded in at changing prices in a free and open market.

STOCK PRICE MOVEMENTS

Within the progress of price history, from day to day – month to month – and year to year, we find three well defined movements, all in progress at the same time. These are the broad Major movements of bull and bear market proportions, the Intermediate decline and rally movements that occur within the larger major swings; and the Minor day to day, and occasionally week to week, fluctuations that go to make up all Intermediate movements.

Major Movements

These are the long term continuous (bull or bear market) price trends that extend over a period of years and which are the primary concern of long term investors for income, having large capital resources and abounding patience. These trends change their course most infrequently seeming to follow closely the cycles of business. They are apparently more influenced by fundamental economic laws than by those supply and demand factors with which we are most particularly concerned in this study.

The Dow Jones Industrial Average chart (Frontispiece) clearly depicts 13 of these Bull and Bear market swings from 1897 to date – six completed cycles and the start of a seventh which, at the date of this writing, has not been completed. Note the characteristic low volume periods from which bull markets habitually have their origin – the ensuing "mark-up" and the warnings of extraordinarily heavy volume, without proportionate price gains, that signal the final stages of these rises. See how bear markets generally start down from bull market peaks with at first a sharp increase of volume and price movement, and then are followed by declining activity until the pressure of offerings has run its course and the foundation is laid for a new Bull movement.

Note the long base that preceded the tremendous bull market from 1924 to 1929, the severity of the bear market that followed into 1932, and the latest bull swing recovery from the latter lows to current date. How clearly this chart reveals the absolute necessity of being on the "right" side of the market and the utter foolishness of believing that "stocks can be put away and forgotten."

Intermediate Movements

Within each major bull and bear market there are many lesser swings – "intermediate" speculative movements – that generally occur several times within the period of a year. These afford excellent profit opportunities for the "technically" informed trader – far greater in the aggregate than are possible for the long term investor holding commitments throughout Major movements.

Very much the same characteristics of price and volume action are found in Intermediate movements as are noted in the larger Major swings of which these Intermediate movements are but component parts. However, because of the more frequent reversals and shorter duration and extent of Intermediate price movements, one to profit repeatedly thereby must employ forecasting methods affording a far finer degree of accuracy than when judging the long Major trend; and it is here that thorough understanding and skillful application of the laws of technical analysis pay largest returns.

Minor Movements

All of those component short term movements that go to make up each Intermediate swing are referred to as Minor trend or Immediate movements – be they a matter of weeks, days, hours or minutes. However only the most nimble in temperament and skilled of professionals can consistently profit from such narrow movements. The expenses of commissions and taxes are disproportionate to the limited extent of these Minor movement possibilities and do not warrant the wear and

This chart reveals the necessity of being on the "right" side of the market.

tear on a layman's nerves and the increased element of capital risk. Minor price movements, nevertheless, do lend themselves to technical analysis and give, thereby, early clue to the direction of price trend from areas of uncertainty, indicate the start of new intermediate swings, and are most helpful guides to the timing of one's market operations.

Major Trends Shown on Monthly Charts

The three principal classifications of stock price movements, as described above, may be seen as they occur in an individual stock on the monthly, weekly and daily charts of American Can (Figs I.1, I.2, I.3). The monthly chart (Fig I.1) covers the period from 1924 to mid-1937, and depicts a major upward or "bull" movement from 1924 to late 1929, a major downward or "bear" movement from late 1929 to mid-1932, and then another major "bull" movement from mid-1932 to late 1935. The downward movement from late 1935 to mid-1937 may be regarded as a major "bear" movement, or as an abnormally extended Intermediate "correction" in the Major "bull" market which started in 1932. Only the future can tell as this is written which of these designations is correct in theory, since the first movement of prices in a new major trend is often indistinguishable from an important Intermediate reverse movement within the old major trend. However, from the point of view of the practical trader the theoretical designation is not important; if he learns to

Fig. I.1

MONTHLY HIGH AND LOW PRICES

AMERICAN CAN
(MONTHLY HIGH AND LOW PRICES)

Fig. I.2

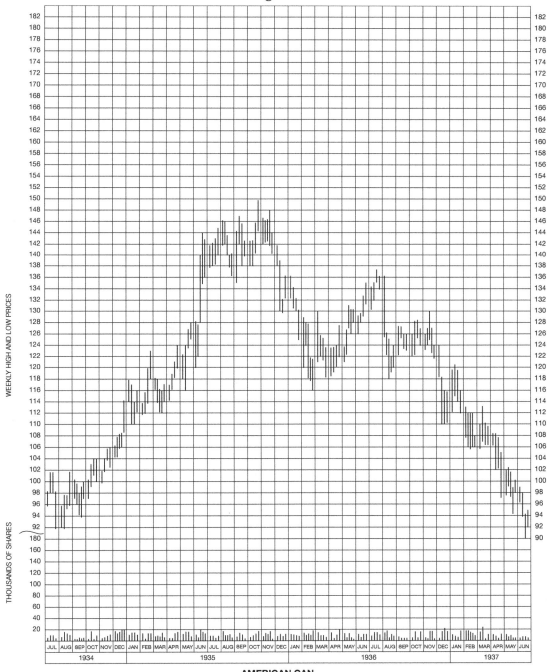

WEEKLY HIGH AND LOW PRICES

THOUSANDS OF SHARES

| | 1934 | 1935 | 1936 | 1937 |

AMERICAN CAN

Fig. I.3

AMERICAN CAN

recognize the Intermediate turning points, if he is able to buy when an Intermediate upward movement starts and sell when it reverses into an Intermediate downward movement, his profits will be safe regardless of the Major trend.

Intermediate Trends Shown by Weekly Chart

Figure I.2 shows the price range of American Can for each week from July, 1934 through June, 1937. Six Intermediate movements appear during this period – up from June, 1934 to October, 1935; down to February, 1936; up to July, 1936; down to August, 1936; up to November, 1936; and down to June, 1937. Each of these price movements (with the possible exception of the limited upward move from August to November, 1936) offered the informed trader a good "swing".

The forecasting of intermediate movements, such as those pictured on this weekly chart of American Can, will be our principal study in this Course since they provide us with the safest and most dependable profits. But, in order to forecast such moves, it is necessary to follow and interpret the minor fluctuations of price as they swing up and down within the path of the Intermediate trends; and for the study of these Minor movements we must turn to the daily charts.

Importance of Minor Movement Study

Figure I.3 shows the daily price range (and volume) of American Can for the months from April through September, 1936. Comparing this with the weekly chart we see that it covers the latter part of the intermediate upward movement that started in February, all of the "correction" that took place in August (an Intermediate movement in the direction opposite to the apparent Major trend is frequently called a Corrective movement), and the first part of the Intermediate up-trend that ran out in

Charts make it easier for us to analyze correctly the technical position of a stock.

November, 1936. Within this 6 months of daily price action we can find at least 20 minor movements, each running from a few days to a few weeks.

The minor movements, it will be seen, were mostly of too limited extent (in per-centage price change) and ran their course too quickly to permit us to trade on them with profit. They served, however, to build the foundations and patterns, or give the signals, which made it possible to detect changes in the intermediate trend of "Can" stock.

The next six studies of this Course are devoted to the analysis and interpretation of the minor movements which signal changes in the Intermediate and Major trends. For the present all we need to fix in mind is the normal habit of stock prices to move simultaneously in these three trends, and the fact that the minor movements are of prime importance because changes which occur within them forecast the changes in Intermediate trends on which it is profitable to trade.

Technical Analysis, is in fact, in a very broad sense, a study of the habitual price movements and volume action of stocks, and the significance of any changes in these habits, or departures from the current habit or trend. Such habits and such changes from the accustomed action are most easily detected, studied and interpreted through the medium of charts. In fact, it would be extremely difficult to understand and analyze them properly without recourse to a complete charted record. That is the reason why this Course is based on the use of charts – not because there is any magic in the charts themselves but because the charts make it easier for us to analyze correctly the technical position of a stock and forecast its probable future price trend.

Study II

IMPORTANT REVERSAL FORMATIONS

Summary of Chart Advantages

In our introductory lesson we observed some of the advantages of stock charts as set apart from the tedious study of figures gleaned from newspapers, in reviewing the trading history of any stock and approaching a study of its technical action. We found that the stock chart not only saves time and offers complete memory but that, through its easy coordination of the trading history, it makes the recorded picture so simple as to permit of delving much deeper into the science of technical action.

And in reference to technical action we noted that it was composed of elements beyond those of fundamental analysis but yet which have a decided bearing on any full and complete study of forecasting future price movements, with special relation to conditions arising primarily from market trading in itself.

When we become quite familiar with stock charts we shall find ourselves looking for various pictures and patterns formed by our charts, but if we are to be complete masters of our study and get the fullest benefits from our own analysis it is important that we do not entirely lose sight of the fundamental basis for the formation of those pictures and patterns.

That fundamental basis is in actual stock market trading, and actual stock market trading is the result of individual actions by many thousands of people, based in turn upon their own hopes, fears, anticipations, knowledge or lack of knowledge, necessities and plans. It is the danger of losing sight of this human element in stock charts that we must guard against, and since this human element is basic it may be wise to fit it into the foundations of our study at the very outset.

Public vs. the Insiders

By and large, there are two classes of stock market traders who have the greatest influence upon prices. They are the public and the insiders.[1] Both are rather large and general terms and neither is all-embracing but they should serve our purposes of explanation.

The public portion of the trading element is made up of all those individuals throughout the entire world who buy and sell stocks in the open market either for investment or speculation, but in a rather casual, amateurish and comparatively small way.

The inside portion of the trading element is made up of those individuals, groups or associations who are professionals at the task, and who make the buying and selling of stocks for profit their important or only business.

---

[1] Insider trading and stock manipulation today are much more difficult than the insider trading described here and carried on in the years before the Securities Exchange Act of 1934.

From such definitions it is not difficult to see why the insiders are generally more successful in their market campaigns than are the public. They are in the minority with respect to numbers but they are much better organized and equipped. Their potential capital is probably a good deal smaller than the potential capital of the total public trading element, yet their smaller capital is a hundred-fold more potent in its purpose because it is professionally organized, is directed in specialized fields of campaign and put to its greatest use by a compact, individual management with one definite aim in view.

That one definite aim of the compact and powerful inside party is confined to raising or lowering the price of one specific issue, a group of issues or even the entire market but, in the final analysis, it is directed fundamentally toward making a profit for the inside party. This must be done in one of two ways. The insiders must buy stocks from the public and sell them back to the public at higher prices, or they must sell stocks to the public and buy them back at lower prices.

Why the Public Usually Loses

If the insiders are able to do this with fair regularity then it stands also fairly apparent to reason that the opposite element in market trading, the public, is going to lose the money that the insiders make through their profitable operations. In other words, the public is the "goat". Many authorities and market writers will take exception to such a bald and sweeping statement. They have done so in the past, but the logic of our argument still holds.

It holds further when we consider that the inside element is in this business from a professional angle. This is their livelihood, their income. They must make a comfortable margin of average profit or they would no longer stay in that business. The unsuccessful insiders therefore drop out, but the successful ones remain to make up the group which takes its major living by buying and selling stocks to the public for a fairly consistent profit.

Though we are convinced that this is the theoretical case, still we would not have the reader assume a fatalistic attitude toward such a situation. That is largely the purpose of this group of studies. In the first place, the insider does not always make a profit. He makes mistakes too, but they are in the minority.

In the second place, and conversely, the public does not always lose. In the third place, the statement is a wide and general one that when the insider profits, the public loses. In countless situations and campaigns both may profit.

And finally, our previous definition of the insider and the public is necessarily also a general one. There is no clear-cut dividing line between the two groups. The man who runs a grocery store in Keokuk might conceivably place himself in the theoretical ranks of the inside element, by extraordinary ability, and reap handsome profits, comparatively just as large as the real insider, even though he is not accepted, strictly speaking, in the definition. He would be our idea of the model student who thoroughly digests this and other studies on successful stock market trading and who therefore, in greater measure than the rest of the public class, makes it his business to profit from stock trading.

How to Become an Insider

We are fully conscious that representatives of both of these general trading classes may read and profit from this course, but its effort is directed more toward aiding the ambitious student in the public class to approach the ability, the technique and the profits of the true insider.

There are two chief methods of accomplishing such a purpose. The first is to study conditions and analyze them along the lines pursued by the insider, who must of necessity be an expert at technical action. The second is to discover what the insider is doing in the market and to follow his lead.

The strongest indications are the result of organized buying or selling.

The first method is to analyze probable future operations of the public trading element. The second is to analyze the probable future operations of the inside element. The technical market student is therefore somewhat between these two classes and, it may be hoped, at an advantage over both.

In many cases it is impossible to differentiate between the technical signals accounted for by public operations or inside activity, but in such cases it is generally also unnecessary. If our chart studies of technical action show us, for instance, that much more powerful buying than selling is going on in a stock we need not worry, for the immediate future, about whether the buying is coming from the public or from the inside element. It would be more likely to justify our complete faith if it came from the inside element but the important thing is that it is present and must be considered the chief forecasting element in our analysis.

So public buying and selling has a most decided effect upon our technical picture, but we must now also realize that the strongest and most important indications are the result of organized buying or selling for a real campaign by the inside interest. We must keep the activities, past, present and future, of both classes in mind, but we shall find activities of the more professional element our most reliable and, fortunately, our most frequent guide.

The Professional Group

The best known and most important element in the past in our group of professional insiders is the "pool".[2] We shall not weary the reader with a detailed explanation of what a pool is and how it operates; old style "pools" have presumably been outlawed by the SEC. The fact remains, however, that professional groups do still operate in the market and do create the same old technical situations. We may define a professional group as an organization of the inside element banded together for a campaign in any stock or group of stocks. That campaign consists in engineering portions of a complete cycle which, in turn, consists of four parts – accumulation, mark-up, distribution and mark-down.

A bull group accumulates, marks up and distributes. A bear group distributes, marks down and accumulates. The former makes a profit by buying stocks from the public, advancing their market price, and reselling them to the public. The latter profits by selling stocks to the public, depressing the price and buying the same stocks back again from the public.

The public, of course, is by no means always the same set of individuals but it is the same general class of individuals. Furthermore, we must not be understood to mean that a bull group is dishonest or unfair in advancing or depressing the price of its favored issue. On the contrary, if the group has made its analysis correctly the stock will move in the right direction largely of its own accord. Suffice it now to say merely that the stock chart helps us to detect such professional operations and to "get aboard" on the right side of the market, through observation of recurring patterns and their subsequent results.

Charts Detecting Professional Operations

The stock chart is constantly giving us a picture of all trading history. It is not always an intelligible picture. In fact, the formations which are replete with forecasting significance, develop rather infrequently; but they are highly important when they do appear. They are important because the science of chart reading is devoted to studying certain standard pictures which help us to forecast future price movement through their successive appearance and the unanimity with which certain future price movements follow such standard patterns.

After we have observed the usual habits of such successively appearing patterns

---

[2] Today the activities of numerous groups of interested parties operating in various stocks along the lines described in the text are no longer referred to as "Pools". These days "Sponsorship" describes widespread operations on stock exchanges everywhere that are not all that far removed from connections with the old pools. The old saying still holds that "the more things change, the more they stay the same".

or pictures we may come to give them technical names. We may find some pictures which generally forecast a reversal of previous price movement and others which mean merely a continuation of the previous movement. According to their relative position with respect to the past movement we may say that they indicate accumulation, distribution, mark-up or mark-down, and we may thus act accordingly, to take advantage in our practical market trading of the promised future movement.

Formations which are replete with forecasting significance develop rather infrequently, but are highly imporatnt.

Some of these pictures can be explained quite logically, Others must be laid to the habits of those interested in certain stocks who always use the same campaign tactics. Other patterns can hardly be explained at all, except by the use of some rather vague and involved theories. But if we find such patterns valuable in forecasting the future price movement of a stock we need not worry too much about what causes the patterns or their subsequent habitual movement. It is enough, for our practical trading purposes, to recognize the pattern and know its probable future significance.

Establishing the Patterns

The following lessons offer as complete a picture as possible of the more important patterns, rules and practices, connected with this field.

The science of chart reading, however, is not as easy as the mere memorizing of certain patterns and pictures and recalling what they generally forecast. Any general stock chart is a combination of countless different patterns and its accurate analysis depends upon constant study, long experience and knowledge of all the fine points, both technical and fundamental, and, above all, the ability to weigh opposing indications against each other, to appraise the entire picture in the light of its most minute and composite details as well as in the recognition of any certain and memorized formula.

Turns Are Most Important

The most important general element of analysis, it will easily be seen, is the judging of important changes in trend, or turning points, in the price movement of a stock. In detail, this will be the greatest part of our future study, but it is not too early to call attention at this time to a few generalizations about the analysis of such reversals.

It is unusual for the price movement of any stock or the general market to remain stationary for long intervals. Prices are usually going places and doing things. They are either going down or up, and are in process of pursuing a trend – generally an irregular trend, but a trend none the less. Once a major trend is established it must be assumed, and quite logically, that such trend will continue until it is reversed. That is a simple statement but it calls attention to the importance of gauging general turning points in chart analysis. And we shall have more to say later concerning the error of bucking such a major trend once it is established.

Suffice it now to say that trends are the important practical money-making aspect of stock chart trading. They should be followed until a reversal is fairly defined. That, of course, is the rub. Detecting reversal formations is not easy, for there are many minor reversals which mislead the amateur and even the experienced student.

In the main, however, there are a few general observations which may assist. A major trend seldom reverses itself suddenly or without warning. Once a trend is established it takes considerable time and power to turn it. Signals of reversal are generally given, therefore, for some time previous to the actual turn.

The most important signal is the beginning of minor reversals, the slowing up of the previous movement, perhaps a gradual rounding off of that movement. After the final extreme price of the previous trend has been established it must be tested by subsequent movements. If such movements tend to depart in the opposite direction of the previous trend then the proof grows gradually clearer that a definite reversal has taken place.

Importance of Volume

But the price range is not the only tool we have for judging such turns. There are, of course, countless minor indications to the practiced student but the most easily apparent, and valuable one, next to the course of actual price range, is the increase in volume, or the activity of trading.

We shall have considerably more to say about volume throughout our entire study, and especially in Study VIII, which is devoted to a detailed study of volume action on reversals. A logical explanation of why volume of sales is important on reversals, however, seems properly in order at the beginning of our studies.

Our charts and our study of technical action go back, as always, to their foundations in actual open-market trading and the balance of buying and selling. We have seen that when buying is stronger or heavier than selling the price tends to advance, and vice versa. So while a stock is in a declining major trend the balance of supply and demand is slightly on the supply, or selling, side. Until there is a change in the technical situation this will continue to be the case.

Why Volume Increases on Reversals

But what is it logical to expect when our awaited change in the technical situation does take place? Naturally, the change will be increased buying power. More and better buying will be the most logical thing that will tend to reverse this technical down trend. Gradually the buying will become more active and will slowly return to a more equal balance with the selling. Finally, if the buying continues to improve, it will exceed the selling and slowly move the balance of power from the selling to the buying side and the major price trend is reversed.

But how can volume be affected by such a change? After all there must be a seller for every buyer. This is quite true, but we must consider that there is a certain amount of momentum to the major trend. Selling may conceivably "dry up" and result in a change of the balance without increased volume. But generally, the selling has sufficient momentum to keep it in steady supply until our friends, the public, begin to realize that the selling was unwise. They realize it long after the trend has been reversed. We are attempting to realize it before the public does.

Volume Needed to Overcome Momentum

Granted then that in most cases the selling will continue in fairly stable volume while the turn is being made, it is going to take a greater amount of buying to turn the major trend than had been normal while the trend was downward. There are still just as many shares sold as are bought but it takes more of both to stem and reverse the momentum of the downward trend. Thus on major turns our index of sales volume will almost show an increase from the previous normal.

If the reader does not immediately visualize the logic of this tabloid explanation he need not worry about the matter just now. This particular explanation for high volume on reversals is not important from a practical standpoint, is admittedly far from a complete explanation, and will be discussed more fully in our later studies.

In fact, if this were the sole explanation then we could not expect volume to increase very greatly on reversals and the change might be so slight as to make our consideration of the phenomenon unimportant. We have given this explanation first because it seems the most basic and automatic one, but there are plenty of others, perhaps more important and more easily understandable.

One of these additional causes for the common tendency for volume to increase is simply because the previous move has begun to meet resistance. Insiders with large blocks of stock to sell or buy must go slowly for fear of forcing prices down or up too rapidly. But when they see the stock absorbing such selling or buying more easily, their first and natural tendency is to increase the speed of their operations, completing them sooner, raising volume of sales and leading to reversal, provided, as assumed, that the new buying or selling power continues its own campaign.

Somewhat the same observations apply to professional operations or other artificial manipulation. The best way for an inside group to buy stock easily is to put it down first, selling a lot of it, perhaps employing matched or wash sales (outlawed under the SEC, but ... ?) to raise volume and attract trading attention, and then suddenly to reverse into buying activity and buy up all the stock which its previous campaign of discouragement has brought into the market. It is easy to see how such artificial manipulation would raise volume of sales on the turn, or reversal.

In Study VIII we shall note a type of exception where high volume comes after the turn instead of before it. This exception to the rule occurs most frequently when a bear trend is reversed into a bull trend, but almost never on the reversal from a bull to a bear market.

The One-Day Reversal

Our volume rule holds generally, however, and leads to what we shall name a one-day reversal. It describes what many call a turnover day, a volume shake-out, or a climax. If the market has been declining steadily on steady volume there may suddenly appear one day of exceptionally high volume, with price weakness in the morning and strength in the afternoon, and with the close not far from the best price and at the opposite end of the range line from the extreme low.

The logical assumption is that the one-day reversal was engineered for the purpose of obtaining stock. They sell recklessly in the morning and catch many stop-loss orders on the way down. Also the sharp decline and high volume of activity call attention to the stock and many unwary traders sell it in anticipation of much lower prices.

Just when this weakness and heavy selling is at its height, they reverse their tactics and buy all the stock there is for sale. They find much more for sale on the way up in the afternoon than on the way down in the morning for many watchers have put their selling orders in just above the market, thinking the rally is only a short one.

The day ends with the price back up near the highest, ready to continue the move upward tomorrow or within a few days, and the insiders have accumulated a nice line of stock for their campaign. High volume is the natural accompaniment of such a movement.

Examples of One-Day Reversal

The one-day reversal occurs at the top of a movement, indicating a change to a downward trend, just as it does at the bottom, and with the same implications. In either case it may be defined as a day of high volume with prices moving early in the day in the same direction as the previous general trend and farther than previous levels, then turning back during the latter part of the day and closing at or near the end of the day's price range opposite its opening thrust.

We can find several examples of the one-day reversal in the charts accompanying this study. Note the following.

Fig II.2 – A one-day bottom reversal on May 14.

Fig II.3 – An excellent example of a one-day bottom reversal on February 5, and a one-day top reversal on February 25 though less typical since the volume did not run as high as on the preceding day.

Fig II.5 – A one-day bottom reversal on April 23.

It should be noted that the one-day reversal in itself is not a forecasting signal to be given undue weight in practical trading. For one thing, not all one-day reversals lead at once to rapid, worthwhile moves in the new trend; days and weeks may elapse before the reverse move really gets under way.

However, as a phenomenon occurring frequently within other patterns or formations that are indicative of impending turns, it gives an important clue to probable trends, and is most useful as a warning to watch closely the chart in which it may have appeared to see what patterns may follow and to be ready for the move when it comes.

Comparative Volume on "Tops" and "Bottoms"

We have been discussing the general rule of high volume accompanying changes in price trends, mentioning incidentally the one-day reversal as a phenomenon frequently appearing at these times. It remains to be noted that volume is a relative matter; i.e., when we speak of high volume we mean a volume of transactions greater than has been prevailing for some time previously. It is particularly important to bear this relativity in mind when comparing the volume which usually accompanies and signals a "top" or change from an upward to a downward price trend, with the volume accompanying a bottom. Each is normally characterized by high volume; i.e., higher volume than has been prevailing, but the high volume at tops is almost always much greater than the high volume at bottoms.

The prime cause for this difference between volume at tops and bottoms is undoubtedly the fact that the public becomes interested and actively engaged to a far greater extent in an upward or bull movement so that more pressure of volume is required to overcome and reverse this optimistic public participation than is required to stem the relatively uninteresting and inactive markets at the end of a downward movement.

Price and Volume Must Be Considered Together

The point of our recent discussion is that both the price picture and the volume picture are important in themselves but that for complete and efficient working analysis of technical formations both price and volume must be considered in combination.

We have spoken previously of the importance of volume in stemming a movement, either up or down, after it has gained momentum. The reader will discover that high volume is helpful in anticipating reversals in many other situations also.

> *For efficient analysis of technical formations both price and volume must be considered.*

The practical trader, by ear, eye or chart, knows full well how often a stock or the general market does quite the opposite of what the public expects and should expect it to do. This is merely a point of insider psychology. The public is generally wrong in its forecast because it would be difficult for anyone to make money in the market if prices always did the obvious thing.

The insider is in business to make money, but he cannot make money by following the crowd and doing the obvious thing. He makes money by dealing on the opposite side from the public.

Volume Showing Insiders Crossing the Public

So it is not illogical to expect that technical action can be a great friend in detecting when the insider is crossing the crowd and preparing to reverse the obvious movement. In October of 1931, for instance, the general market turned from a major decline into an intermediate recovery. At about that time Woolworth declared an extra dividend and there was very bullish enthusiasm in the press and brokerage gossip about the split-up of its British subsidiary.

There appeared no reason for any further bear market in a stock seemingly so well placed as this one. The public bought avidly. It advanced from 45 to 55 in a few days. But just about when the best news was coming out the stock began to hesitate. Volume of sales was terrific but the price barely advanced for several successive days.

The reader is right. It was inside distribution. The public was buying, but the stock was not going up as fast as it should under such conditions. Why? Because the insiders were selling tons of it. The stock barely got above 55 around the end of October and before the close of the year it was back down to 35.

Another example of how high volume bears out a turn when prices cross public psychology may be recalled when Lorillard suddenly resumed dividends around the first of December, 1931. The stock rose only two points on the day of the announcement and could get no further. The volume was tremendous, with nearly 40,000 shares traded in a single day, compared with a normal average of less than 10,000 shares a day. In the following week the stock not only lost those two points of gain but was back down near its extreme low once more.

Again on about November 3rd, 1931, the general market was faced with a most melancholy situation. RKO had just gone into receivership and was dragging Radio down with it. Wabash had just gone into receivership and it looked as though a number of the other weakened roads would go within the next couple days. In fact, two or three names were mentioned about the street which were about to announce default. The railroad wage controversy had just taken a disappointing turn. Everything looked exceedingly bad for the stock market. Naturally, the public sold. What happened?

The market dropped fairly swiftly in early trading but only went down about one full point from the previous close on the accredited averages. From then on there was a slow but steady recovery, and the market closed with a net gain of nearly three points. Technically, it was a one-day reversal. Volume of sales was heavier than it had been for many days but yet it was not terribly high. The important point for the student was that the public must have sold heavily on the bearish news, and yet prices went up. The only logical conclusion was that the insiders were buying heavily in spite of the bad news. In just four days the market had touched a new high for two months past and showed a further gain of over 12 full points on the major averages from the day when the powerful support and accumulation showed itself in technical action.

Introductory Review

We have thus built, it may be hoped, some further foundation of introduction for our study of stock charts and technical action. We have tried to show why technical action is highly important and how the charts can help us in studying it. We have noted in particular the value in detecting early signs of reversal in any major or long-continued trend. We have seen that it is important to analyze the development of such reversals in advance of public recognition. We have seen that such reversals often result from operation of powerful inside factors and we have attempted to discover some logical explanations of why technical action often warns us that the market is not going to do the obvious.

Finally, we have found that volume is quite as important as price movement in making up our complete picture of the trading record, and we have noted that we may find individual patterns and pictures which recur not infrequently and which give us a reliable clue to probable future action from which we may reap practical trading profit. We may now go on to a more detailed study of the most frequent and dependable of such technical chart formations.

Major vs. Minor Reversals

In taking up a study of the more important chart patterns, or formations, it is logical to begin with the pictures which generally indicate a reversal of the previous trend, for we have already noted the rather apparent importance of such turning movements. From a practical trading standpoint, they warn us to switch our short-term speculative operations from the side of the previous main trend to the side of the newly developed or reversed trend.

Reversals, of course, often occur when the long-term or major trend does not truly reverse itself. This is somewhat of a technicality, however, since the intermediate reversals may be quite worth playing. The longer the time taken for the chart to form the picture of any formation the stronger is the forecasting significance of that pattern and the longer will be the ensuing move. The length, size and strength of our formation, then, gives a good idea of whether it is going to be a major reversal or a minor one, and thus whether it is worth switching for.

Description of Head and Shoulders

Our first important formation which usually signals a reversal in trend is the Head and Shoulders pattern. It consists roughly of a sharp point in the direction of the previous trend, followed a little later by another sharp thrust carrying prices beyond the level of the first, and then another movement in the same direction as the two preceding ones, but going only about as far as the first movement noted, and therefore not as far as the second.

The furthest turning point of this third sharp movement is the last objective of the previous trend in the former direction, and is followed by gradual development of the new trend in the opposite direction from the third small turn and in the direction of the reversed, or new trend.

> *Our first important formation which usually signals a reversal is the Head and Shoulders pattern.*

The formation is equally applicable in either direction, as is the case with most of our chart pictures. If the preceding movement has been up and the reverse formation is a top reversal then this picture is called the Head and Shoulders top. If the previous trend has been down, then the formation is a bottom reversal and is termed the Head and Shoulders bottom.

Its terminology is more easily traced by reference to the Head and Shoulders top. The first extreme level of the three we have mentioned is called the left shoulder, the second, which goes a little higher, forms the head, and the third or last, extreme level, equal in height with the left shoulder, is called the right shoulder and completes the pattern, similar in anatomical formation to the figure of human head and shoulders.

The Head and Shoulders bottom takes its name as the reverse of the Head and Shoulders top, being the same picture merely turned upside down, though the pictorial relation to the human figure is that of a somewhat unusual posture. The Head and Shoulders bottom picture is sometimes termed the pendant bottom, since it also resembles somewhat the shape of a pendant and this terminology for the bottom picture is a bit more logical for this particular reversal.

Chart Examples of the Head and Shoulders Top

If the mental picture of the Head and Shoulders formation is not yet quite clear to the reader a few specific chart examples should make it so. A nearly perfect Head and Shoulders pattern appears plain to see in the chart of Republic Steel at its bull market peak in 1929 (Fig. II.1). Considering for the moment only the larger and more conspicuous picture, the upthrust of prices to point B in the last week of August formed the first or left shoulder of the pattern. The small recession from that point to point C established the left side or base of the "neck". From here another strong upward movement carried prices in the third week of September to F where a reversal day occurred and the pattern of the price range culminated in a head. From this point prices dropped off sharply to point I, locating the right neck line, then up to J to make the right shoulder. At this point a reversal day again appears and prices then drop off rapidly in the new downward trend – a major trend which continued for about three years.

When we introduced this pattern we referred to it as "nearly perfect". In a perfect Head and Shoulders formation the price levels attained by the right and left shoulders, and the levels of the two sides of the neck should be approximately the same, which is not the case here. Nevertheless Fig II.1 shows an excellent and a typical Head and Shoulders. The size of the pattern, requiring two months for its completion and ranging through points in price, indicated a reversal in trend of major importance.

Typical Volume in Head and Shoulders

The volume action during the formation of the Head and Shoulders in Republic Steel was also typical. Note the high volume accompanying the formation of the left shoulder, the somewhat higher volume at the head, but only slightly increased volume on the right shoulder. This is the typical volume picture to be looked for on the Head and Shoulders formation, but it should be noted here that the relative volume

Fig. II.1

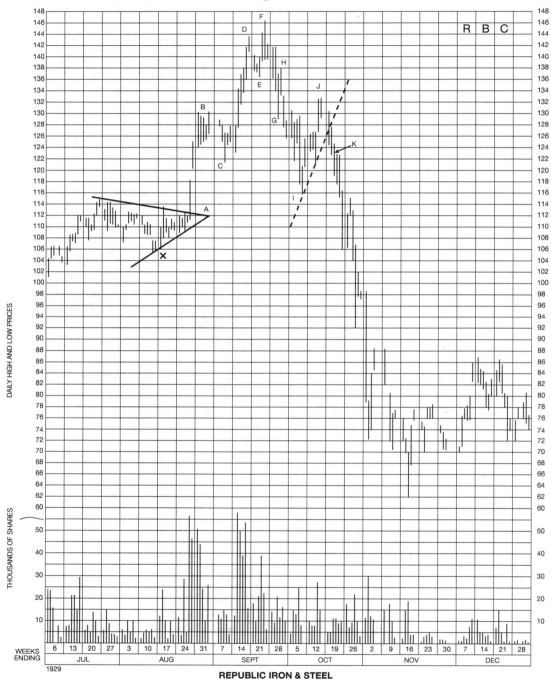

REPUBLIC IRON & STEEL

on the two shoulders and the head does not always follow this typical formula; volume on the right shoulder may, for example, be greater than on the left and, infrequently, greater than on the head. In general, however, increased volume accompanies the formation of both shoulders and the head which, of course, is to be expected from the operation of our general rule previously discussed of high volume on reversals.

We shall revert to the implication of the formation of the neck line at different levels, and discuss other interesting points appearing in Fig. II.1 later on. Let us turn first to another example of a Head and Shoulders top in which the pattern is not quite so obvious to the beginner but in which shoulder and neck levels conform more closely to the ideal picture.

"Breaking the Neck"

In the chart of Western Union for the first six months of 1934 (Fig II.2), we have a left shoulder formed by the area ABCD, a head at E, and a right shoulder at FGHI. The nearly equal time consumed in the formation of the two shoulders, the high volume on the head, and the almost horizontal neck base area BDFH – all conform with the ideal pattern, and

> *Our signal of a genuine Head and Shoulders reversal is the breaking of the neck line.*

point to an eventual price drop of substantial proportions. In this chart the volume that accompanied the formation of the left shoulder exceeded for one day the volume at the head, which is often the case; while the volume on the right shoulder increased only slightly over the days preceding it.

We may proceed now to a consideration of the neck line which might be called the vital point in the Head and Shoulders pattern. Note first that it is the retreat of prices from the right shoulder at I to and below the line established by the base of the left shoulder and the retreat from the head which completes the Head and Shoulders picture. When the market reacted from point I on February 17 we might have been justified in suspecting that a Head and Shoulders reversal was in process of forming; in fact, a bold and well-financed trader might even have hazarded the selling of Western Union stock at this stage; but, conceivably, the reaction from I might have stopped at the 61 level and than turned up again. If that had happened we should not have had a Head and Shoulders, and our too bold trader might have had to take a small loss or, at least, wait for some time for his suspicions to be borne out and his trade to show a profit.

Our important signal of a genuine Head and Shoulders reversal is, therefore, the breaking of the neck line which in the case we are now studying took place on February 23 when the market closed at 59½, below the outer neck line B-H. Note here

Fig. II.2

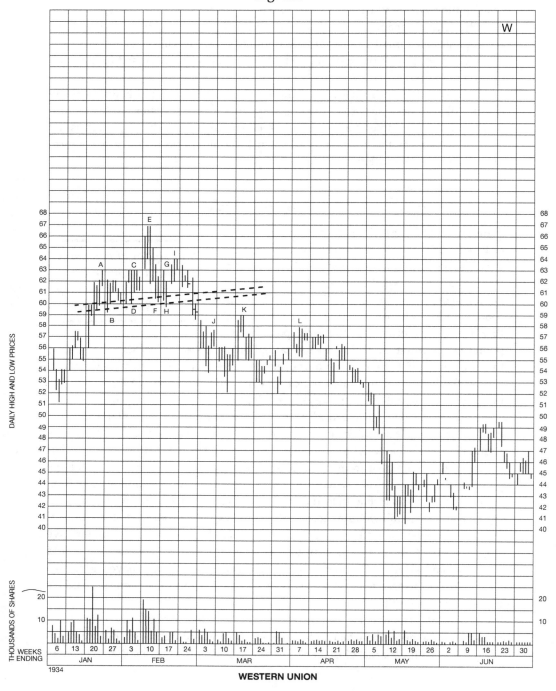

WESTERN UNION

the increase of volume, conspicuous when compared with the volume on the days which preceded, which accompanied the breaking of the neck. This confirmed the signal given by the closing of the day's market below the neck line and is typical of the true Head and Shoulders formation, in which the neck line is nearly horizontal.

Varying Width of Shoulders

Before proceeding to a more definite and practical conclusion of the point brought up in the last paragraph, let us turn for the moment to some examples of the Head and Shoulders pattern in which other variations occur – variations that we may expect to appear quite frequently and must learn to recognize and interpret. In the chart of US Industrial Alcohol for the first half of 1931 (Fig II.3), we have a right shoulder (at F) which took considerably longer to form than did the left shoulder. the rally from E to F gave us a neck line C-E which was broken on March 12 but the volume of sales was very light, failing to confirm decisively the breaking of the trend and indicating that buying power was not yet exhausted. The rally from G gave us another neck line across C-G; this was broken with decisive volume on March 19, and our reversal picture was complete.

In passing, note the fairly typical volume action in this chart, including the one-day reversal on March 10.

Now turn to Fig. II.4, showing the action of Borden during the first six months of 1931. In this case we have the reverse of the picture presented in Fig II.3 in that the left shoulder is heavier and took longer to form than the right shoulder. The neck line B-D was decisively broken with volume on April 15.

Comparing these two charts, Industrial Alcohol and Borden, we may now attempt to explain the reasons for the differing width of shoulders. Where the left shoulder is wider, as in the case of the Borden pattern, large holders of the stock have evidently been ready to take their profits in the neighborhood of 73–74 and distribution has been nearly completed while there was still considerable buying power. Consequently, after the final thrust, the floating supply had fallen largely into the weaker "public" hands; the subsequent rally to the right shoulder at E was very narrow and weak. In the case of Industrial Alcohol, strong holders were not yet ready to distribute their stock when prices attained the peak of the left shoulder at B. The public was still buying. At D distribution began in earnest and continued until the strong buying interest in the stock was finally exhausted at H and prices dropped off precipitately from then on.

This explanation is admittedly reduced to the simplest terms and does not take into account any number of other factors which may have contributed to the reversal in trend, but we must bear in mind that we need not, after all, concern ourselves

Fig. II.3

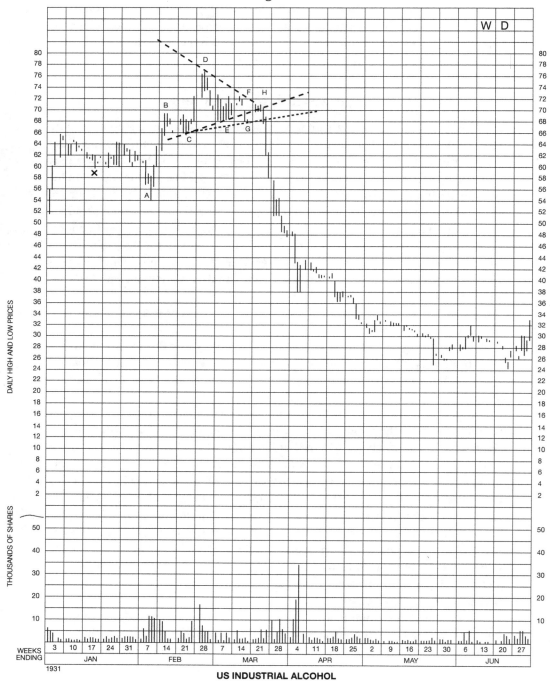

US INDUSTRIAL ALCOHOL

Fig. II.4

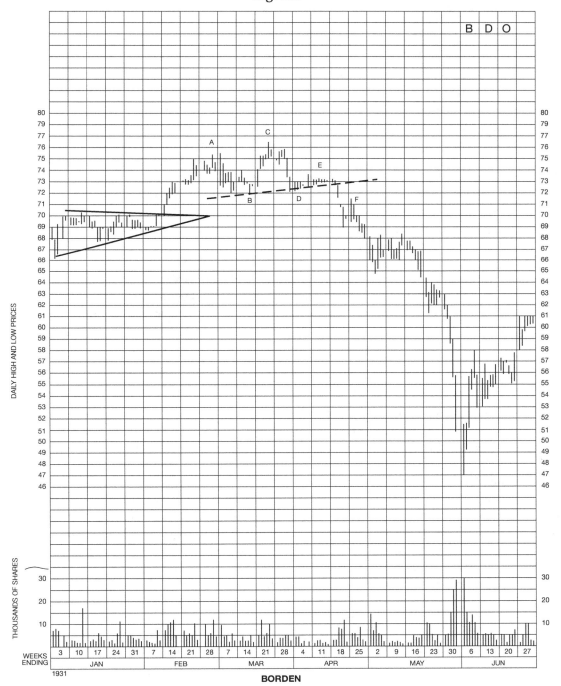

BORDEN

too much with the "whys". So long as the market runs true to form we need not care why it does so.

The Time to Act

We may return now to the point brought up when we called attention to the break-ing of the neck line on page 47. We have seen how the Head and Shoulders pattern is completed when this vital line is broken, how the break away is typically con-firmed by increased volume. Obviously, and without any further explanations being required, the time to put in an order to sell the stock is as soon as the neck line is deci-sively broken. Depending on the size of the pattern, its range and the length of time it consumes in forming, the resulting movement in the reverse trend will be of greater or less extent before an important recovery occurs. A clear Head and Shoul-ders is followed normally by a worthwhile movement and offers the watchful stu-dent an opportunity for considerable profit or, if he is already "long" of the stock, an imperative signal to take his profits and stand aside.

In all of the examples we have shown, except Republic Steel (Fig II.1), and in the great majority of clearly recognizable Head and Shoulders formations, the signal to sell, evidenced by the breaking of the neck with increased volume, comes before the downward movement has gathered momentum and allows ample time for prof-itable action. Let us now study Fig II.1 more thoroughly.

Warning in Drooping Shoulder

In highly excited markets, with the public deeply involved, such as those that occurred at the end of the bull movement in 1929, a new technical situation often develops very rapidly and the reverse trend gets under way with startling speed.

A "drooping" neck line on a Head and Shoulders top is usually indicative of rapidly developing technical weakness. Such a drooping line is, of course, produced when prices drop down from the head to a lower level than the neck base previously formed between the left shoulder and the head, exemplified in the action of Repub-lic Steel (Fig II.1) when the bottom at I formed below the bottom at C. This is defi-nitely a warning, and a warning which is not cancelled by a high right shoulder following it. In the case of our Republic Steel chart, the fact that the rally from I to J carried prices higher than the left shoulder at B, did not change the bearish implica-tions of the picture. This rally might conceivably have carried even higher, higher than the head at F, and still produced an important reversal pattern, as we shall see later on in Study IV when we take up the Broadening Top formation.

On the other hand, the neck-base line remains the critical line in the pattern. Until it is broken decisively the Head and Shoulders formation has not been completed and a reversal signal has not been given. In the case of our Republic Steel example the neck-base line (a line extended across C and I not shown in our illustration) was not penetrated until Saturday, October 19, when the price dropped to 106 and closed at 111.

Fortunately, there are often to be found in these fast developing Head and Shoulders tops with drooping neck lines other critical lines and technical indicators which give us a reliable reversal signal before the neck line is finally penetrated. It would lead to confusion to enter here into a discussion of all the other formations and critical lines which may appear within a Head and Shoulders reversal: they will come up in more logical sequence later on in our Course.

Patterns within Patterns

There is one minor pattern or formation in Fig. II.1, however, which is logically a part of this Head and Shoulders study. So far we have considered only the large, conspicuous pattern which did not begin to suggest itself until the right neck base had been formed at I, or possibly not until the reversal day at J. But closer inspection will discover that we had already formed a smaller and very bearish Head and Shoulders at D, E, F, G, H. This pattern was not strong enough, perhaps, to have convinced us that the long major uptrend had been broken; it might have forecast only a minor or intermediate reaction; but it did sound a warning of technical weakness, putting us on the alert for further developments. And it did, of course, honestly forecast an intermediate reaction for that is what we would term the movement from F to I.

At this point it may be well to refer to the other lines and notations drawn upon the charts accompanying this lesson, which the student has doubtless noticed. These have to do with other formations and significant price actions which will be taken up later on in the Course, and referred back to in due time.

Action on Ascending Neck Lines

In stressing the point, exemplified by Fig II.1 that the Head and Shoulders Top with a drooping or descending neckline shows weakness and forecasts rapid price action, we do not want to convey the impression that the other type, where the neck base forms on the right at a higher level than on the left, is not also bearish. All Head and Shoulders Tops are bearish in their implications. The point to note about the ascending neck line, as illustrated in the chart of Borden, is that the ensuing downward movement does not get under way so rapidly and that the profit possibilities are all the greater because the "sell" signal comes in time to catch the full extent of the decline. Head and Shoulders patterns with an ascending neck line present, as a rule, the most distinct signals and, if prompt action is taken, the greatest potential profits.

An increase in volume on the breaking of the neck line is more to be depended upon in the ascending neck line formations than in the case of the drooping necks. With the latter types, the break may come on comparatively very little increase in activity, and then the volume picks up rapidly as the movement gets under way. In brief, the formation with the descending neck line is by far the more "tricky" and demands greater agility on the part of the trader to make it pay maximum returns.

Advantages of Charting Several Stocks

Our discussion of drooping shoulders, and the greater agility they demand of a trader, brings up one of the important advantages of keeping charts constantly on a number of different stocks.

The Head and Shoulders formation is most frequently encountered in quickly recognizable form at the tops of major and strong intermediate upward movements. That is why we find so many fine examples of this pattern at the 1929 tops and at the tops which followed the big upward surge of stock prices in the first half of 1933. But, as we all know, not all stocks make their tops at the same time; some "top out" weeks (in the case of intermediate moves) or months (in the case of major reversals) before others reach their peaks. When the student sees that some of the issues he is charting have made Head and Shoulders patterns (or other reversal patterns which we shall take up later) he should begin to expect the same performance from others which his charts may indicate are still in an upward trend.

Speaking very generally, Head and Shoulders Tops with the ascending type of neck line are most apt to be found in stocks which are making their tops ahead of the market as a whole and before general liquidation has begun. Stocks which top out later, when the whole market has become weakened, are more apt to show descending neck lines and more precipitate declines.

Therefore, the student who charts a goodly number of stocks and sees that several of them have reversed their trends, is forewarned of probable reversals in his other charts and is ready to act quickly and decisively as these reversals develop.

Head and Shoulders Bottoms

Up to now we have been discussing the Head and Shoulders pattern primarily as a top, forecasting a reversal from an upward to a downward price trend. But we mentioned the fact that the Head and Shoulders is equally valid as a reversal formation at the bottom of a declining price trend, being sometimes called in this position a pendant bottom.

Before proceeding to a closer examination of some typical Head and Shoulders

Bottoms, we may make some general comparisons. In our preliminary study of the significance of volumes at reversals in the market we mentioned the fact that activity in stocks as expressed in volume of sales is characteristically less after a period of declining prices than after a bull movement. This is particularly notable at the end of a major bear market – as in 1932–1933; the public generally has lost interest in stocks and trading is largely in the hands of professionals and those who enter the market through necessity. (Of course, the public, so-called, is never entirely out of the market.) This general rule of lower volume at bottoms than at tops is reflected in the typical Head and Shoulders Bottom picture. Since activity is at a lower ebb, the patterns are apt to be somewhat smaller or take longer to form, and the higher volume which we have learned to expect at the culmination of the head and the shoulders (as well as on the day when the neck line is broken) is apt to be less conspicuous. Also, for the same reason of less activity, the upward move in the new trend is frequently slower in getting under way. That means, in many cases, that more demands will be made upon our patience when we act upon Head and Shoulders bottom formation than is the case when we trade on a top.

In fact, by its very nature, being built up as it is by fairly wide fluctuations in the price level, good Head and Shoulders patterns appear less frequently at bottoms than at tops. Nevertheless, they do appear, and are just as important and reliable in the one position as the other.

Examples of Head and Shoulders Bottom Reversals

Figure II.5, shows the action of Woolworth through the first six months of 1936. Readers who have followed this stock will recall the long slow decline which preceded the period pictured in this chart as well as its subsequent fairly rapid rise to 63 by the middle of October. Note first the large pattern formed by the left shoulder at A, the head at D, and the right shoulder at H – a nearly perfect formation and one of such size and strength as to forecast a considerable move. The neck line B-G was broken on June 9 with a sharp increase in volume. The volume on the two shoulders and the head was not conspicuously greater than during the intervals between, but this as we have already noted is quite apt to be the case on bottom reversals.

Note in this chart (Woolworth) also, that we had another Head and Shoulders formation at C-D-F, smaller and less distinct but certainly valid. We were warranted in buying the stock when the neck (dotted line through E) was broken on May 13. The reaction, which came after the upward move to point G, might have tried our patience; it is, however, quite often the case that a reaction brings prices back to the level of the neck base before the true major movement gets under way. Conservative traders would doubtless prefer to wait for the completion of the larger and more positive formation before buying.

Fig. II.5

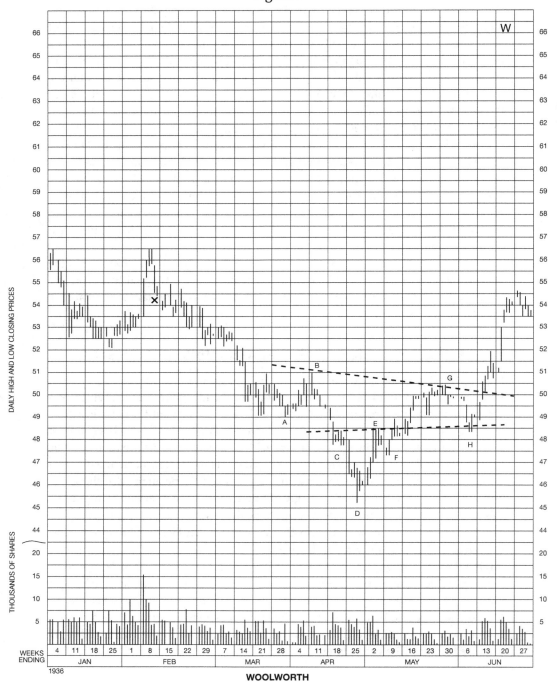

WOOLWORTH

Fig. II.6

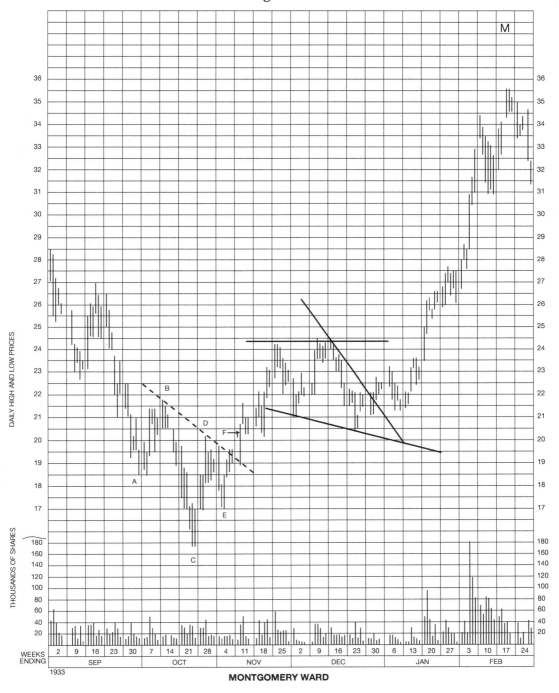

MONTGOMERY WARD

Fig. II.7

DU PONT

Typical Variations in Head and Shoulders Bottoms

We have referred in our discussion of Head and Shoulders Top Reversals to the wide variations in height and width of shoulders which are to be expected. These same varieties occur in bottom reversals. Figure II.6, for example, shows Head and Shoulders pattern with descending neck line, B-D, which reversed the downward trend in Montgomery Ward in October 1933. Figure II.7 illustrates a pattern with a wide left shoulder and narrow right shoulder which formed at the same time in the reversal of Du Pont.

In the case of Montgomery Ward the neck line was broken at F on November 7 with a significant increase in volume. The movement of prices in the new up-trend did not extend very far before meeting resistance and nearly two months of indecisive price action ensued before the upward push got under way in earnest.

In the case of Du Pont, the narrower right shoulder was indicative of a more rapid get-away. The neck line B-D was barely "dented" at F but, although the volume indications were encouraging, prices on this day (November 3) came back and closed just within the pattern. The more decisive and final breakthrough came on November 7 with high volume, and prices closed the day more than a full point above the vital line, indicating definitely that demand had finally overcome supply.

Flat Shoulders

In our first explanation of the Head and Shoulders formation we described the three parts as being sharp movements in the direction of the preceding trend. This is the clearest way of explaining the picture to the novice but it is not always accurate. There are always three stages, as described, but very often they are not sharp thrusts so much as they are merely flat or gently sloping levels beyond which the price movement is unable to penetrate.

This is particularly true of the shoulders which may be either pointed, rounded, flat or sloping. The point to note is simply that the stock is trying to continue its previous main movement but is restrained from doing so on successive occasions by the development of technical power or pressure in the opposite direction, which we shall later discuss as support and resistance.

The head itself may also be rather flat instead of sharp, but this is the exception rather than the rule; the final thrust frequently takes the form of a one-day reversal on high volume, as described earlier in the present study.

Several good examples of such sharp thrusts are to be found on the charts accompanying this study.

Tops Must Follow Advances

This is a point which will seem quite simple and apparent to the practiced chart student but our experience with beginners leads us to stress it here. Many "freshmen"[3] are so eager when they discover a common chart picture that they neglect to analyze it in its proper relations with the major movement.

Let it be remembered, therefore, that a top reversal formation can come only after a previous rise, and a bottom reversal only after an appreciable decline. This applies, of course, to all reversal formations as well as to the Head and Shoulders pattern.

Thus, an apparent Head and Shoulders pattern occurring in a period during which prices for some time have had no definite up or down trend but have been moving "sidewise", has no special technical significance. The student may find Head and Shoulders pictures in their upright position in the course of a downward price trend in a certain stock or, vice-versa, will find the pendant or upside-down picture in an upward trend; such patterns are not to be taken as indicating a reversal in trend. In fact, they frequently develop

Close inspection of any collection of charts will turn up formations which looked as though they might become Head and Shoulders reversals.

into continuation patterns, which we shall study and learn to recognize later, and which forecast a resumption or continuation of the same trend.

Uncompleted Head and Shoulders Patterns

Another common freshman error is to "jump the gun" on what has the appearance of becoming a Head and Shoulders pattern without waiting for a decisive penetration of the neck-base line. The temptation is admittedly great, especially when the familiar formation shows signs of developing at a time when a reversal of trend might reasonably be expected.

Figure II.8 shows a pattern which had every appearance of becoming a Head and Shoulders bottom in May and early June, 1937. If you will cover that portion of the chart to the right of the heavy vertical line between the first two weeks of June, you can see why many traders became bullish on Chrysler at that time. But the neck line (N-N) was never broken; the rally the first week of June failed to carry Chrysler above 115, and the stock did not reverse its down trend until it touched 94 on June 30.

A close inspection of almost any collection of charts of active stocks will turn up

---

[3] "Freshmen" is a US term for first-year students in high schools or colleges.

Fig. II.8

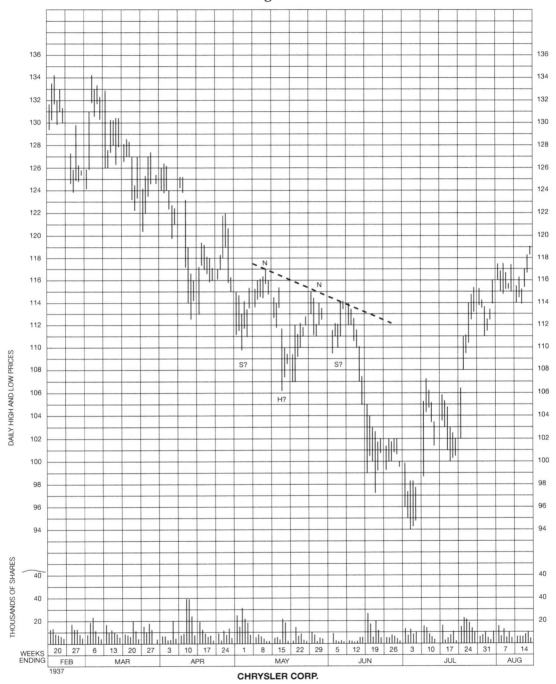

CHRYSLER CORP.

a number of such formations which looked at the time as though they might become Head and Shoulders reversals but which were never completed.

Wait for Clear Confirmation

The beginner in this interpretive science may find our frequent reverting to counsels of caution somewhat disconcerting. It is admittedly trying to the inexperienced trader to see where he may have lost a point or more of potential profit by waiting and abiding by certain rules of conservatism. In actual practice, however, over the long pull, the student will find that he sacrifices little or nothing in profits and frequently saves himself from nerve-wracking if not actually dangerous false moves by avoiding premature action. It is a matter of common knowledge in "the street" that the trader who tries to buy at the very bottoms and sell for the last eighth of a point at the tops loses more opportunities than his occasional lucky hits can ever recompense.

In our study of the Head and Shoulders formation we have stressed the fact that the pattern is not completed, and the forecast of a reversal of trend is not to be considered as established until the neck base line has been broken decisively. And we have called attention to the fact that this decisive breaking is usually, though not invariably, confirmed on our charts by an appreciable pick-up in volume. Caution and experience have led to our recommendation of certain further rules to be followed, by the beginner at least, in determining when to act upon the implications of his charts. In general, it is wise to wait until prices have closed at least a full point beyond the vital line in the case of a stock selling between, say, 50 and 100, that is fairly stable in its market movements. In the case of a stock that is prone to violent and erratic fluctuation this margin of safety may well be doubled. With lower priced stocks of stable habits the margin may be reduced to half a point, and with stocks selling over 100 it should be correspondingly increased.

This rule of caution is introduced at this point in our Course chiefly for the sake of those bold and impatient students who may recognize their own proclivity to rash action and the consequent need of arbitrary restraints.

Patterns in Weekly and Monthly Charts

Before closing our discussion of the common Head and Shoulders reversal, we may find it interesting to examine its occurrence in long-term charts. Study Fig. II.9 which shows Head and Shoulders formations which appeared in a weekly chart of Atchison during 1934 and 1935, and a fine example which developed in the reversal of the long-term down trend in 1932 on a monthly chart of Allied Chemical.

Aside from their purely academic interest to the technical student, their occurrence is useful to the long-term trader or investor as confirmation of the change in the long cycle. Also, their appearance, and the accuracy of their forecast, in weekly and monthly charts is additional evidence of their reliability. Moreover, they serve occasionally to guard the practical trader from taking a relatively unprofitable position in a stock against its major trend.

Finally, they may call to our attention a strong long-term movement in a certain stock which we can then turn to account in our study of the daily chart. We shall be encouraged to watch the daily chart for profitable buying or selling points, as the case may be, in the direction of the major movement, and we shall not be so readily discouraged by false moves against the trend our weekly chart has predicted.

Reliability of the Head and Shoulders

In completing our observation of the Head and Shoulders formation it may be repeated that this pattern is not only the most frequent, popular and well-known of the reversal formation series, but that it is deservedly so, because it is the most important and the most reliable in actual practice. It is not infallible any more than the other forms we shall discuss. They are all subject to exception to which we shall refer later, but it still holds that disappointments in the Head and Shoulders formation are comparatively few.

The reader may test this, as well as other formations, constantly as he continues his perusal of this Course, for the charts which will appear in later studies, while they are inserted primarily for exemplification of other technical patterns, have also been selected for their value as vehicles of review and many of them contain good Head and Shoulders reversals.

Measuring Extent of Movement

We have stated early in this study the general proposition that the size and duration of the formation may give us some idea of the extent of the movement to follow. Such suggestions of measuring and timing formulae always fascinate the beginner and frequently lead him into loss and confusion, or at best divert him from more reliable and profitable considerations.

It is only fair to state in the plainest terms before we proceed any farther in this Course, that we have never found a reliable time factor or timing formula, and we have examined and tested hundreds. That security prices move in cycles is undeniably true, but a very brief study of the long-term chart (frontispiece) shows that the cyclical periods vary in duration too widely to permit of any but the very broadest generalizations with respect to time – certainly too widely to permit us to buy or sell

Fig. II.9

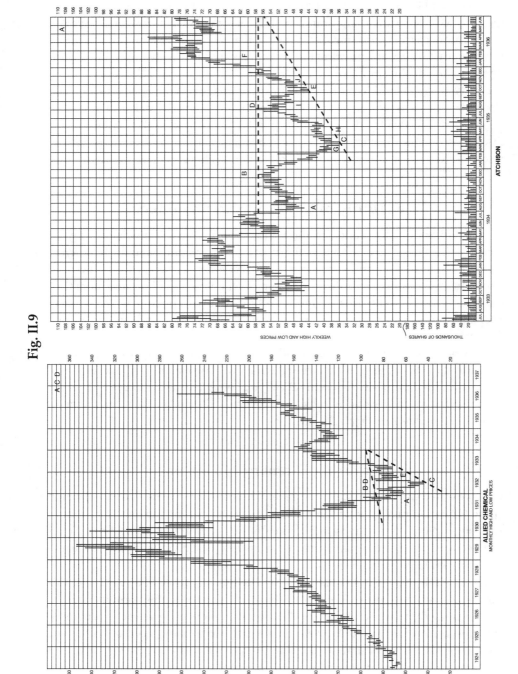

with profit on such deductions. And this variance in time as between intermediate rallies and reactions is even greater – and still more noticeable in the case of individual stocks in which we have to do our trading. In brief, there are the best of reasons for believing that a timing formula that can be converted to a profit in intermediate or short-term trading, will never be discovered.

However, there are measuring inferences (in terms of prices) to be drawn from certain technical patterns. One such in connection with the Head and Shoulders formation we shall mention briefly here, with the promise that its possible uses will be taken up later on in this Course, and with the urgent recommendation that the student simply note it for the present, check it on his charts, but not attempt to make use of it in actual trading until we have given it that later more detailed examination.

This measuring formula has to do with the probable level at which prices will meet their first important resistance to further movement after breaking out of a Head and Shoulders pattern. If we measure the vertical distance on the price scale from the tip of the head to the neck base line, and then measure off this same distance vertically in the same direction from the point where the neck line is finally broken, the point thus determined frequently falls on or very near the price level at which the first important reaction or congestion occurs. This reaction or congestion may be brief or long-continued before the newly established trend is resumed. There are many exceptional cases and the measuring is, at best, only approximate.

The most important and reliable deduction to be made from the Head and Shoulders formation is that our stock has reversed its trend and that the new trend will continue at least long enough to permit worth-while profits to be taken.

Logic of Chart Patterns

It is only natural that technical students should ask for a logical explanation of why certain definite chart formations forecast reversal of the previous movement, and the Head and Shoulders pattern has been one of the favorite subjects for such questions.

We have previously noted that there are various such formations whose efficacy in the matter of forecasting is well demonstrated, but for which the logical explanations are rather indefinite and vague. We have always taken the attitude that it is much more important to discover and establish the practical uses of such formations than to explain why they act as they do, but, in most cases, a little thought will furnish the clue to the underlying explanation of the individual phenomena.

Such explanations, almost without exception, take us back to our fundamental basis of technical action – the human element of trading, the relative balance between buying and selling, as well as, indirectly perhaps, to unprovable but probable personally directed campaigns by insiders.

We have already noted that most reversals are accomplished gradually, by the slow overcoming of excessive buying power by growing selling pressure, or the slow overcoming of previously excessive selling pressure by the growth in strength of buying.

Logic of Head and Shoulders Reversal

In the case of the Head and Shoulders formation the reversal is still slow and rounding but not quite so apparently thus as are other reversals where the turn is made in a more regular fashion. This differentiation in the case of the Head and Shoulders pattern is probably accounted for by the more rapid movement, the sharper swings, of certain stocks at certain times, indicating that they are more definitely in the popular eye or, perhaps, that they are under the influence of professional manipulation.

The entire picture is composed simply of three particular points in the rapid movement of an active stock where the momentum of the preceding trend is met and stemmed by the rising tide of technical strength tending toward reversal of that previous movement.

Study III

IMPORTANT REVERSAL
FORMATIONS
CONTINUED

The Gradual Reversal

In our first study of technical action and the shifting balance between buying and selling power in the market, we noted that changes in technical condition do not generally take place overnight but are usually spread out over a considerable period of time. Gradually a previous major trend is reversed by the growing superiority of buying over selling power, or vice versa, and we usually have plenty of time to watch this turn in the balance of power on our charts.

In the immediately preceding study we also had occasion to note that our Head and Shoulders formation, the first and most important of the reversal patterns, is simply a specific and rather sharply integrated style of this gradual turning movement which signifies a change in technical position and therefore in the main trend.

Our second type of reversal formation, the Common or Rounding Turn, is a much more natural example of this change in the balance between buying and selling power. In fact, it is the simplest and most easily understandable of all the many chart formations which forecast probable reversal of the previous movement.

Definition of the Common Turn

The Common Turn is simply the gradual and fairly symmetrical change in direction of the preceding major trend and is very directly the result of a gradual shift in the balance of power between buying and selling. If, for example, the buying has been stronger than the selling for some time past, we now know that the result will have been a general upward trend in the price of our stock or stocks, as indicated by our pictorial chart record of the trading history.

So long, therefore, as the buyers of the stock remain more anxious, more numerous, more aggressive, more powerful, than the sellers, that preceding upward trend will continue. Now, however, suppose that the selling grows a little stronger, while the buying either weakens slightly or remains stationary at its previous strength. This slight change in the technical balance will be indicated by a slowing up of the previous advance.

As the selling increases in relative power it will finally become equal to the buying power and the result is a theoretically equal balance between the two, with the result that the market level moves neither up nor down, but remains for a time quite stationary.

Now assume that the new development continues and the selling grows still more powerful with respect to the buying, until it is finally stronger. Now the balance is moving the other way. There are now more sellers than buyers and the result will be a gradual decline in the price of the market quotations for the stock. If this change in the balance of power is fairly steady and continues to its logical conclusion, we can see, even without the aid of a chart, that our picture of the price movement for that stock would be one of a long advancing trend slowly beginning to round off, holding in stationary suspense for a time, and then commencing a retreat, reversing the previous upward movement into a new downward trend.

The technical chart picture thus resulting would be our Common Turn, or Rounding Top, the second of our reversal patterns. In truth, it is nothing more or less than a chart picture of the gradual shifting of the balance of technical power from the buying to the selling side, or vice versa, to indicate a reversal of the technical position and therefore a reversal of the preceding trend. The picture is also known as the "bowl" formation, since it resembles such a receptacle, the common up turn in normal position, the down turn in position of an inverted bowl.

Chart Example of the Rounding Top

The formation is such a simple one that it probably needs little further explanation or example, but we may pause to glance at the Rounding Top, or common down turn, shown in Fig III.1, the chart for United States Steel in March and April of 1930.

The general trend had been upward since the panic low of 150 in November, 1929. Finally, came the last steep ascent from under 185 to above 195 at the close of March, 1930. Several one-day reversals on high volume, or turn-over days, may be noted in the formation, but the pattern is a clear one showing the gradual accretion in strength of selling over buying power, the final victory for selling and the resulting reversal in the technical position of the stock and the major trend.

As usual, the picture here of the Common Turn is merely one of a rounding off of the previous movement as the reversal develops into the new and opposite trend. The similarity of the Rounding Turn to other reversal patterns, notably the Head and Shoulders picture, is readily apparent. They are all pictures of this technical phenomenon of a change in the balance between buying and selling power, only in the Common Turn the change is more gradual, more steady, more symmetrical, than the sharp moves and points of the Head and Shoulders pattern. Even in our accompanying picture of the Rounding Top, in Steel, the reader may note the similarity to a Head and Shoulders Top.

The dividing line between the two formations is sometimes difficult of detection and it is often merely a matter of personal judgment whether the chart reader will label such a formation a Rounding Turn or a Head and Shoulders picture. Fortunately, and rather naturally, the judgment in such a case is relatively unimportant because both formations mean the same thing and are about

They are all pictures of this technical phenomenon of change

Fig. III.1

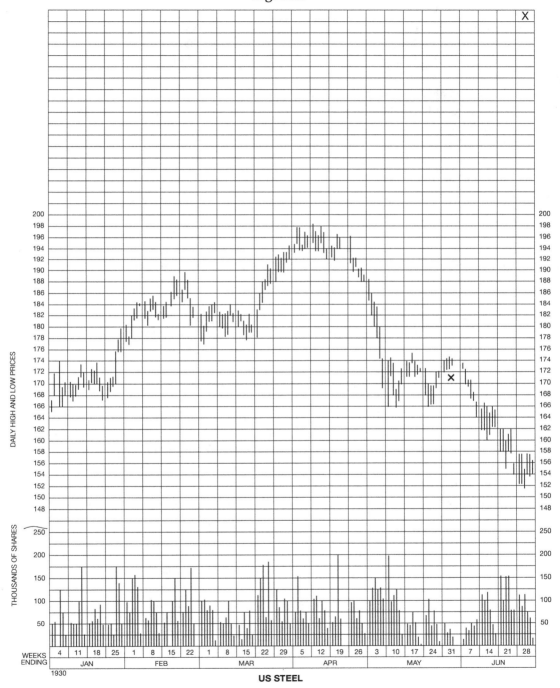

US STEEL

equally powerful and equally definite in their implications of a more or less permanent reversal of the previous trend.

Just as this rounding top in Steel might easily have been a Head and Shoulders top if the potential head and shoulders had been a little sharper and better defined instead of blending symmetrically into the gradual turning picture, so we may glance back at Fig II. 4, and notice how the formation in general might be construed as somewhat of a Rounding Top, though its sharper points place it actually in a class with the Head and Shoulders top.

We may find many additional examples throughout the charts in this Course of the Rounding Top. The averages themselves present a very satisfactory one in April of 1930 which ended the post-panic recovery and reversed the main trend of stock prices back into the long bear market movement.

Chart Patterns in the Averages

In passing we may also note how and why the average, or index, charts often give very good chart pictures. They are made up of many individual stocks so they give us a composite picture of all the various patterns under way in the individual issues which go to make up the average chart. When enough of these individual issues are forming definite pictures, the composite picture in the averages is quite likely to produce a pattern of similar import, and when such a formation appears in the average chart its power and importance are multiplied many times over for it shows an unescapable unanimity of action.

For example, if many individual issues were to make strong Head and Shoulders formations at exactly the same time, the average chart would, obviously, show a similar Head and Shoulders. However, since the many different stocks do not, as a rule, make their "peaks and valleys" on precisely the same days, the average chart is apt to show a less specialized and distinct pattern. We should, for this reason, expect the averages to show Common or Rounding Turns more often than do the charts of individual issues at times of important reversals, and this is in fact the case.

We have just noted the Rounding Top in Steel during April of 1930. Now we find that the averages themselves also presented the same picture at the same time. The natural inference is that other representative stocks, in addition to Steel, were forming their reversal patterns at the same time. The other pictures may have been most any type of reversal yet there were enough similar to the Rounding Top to give that formation's appearance to the general averages themselves. The technical top formation was therefore a very strong and important one, befitting its subsequently revealed position as the formation which turned the

Note how and why the average charts often give very good pictures.

long and strong recovery following the 1929 panic back into the much longer bear market which followed.

The Rounding Bottom

The Rounding Bottom or Common Upward Turn is, of course, the reverse of the Common Down Turn, being simply the latter turned upside down, and with the opposite implications, forecasting an advance instead of a decline. The Rounding Bottom is the chart picture resulting from the gradual accretion of buying strength, finally to overcome the preceding balance of selling pressure and lead to reversal of the technical position from weak to strong, and reversal of the previous down trend into one of advancing prices.

Rounding Bottoms are somewhat more common than Rounding Tops for reasons which we shall discuss under the heading of volume but, before proceeding to that point, we may first examine two charts which depict this formation in its simplest and most typical aspect. Figure III.2 shows the rounding off and reversal of the long bear market downtrend in Case in 1932. Prices had been declining for nearly three years with alternating rallies and reactions in swings that tended to become narrower and narrower until finally in May of 1932 the trend began to flatten out. On June 10 there was a burst of buying, due perhaps to impatient inside accumulation, which drove prices up 10 points in two days. Thereafter prices sagged back roughly into line with the lifting trend already noticeable at the bottom, and then worked up with volume increasing rapidly as the curve accelerated.

Figure III.3 shows a Rounding Bottom which reversed an intermediate reaction in Goodrich, turning it into a new upward movement from 7 in October, 1935 to 21 in February, 1936. In this chart, as in Case, we see a brief spurt of activity at the bottom which broke the regular curve for a few days but did not appreciably distort or confuse the typical "bowl" picture and again, as in the preceding chart, we note volume picking up rapidly as the upturn developed.

(Formation A-B-C appearing on Goodrich chart will be discussed in Study VI.)

Volume on Rounding Turns

We mentioned above that Common Rounding Turns occur more frequently at bottoms than at tops. This naturally follows our experience with volume which we have noted is apt to be high at the culmination of bull movements and to dwindle away in long declines. The Common or Rounding Turn in its simple form is a picture of a very gradual and regular change in technical balance. This gradual and regular change, obviously, would be thrown into irregularities by any sudden, sharp

Fig. III.2

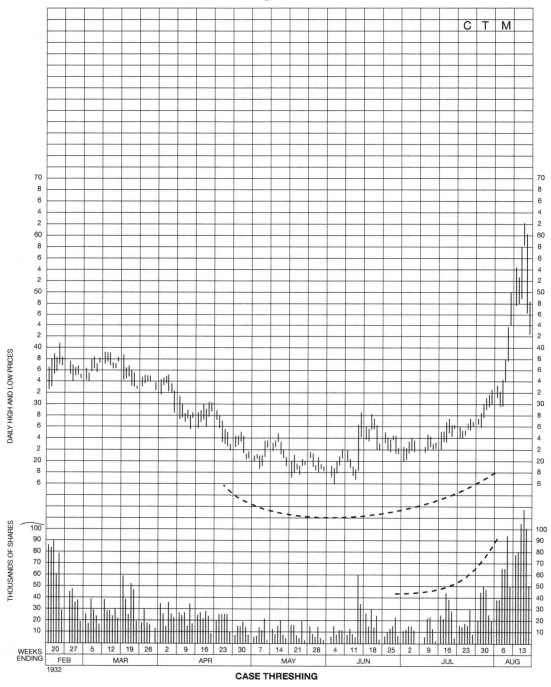

CASE THRESHING

Fig. III.3

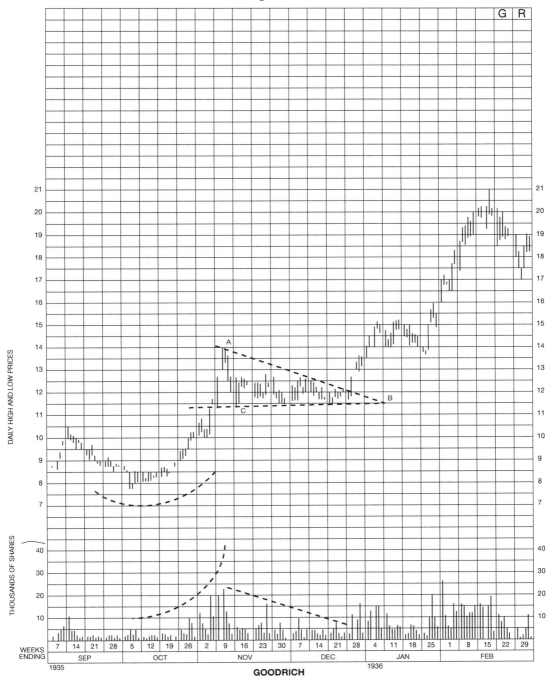

increases in activity. This is the reason why simple Rounding Turns are found less often at the active peaks, than at the dull bottoms.

Volume Increase on Common Turns

If the student will refer again to the charts of Rounding Turns we have been discussing, he will note that, in every case, volume picks up rapidly as the curve swings past "dead center" and around into the new trend. This noticeable increase in activity is an almost invariable accompaniment of the Common or Rounding Turn, an important confirmation of the formation that gives us our signal to buy or sell, as the case may be.

Common Rounding Turns occur more frequently at bottoms than at tops.

The student of this course will find that many of the charts of other reversal formations to follow, as well as several of the Head and Shoulders patterns in the preceding study, partake somewhat of the nature of Common Turns. This is particularly true of the Head and Shoulders formations in which the reversal is accomplished without wide fluctuations or sharp thrusts. Refer, for example, to the chart of Borden, Fig. II. 4. In any case, whenever either construction is possible, it will be found, as usual, that both constructions lead to the same conclusion or forecast.

So simple is the Rounding, or Common, Turn formation that we need spend no further time in its study. It is probably the most logical and most easily comprehended formation in chart reversals. It is fallible just as are all chart formations, but it is sufficiently definite in its forecasting implications to give it a high place in our technical studies.

The Triangle or Coil

The third of our most important reversal formations is generally known as the Triangle, or Coil, because of its similarity in appearance to those descriptive appelations. We prefer and shall use the term triangle, because it seems to us to be more descriptive of the pictorial pattern and because it makes easier the description and classification of its varieties, but various authorities use the term "coil" because it gives the suggestion of a spring being wound up tighter, as the formation comes to its apex, until it is finally released and breaks out of the receding formation with a pent-up, or wound-up, force.

As usual, the picture of the Triangle is formed by the action of the price range on our chart. In its basic form which we will take up first, it has the appearance of an equilateral triangle lying on its right side, with its base a perpendicular line at the left side of the formation, and its median line a horizontal one extending to the right.

Its apex is also formed to the right, therefore, and the entire triangle points in that direction, to the future chart formation instead of the past. We shall refer to this basic form hereafter as the Symmetrical Triangle.

Thus the basic formation is the result first of comparatively wide swings of the price range on the chart, with a subsequent gradual and symmetrical narrowing down of such swings to bring the price range into smaller and smaller proportions until the apex is reached at a point where the daily ranges for the stock are abnormally small and the volume, therefore, naturally also at a low ebb, as interest and trading in the stock diminish.

Actually, of course, this basic pattern is never perfect and is commonly broken up by irregularities. Much latitude, must, therefore, be taken in the interpretation of the triangular pattern but the general picture is one of the most common and important of chart patterns.

Triangle Unreliable as a Reversal

Since we are studying, in this section, cardinal reversal formations, this current study will be confined to a consideration of the Triangle as a form of reversal, but it is only fair, and, indeed, quite important, that we realize immediately that the Triangle is by no means always indicative of a reversal in technical position. In fact, the Triangle appears more often as an intermediate or continuation formation than a reversal formation, and we shall study it again under the former connotation in Study VI.

For the time being, it is sufficient if we realize that the Triangle can be either a continuation or a reversal pattern. That is the chief reason why it is not so important a reversal formation as is the Head and Shoulders picture. We rank it second in importance to that formation because the Head and Shoulders pattern is practically always indicative of reversal while the Triangle, though found more often, must be content with second place because it is not as definite or as reliable in its implications.

This disadvantage of the Triangle as an example of the reversal type of formation is a practical one because there is no sure way of telling during its formation whether a Triangle will be intermediate or a reversal. Of course, the chart student must always watch carefully the direction and character of the subsequent movement, after the completion of any formation, to be certain that he has made a correct analysis and that the pattern noted is a genuine one but, in the case of other chart pictures, he is almost always able to form a definite advance opinion of what the next move *should* be from the character and style of the pattern itself, before it reaches completion.

In the case of the Triangle, we know of no certain rule whereby the student may satisfy himself that the triangular formation is going to be intermediate or a reversal until the subsequent movement has broken away from the apex of the Triangle. Compared with our other reverse formations, therefore, the Triangle does not give as early a forecast suggestion.

The Break-away Move

From our description of the Triangle itself, it stands to reason, that, as the price range and activity gradually narrow down to form the point or apex, a critical period approaches when the abnormally small range must give way to a wider and more definite movement.

The beginning of this subsequent movement, following the apex of the triangle, is called the break-away, and it generally indicates the direction of the large, profitable price movement to follow the formation. In some cases, the apex will be followed by what is known as a false move, in a short and temporary shift of the price in the opposite direction from the later and true major movement. Such false moves will be discussed at greater length in Study IX. They are comparatively infrequent, but when they do occur they interpose still another disadvantage in the triangle formation.

We would not give the reader the impression that we scorn or distrust the Triangle. On the contrary, we consider it a very important and very useful chart formation. We are merely trying to give a clear and complete view of the drawbacks of this pattern, particularly as an indication of reversal, which are somewhat greater than in other technical pictures.

Denotes Continuation More Often than Reversal

It is only fair to state again that, while the Triangle is both common and important as a form of reversal, still it is more common and more important as a continuation formation. In other words, other things being equal, the Triangle denotes continuation of the previous major movement more often than it does a reversal of that preceding trend.

The break-away generally indicates the direction of the price movement to follow the formation.

We have said that while this formation is in process of development it is difficult to be certain, from the pattern itself, whether it is going to turn out to be a continuation or a reversal. This statement is qualified by the paragraph above, for it follows naturally that it should *generally* be assumed a Triangle in process of formation is going to be a continuation, or intermediate formation, until the contrary is proved to be the case.

Aids to Advance Judgment

Another helpful consideration is the pattern of the whole movement preceding the beginning of the Triangle's formation. If the preceding move has been long and begins to show other signs of possible exhaustion, then the chances are more favorable that the Triangle will signal a reversal. If the previous major trend has been a short one, however, and other indications suggest continuation of the trend then the chances are naturally better that it will really turn out to be such a continuation, rather than the rarer form of reversal.

Analysis of other and more fundamental factors is also frequently important, and helpful, in connection with the chart analysis of the Symmetrical Triangle. Here the technical picture by itself fails to give the usual definite forecasting signals; the Symmetrical Triangle simply emphasizes the indication that somewhere near the apex it is forming there is going to be a very wide, rapid and worthwhile movement in the price of this particular stock. Which way? We are obliged to look elsewhere or await the break-out to answer this question.

We have pointed out one possible guide but, in the main, the most helpful indications in such a case are generally those dealing with fundamentals, or at least with aspects not immediately present in the technical formation itself. How are earnings? What are the future prospects? What surprise news is possible on this stock? What is the future for general business? Is the technical position of other stocks, and of the general market itself, strong or weak? Such pertinent questions, while not all fundamental by any means, often give the correct answer to our technical problem as to whether a Symmetrical Triangle in process of formation is going to turn out to be a real reversal of technical trend, or merely a continuation formation (a temporary halt or congestion leading to a strong resumption of the previous trend).

Examples of Triangular Reversal

We have felt it necessary first to bring out the drawbacks in this introduction to the Triangle formation, but we may now take up our more immediate interest, the study of the Triangle, not in general, but as a clear-cut reversal of the previous major movement.

When a Triangle reverses the movement from up to down it is called, quite logically, a Triangular Top; when it reverses the previous trend from down to up then it is called a Triangular Bottom.

Figure III.4 shows a good example of the Symmetrical Triangle as a reversal, occurring in Auburn at the "April Tops" of 1936. The student will have no difficulty in seeing the triangular picture suggested by this chart even without the aid of the boundary lines that have been drawn on it from points A and B respectively to the apex at C. Point A is at the peak of the intermediate bull movement which took Auburn to 54¼ on March 5; point B is the bottom of the minor reaction which preceded this final upthrust of prices. Up to these points the Auburn chart had shown for some time previous a picture of constantly higher tops and higher bottoms on each minor swing of the price range. Now, however, although the bottoms continue to hold within a slightly upward trend, the minor rallies become progressively weaker, with the result that the price range narrows appreciably, converging into the apex at C. During this same period of narrowing price range, note that the volume of transactions tends to "dry up" each week's volume appreciably less as the apex of our price formation is approached.

But, as we have remarked in our general introduction to the Triangle pattern, we had no way of knowing from this chart alone in which direction prices would eventually break out. If we were following a number of charts, however, we should have seen that many of them were developing at this same time formations indicative of reversal, so we should have had reason to be slightly suspicious of our Auburn Triangle.

Break-out Confirmed by Volume

Our suspicions were at least partly confirmed on April 11 when prices broke through our boundary line on the down side and the volume (making allowance for the fact that this was a Saturday with only two hours of trading[1]) showed a definite increase. The market closed, however, with the last transaction of the day practically back to our pattern – certainly not a decisive break-away, and possibly, so far as we could tell then, only a false move (which we shall discuss later). But Monday told the story. The volume exceeded any day for two weeks back and prices broke away definitely, closing over 3 points below our pattern. Time to sell Auburn!

We have stressed the volume action in our study of Fig. III.4 because it is typical of the Triangle formation, whether reversal or continuation. The shrinkage of volume as the pattern works towards its apex is always quite apparent though not necessarily at a regular rate from day to day. Distinctly higher volume when prices break out of the pattern is always to be expected, and any slight break on dull volume may well be regarded with suspicion. The genuine break-out, into the new trend (or rapid resumption of the old trend), is almost invariably confirmed promptly by noticeably greater volume. The student will note that the rule of volume on the definite break out of formation is the same in the case of the Triangle as in the other patterns previously studied, and it may be further noted here that this

---

[1] For many years the New York Stock Exchange traded half a day on Saturdays; this was eventually phased out.

general rule – that volume picks up noticeably with the break of prices into a new trend or out of a congestion – holds with practically every important technical pattern.

Apex Not Always Reached

One more point may well be discussed before we drop our study of Fig. III.4 lest it cause confusion in the student's mental picture of the Triangle.

It is not necessary that prices shrink into the absolute apex of the pattern before they break-out into the new movement. As a matter of fact, they very seldom do, and frequently the break comes some distance away from the projected apex on our charts. As soon as it becomes apparent that the price range is converging and a triangular pattern forming, we must draw our boundary lines, tentatively

Volume picks up noticeably with the break of prices into a new trend.

at least, and be on the watch for their being broken with an accompanying volume signal. In very active stocks, leaders with a large floating supply and a big public following, the break may be expected to come well ahead of the apex. In relatively inactive stocks, on the other hand – those which normally attract public attention only in periods of rapid mark-up or mark-down – volume and price range may dwindle almost to nothing, right into our theoretical apex, before breaking out.

Break-out may Come Quickly

No special significance attaches to either an early or late break out of a Symmetrical Triangle Reversal, the forecast in either case being the same. However, the Triangle in which the price range converges far into the apex does call for a more critical examination of any out-of-bounds movement that may appear. The price range in the apex becomes so small that a very slight change in price, effected perhaps by just a few transactions, may pierce our theoretical boundary lines and yet not constitute a genuine break-out signal. The longer and narrower the formation, the greater the necessity for awaiting a decisive break-out, closing well out of the pattern and confirmed by a good increase in volume, before placing a "buy" or "sell" order in the stock.

Varieties of Triangular Tops

In Fig. III.5 we have a very interesting chart which will repay close scrutiny. This chart pictures the price and volume action in Houston Oil at the time when the stock

Fig. III.4

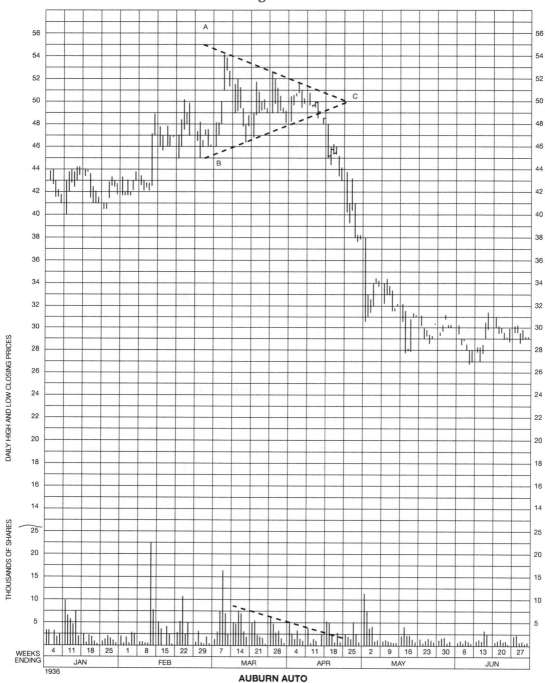

AUBURN AUTO

Fig. III.5

HOUSTON OIL

had made a very impressive intermediate rally and then turned again into the long bear trend. The top of this movement formed a pattern which illustrates very well the point we made on page 70 when we stated how certain formations may be classified in more than one way but will, nevertheless, indicate the same forecast.

The top formation on this chart may be construed, for example, as either a Symmetrical Triangle or a Head and Shoulders Top. Some chart students will see the formation developing as a Head and Shoulders (with Head at D and Shoulders at A and E) while others will see more readily the triangular suggestion of the price trend converging within the lines A-C and B-C. Either construction is perfectly valid and, as noted above, both have the same significance. It happens in this case that the boundary line B-C of the Triangle is also the neck-base line of the Head and Shoulders pattern. This line was broken with high volume on August 8.

Strict Construction of Boundary Lines

In drawing the boundary lines for the Triangle A-B-C we have disregarded the one-day peak at D, a latitude which, we have noted on page 75 it is sometimes necessary to take in construing the triangular formations. A very strict technician might object to this as a violation of one of the rules of this science which states that pattern lines should always be projected across the outer limits and never through any portion of the price range. And, generally speaking, we agree and would caution the student against taking such liberties with his chart until he has had considerable experience. In this case, the triangular pattern is quite evident to the eye and the line A-E-C does bound the outer limits of the important congestion.

Early Break-out Reliable

This Houston chart illustrates also a typical break-out early in the development of the Triangle, less than half way, in fact, from the start of the pattern to the theoretical apex at C. Such early break-outs, as we have noted above, are almost invariably genuine and call for prompt trading action – in this case, selling.

A sale of Houston shares following this break-out signal would, presumably, have been executed at a price around 75, and then we should have had a period during which our forecast apparently refused to come true. But note that prices in the ensuing rally did not go above the level of break-out, and that the downward implication of our reversal formation was eventually borne out, bringing a very substantial profit to the technical trader with the courage of his convictions. This rally failing to return to the level of the break-out, or to the neck-base line of the Head and Shoulders pattern, is a frequent occurrence which will be taken up later on in this course in the study of resistances and the placing of stop-loss orders.

Still another feature of our Houston chart is the large Triangle A-G-F. Strictly speaking, this partakes more of the nature of a Right-Angle Triangle than a Symmetrical Triangle. We will take up the significance of the Right-Angle Triangles further on in this study. In the meantime, it will suffice to state that this larger pattern gave an even stronger forecast of an approaching decline of major proportions. The break-out accompanied by high volume on September 22 is decisive and typical.

Triangles on Weekly and Monthly Charts

Figure III.6 shows Triangle Reversal formations we may expect to find in long-range charts – one in a weekly chart of Standard Oil of New Jersey and the other in a monthly chart of Public Service of New Jersey. These have the same uses for the student as have the long range Head and Shoulders which were illustrated and discussed in Study II, and it is suggested that the reader turn back at this point to page ref. and review our explanation of their practical value.

Triangular Bottom Reversals

We can dismiss with a brief reference to two typical examples, the subject of Symmetrical Triangle Bottom Reversals, which signal the turn from a downward to an upward price trend.

Figure III.7 shows a Symmetrical Triangle Bottom Reversal in Auburn in the Fall of 1933. Prices penetrated the boundary line on the up-side – but not decisively – on November 3. On the following day which was Saturday, if we double the volume shown on the chart in order to bring it into fair comparison with the full trading days preceding it, we have our break-out confirmed and the reversal of trend established.

Figure III.8 pictures a Symmetrical Triangle which formed in the upward turning of Johns Manville in March, 1935. In this chart it is important to note the movement of prices on April 3, falling below the lower boundary of our pattern but returning and closing the day within it. Refer back at this point to our discussion on page 79 of the likelihood of false moves in Triangles that work well out into the apex before breaking out. The volume of transactions on April 3 was insignificant which, in addition to the fact that the closing price for the day fell inside the pattern, would have prevented us from making an incorrect interpretation and from taking any premature action. On April 5 there was a similar price movement, again closing practically within the pattern, but note this time the increase in volume – an important clue to the probable significance of our Triangle. The volume action on the several days following confirmed the forecast of a reversal.

Fig. III.6

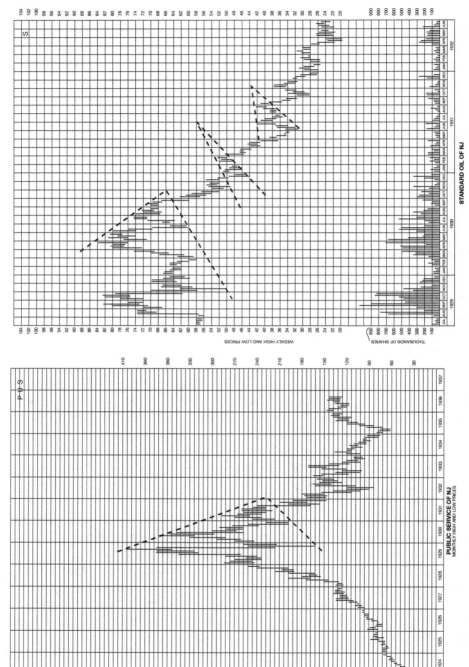

Fig. III.7

AUBURN AUTO

Fig. III.8

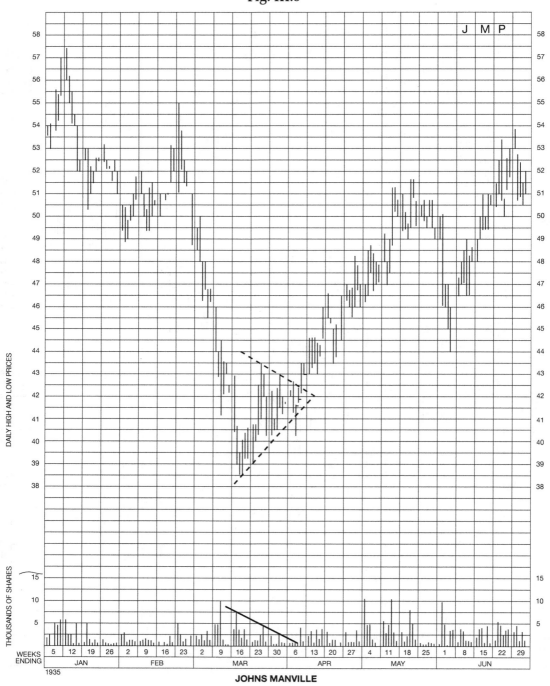

JOHNS MANVILLE

Relation of Price Move to Pattern Size

We have mentioned previously, in our study of the Head and Shoulders formation, the general principle that the greater the price range and the greater the time duration required in the formation of any technical chart picture, the greater is that picture's importance, and the greater the subsequent move which the formation forecasts. This general principle applies as well to the Symmetrical Triangle Reversal, but we must again stress the point that the rule is to be construed only in the most general way and is subject to many exceptions. We do occasionally have very long and continuous movements developing out of surprisingly small Triangles and, vice-versa, large Triangles do infrequently lead to disappointingly short moves. The rule, nevertheless, is a useful one to have in mind and our word of caution is introduced chiefly to remind the student that the technical picture may change at any moment and that he cannot put away his chart and forget it after taking a position in a stock.

The student will find it interesting at this point to review the charts we have shown so far in this study and compare them as to size of pattern and ensuing price movement.

Wave Movement Following Apex

Before leaving the Symmetrical Triangle as a reversal, it is not out of order to mention in passing a rather unusual type of action that follows in rare instances the completion of the Triangle's apex. We have seen that at that point, or more often before it is reached, the movement usually takes the form of a break-away, with a fast and worth while advance or decline immediately following. In exceptional cases, especially when the Triangle is somewhat irregular and dogeared, and

The greater the price range and time duration the greater is that picture's importance.

also when the general market is inactive or indecisive, a Symmetrical Triangle will develop a good and true apex, but there will be no break-away or sharp following movement. Instead, the stock remains comparatively inactive and lethargic, and the price range widens out only moderately from the apex.

In such cases it is generally found that this indecisive wavering will not only continue for a week or more but that the price range will vibrate around the level of the preceding apex. In other words, the triangle has been left behind and the stock will fluctuate in a wider range than at the apex, but it will not go very far in either direction. It will show a gentle decline for perhaps three or four days to perhaps three or four points below the previous apex level. Then it will lackadaisically reverse itself and swing up for three or four days to a range perhaps three or four points above the preceding apex level. There may be four or five of these quiet and disinterested reversals before the stock finally comes to life and decides to go somewhere in particular: and even then the next major move is seldom a sharp or rapid one, and often requires another small technical formation preceding such a major move, even to stretching out the previous Triangle formation still further and coming to another gradual apex.

This rare "wave motion" is the alternate subsequence to the apex of a fairly long Triangle and the exception to that Triangle's normal forecast of a fast and powerful break-away movement. When observed in time it offers an opportunity for short-swing operations, buying a few points below the previous apex level and switching for renewed decline a few points above that level. Such trading switches amount almost to scalping[2] however, and, while they may well prove quite profitable they still carry dangers, should always be protected with stop-loss orders, and are not recommended for the average chart trader.

Right-angle Triangles

Thus far in our study of triangular reversals we have considered only the Symmetrical Triangle, which has a more or less indefinite vertical line for its base and two equal legs that come to a symmetrical apex. The Symmetrical Triangle is more common but not so easily analyzed as are the various types of Right-angle Triangle. The Right-angle Triangle is similarly formed by a converging of the price range, and its base line is the same, a more or less imaginary vertical line on the left of the pattern. The difference lies in that instead of having symmetrical legs projected at approximately equal angles from the base, the Right-angle Triangle has one leg extended horizontally, forming a right angle with the base, while the other leg completes the enclosed triangle as the hypotenuse. The form of Right-angle Triangle, with its hypotenuse slanting down from the beginning of the pattern to its conclusion, is called a Descending Triangle, and almost invariably forecasts a downward movement to come. The Right-angle Triangle with its hypotenuse slanting upwards is called an Ascending Triangle, and it almost invariably forecasts a subsequent advance.

More Reliable as Forecasters

The Right-angle Triangles are, therefore, much more valuable for the purposes of

---

[2] The term "scalping" refers to the measured taking of tiny profits on trades, regardless of whether the trade or trades go higher or lower after the scalper pockets his acceptable small profit.

practical forecasting than the Symmetrical Triangles. We have seen that the Symmetrical Triangle offers the decided drawback of not forecasting, in itself, the direction of the subsequent movement. The Right-angle Triangle *does* make such a forecast, according to the direction of the hypotenuse. If the hypotenuse as it takes form on our charts points downward the forecast is down, and vice-versa.

As in the case of the Symmetrical Triangle, the Right-angle Triangles appear more often as intermediate formations, signifying continuation of the previous movement, with the hypotenuse inclined in that previous direction of trend. By no means infrequently, however, the Right-angle Triangle is found with the hypotenuse inclined in the opposite direction from the preceding movement and, in such cases, the formation falls into our current study of reversals, which change the preceding trend to a new and opposite direction. It will easily be seen then that only the Descending Triangle can be expected to form a top *reversal* formation, and that only the Ascending Triangle can be expected to form a bottom reversal formation.

The Descending Triangle as a Reversal

The strongest reversal patterns, as we have previously noted, are formed at the tops of major or important intermediate rises or, to put it another way, at the beginning of major or important intermediate downward price movements. This is especially true of the Head and Shoulders formation, taken up in Study II, which seldom appears in useful form at the reversal of minor trends. The Right-angle Triangles of the descending type also appear at their best on the tops of important moves, but they are formed with fair frequency, as well, in the top reversals of less extensive rallies, and are very useful to the technical student in forecasting such reversals.

An excellent example of a large Descending Triangle, presaging an important decline, is shown Fig. III.9. Glidden had worked up in the post-panic recovery in 1930 to over 37. From its peak on March 20 (point A on our chart) it made a series of reactions and recoveries – each reaction bringing the price down to around 34–34½, but each following rally failing to carry up quite as high as the preceding. Thus we had the first indication of a turn in the upward movement – the formation of a Right-angle Triangle with a descending hypotenuse (from A to B to C to D), and with the other leg extending horizontally through E, F and G.

Note that we already had within this pattern, before any break-out occurred, a strong suggestion of reversal in the price trend and of a declining market to come. This inference would not have appeared if our Triangle had formed a symmetrical design with the lower leg slanting upward at about the same angle as the upper leg slanted down; in

The strongest reversal patterns are formed at the beginning of major intermediate downward price movements.

Fig. III.9

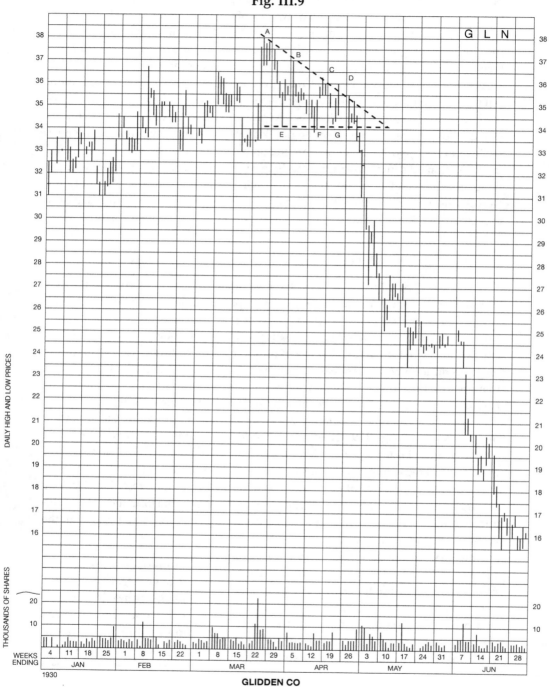

GLIDDEN CO

that case, we should have had to wait for the break-out before knowing which direction prices would take. By the same token, if the upper leg had extended out horizontally, and the lower leg had slanted strongly upward, the forecast would have been one of continuation of the previous up-trend rather than reversal. In brief, if we recognized this typical descending pattern as it developed, and if we happened to be "long" of Glidden stock we should have been warranted in selling and taking our profit at once.

Volume on Initial Break-out Not Essential

Before taking a short position in a stock, however, it is safest always to wait for the break-out. In our Glidden chart prices broke out and closed out of the pattern on April 24 – with no increase in volume. On the following day, the price movement was conclusive but volume was not. This low volume action on the initial break-out is a frequent occurrence with Right-angle Triangle Reversals, differing in that respect from the break-outs with decisive pick-up in volume which we demand of Symmetrical Triangles before taking a position. Since the Descending Right-angle Triangle is already expressing a growing technical weakness in the market, it follows naturally that no excessive selling is required to push prices out of the pattern. The support along the level of the bottom leg eventually has to give way. Consequently, any closing of prices by a fair margin out of the bottom of the pattern – *in the direction which the pattern has already forecast* – may be considered a valid break-out and a sufficient signal to sell.

We do not mean to imply that this failure of volume to appear on the initial break-out of Right-angle Triangles is the rule, for it is not; in the majority of cases, perhaps, a sharp volume increase accompanies the break and usually the price movement is proportionate. What we do wish to bring out is that we need not wait for a volume signal to confirm an otherwise valid break-out on the down side from a good Descending Triangle (or on the up-side from an Ascending Triangle).

Out-of-Line Movements

In the preceding paragraph, however, note that we specified "an otherwise valid break-out", meaning a break-out closing out of the pattern by the decisive margin which we discussed in Study II, page 60 under the heading "Wait for Clear Confirmation". The need for this caution is shown by our next example, the Descending Triangle Reversal in Nash Motors in 1929 (Fig. III.10).

Nash reached its top on August 5 (over two months before the majority of stocks made their final spurt) where it showed a typical one-day reversal. Thereafter, it formed a large Descending Triangle with horizontal leg or support line at the 84

Fig. III.10

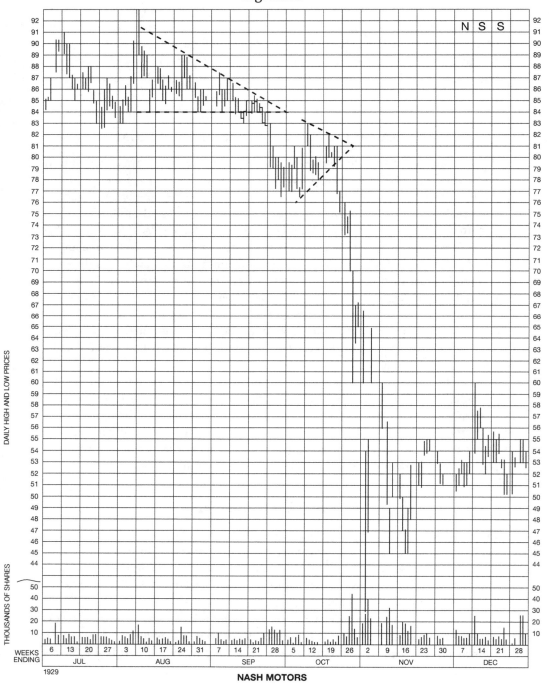

NASH MOTORS

level. On September 12, this support line was pierced but by only half a point; on the following day the price fell a full point below the boundary line but worked back and closed the day inside the pattern.

After the 14th of September prices ranged within the pattern and did not break out again for nearly a week. Not until September 21 did we get a break confirmed by volume. (Here, again, doubling the Saturday volume gives us our clue.)

Such brief out-of-line movements (of prices) as occurred in Nash on September 12 and 13, are by no means a rare phenomenon in Right-angle Triangles. They are not to be classed as false movements since they break out, in fact, in the same direction as the anticipated true movement. More often than not, the out-of-line movement occurs all within a single day and is then called a "one-day out-of-line".

It is reasonable to assume in the case of the out-of-line movement in Nash, that professional interests engaged in distributing a large quantity of the stock were supporting the price at or around 84, withdrawing their offers whenever this level was approached. On September 12, however, the market in Nash had developed so much technical weakness that the movement got out of hand for a couple of days; probably the operators in Nash had to do some buying at this time to prevent a collapse and permit them to complete their distribution at profitable levels. This explanation is, possibly, too simple to account for all out-of-line movements but, as we have noted before, the exact explanation does not matter so long as we recognize the phenomenon and are not misled by it.

Taking a Short Position

From our study of the out-of-line movement we can now see why it is safest to wait for a decisive break-out before selling a stock short. In the case of Nash we should have been safe in closing out a long position and taking our profit it as soon as we were reasonably certain that a Descending Triangle was in process of formation. But if we had sold the stock short at, say, 83½ on the strength of the piercing of the support boundary on September 12 and had placed a stop-loss order at, say, 85, our stop would have gone into effect a few days later and our transaction would have been closed out with a small loss. By waiting for a decisive break we avoided that risk. (The value and placing of Stop-Loss Orders will be taken up in Study XI.)

Effect of General Market on Individual Issues

The Nash Chart (Fig. III.10) illustrates not only the occurrence of out-of-line movement, but also another phenomenon which is worth a little attention at this point although a full discussion of it belongs more properly in our later consideration of market tactics.

Note that the downward movement in Nash, after the break-out on September 21, ran into buying very quickly and was halted for nearly a month around the 79 level. The technical trader who sold Nash short on the break-out might have been concerned about the correctness of his position during this waiting period before the down movement was resumed. Quick halts and periods of congestion following a break-out from a strong reversal pattern are often attributable to a "braking" effect which the strength of the market as a whole has at times upon the weakness of an individual stock (or vice-versa). What happened in Nash at the time of our chart was very plainly due to the fact that Nash made its top in early August, whereas the majority of stocks in which the public was actively trading during those epic days did not make their tops until the last half of September, and the general market did not make its last spurt until October. Nash had headed downward definitely in August but the general market was still strong; the new owners of the Nash stock that had been distributed during August and early September were under no pressure to liquidate and the strength of the general market probably led them to believe that their stock would go higher again. Consequently, the downward trend in Nash, already so clearly forecast in our technical pattern, did not get into its stride, so to speak, until the whole market changed its tone.

This "braking" effect of the general market on a single stock's technical action is a phenomenon which occurs just often enough to create doubts in the mind of the inexperienced technical trader, and this has led us to discuss it briefly here.

A similar action in the opposite trend may be observed by the student who cares to look up and analyze the charts of leading Copper stocks in the early Spring of 1936. Several of them developed very strong patterns indicating a good mark-up impending. But the whole market at this same time began to show technical weakness, culminating in the April drop (amounting to almost 20 points in the Dow Jones industrial average) which may be seen in the frontispiece. The strong technical position of the Coppers was held in check until the general market correction had run its course; then, however, it made itself felt in an extremely rapid advance that more than made up for all the lost time and setbacks.

Ascending Triangle Reversals

Just as the Descending type of Right-angle Triangle forecasts the reversal of an upward into a downward trend, so the Ascending Triangle forecasts the reversal of a downward trend into a stage of mark-up. Everything we have noted above in our study of Descending Triangles, applies as well to the Ascending Triangle when it occurs in a downward trend, although the forecast is, of course, reversed.

Figure III.11 shows the Right-angle Triangle (A-B-C) of the ascending type which forecast the change to an upward price trend in Hudson Motors in the Fall of 1933.

It is interesting to observe the tendency of prices to lift away from the hypotenuse (A-C) as the apex of the Triangle was approached, suggesting a rapid accumulation of technical strength. There was an attempt to pierce the resistance line B-C on November 20 with good volume, emphasizing the growing strength of the picture. Another push on November 25 and 27 carried the price out of the pattern but the decisive break did not come until December 1. The stock halted at 15, built a strong continuation Ascending Triangle, and then moved up rapidly to 23.

Figure III.12 depicts an Ascending Triangle Reversal in Johns Manville which came at the end of the April drop in 1936. The technical student may see in this the suggestion of a Head and Shoulders bottom, with the head formed at C and a long double right shoulder (E and G), but the pattern is, at best, irregular, and most observers would see it more readily as an Ascending Triangle. The failure of the recession from H to carry back down to the hypotenuse before turning up again at F, indicated rapidly growing technical strength. The gap in prices at J (discussed later on under the subject of Break-away Gaps) further emphasized the importance of the rise to follow.

Right-angle Triangles in Weekly Charts

Descending Triangles are fairly common at the end of long-range major uptrends. The Ascending Triangle appears less frequently at the bottom of major down-trends, but is just as important and valid when it does appear.

A good example of a Descending Triangle Reversal on a weekly chart is pictured in Fig. III.13.

The Wedge Formation

Related to the Triangle in appearance at least, although probably brought into being by an entirely different set of fundamental causes, is the Wedge Formation. It belongs in our discussion of Reversals because it forecasts a reversal of the trend in which it is formed, but it is not so easy to explain why it should act the way it does.

The Wedge Reversal formation is produced by a progressive narrowing of the price range but without any great slowing up of the prevailing trend. Instead of the convergence being produced by successively higher bottoms and lower tops in the minor fluctuations that form the pattern, as is the case with the Symmetrical Triangle, the Wedge pattern converges to a point by a process of both higher tops and higher bottoms (or both lower tops and lower bot-

Descending Triangles are fairly common. The Ascending Triangle appears less frequently.

Fig. III.11

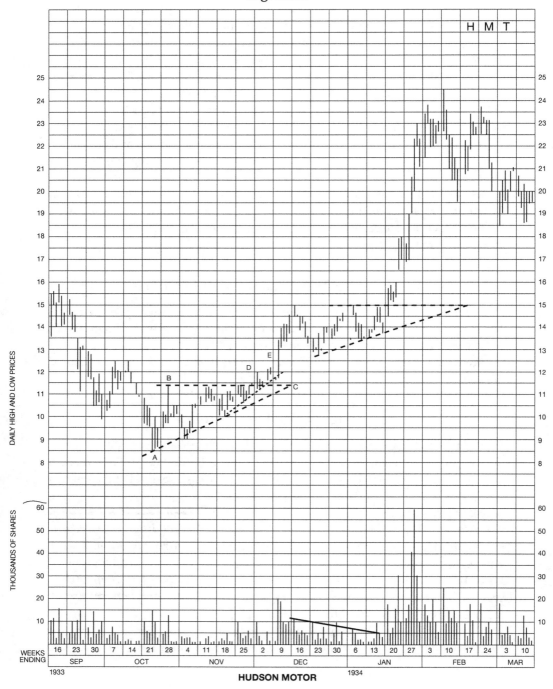

HUDSON MOTOR

Fig. III.12

JOHNS MANVILLE

Fig. III.13

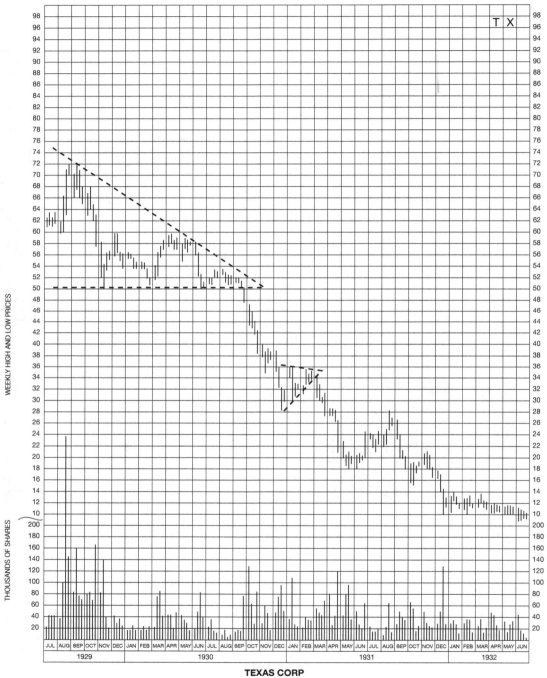

TEXAS CORP

toms if the prevailing trend is down) but the spread between minor tops and bottoms grows less and less until the stock is fluctuating within a much narrower range than is its normal habit. The forming of the Wedge is accompanied by a progressive perceptible decrease in activity, the declining volume as the pattern tapers to its point being analogous to the declining volume that accompanies the forming of a Triangle.

Somewhere near the theoretical tip or apex of the Wedge, prices break away from the pattern, with or without volume increase according to its direction. Thereafter, prices move away, more or less rapidly, in a trend *opposite* to that which formed the Wedge.

Examples of the Wedge Formation

Before proceeding to a further analysis of the Wedge pattern we had best get its appearance fixed in mind by reference to typical examples. Figure III.14 shows a Wedge formation in New York Central in 1931. Note the price trend working up during January and February in a clearly-defined, narrowing track bounded by the lines A-C and B-C. At the same time, the volume (except for two lone days of sharp rally, Feb. 10 and Feb. 21) is very gradually but perceptibly declining. On February 29 prices broke out of, and well away from, the pattern on the down side, with a spurt in activity that is conspicuous when we follow the rule of doubling Saturday's volume. The decline that followed carried New York Central from 124 to 74 in three months' time, although a movement of this extent is by no means always indicated by the Wedge pattern. However, the rapid break-away and decisive movement in the new trend is typical of the Up-Turned Wedge Reversal.

Up-turned and Down-turned Wedges Compared

Figure III.15 shows a Down-turned Wedge which formed in the daily chart of Electric Auto-Lite in the Spring of 1932. Compare the volume picture and price action following the completion of the Wedge in this chart, with the New York Central chart (Fig. III.14). Note the indecisive and dull period which followed the turn of prices out of the Down-pointed Wedge pattern before the new upward trend really started; this is typical of the price (and volume) action to be expected following a Down-turned Wedge, and is, as we have seen, quite different from the characteristic action following the Up-turned formation. Each presages a reversal of trend, but the move is delayed for an indefinite period in the case of many Down-turned Wedges. The practical trader will therefore take prompt action when his chart shows a break-out from an Up-Pointed Wedge Top; whereas he may safely delay action at a Bottom until the price and volume action indicate that the new uptrend is really started.

Fig. III.14

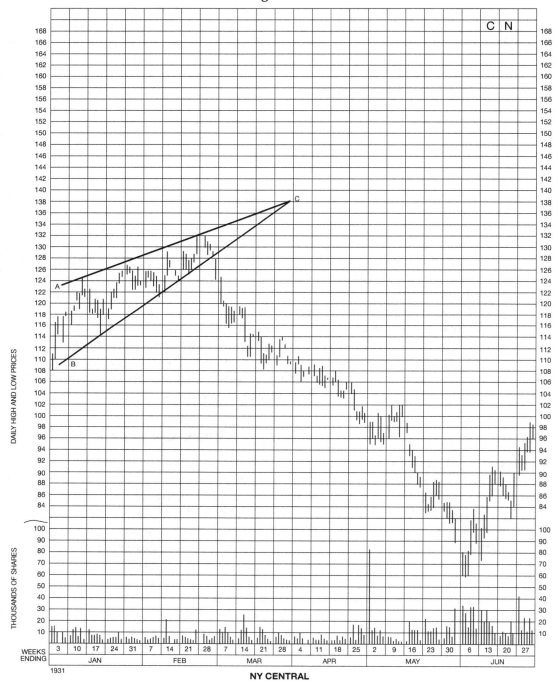

NY CENTRAL

Fig. III.15

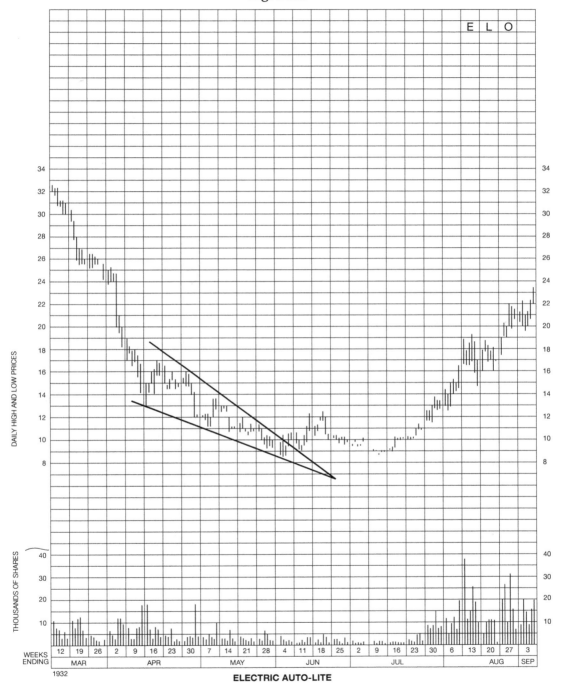

ELECTRIC AUTO-LITE

The Wedge Must be Strictly Defined

A word of caution to the student is in order at this time. The Wedge Pattern is reliable as a reversal formation only when it conforms strictly to the description given herein. The boundaries of the Wedge must be clearly defined and well filled with price action. The Wedge must point *sharply* up or down. A converging pattern which is projected on the chart in a nearly horizontal direction is more apt to partake of the nature of a true Triangle, and the student will note that the forecast in that case would be quite different.

The Wedge, in fact, is not a common formation. It is taken up here in connection with our study of the important reversal patterns only because of its pictorial similarity to the triangle, and its reliability when it is strictly defined.

Summary of the Triangle Reversal Group

Let us now review the Triangles and related formations which may indicate a reversal of price trend, which we have been studying in this section of our Course.

The Symmetrical Triangle may signal either a reversal or a continuation of the previous trend, the latter more often than the former. It does not tell us, in itself, which direction the subsequent move is going to take until the break-away, generally near the apex, gives us this important information.

The Wedge Pattern is reliable only when it conforms strictly to the description.

The Right-angle Triangle also appears more frequently as an intermediate or continuation formation than as a reversal, but, unlike the Symmetrical pattern, it does give us a fairly reliable intimation, in advance of the break-out, as to the direction of the next move.

Right-angle Triangles with the hypotenuse slanting upward from the origin of the pattern are called Ascending Triangles and are "bullish". Those in which the hypotenuse slants downward from its origin are called Descending Triangles and are "bearish".

Wedges are clearly defined patterns of converging price trend, pointed sharply up or down; they forecast a reversal of the trend which forms them.

All of these formations are generally characterized by progressively declining volume as prices converge toward the apex, with a sharp pick-up when they break out of pattern and the new move gets under way.

We have noted that the Wedge must conform strictly to rule but that a certain amount of latitude is permissible in construing the Triangles. It will not be out of place, however, to add here the advice to the beginner that he confine his trading at the start to only those situations where the pattern and its forecast are reasonably clear, and to await more data and experience before attempting to fit definite patterns to any more loosely constructed and irregular areas of price congestion.

Probable Causes for Triangles

Before closing our study of this group of Reversal patterns it will be interesting to discuss briefly the probable factors of supply and demand which produce them.

The Symmetrical Triangle is typically a picture of hesitation, doubt, or delay pending some event that will clarify the stock's prospects for the future. It does not necessarily indicate manipulation or even concerted inside trading. One of the sets of factors which may produce a Symmetrical Triangle is exemplified by the large patterns which developed in the charts of several large utility holding companies prior to the 1936 national elections, starting several months before. In other cases the hesitation may be due only to a temporary exhaustion of buying – or selling – and a disposition on the part of traders to catch their breath and hold fast until they can re-appraise the situation.

The Right-Angle Triangles, on the other hand, do indicate some degree of concerted inside action. The Descending Triangle plainly pictures increasing offers of the stock met by a more or less definitely organized willingness to buy at a certain demand or support level. The Ascending Triangle pictures growing buying power meeting more or less organized selling at a certain resistance or supply level.

In the case of the Descending Triangle we may have, as was suggested in connection with the Nash chart Fig. III.10, certain interests engaged in distributing large holdings of the stock to the public and "supporting" the market at a certain level until they have unloaded all their shares. The level at which they throw in their support by bidding in any stock offered at that price, becomes the horizontal bottom leg of our Triangle. In the case of the Ascending Triangle we have, on the other hand, a picture of professional accumulation. The interests engaged in buying do not want to attract any public following until they have acquired a substantial quantity of the stock, so they "resist" any rise in prices beyond a certain level by throwing part of their accumulation back on the market whenever bids reach that level.

As their buying progresses and they pick up the floating supply in weak hands, they find less and less of the stock available at low prices; hence the upward slant of the bottom leg of our Triangle. Finally, a point is reached where they would be obliged to sell out too much of their accumulation to prevent prices from rising above the level they are willing to pay. Their "resistance", which caused the horizontal top leg of our Triangle, is then withdrawn. Other buyers now find the weak floating supply exhausted and are forced to raise their bids sharply to secure any of the stock; the sudden upward movement attracts the attention of still other buyers and the mark-up stage appears on our chart.

It must not be taken for granted, of course, that every Ascending Triangle is brought into being by the operations of a single powerful trader or a single organized group. There may, for example, be several interests or large operators engaged in accumulation independent of each other, while other groups who are not so optimistic about the stock's prospects are, consequently, willing to distribute their holdings whenever the price reaches a certain level. The net result, so far as the chart shows, is the same.

The factors which produce the less common Wedge formation are difficult to analyze. The most important factor in its creation is probably a shrinkage of activity in the stock as the feeling grows that it is temporarily over-running its true relation to underlying values. However, as we have remarked before, the causes are not important so long as we know the probable effects.

The next study will take up other reversal patterns of a more complex nature.

Study IV

IMPORTANT REVERSAL FORMATIONS
CONTINUED

The Four Previous Reversal Patterns

We have seen from our study, thus far, of technical reversal pictures, that they partake of various shapes and patterns but that, in the end, they are all varying aspects of the same essential phenomenon, the more or less gradual switching of the balance between selling pressure and buying power.

Neither are as reliable in forecasting a major reversal as the authorities might lead us to believe.

We have noted that the Rounding Turn is the most logical and simple of all such technical chart reversals; that the Head and Shoulders formation is only a less regular, more pointed, more widely swinging or vibrating reversal; that the Triangle, while not always a reversal formation, often manifests itself as such, by a sort of wearing out of the previous move and consequent reduction in activity; but that the Wedge, occurring more rarely, is hard to explain on any logical basis yet gives us a thoroughly reliable reversal forecast.

A Much Misunderstood Formation

We come now to a formation which is one of the most loosely and glibly discussed of all reversal patterns – the Double Top (or, in its opposite manifestation, the Double Bottom). The layman who has followed the financial columns in the daily papers or listened to board room gossip has undoubtedly heard it mentioned frequently. It is referred to so often by superficial writers that the beginner is likely to believe it a common and reliable indication of technical reversal, requiring little study. Unfortunately, this is not the case. Neither Double Tops nor Double Bottoms are as reliable in forecasting a major reversal of trend as the surface authorities might lead us to believe. Probably not more than a third of them signaled reversal; and most of the patterns which are popularly alluded to as "looking like a Double Top", carry no such suggestion to the informed student.

Nevertheless, the true Double Top and true Double Bottom, and their related patterns, do appear frequently enough as reversals of major trends to find a place in our discussion of the standard and important reversal formations. We must study first how to recognize the development of what may turn out to be a genuine Double Top Reversal.

Relation to Preceding Price Movement

One of the first considerations in interpreting the Double Top pattern is the extent of the movement which preceded it. If the stock has been in a long-continued up-trend, the Double Top is more likely to develop into a reversal. If, on the other hand, the preceding movement has been short, then the apparent Double Top is more likely to be broken and the upward trend continued. In this connection, the formations appearing on our other charts and in the averages also are helpful; if they are showing signs of an important reversal in trend we may suspect a true Double Top is forming.

Other helpful indications appear in the pattern itself.

How the Typical Double Top Forms

Frequently in very active markets, a stock will work up rapidly to a peak accompanied by high volume and then, without building any apparent reversal formation, drop off for several points and remain, more or less inactively, at a lower price level for several weeks. This is followed by another run-up with increased volume to approximately the same level as the preceding top, and again the stock backs away with volume again declining. The two sharp advances, meeting a large volume of selling at about the same level, appear now to have exhausted the buying power in the stock. It declines to the level of the previous reaction between the two tops, often hesitates there for a time, and then drops off in the new downward trend with volume usually increasing as the movement progresses.

Before entering into a detailed discussion of the significant points in the typical Double Top pattern described above, it will be helpful to study a few examples.

Examples of Double Top Reversals

Figure IV.1 shows a nearly perfect Double Top which formed in American Radiator and Standard Sanitary in 1929. The price movement which preceded this formation is not shown on our chart; probably, however, the student does not need to be told that the stock had been in a "bull" trend for many months before and was marked up very rapidly during the first half of 1929. In July it made its first top at 54½ with a large volume of transactions taking place around that price level. It dropped off precipitately from this first top and fluctuated for five weeks between 45 and 49 with comparatively little volume. In the first week of September it was again marked up rapidly on very high volume, reaching for one day a level slightly higher than the preceding top, but failing to penetrate it by a margin we should regard as significant. The movement that followed requires no special comment.

Figure IV. 2 shows another good example of the Double Top which formed in Houdaille-Hershey-B in the Spring of 1930. This stock had made a strong advance from the panic low to over 28 in the first week of February. The top at that level was accompanied by extraordinary volume. Dropping back quickly to 24, it began another very gradual advance with several days of high activity around the 27 level. On April 9 it touched 28⅞ but dropped back and closed at the bottom of the day's price range, making a one-day reversal on high volume which, as we have seen in Study II, frequently indicates a change in trend. This second top completed the Double Top Reversal, and the stock dropped off rapidly to 10 (and lower, later).

The picture in Houdaille-Hershey-B is not so typical in every respect of the true Double Top Reversal as that shown in American Radiator, but both conform in their important features to the requirements of that pattern. Both made a first top on high volume after a long advance and dropped off quickly without any top congestion or pattern of consequence. Both declined in the neighborhood of 20% from their top levels in the interval between their two tops. In each case, a period of sev-

> *More important is the extent of the decline from the first top and the duration of the interval between tops.*

eral weeks of decreased activity elapsed before the first top was again approached. In each case the second top, accompanied by high volume, was made quickly at approximately the same level as the first. All of these points require some brief consideration in our study of the practical use of the Double Top formation.

To begin with the first top, the factor of volume is important. We have noted in Study II the general rule of high volume at points of reversal, and we must expect this rule to apply quite strictly in the case of a true Double Top. The second top is also made, as a rule, on noticeably high volume but this volume need not be as great as that which accompanied the making of the first top, and it is often made on only a slight increase over the average volume during the interval between the tops. It is not necessary that the two tops be made at exactly the same level; the second top may rise slightly above or fail by a small margin to attain the highest point of the first top. A difference of a full point in the case of a stock selling under 100 does not invalidate the pattern. The general level of the two tops should be approximately the same, taking into account the price level and normal habits of the stock under study.

More important even than the volume factor, is the matter of the extent of the decline from the first top and the duration of the interval between tops. The decline should be of some consequence in terms of the stock's price level. We have mentioned the fact that this decline amounted to approximately 20% in each of the two examples shown so far. It might be considerably more but it should not be a great deal less than that, percentage-wise, to make a good Double Top Reversal. And, there should be more than just a few days' elapse before the second attempt is made to run the stock up through the previous top level. Speaking very generally, the longer the time interval between the two tops, the more important the pattern becomes as a signal of a major reversal.

Fig. IV.1

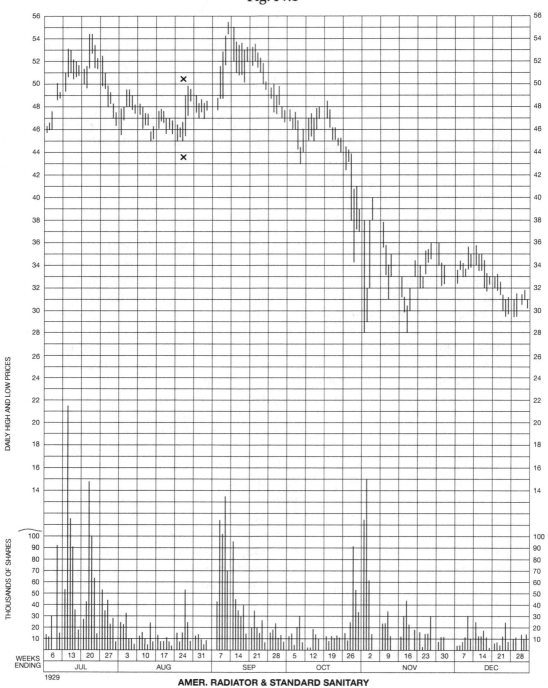

AMER. RADIATOR & STANDARD SANITARY

Fig. IV.2

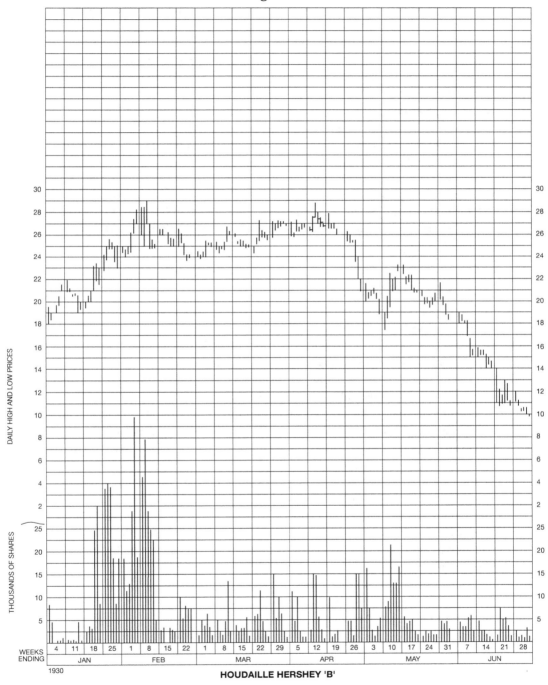

HOUDAILLE HERSHEY 'B'

The forecast of such reversal may be considered to be definitely confirmed when the price drops back and penetrates by a decisive margin the low range made during the interval between the tops.

The Double Top formation may be compared to successive assaults made by an army on a strongly defended enemy line. The first attack is made in force but is stopped short and quickly repulsed. The attackers drop back to a safe position, consolidate their forces, rest and gather strength for another assault on the enemy trenches. Again the charge is made; the first line of enemy trenches may be slightly penetrated or the attack may be stopped before it quite attains that objective; in any event the attack is repulsed and, this time, the beaten army has spent its strength and retreats in defeat. The tide of battle has turned. To carry our analogy further, the longer the time spent in preparation and the greater the force exerted in the second onset, the more decisive and significant is the failure to pierce the enemy line.

The student may, if he chooses, apply this comparison with an attacking army to our further study of variations in the Double Top or Double Bottom patterns.

Shorter Intervals Between Tops

Figure IV.3 shows a Double Top which formed in Pullman in 1932. It will be noted that this picture does not comply with our requirements for a major reversal in one important respect: the time between the two tops is too short. Despite the other elements in the pattern which do conform to the Double Top definition, this one defect should have made us doubt that any extensive movement of Pullman in a new down trend would result. The downward move was, in fact, halted too quickly to permit any but the most nimble of "scalpers" to profit by it.

This Pullman chart is included in our study to illustrate the danger in making a heavy commitment in a stock on the strength of a Double Top which does not conform in all respects to the requirements we have set up for a true reversal formation. It must be admitted, however, that stocks do occasionally reverse their trend after making two tops only a few days apart. In many of these cases there are other formations in the chart which give a more dependable clue to the reversal – an Inverted Descending Triangle, for example, which we shall take up in a later Study. In fact, the closer together the two tops stand on the chart the more likely they are both to be elements of but a single technical pattern which may, as it develops, indicate either a reversal or a continuation. The reader will find plenty of instances in the charts illustrating these studies – those that have preceded as well as all to follow – where stocks make two tops at approximately the same level but quite close together, and no reversal follows.

As for these rare cases where a major reversal does follow no apparent pattern except what might, by a stretch of the imagination, be considered a Double Top

Fig. IV.3

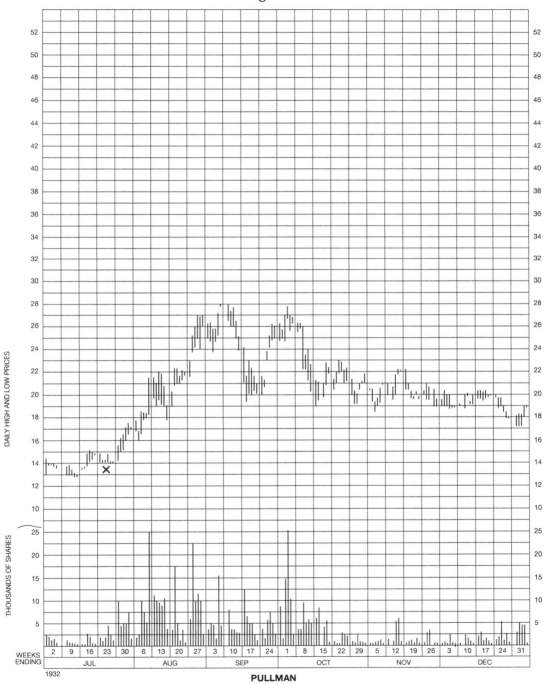

PULLMAN

formed within a few days of high activity, it must be recalled that many important moves take place without any forecasting patterns appearing on the chart. This is particularly true in very thin and erratic stocks in which the technical factors of supply and demand can change with great rapidity, although it may happen in any issue at times. The technical trader is well advised to watch for genuine and dependable chart patterns, of which there will always be plenty, and to pass up the doubtful pictures.

(To digress for a moment, the reader may find it interesting to observe in Fig. IV.3 the small Symmetrical Triangle which formed at the second top in Pullman in the first week of October. This was a good clear pattern, forecasting reversal, but its small size, plus the brief extent of the move which led up to it, indicated that only a limited decline would follow.)

Examples of Double Bottoms

The Double Bottom is, of course, the Double Top turned upside down, and is subject to the same conditions and same interpretations. The volume to be expected on the two bottoms is typically less than we should expect at tops, but the *relative* volume at the bottoms, and during the interval between them, follows the same rules as for the formation of a genuine Double Top. When a Double Bottom, meeting all the specifications we have analyzed above, appears on our charts we are warranted in predicting an advance of goodly proportions to follow. This type of formation gave technical students clear warning of a reversal out of the sharp declines in many leading stocks in the Spring of 1936, and of the long profitable advance to follow. Figs IV.4 and IV.5 on the following pages are excellent examples. We suggest that the student examine these carefully, checking price, volume and timing with the specifications laid down for testing the reliability of a Double Top, and noting further, as a point of interest, the typical halt or congestion of the new upward trend at or near the level of the farthest extent of prices between the two bottoms.

Multiple Tops and Bottoms

Technical factors similar to those which produce Double Tops and Bottoms, may on occasions produce triple and sometimes even quadruple or quintuple formations having the same implications. The tops (or bottoms) in these multiple patterns are characteristically closer together than is the case with true Double Reversals, and it is perfectly logical that this should be so. If we may once again employ our comparison with an attacking army, we should naturally expect that a large number of unsuccessful assaults on an impregnable enemy position, even though each were delivered with comparatively little power and with little time taken for gathering of

Fig. IV.4

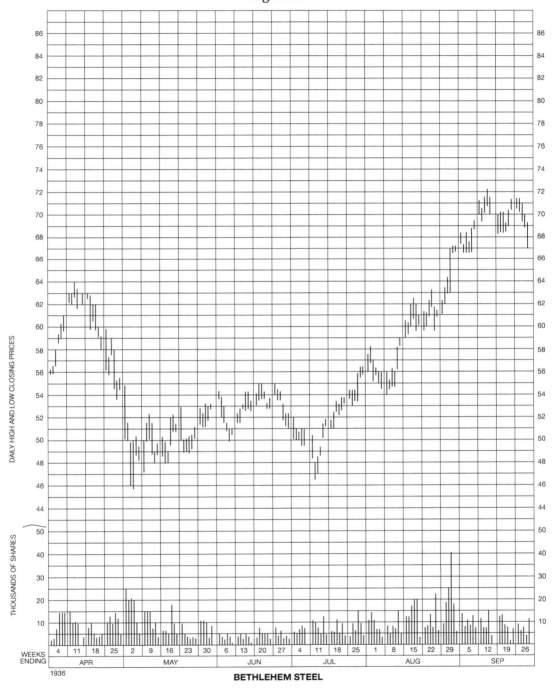

BETHLEHEM STEEL

Fig. IV.5

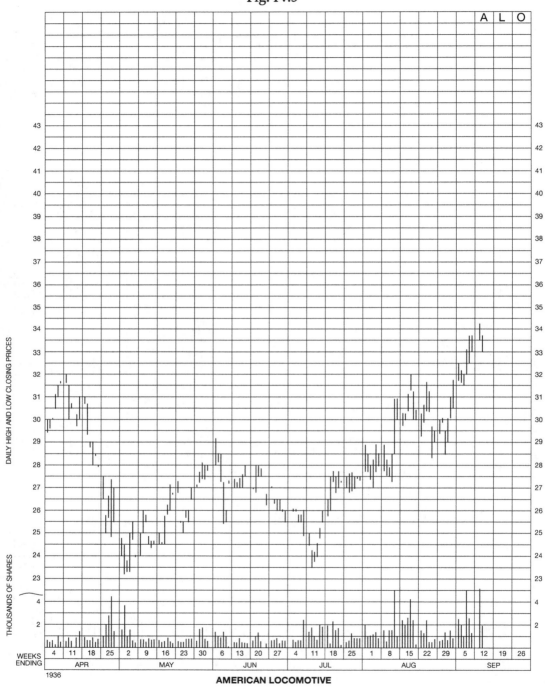

AMERICAN LOCOMOTIVE

forces between, would eventually wear down the besiegers and throw them into rout. In any event, whether or not the analogy is fairly drawn, it is safe to assume in the technical analysis of our charts that, whenever prices attempt and fail to penetrate certain levels on successive occasions, each failure adds weight to the indications of reversal; also that the longer the attack persists the greater the importance of the move to follow.

However, it should be noted that many chart pictures which show multiple tops or bottoms are more correctly to be regarded as falling into the classification of some other, perhaps more dependable, technical formation which may even have an opposite implication . . . for example, a Right-Angle Continuation Triangle.

Volume Action in Multiple Reversals

In those cases which permit of no other construction – where the only clear picture is one of Multiple Tops or Multiple Bottoms – high volume accompanies the formation of the first reversal but thereafter the volume picture is usually confused and irregular, offering little aid in forecasting until it again picks up sharply as prices break away into the new trend. Figure IV.6 shows a Multiple Top which reversed the trend in Timken Roller Bearing early in 1931. Four successive rallies in a period of about six weeks failed to carry the stock above 59. The first top was made on good volume but note that it took the form of a one-day reversal – in itself a caution signal. However, perhaps the first confirmation of a major reversal – making this a Multiple Top pattern – was the breaking of prices on April 7th down through the level at 52 of the minor bottoms which followed the making of the first two tops; this break it will be noted occurred on volume appreciably higher than the average for over two weeks before. The decline took prices down to 32 in the first week in June. At this time a formation developed which might be construed as a weak and rather doubtful Double Bottom, but really is better interpreted as a Symmetrical Triangle reversal followed by a type of false movement which we shall refer to in a later study as an "End Run".

An Illustration of a False Double Top

Note also in the 1931 Chart of Timken Roller Bearing the tops made at 48 in the first part of January and again in the last week of that month. Here is an excellent example of the type of price action which is so often referred to by superficial chartists as a Double Top. In fact, we haven't the slightest doubt that more than one market commentator mentioned this very action on January 29th with the remark "TKR looks as though it had made a Double Top". The student of this Course will quickly see

Fig. IV.6

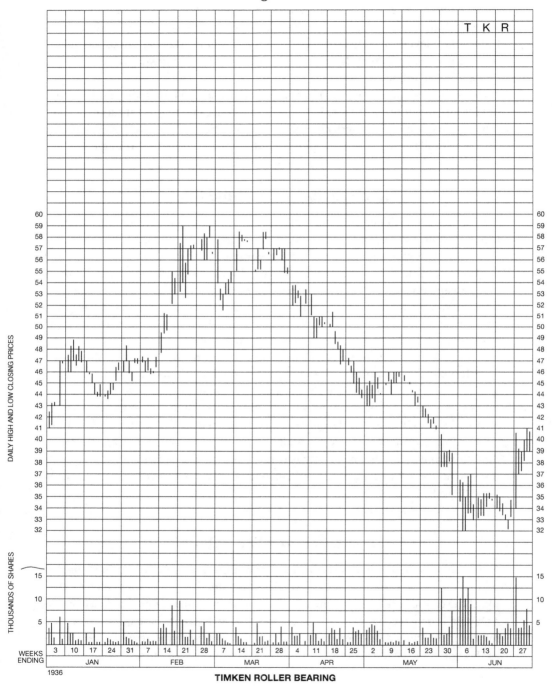

TIMKEN ROLLER BEARING

that neither the interval of time nor the extent of the reaction between the two tops bear out the Double Top interpretation.

He will see also that these minor tops were actually constructing the horizontal top or "resistance" boundary of an Ascending Triangle which called for higher prices rather than a reversal at this stage.

A Multiple Bottom Formation

Figure IV.7 illustrates a Multiple Bottom Reversal, fairly typical of this formation, which appeared in the Chrysler chart in May, 1936. The first bottom (at 91¾) was made with high volume on April 30, but note that the closing transaction on this day was at 95½), the very top of the day's price range – a perfect example of a one-day reversal which, in itself, gave warning that the previous trend had run its course, although this action alone did not warrant a conservative trader's taking a "long" position. On May 12, Chrysler again touched 91¾ and again bounced back. Selling pressure once more forced the price down on May 19 to 92½ practically the level of the previous bottoms. The first suggestion that this chart was developing a good multiple bottom came on May 26 when prices closed well above the levels reached by the previous minor rallies. The volume at this stage was not conclusive, however, and another and a final attempt to penetrate the previous bottoms had to be made before Chrysler's growing technical strength finally won out and the new up-trend was definitely established. An ultra-conservative trader would get all the confirmation he might ask in the decisive break-away of prices from congestion on June 20 if he remembered to double the Saturday volume.

Double Tops and Bottoms on Long-range charts

Good Double Tops are by no means uncommon in weekly and monthly charts of individual issues. Good Double Bottoms also appear, and apparently with greater frequency than Tops. In both phases they are of greater academic than practical interest. (Refer back to our discussion in Study II of the Head and Shoulders formation in weekly and monthly charts.) The volume indications are, quite naturally, lacking on weekly charts, especially in the case of Double Bottoms, because the volume on break-outs, etc. usually comes on one or two days only and does not show up conspicuously in the week's total.

Figure IV.8 shows a fine Double Bottom pattern in a weekly chart of American Bank Note. The two bottoms at the 11–12 price level occurring a year apart might conceivably bear no relation to each other yet it is reasonable to assume that a "stone wall" of resistance based on sound fundamentals did (and possibly still does) exist at that level, and that it did turn the stock back and form the foundation for the long

Fig. IV.7

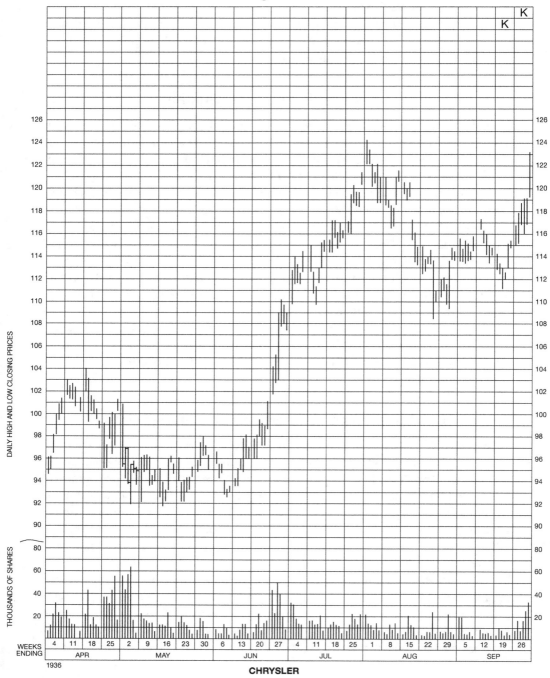

CHRYSLER

and very profitable advance that carried this issue to 55 early in 1936. What makes this especially interesting is the form taken by the two bottom reversals. At the first bottom, in October, 1933, an Ascending Triangle signaled the upturn (with good volume confirmation) and was followed immediately at the turn of the year by a strong Symmetrical Continuation Triangle. The second bottom, in the fall of 1934,

> *Good Double Tops are by no means uncommon. Good Double Bottoms also appear, apparently with greater frequency.*

was part of an excellent Head and Shoulders formation, with shoulders in July and December.

"M" and "W" Formations

Certain financial writers have in the past referred to chart pictures bearing a fancied resemblance to the capital letters "M" and "W" as distinct reversal patterns. However, careful examination and study of many hundreds of stock charts leads us to consider the "M" and "W" formations as simply rather natural and not uncommon variants of the Double Top and Double Bottom, respectively. Generally speaking, the same requirements as to volume action, extent of price movement and timing apply, and the interpretation is the same.

The "M" formation is a Double Top in which prices move up very sharply to the first top and down at an equally sharp angle from the second top, and form, in the interval between the two tops a fairly deep V-shaped price track. The illusion of a capital "M" is further carried out in many cases by the halt or congestion which we have learned to expect in many charts at about the level of the bottom formed between the two tops. As might be expected, the "M" formation appears usually in stocks that have habitually rapid movements and sudden reversals in trend.

The "W" formation is simply the "M" turned upside down, and is a similar variant of the Double Bottom. The weekly chart of American Bank Note (Fig. IV.8) pictures a good example of the "W" type of Double Bottom, and so does the daily chart of American Locomotive (Fig. IV.5).

Rarely also a good "W" picture will appear in a Triple Top Reversal; its forecasting value differs in no wise from that of any strong Multiple Top. Such a "W" variety of Triple Top is illustrated in the chart of National Power and Light for the first half of 1931, shown in Fig. IV.9. Remember to double the volume shown on the chart for Saturday, March 28, when studying the volume action in this illustration.

Double Tops and Bottoms in the Averages

Perhaps one of the reasons why the inexpert public and many newspaper financial

Fig. IV.8

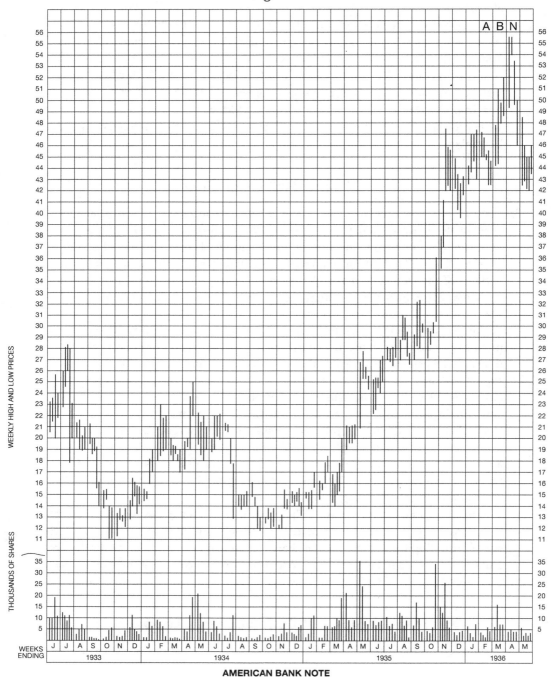

AMERICAN BANK NOTE

Fig. IV.9

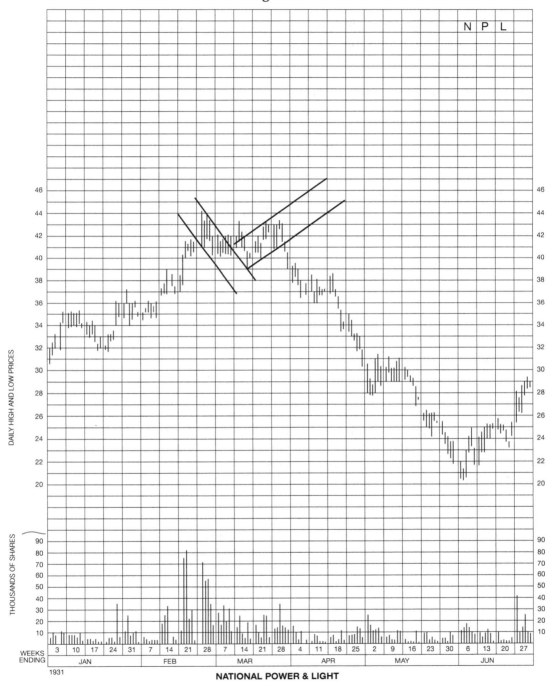

NATIONAL POWER & LIGHT

writers speak so confidently about the Double Top and Double Bottom as a positive indication of a reversal is because there have actually been several occasions when Double formations appeared in the widely published average charts at the end of long bull or bear markets. The most notable example which writers are prone to submit is the close of the bear market of 1921 which does show, with a little imagination, a satisfactory example of the Double Bottom.

Going back still further on the Dow-Jones Industrial average, we find that Double Bottoms apparently ended the long bear markets in 1897, 1903, and in 1914–15. Double Tops are no less common at the close of long bull markets, notably in the Industrials in 1899 and 1906, and in the Rails in 1918–19.

Attention is called rather naturally, however, to those formations, because they stand out as reversals in the chart picture, but we must call the reader's attention also to the myriad additional multiple formations occurring in the long-term average charts which might have been reversals but were not. And because they were *not* reversals they melt into the general picture and are comparatively unnoticed by the casual observer.

Despite this slightly optical illusion, however, the Double formations do appear quite logically to have greater reversal strength and importance when appearing in the averages than when noted merely in the chart history of an individual issue.

The Complex Pattern – a Reliable Forecaster

The sixth type of reversal formation, which we are now ready to study, is the Complex Formation and it allies itself strongly with the Head and Shoulders and the Common or Rounding Turn patterns as being a reliable forecaster, in itself, of a reversal from the previous trend into a new direction of price movement. The Complex Formation is, in addition, one of the strongest of all our reversal patterns. It stands so far ahead of the others in this respect that if it were a more common development it would, with little doubt, take the crown of importance away from the Head and Shoulders formation, and lead our entire list of reversal pictures.

The Complex Reversal is, as a matter of fact, merely a stronger, longer and more detailed form of the Head and Shoulders picture. For that reason it is found less frequently but, also for that reason, it is one of our most reliable indicators of definite reversals in the comparatively rare cases where it *is* found.

The Complex Formation divide themselves into two more detailed aspects of the Head and Shoulders pattern. These are the shoulders and multiple head type, and the head and multiple shoulders type. Their appelations suggest rather clearly their definitions. The shoulders and multiple head form is simply our old friend the Head and Shoulders, but with a double, or multiple, head. The head and multiple shoulders form is also like the regulation Head and Shoulders picture but while the head is single, the shoulders are in multiples. Both of these Complex Formations are reversals and they appear, therefore, either as tops or bottoms.

Relation to the Double Tops and Bottoms

In addition to its close relation to the Head and Shoulders formation, the Shoulders and Multiple Head classification partakes also, of course, of the nature of the Multiple formations which we have just studied – especially the Double Tops and the Double Bottoms. However, the Complex pattern we are now considering, when it has two or more heads, makes these heads too close together to be defined as a Double or a Multiple Top. Moreover, the Complex Formation, as we have stated above, is stronger than the Multiple Formation and is more quickly recognized, permitting us to take a somewhat quicker and more profitable trading position.

The Double Head and Shoulders Top

We have noted in our introduction to the Complex patterns that they are not common; ideal formations, perfect in every respect, are indeed extremely rare. We may, therefore, be pardoned if we go back in the files for a classic example in order to give our readers a first look at this interesting formation. Incidentally, this illustration serves also to point the fact that previous bull market produced the same technical pattern we found in 1929, and are finding today.

Figure IV.10 shows the price action in Crucible Steel from November, 1922 to May, 1923. (A reference to the long-term chart of the Dow-Jones Industrial Average at the beginning of this Course shows that a general reversal in the market occurred at this time.) In November, 1922, Crucible Steel after a rapid drop down to 60 from above 80, reversed its trend with a perfect Head and Shoulders pattern of the ordinary type at A-B-C. Thereafter the stock worked up in a few months to 82 at point D, where it met resistance and formed the left shoulder of our Double Head and Shoulders Top. After a brief reaction the stock succeeded in getting up through that one previous point of resistance but was again stopped dead on two successive occasions, points E and F, at the 84½ level. The stock backed away once more from the double head and, finally, staged one more rally to point G, the right shoulder, in a vain effort to renew the advance. But selling pressure was now too strong; the technical balance had definitely changed and, at H, the neck-base line was broken and the reversal formation was completed.

Variations as in Simple Head and Shoulders

The Crucible Steel chart shows the Complex Top with double head and a single pair

Fig. IV.10

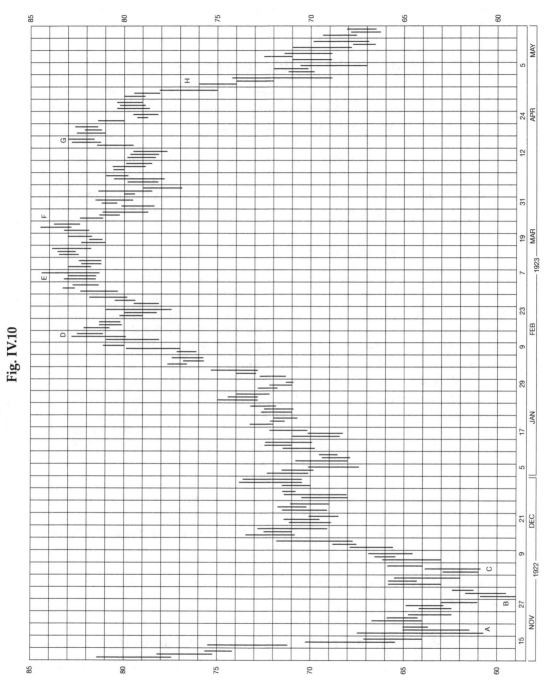

CRUCIBLE STEEL

of shoulders in as nearly perfect form as we are likely ever to encounter it. With this typical picture in mind, we may now proceed to a consideration of its more probable variations.

The Shoulders and Double Head occurs with the same differences in width and height of shoulders as the simple Head and Shoulders pattern. The neck-base line may slope up or down although the extremes in this respect do not appear so often. The two heads may be made at slightly different price levels. Generally speaking, however, the symmetry of the pattern is well maintained and the student will find the "rhythm" developed by these Complex Formations interesting to observe.

Fig IV.11 shows a rather unusual yet perfectly valid – and extremely powerful – Shoulders and Double Head Top that reversed the major trend in Chesapeake and Ohio in 1929. In this the two heads, B and C are made at different levels yet are clearly related and clearly twin heads. The left shoulder at A is unusually high and is characterized by an "Island Reversal", a valuable forecasting formation which we shall take up in detail in Study V and which in itself signaled the exhaustion of "good" buying. The rhythm of the pattern is notable.

Trading on the Shoulders and Double Head

Conservative traders may, and we think that beginners should, follow the rule laid down in our discussion of the common Head and Shoulders pattern, of waiting for the breaking of the neck base line before selling the stock, or buying in the case of a bottom pattern. However, due to the characteristic symmetry of these Complex patterns, it is frequently possible to anticipate the break-out, especially when the previous chart picture or other considerations suggest the probability of a reversal. In the Chesapeake and Ohio top, for example, after the emphatic reaction on Saturday, October 19 from the top of the right shoulder at D, the picture was sufficiently definite to warrant selling the stock. Obviously, in this particular case several extra points of profit would have been gained.

However, before attempting to "jump the gun", the trader should be certain of his picture. If it is not entirely clear, if it is not patently symmetrical, if the retreat from the right shoulder is not plainly evident, wait for break-out confirmation.

Let the student not take from the above remarks, which apply only to the perfectly symmetrical Complex Reversals, any implied permission to "jump the gun" with the simple Head and Shoulders formation which is not completed and does not signal a reversal until the neck base line is broken.

Head and Multiple Shoulders Types

This division of the Complex Reversals is somewhat more common than the type

Fig. IV.11

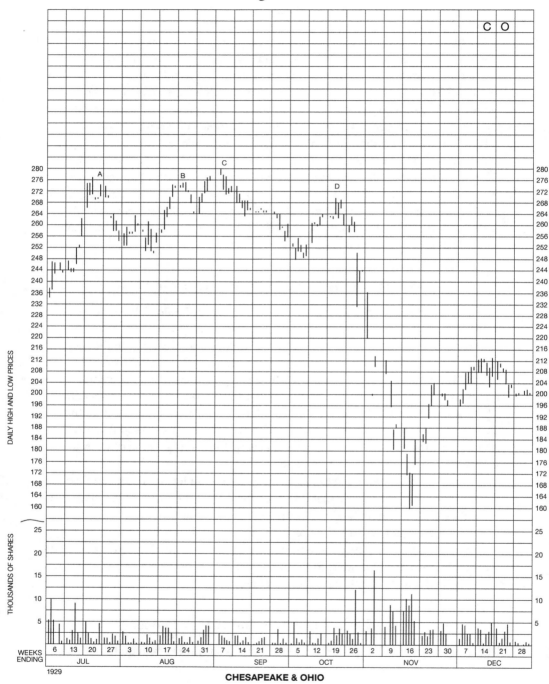

CHESAPEAKE & OHIO

that has two or more heads and only a single pair of shoulders which we have just discussed. In fact, multiple Shoulders show up "under the microscope" in a great many patterns ordinarily classed as simple Head and Shoulders reversals. (Note, for example, in Fig. II.2 the two sets of shoulders A-C and G-I, in the chart of Western Union.)

The rule of rhythm or symmetry applies to this type as well as to the multiple head type previously discussed, although it is sometimes necessary to look very closely to find the proof, and there are, of course, exceptions as there are with all technical patterns. A Head and Multiple Shoulders Top in the 1931 chart of General Theatres Equipment is shown in Fig. IV.12; this may be analyzed into three shoulders on the left, formed in quick succession at A, B, and C, a head at D, and three "broader" shoulders on the right at E, F, and G.

We might extend our discussion and our illustrations of Complex Tops almost indefinitely, since we can have both multiple heads and multiple shoulders in the same formation, with all the combinations thereof which the student may work out and classify if he wishes. Suffice it to say that they are all subject to the same limitations and interpretations as the types we have already considered.

Complex Bottoms in Same Varieties as Tops

We need not consider in detail the Complex Formation as a bottom reversal. Complex Bottoms appear in all the different forms found in Complex Tops, and are equally strong and reliable as indications of reversal. We can dismiss their study with a brief analysis of Fig. IV.13. The chart of Pullman in the Fall of 1934 shows a Complex Bottom Reversal with two distinct heads at C and D and with shoulders at A-B and E-F. The student may regard these as a single pair of irregular shoulders, or as two sets of shoulders with the two on the right somewhat confused by the greater congestion as the formation approached completion. The right shoulder area may also be construed as a small Symmetrical Triangle, and the decisive price action on November 7, with a sharp increase in volume, breaks both the Triangle and the neck of the Complex Reversal, doubly confirming the forecast of higher prices.

The reader has probably noticed the appearance of a Double Bottom in this Pullman chart, but as we have already noted in our earlier study, Double Bottoms or Tops which occur quite close together are almost always elements of a larger pattern and are best interpreted in the light of the larger and more dependable formation.

Refer back to Fig. II.7, for a Head and Shoulders Bottom which may also be construed as a Complex Formation with one head and two pairs of shoulders, the first left shoulder forming on September 21. The significance of this chart is in no wise changed by such a construction, except that the forecast of a reversal is slightly strengthened.

Fig. IV.12

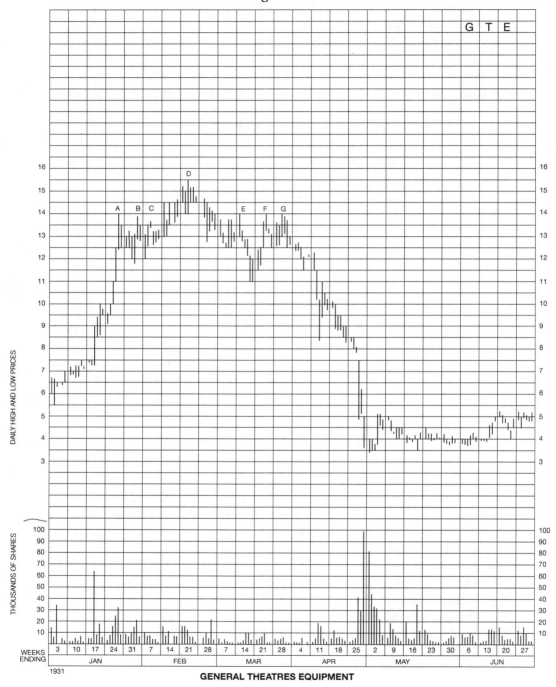

GENERAL THEATRES EQUIPMENT

Fig. IV.13

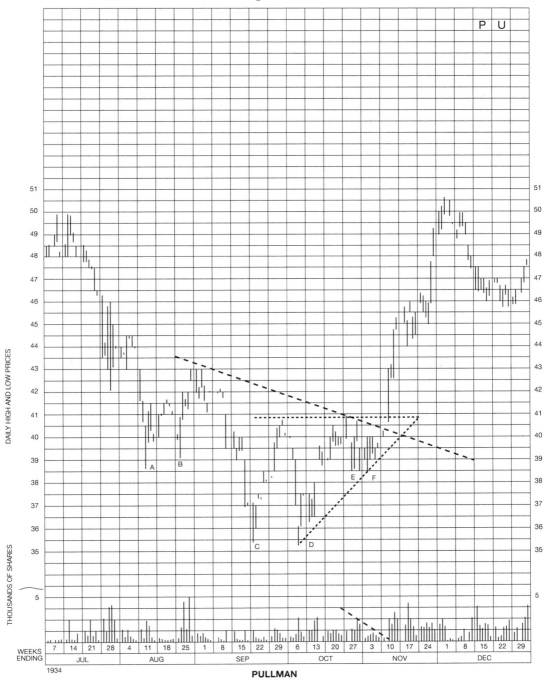

PULLMAN

Volume Indications in Complex Reversals

The reader has observed, very likely, that we have made practically no comment on volume action in connection with the Complex patterns. The reason is that no very definite volume pattern can be depended on to occur during the formation of a Complex Reversal, due possibly to the very complexity of the formation and the number of price fluctuations involved in changing the tide of technical strength. We might say that the Complex pattern looks as though it has difficulty making up its mind, but when it does decide, the decision carries considerable weight. One general rule of volume is carried out with very few exceptions; i.e., the sharp increase that breaks the neck-base line.

Shoulders at Different Price Levels

We have already commented in Study II on the occurrence of Head and Shoulders formations with an additional pair of shoulders formed on either side at a much lower level in the case of tops, or higher in the case of bottoms, than the pair next to the head. The student will find many examples. We do not classify these as Complex Formations because the inner pair of shoulders completes the picture, and the breaking of the inner neck-base line, which they define, indicates the reversal of trend.

The Broadening Top – a Rare and Intricate Pattern

The Broadening Top is the seventh pattern we shall take up in our study of formations which appear at major reversals in price trend. Due partly to its rarity and partly to its intricacy it is unquestionably the most difficult of all to discover and to analyze. For these same reasons it should possibly be placed at the end of our reversal studies, but we are inserting it here because it seems to form the transitional picture between the Head and Shoulders types already examined and the Inverted Triangles which we shall take up in the next section of this Course.

The Broadening Top, in its simplest and purest manifestation, might be described as a simple Head and Shoulders Top with a downward slanting neck-base line and a right shoulder reaching up to a higher level than the head. In its less simple (and more frequently found) form it suggests a triangular pattern faced about, with its apex at the left or beginning, and its broadest end at the right or completion of the congestion. It might, in fact, be logically included in the Inverted Triangle classification were it not for the fact that it must conform strictly to a certain "rule of five", of which more later.

When a Broadening Top is found in our charts it has a forecasting value of nearly the same rank as the Head and Shoulders. Moreover, it usually foretokens a movement of more than average proportions. It allies itself with the Head and Shoulders and Rounding Turn patterns in that it signifies, within its own formation, a reversal of the previous trend. It differs from the standard Triangles in that the Broadening Top does not indicate a continuation whereas the Triangles indicate a continuation more often than a reversal of the previous trend. Of course, it must be kept ever in mind that no technical pattern is 100% reliable in forecasting market changes.

Description of the Broadening Top

The Broadening Formation is made up of five separate and distinct minor reversals of trend, with each reversal going farther than the last, which gives it its characteristic broadening appearance and which, as we have already noted, causes it to resemble an Inverted Triangle. But an Inverted Triangle may be built up of any number of minor reversals whereas a Broadening Top must have five, and only five, fairly compact, broadening swings of minor or short intermediate price reversal. If a sixth reversal appears, then the formation is spoiled, and incidentally that sixth swing carries the previous major movement on into a continuation, whereas we know that our Broadening Formation, to be called such, must be a reversal of the previous major trend.

Since the Broadening Top must have five turns, or reversal in minor or intermediate trend, and never show a sixth turn, the first reversal of trend will be in the opposite direction from the previous major trend, while the fifth and last turn will also point the price trend in the opposite direction from the preceding major movement and set it on its new course opposite that previous direction. Thus the first turn in a Broadening Top must be a down-turn.

However, all this theoretical description may sound a bit involved to the unfamiliar student. We have previously allowed that the Broadening Formation is the most difficult of all of our major reversal chart pictures and before we go further in our discussion it may clarify our study to examine some examples in black and white.

Chart Example of the Broadening Top

Let us look first, then, at Fig. IV.14, the chart of Air Reduction from the late Summer of 1929 through the memorable panic of that Autumn. The stock was no laggard in the general action which attended the last, final, spectacular uprush during the Summer of 1929. From a low point around 95 in April, Air Reduction was in an almost constant and rapid upward movement, gaining nearly 130 points and much more than doubling in value in less than six months.

Fig. IV.14

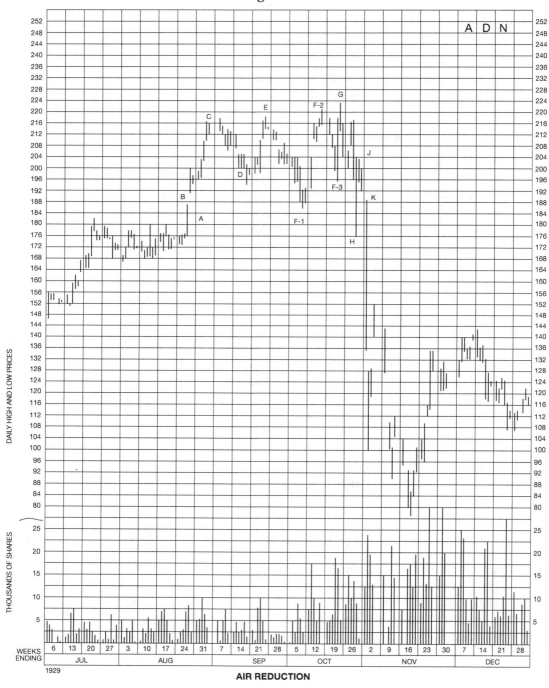

AIR REDUCTION

The first sign of final selling resistance, which was to end the longest and greatest bull market in history, came at Point C, where we had our first reversal of the previous major trend, the downward turn which we have just noted we must have for a Broadening Top. But buying again turned the technical balance temporarily, after a moderate reaction, and at Point D we had our second reversal. This second turn was not confirmed as a useful part of our formation, however, until the ensuing upward movement broke through the previous resistance at Point C, and went higher than that point, for we have learned that each successive reversal or turning swing must go farther than the last swing.

But almost immediately after the reverse swing at Point D had been confirmed as such by the movement going slightly higher than at Point C, we got our third reversal. This third turn at Point E, however, was not confirmed as a useful part of our formation until the new down-swing went still further down than the previous reverse swing at Point D. And just after the new down-swing, following Point E, had been thus confirmed our fourth reversal came at Point F-1.

This fourth reversal at Point F-1 was not confirmed as such until, once more, the new swing, this time upward, exceeded the previous up-swing at Point E. and, finally, after that fourth reversal at Point F-1 had been confirmed, we got our fifth, and last, reversal at Point G.

Let the reader note carefully, however, that while the fifth and last turn was made at Point G, it was not confirmed, did not become official, so to speak, for our purposes, until the ensuing reaction had gone down through and below the previous low point at Point F-1. The moment that the decline, which started with the fifth intermediate reversal at Point G, broke below 186, the level at which the fourth turn was made at Point F-1, our Broadening Top was technically completed.

Completion of the Pattern

Instantly, the forecast was for a large and rapid decline to follow. It might have ensued immediately; the price of Air Reduction might have continued straight on down from the day it formed Point H, below Point F-1. Actually, however, there was a moderate recovery from Point H, and such a partial recovery is generally to be expected following the completion of a broadening pattern. In the majority of cases, after the fifth reversal has carried prices below the fourth turning point, there is an attempt to rally and resume the previous major trend, but this rally seldom gets beyond the half-way level between the last top and last bottom of the pattern.

With this good example before us we may now see more clearly the resemblance of the Broadening Top to a Symmetrical Triangle inverted or turned about with its apex to the left and its base line to the right. We may also note how each successive reversal must go further than the preceding one before it is confirmed as a useful portion of our picture, and we may easily see, too, how the formation gets its name of the Broadening Top.

We may recall once more, with this example before us, our previous statement that since the Broadening Formation must be a reversal to deserve that name, and since it must also have in it five minor reversal turns, it follows that the first of these five turns must be a reversal in itself – that is, the first turn must reverse the previous major trend. So the first turn in the beginning of the Broadening Top must be a down-turn, while the first turn in a Broadening Bottom would be an up-turn. Likewise the last turn will also be in that same direction.

Major Importance of the Broadening Pattern

In the example just studied, in Air Reduction, the Broadening Top ended the longest and most spectacular bull market in the history of this stock; in only about two weeks after the Broadening Top had been formed the tremendous declines of the succeeding panic market had carried the price back down under 80. The broadening formation is not as infallible as we might wish but, when it does work, it works hard and profitably.

Some Important Technicallties

In the light of this example we have, it is hoped, cleared up a few of our previously obscure statements at the beginning of the chapter. Suppose for example, that Air Reduction, in Fig. IV.14 had continued the recovery which materialized from Point H to Point J. Suppose that recovery had gone up until it went through the previous high point, at Point G. Instantly such action would confirm a sixth minor or intermediate reversal, started at Point H. Our Broadening Top is allowed only five such full reversals and even if the movement had reversed a seventh time, our picture would already have been technically spoiled. The probability is that our previous broadening formation would then have turned into a plain Inverted Triangle, with the same forecast for major reversal, but in any case, confirmation of a sixth intermediate reversal would immediately have destroyed the formation as a Broadening Top.

One more point may here be touched upon which seems difficult for beginning students completely to grasp. That is the necessity for each successive intermediate reversal in the broadening formation to exceed the previous high or low point of the preceding reverse swing, before the intermediate reversal under observation is definitely confirmed.

Between Point F-1 and G, which were properly counted as real turns, we have Point F-2 which exceeded the previous high point at turn E. But the next downswing ended at F-3, well short of the previous low point at F-1, and immediately gave way to another upward movement to Point G. Neither Points F-2 or F-3 could properly be counted as confirmed turns in our needed five reversals, because the movement following Point F-2 had not gone down far enough to confirm it as a real turn, below the previous turn at Point F-1.

And incidentally, if the recovery from Point H to J had continued on back up to around 215, or even just slightly below Point G, and then turned back down, our Broadening Top picture would not have been disturbed. The sixth turn, at Point H, which would have spoiled the entire formation, would not have been confirmed as such unless and until the new recovery actually exceeded Point G, the highest point of the fifth confirmed turn, which, of course, it did not do.

Ending Bull Markets

As has previously been noted, the Broadening Top is rare and is not infallible but, when it does work, it is exceedingly important, and generally marks a critical turn from a "bull" to a "bear" market. This is comforting to the technical student because it means that there is still an ample swing for profit on the downside even after he has waited for some time to be sure that the Broadening Top was a bona-fide reversal pattern.

Figure IV.15 shows the Broadening Top which preceded the long decline in US Steel from the vicinity of 60 to 37 in the Spring of 1934. It will help the student to recognize the Broadening Top when, as and if it shows up in his charts, if we take the time to analyze the pattern in "Big Steel" as carefully as we did that in Air Reduction.

The first reversal in trend appears at point 1, when a three-day reaction carried the stock from $57\frac{3}{8}$ back to $55\frac{1}{8}$. The second reversal here (at 2) sent the price up again in two days to $58\frac{3}{8}$ (at 3A). Here we had what promised to be our third reversal but note that the reaction from 3A carried only back down to $55\frac{5}{8}$ (at 3B) before prices turned up again. The reversal at 3A was, therefore, not "confirmed" and could not be counted as the third reversal in our Broadening Top picture. The upward movement continued to $58\frac{3}{8}$ (at 3C) before another reversal appeared. Now we have to disregard the turns at both 3A and 3B and look upon 3C as our third reversal if it should be confirmed by prices falling below the level of the second reversal at 2. The reaction from 3C did carry down to $54\frac{1}{2}$ and 3C was thereby established as the third reversal in what might become a Broadening Top.

The fourth turn (at 4) had to be similarly confirmed by a movement to a level higher than 3C before we could count it as the fourth of the five reversals of a Broadening Top. This confirmation came in short order for the price of "Steel" worked up quickly to $59\frac{7}{8}$ on February 19 (point 5). The movement of prices on that day suggests a one-day reversal. A week later the price had dropped to $54\frac{1}{8}$, lower than the level of the fourth reversal; the fifth reversal (at 5) had been confirmed and the Broadening Top pattern was complete. Two brief rallies followed, which we have noted as being quite characteristic of this reversal formation, but they "got nowhere". Nothing short of a recovery to 60 or better would have spoiled our Broadening Top. The ensuing movement needs no comment.

Rally Following Completion of Broadening Top

We have referred in the paragraph above, as well as on page 136, to the partial recovery which usually follows the completion of a Broadening Top pattern. This rally, we have noted, frequently carries prices about half way back to the level of the last top or fifth reversal point of the pattern. In the Air Reduction top (see Fig. IV.14) the rally from H to J retraced almost exactly half the decline from G to H. In the US Steel top (Fig. IV.15) the Broadening Top formation was completed on March 1 when the price touched 53 after having attained $59\frac{7}{8}$ at the fifth reversal point. The rally on March 2 carried to $56\frac{3}{4}$, again half the extent of the preceding decline.

Naturally, we cannot expect such a close approximation of the half-way level on every rally after a Broadening Top has formed nor, for that matter, can we expect a rally of any extent always to follow promptly after the decline from the fifth reversal point has carried prices below the fourth reversal. In *most* cases a rally will develop shortly after the level of the fourth reversal has been "broken", and in *most* cases this rally will carry prices about half way back, but the exceptions are frequent enough to suggest the practical danger of counting on it, and to advise the immediate sale of any "long" stock as soon as the Broadening Top is completed without waiting for a rally. When it comes to taking a "short" position, however, a more conservative and frequently more profitable policy is to wait for a rally and to sell when prices have recovered about 40% of the preceding decline which completed the Broadening Top. Since these rallies are usually very short-lived, it is also good policy to place an order with one's broker to sell short at the specified price – the level to which the hoped-for rally might be expected to carry – as soon as the requirements for a Broadening Top formation have been carried out and before the rally has actually started.

> *When it comes to taking a "short" position wait for a rally and sell when prices have recovered about 40%.*

Distinction Between "Long" and "Short" Trading

This distinction in policy between disposing of "long" stock and selling "short" when a top reversal pattern appears on the charts, is based upon all important con-

Fig. IV.15

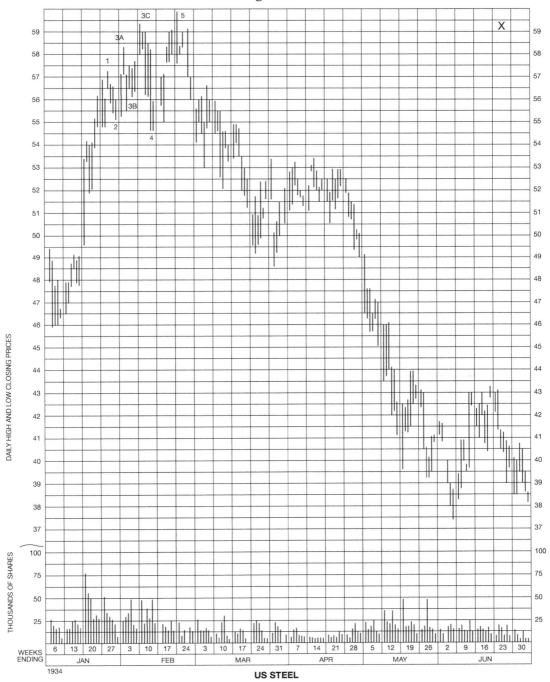

US STEEL

siderations of safety. Needless to say, it is better to miss a dozen opportunities to trade through following the rules of caution, than to suffer an actual loss by holding out for a rally which may never come. Technical patterns are not infallible, a fact we must keep ever in mind. The Broadening Top is an important and remarkably reliable reversal formation yet it may fail. The trader who sells his long stock as soon as a Broadening Top signals a reversal of the previous up-trend, loses only a part of his hoped-for profit if the reversal does not eventuate. On the other hand, the trader who waits for a rally before selling short is just that much better off in case the trend should go against him.

Broadening Bottoms Extremely Rare

The Broadening Bottom has appeared so rarely in the charts that any discussion of it may be considered as almost entirely theoretical. It is, of course, simply the same chart picture as the Broadening Top but coming at the end of a long down trend and signaling the reversal into an extensive upward movement. The first of its five turns must, naturally, be an upward one, reversing the previous major decline.

It is better to miss a dozen opportunities to trade than to suffer an actual loss.

Since a broadening formation by its very nature can be built up only by a fairly active market such as does not ordinarily exist at the end of a "bear" trend, we can understand why true Broadening Bottoms so seldom appear. The few bottom patterns which have conformed to the analytical requirements of a Broadening Bottom, have also presented as a rule other and more obvious patterns of bottom reversal. The student may, therefore, safely forget the Broadening Bottom – at least, he need waste no time trying to find it.

Broadening Formations Which Fail

We have stated that the Broadening Top is not infallible; also that a formation which apparently starts out to be a Broadening Top may fail of ultimate completion. Such uncompleted and violated Broadening Tops seem, nevertheless, to have a practical significance for the technical student. For the very attempt of a stock to make a Broadening Top seems to be a reliable warning that an important reversal is soon to be expected. There were, for example, many stocks which showed in their charts what promised at first to be typical Broadening Tops in the Spring of 1929. These formations failed of completion and prices moved up out of them in the final drive of the 1929 market, but they gave technical students cause to anticipate an impending break and to be prepared for genuine reversal patterns.

In the same way, many stocks tried but failed to make Broadening Bottoms in January and February of 1932, just a few months before the actual bottom of the long "bear" market was reached.

Possible Explanation for the Broadening Top

It may serve no very useful purpose to attempt to deduce the market factors which produce a Broadening Top in the chart of a stock. The value of the formation is sufficiently demonstrated even if a satisfactory explanation is difficult to find. However, a study of the history of the stock market at those times when Broadening Tops have appeared, suggests an explanation which seems logical and is very likely correct. The Broadening Top forms apparently in very active and excited markets after professional traders have already distributed their important holdings and have stepped aside. Heavy public participation, however, keeps the market active; prices, out of professional control, fluctuate in ever widening swings until it becomes evident that there is no real support or basis for further advance; no buyers appear for the shares the public now wishes to sell and the market collapses. Such conditions develop only at or near the end of fast "bull" markets that have run completely out of bounds.

As for the rule of five reversals, there is no conceivable logical basis for it, yet experience and a critical examination of many hundreds of stock charts indicate that a fifth reversal, in other types of congestion as well as in the Broadening Top, more often than not terminates a reversal pattern and signals the final exhaustion of technical strength.

A Brief Review

We have examined and studied in this section of our Course three types of technical patterns which are important as indicating a reversal in price trend of major proportions.

The Multiple Formations, of which the commonest manifestations are the Double Top and Double Bottom, are reliable when they conform quite strictly to certain specifications. The tops (or bottoms) must be made with a fair interval of time and a fair price movement between them, and the "valley" between the tops must be broken before the formation is complete.

The Complex Formations, closely related to the simple Head and Shoulders, are among the most reliable of all reversal forecasters, and would qualify for top place among reversal patterns if they appeared more frequently.

The Broadening Top is an even rarer formation, requiring careful analysis, and is not as dependable as the Head and Shoulders and the Complex patterns. But it is definitely indicative of a long and important movement in the new trend when it does form at a reversal, and it is this indication which warrants our including it among the important technical reversal formations.

Study V

MINOR REVERSAL FORMATIONS

Summary of the Major Reversal Patterns

In the three preceding studies we have analyzed seven types of technical formations which occur at reversals in stock price trends and have discussed their usefulness in forecasting. Of these seven, five are of major importance because of their frequent appearance, or great reliability, or both. These are:

1. The Head and Shoulders
2. The Common or Rounding Turn
3. The Triangle
   a. Symmetrical
   b. Right-Angle, Ascending and Descending
4. The Multiple Tops and Bottoms
5. The Complex Patterns

The other two formations – the Wedge and the Broadening Tops – were studied with the above not because of their major importance but rather because of their pictorial relation to the major types.

Reversal Patterns of Less Frequent Appearance

In this study we shall take up four more technical formations which may appear at reversals in price trend, and which are an essential part of the technical trader's "kit of tools" although an opportunity to use them may not come very often. Two of these – the Inverted Triangle and the Diamond – are somewhat related to reversal patterns previously examined. The other two – the Rectangle, with its variations, and the Island – are quite new and distinct.

The Inverted Triangle

We have referred to the Inverted Triangle (in our study of the Broadening Top) as a pattern of price congestion resembling a normal Triangle turned about so that it forms its apex first, and its wide end or base at the completion of the picture. The Inverted Triangle, in other words, is formed by a price action exactly opposite to that which forms a normal Triangle. In the Inverted pattern prices at first fluctuate within a narrow range but, as time goes on; the fluctuations tend to broaden; the lines which bound the price track diverge farther and farther apart.

We have in the Inverted Triangles the same two main divisions which we found in the normal Triangles – the Symmetrical and the Right-angle forms. And we find Right-angle Inverted Triangles both with ascending and descending hypotenuses.

Also, the Inverted Triangles, like the normal Triangles, may signal either a reversal or a continuation of the previous price trend. There, however, the analogy stops and, before proceeding to a detailed study of examples, we should give some consideration to general respects in which they differ from the normal Triangles and other more normal patterns of price congestion.

Differences Between Inverted and Normal Triangles

Among these points of difference, the Inverted Triangle is found much less often than the normal pattern – perhaps in the ratio of only one Inverted to 30 or 40 normal Triangles. The Inverted picture is typically looser and less regular, although occasionally a compact and well defined pattern will be found. The interpretation of the Inverted Triangle is difficult and the profit possibilities are much more limited as a rule than in the case of the normal Triangles. In fact, unless other helpful technical patterns appear, many Inverted Triangles offer the technical trader no good opportunity to take a profitable position in a stock.

The Inverted Triangle is formed by a price action opposite to a normal Triangle.

However, it is only fair in this study which deals primarily with the formation as a reversal, to state that the proportion of reversals to continuations is considerably greater with the Inverted Triangles than is the case with the normal patterns.

Another important difference appears in the volume chart. The volume action which accompanies the building of a normal Triangle is already familiar to us; almost invariably we have the base or wide end of the normal Triangle made on relatively high volume, and this is followed by a progressive shrinking of activity as the price range converges toward an apex, getting less and less until finally the break-out occurs and volume again picks up with it. In the Inverted Triangles, however, the volume picture is quite different. The beginning or narrow end of the pattern is frequently made on good volume. Thereafter, activity drops off at first to a lower level but does not continue to shrink; on the contrary, it is apt to be quite irregular and, more often than not, tends to increase somewhat on the average as the pattern broadens. A little thought would, of course, show us that higher volume must accompany wider price fluctuations. This volume action in Inverted Triangle patterns adds to the difficulties in trading on them since it often makes the break-out difficult to identify with confidence.

The Symmetrical Inverted Triangle

The chart of General American Transportation (Fig. V.1) shows an Inverted

Fig. V.1

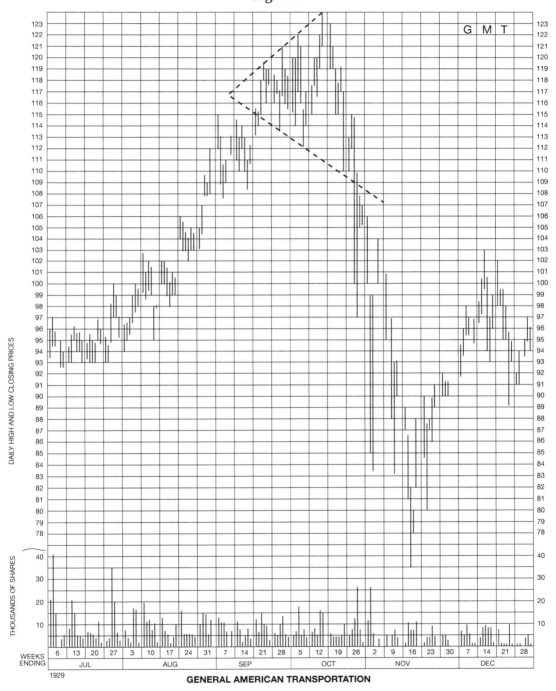

GENERAL AMERICAN TRANSPORTATION

Symmetrical Triangle which formed the 1929 top in this stock. The resemblance to a Broadening Top will be seen at once; in our previous study we stated that the Broadening Top might be considered a special form, or at least closely related to, the Inverted Symmetrical Triangle. The Broadening Top, however, need not be a compact pattern of price congestion, and its tops and bottoms need not fall along quite definite boundary lines as they do in the Inverted Triangles. On the other hand, the "rule of five" need not be applied to the Inverted Triangle, although it is carried out in the example before us. Inverted Symmetrical Triangles may also be built up of seven or, rarely, nine reversals. (And when they become continuation instead of reversal formations, they may have four, six or any larger *even* number of minor reversals within them. Inverted Triangles as continuations will be taken up in Study VI.)

In our present example of the Inverted Triangle, the price pattern requires no detailed study, but it will be interesting to analyze the volume action. Note that the four tops, on September 19 and 26, October 2 and 11, were made on relatively high volume, with activity falling off each time prices declined. Incidentally, the last two tops were good one-day reversals. The first change in the volume pattern appears on Saturday, October 19, when conspicuously high activity accompanied the making of a bottom; this, in itself, was definite warning of technical weakness. The lower boundary line was broken on October 23. Noting the drastic extent of the break-out of formation on that day, the closing of prices at the bottom of the day's range, and the increasing volume, the technical student needed no further confirmation of an important reversal of trend.

It must be admitted that this chart of General American Transportation presents an almost ideal Inverted Triangle pattern, extremely rare and, unfortunately, not typical of the formations of this classification which the chartist is likely to encounter at the more frequent intermediate reversals.

A More Typical and Less Profitable Example

The chart of Sharon Steel Hoop (Fig. V.2) shows an Inverted Symmetrical Triangle which signaled the reversal at the April tops of 1936. The reader will see in this a valid pattern of reversal which, nevertheless, did not give a dependable signal upon which to take profitable market action. The appearance on our charts of a congestion which takes on, as it forms, the appearance of an Inverted Triangle, is not in itself a reliable indication of a reversal, but there are frequently other factors, perhaps other charts forming true reversal patterns at the same time, which do give help. The trader who is "long" of the stock may well take his profit and stay out of the stock until a definite signal of the next trend shows up. The trader who does not already hold the stock had better not try to trade in it; he can find plenty of other opportunities more clearly forecast and more profitable.

Fig. V.2

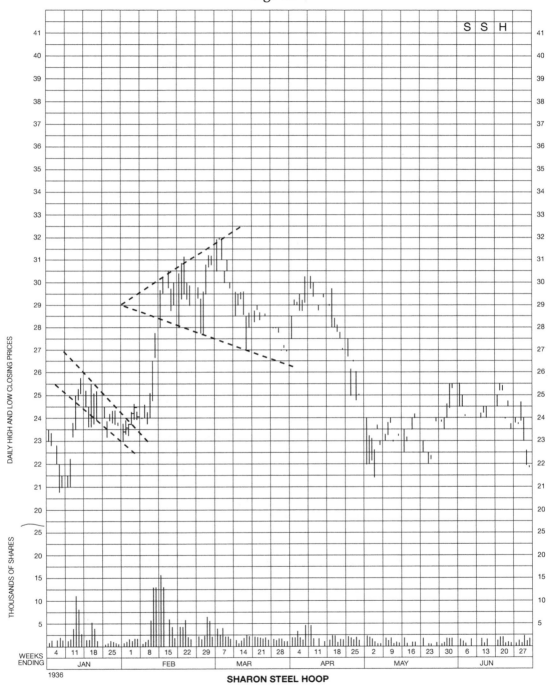

SHARON STEEL HOOP

Inverted Right-angle Triangles

Inverted Triangles with one boundary line extended horizontally and the other (the hypotenuse) slanting strongly either up or down from the origin or theoretical apex of the formation, are roughly comparable pictorially with the normal Ascending and Descending Right-angle Triangles previously examined in Study III (refer to pages 88–94).

However, the direction of the hypotenuse in the Inverted Triangle does not give us a dependable indication of the future course of prices as it does definitely in the normal Triangle. This failure of the hypotenuse to forecast is conspicuous in both reversal and continuation patterns and should be kept constantly in mind by the technical trader in his practical use of the Inverted formations.

The Inverted Triangle with Descending Hypotenuse

In some Inverted Triangles a horizontal leg forms the top boundary line, and the hypotenuse slants downward from the origin of the formation and forms the bottom boundary line of the price area. A conspicuously clear and strong example appeared at the 1929 top in American Can (Fig. V.3). The volume action during the formation of this reversal pattern is fairly typical of the Inverted Triangles. The sharp downward slant of the hypotenuse certainly suggested technical weakness, yet as is so often the case in Inverted Triangles, there was no definite and final confirmation of a reversal in the major trend until the extreme top price had already been left far behind. The first breakout occurred with high volume on October 24, but the movement reversed itself on that day and the closing price was back within the pattern and practically at the top of the day's price range. The next two days' range fell within the pattern. It was entirely possible at this stage, from all we could tell by the chart, to get another rally back to the 160–162 level which would be a normal recovery. Not until October 28 did prices leave the pattern behind definitely, and conspicuous volume pressure did not show up until the following day, when American Can had already fallen from its top of 183 to 132.

Difficulty of Trading on Inverted Triangles

In analyzing the Inverted Triangle top in American Can we have again stressed the difficulty of taking profitable market action after these patterns are decisively completed. Our advice to the beginner must be to leave these inverted patterns alone unless he happens already to own the stock, and to take new positions only on formations of clearer implications. Of course, the trader who was "long" of American

Fig. V.3

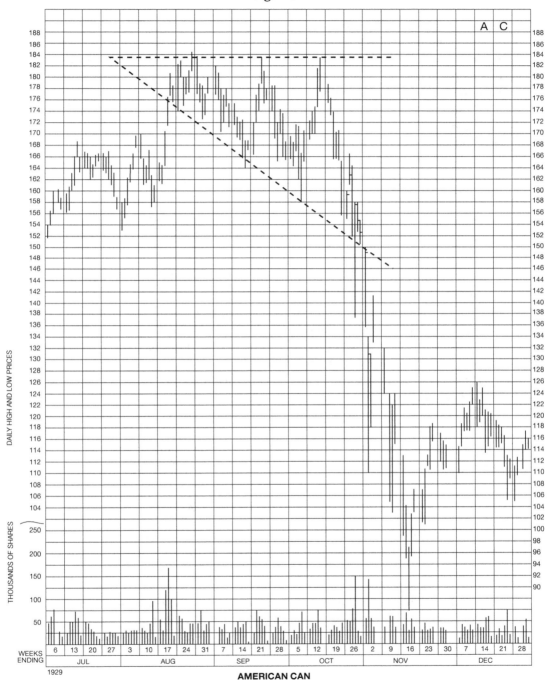

AMERICAN CAN

Can should have suspected that the trend had turned down when the rally on October 11 reversed without exceeding the previous tops; he was warranted then in taking his profit; he might even have arrived at this conclusion on September 20. But taking a long profit in a doubtful situation and selling short are two very different matters. A well-financed trader of long experience might have sold the stock short on October 12 but even then he should have placed a stop-loss order at, say, 187, and been ready to reverse his position if his stop was caught by a subsequent rally.

It is interesting to note, although it has no special significance, that there are nine minor or short intermediate reversals plainly to be seen in the formation of the Inverted Triangle top in American Can.

The Inverted Triangle with Rising Hypotenuse

A good example of an Inverted Triangle with a practically horizontal bottom boundary and an ascending hypotenuse is shown in the chart of General Foods in Fig. V.4. The pattern is long and rather loose but the diverging boundary lines are well defined and the triangular construction is clear.

The student will presumably have already observed that this is an example of the Inverted Triangle in which the break-out proceeds in a direction opposite to the direction of the hypotenuse (as it forms as time progresses) and, consequently, in the direction opposite to what we should have expected in the case of a normal Triangle with a rising hypotenuse. However, we have noted that the slant of the hypotenuse is not to be taken as a guide in Inverted Triangles.

There was a premature break-out, with volume, on April 23 which we have learned to recognize (Study III, page 91) as a one-day out-of-line movement. A decisive break, made on volume and closing a full point out of pattern, came on April 27. The rally in May carried prices back up to the level of the bottom of the pattern but stopped there. Note that activity dwindled away as this rally was made – the best of evidence, as we shall later see, that the rally was contrary to the basic trend.

Explanation for Inverted Triangles

The Inverted Triangle is difficult to explain. Although the ascending and descending hypotenuse types suggest (by their horizontal sides) support and resistance, respectively, or at least well defined demand or supply levels, yet the picture as a whole is one of a market which reflects wide differences of opinion without leadership, with the final decision as to future price trend awaiting some resumption of control or some decisive news. This explanation for the formation of Inverted Triangle patterns, if it be true, serves also to explain the difficulty of forecasting from them.

Fig. V.4

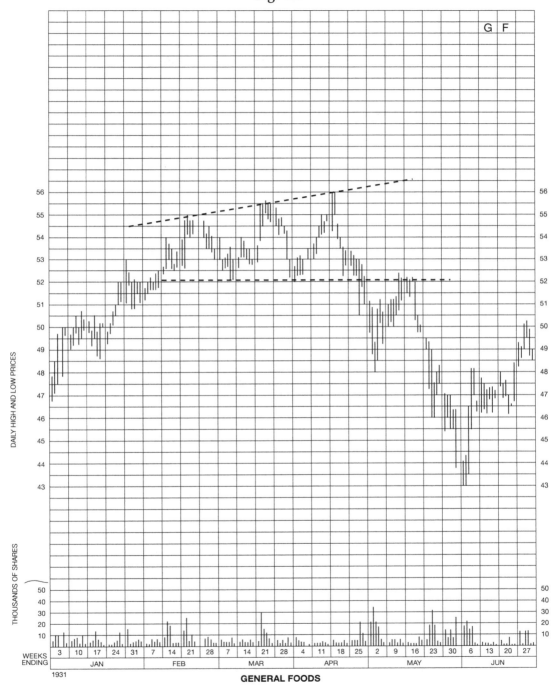

GENERAL FOODS

The suggestion of professional support at the level of the horizontal side of an Inverted Triangle with rising hypotenuse, or of professional selling at the level of the top boundary of an Inverted Triangle with descending hypotenuse, is seemingly corroborated by the fact that any break-out through these horizontal boundaries is nearly always emphatic and reliable. We have stressed the difficulty of trading profitably on Inverted Triangles, but we should point out that a decisive break through a horizontal side, representing as the case may be a support or a resistance level, is a more important signal for the technical trader and does frequently permit us to take a very profitable position.

The fact that Inverted Triangles are formed as a rule with fairly high and irregular volume action accounts undoubtedly for their appearing more often at tops than at bottoms.

The Diamond Formation

Our next reversal pattern gets its name from its quite evident pictorial resemblance to the conventional four-sided design which is commonly called a "diamond". This pattern might be considered a variant of the Head and Shoulders. It may be more accurately described, however, as a formation built up of two Triangles base to base with their apexes pointing in opposite directions – an Inverted Symmetrical Triangle merging into a normal Symmetrical Triangle. It is rarely found in perfectly symmetrical and clearly defined form; a certain amount of latitude must be taken and is permissible in drawing its boundaries. However, when it does appear, it is a reliable formation and one which permits the trader to take a profitable position. It is found more often at tops than at bottoms.

Examples of Diamond Reversals

The chart of Standard Oil of New Jersey in the first half of 1930 (Fig. V.5), contains a very good illustration of a Diamond Top. From 70 in December, 1929 the price of this stock had fallen to 58 in February, 1930. A rapid recovery swept it back up again to 80 before important resistance was encountered. A brief reaction and then another drive took it up to 84. Those readers who were following the market at that time will recall the public optimism that prevailed, leading many to predict that stocks were headed back for their 1929 tops. Several days of heavy volume in the 82–84 zone, however, exhausted the "good demand", and the price dropped 13 points in four days. The next rally carried only to 81 – but we need not follow the ensuing movements in

Our next reversal pattern gets its name from its resemblance to a "diamond".

Fig. V.5

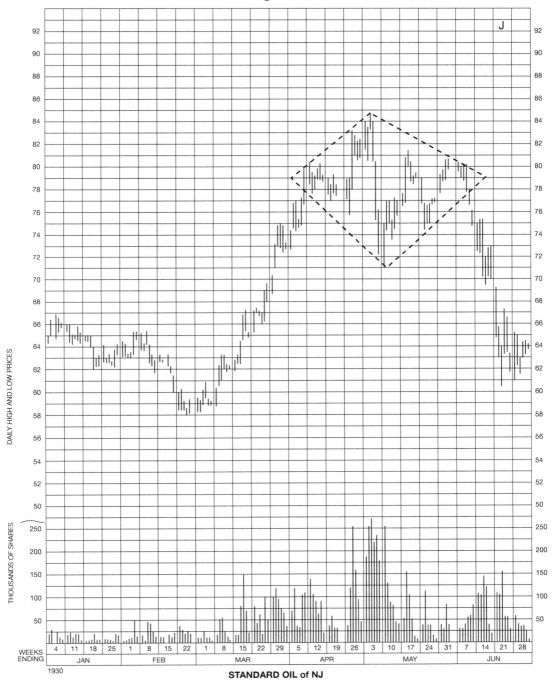

STANDARD OIL of NJ

detail; the Diamond picture soon became quite apparent and, no matter how loosely we drew its boundary lines, an obvious break-out occurred on May 7 with decisive pick-up in volume. (Remember to double a Saturday's volume in interpreting your charts). From the break-out in the neighborhood of 78 the stock dropped rapidly to 61, and continued on down in the long bear market.

The reader will note the resemblance of the 1930 Diamond Top in Standard Oil of NJ to a complex Head and Shoulders with a downward sloping neck-base line. The Head and Shoulders formations with down slanting neck-base lines ordinarily present poor opportunities to take profitable trading positions, but when they permit of the Diamond construction also, a good break-out signal is given at a much higher and more profitable level.

At the 1936 April Tops

Another example of the Diamond, in which the resemblance to a Head and Shoulders was not so apparent while the pattern was forming, appears in Fig. V.6, the 1936 chart, of Virginia-Carolina Chemical 6% Preferred stock. The break-out on April 13 was confirmed by a good pick-up in volume and by the fact that it closed well out of pattern, at the bottom of the day's price range.

Diamond Bottom Reversals

The Diamond appears at bottoms as well as tops, and is equally reliable as a reversal in either position.

The chart of Sears Roebuck Fig. V.7, shows the Head and Shoulders which formed at the bottom reversal in this stock early in 1935. But this pattern, although a good and valid Head and Shoulders, was confused by the extent of the sharp rally on February 18, and it is doubtful on that account if many chartists would have been looking for the Head and Shoulders development. The Diamond pattern is, however, quite obvious, and the break-out on April 5 was decisive in every respect and gave ample play for substantial profit.

We need not take the time to seek an explanation for Diamond formations since it is plainly evident that they are produced by the same sequence of technical factors which produce Head and Shoulders Reversals.

The Rectangle as a Reversal

We come now in our study of patterns which form at reversals of price trends, to a formation that bears no pictorial resemblance to any we have yet studied. We shall call this the Rectangle because it is a pattern of price fluctuations between two fairly

Fig. V.6

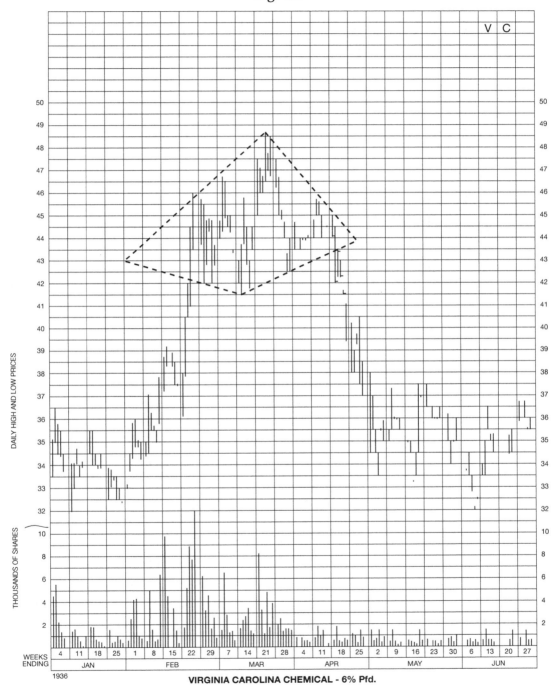

VIRGINIA CAROLINA CHEMICAL - 6% Pfd.

Fig. V.7

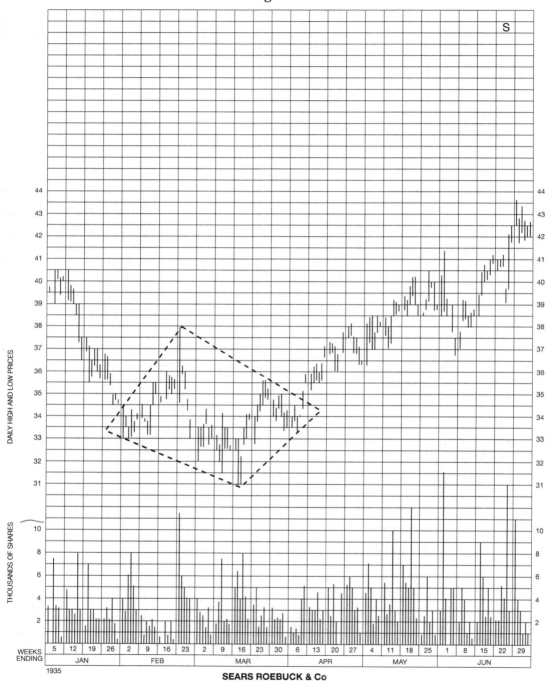

SEARS ROEBUCK & Co

definite horizontal lines and thus has the appearance of the geometrical rectangle. It may be long, extending over a considerable period of time, and thin, built up of fluctuations within a narrow price range – or it may be quickly formed of comparatively wide fluctuations, approaching a square in proportions. Generally speaking, the volume action during the formation of a Rectangle is the same as the volume in the formation of a Triangle. The first movement of prices into the pattern is usually made on good volume; thereafter, activity diminishes, frequently becoming almost nil as the formation nears its completion; finally a break-out occurs with a notable increase in volume.

Interpretation Like That of Triangle

Like the Triangle, the Rectangle may signal either a reversal or a continuation of the previous price trend. Like the Triangle, it is much more often a continuation or intermediate formation than a reversal. And, again like the Triangle, the direction of the ensuing price trend is determined by the direction of the break-out which must conform to the general specifications, as to closing well out of pattern with volume confirmation, which we have required of break-outs from other formations previously studied.

As a reversal, the Rectangle may occur either at a top or bottom. It is found rather more often at bottoms than at tops, this being particularly true of the long extended, narrow type of patterns. Its forecasting value is of even greater reliability than that of the Triangle and it would rank in importance with the Triangle if it were only formed more frequently.

Rectangular Bottom Reversals

A very interesting formation which made the 1932 bottom in Johns Manville is shown in Fig. V.8. This pattern is of the relatively long and narrow type. Note the decline through March and early April to the 10 level, followed by four months of fluctuations between this bottom price and the general level of 14. There are, in fact, two top boundaries to be seen – one at about 13½ bounding the majority of the rallies, and another at 14⅜ bounding the two sharp thrusts on April 27 and June 15. Since practically all of the price action takes place below the 13½ level we are warranted in considering the lower of the two top lines as the pattern's true boundary. Note also the gradual decline in activity from an average level of 4,000 or 5,000 shares daily during the middle of April at the beginning of the formation, to only 1,000 or so shares daily in

The Rectangle is much more often a continuation formation than a reversal.

Fig. V.8

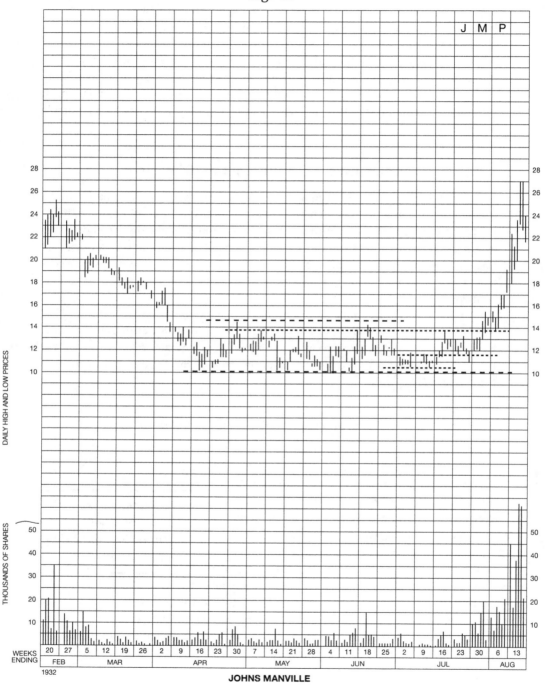

JOHNS MANVILLE

early July when the bottom boundary was last touched. And, finally, note the pick-up in volume as the stock at last turned up, reaching 20,000 shares on the day a decisive break-out occurred with prices closing out of the pattern.

The failure of prices to close at the top of the price range on the breakout day suggested some further consolidation before a rapid mark up, and the brief reaction on August 2 to the level of the top boundary of the Rectangle was a normal expectation with no negative implications.

A closer inspection of Fig. V.8 shows a small Rectangle bottom formed in the first two weeks of July within the bounds of the large Rectangle we have been studying. It is interesting to observe the increased volume, as compared with the preceding days, that signaled the break-out from this small pattern. We could not reasonably expect an immediate upward movement of any consequence to proceed from such a small congestion. The break through the top or resistance boundary of the large pattern, however, could be expected to lead to an important price movement in view of the four months' "foundation" it had laid.

> *The trader may watch carefully any well defined rectangular trading areas that form.*

Importance of the Rectangle

In our introductory remarks on the Rectangle we mentioned its great dependability. This holds even though the formation is built on a very small volume of transactions. A conspicuous and typical example occurred at the bottom in Mack Trucks in May-June, 1936, pictured in Fig. V.9. Dropping precipitately from a price of 37 reached in early April, selling pressure was quickly exhausted and after hitting the extreme low point of 28 on April 30, the stock fluctuated for nearly six weeks in a seemingly aimless fashion on very light volume between the approximate price levels of 28$\frac{1}{2}$ and 30$\frac{1}{2}$. The pattern appeared hardly compact enough to carry much significance yet once prices broke out decisively with a notable pick-up in volume as they did on June 8, a substantial movement in the new up-trend followed. The technical trader may well watch carefully any well defined rectangular trading areas that form on his charts.

(The downward slanting formation in the Mack Trucks chart between June 15 and July 9, resembling a Wedge, is a type of continuation pattern known as the Pennant which will be analyzed in Study VI.)

The Rectangle as a Top Reversal

The Rectangles, as we have noted in our introduction to their study, occur more

Fig. V.9

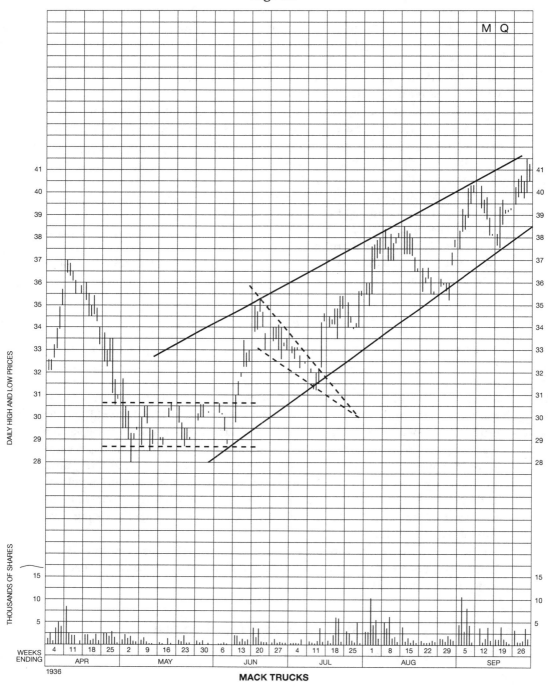

MACK TRUCKS

Fig. V.10

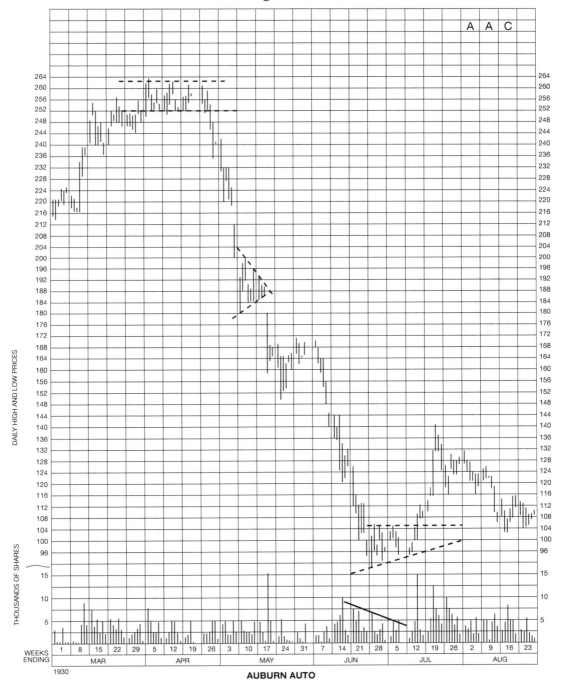

AUBURN AUTO

often at bottoms than at tops. Rectangular Tops do appear occasionally, however, and have the same forecasting value.

A good example appears in the 1930 chart of Auburn, shown in Fig. V.10. This stock had rallied from an intermediate bottom at 176 in January of this year to a top at 264 on April 1. Thereafter, it fluctuated for nearly four weeks, with volume generally declining, in a well defined rectangular area which was broken on the down side on April 24 with a decisive pick-up in activity. The extent and rapidity of the decline which ensued could hardly have been foreseen from the size and range of this Rectangle alone, but we know that Auburn is a stock that has been characterized by wide and frequently startling swings.

Break-out of Dormancy

Our next subject for analysis is a formation which we may consider as an extremely long extended and extremely narrow Rectangular Bottom, or as a distinct pattern deserving to be separately classified – or even as no pattern at all in the usual sense of the word. We have chosen to take it up here, as an extreme variant of the Rectangle, since it follows the same general rules, and since every conceivable intergradation between it and the broader normal Rectangle bottom formations is to be found in the charts.

When a stock has declined in a long bear trend to the point where all pressure of liquidation has been exhausted, there frequently ensues a considerable period of time during which no one cares to buy the stock at any price and the holders prefer to keep it rather than sacrifice it at such low levels. Until such time as the prospect of better earnings or a pick-up in the industry generally attracts the attention of shrewd operators looking for bargain situations, the stock remains practically dormant. Transactions are few and far between and take place at a more or less constant level. Suddenly, however, there will come a day of real activity in the stock and both the price and volume lines fairly jump up on the chart. If this sharp rally continues for several days, getting attention in the press, and if, in the meantime, good news regarding the industry comes out, the public is attracted into the stock and the mark-up continues into a substantial upward movement. On the other hand, the sharp break may be met immediately by offerings from owners of shares who were not willing to sell at the bottom but are now tired out and willing to let go on any reasonable recovery. Depending on the quantity of such offerings the interests engaged in accumulation have to absorb, the movement may be halted for a time, but even so the stock does not again become dormant as a rule, or drop back to its previous bottom. Such breaks out of dormancy offer the technical student of the market who is willing to wait many months if necessary, an opportunity to take a substantial long-term profit, since almost invariably such breaks signal the beginning of a major bull trend.

A Common Long-Term Bottom Picture

The student who has available charts of low-priced, relatively inactive issues covering the 1932–1933 period will find any number of Breaks-out of Dormancy. We will consider briefly two typical examples, one from the 1933 bottom and one which broke out two years later.

Figure V.11 shows the action of Omnibus Corporation from March to November, 1935. During the first four months of this chart (and for some time before) this stock was extremely inactive; for days at a time no transactions whatever were registered and on many other days there were only single lots of one hundred shares traded. The price during this long period of dormancy ruled at $3\frac{1}{2}$ to 4. We are hardly justified by the evidence of the chart in calling this a picture of accumulation yet it is evident that stock was moving slowly and irregularly, but surely, out of weak and into strong hands. Many small holders must have become discouraged by the stock's failure to move with the rest of the market, and any technical trader who was following the chart must certainly have despaired of ever getting any action.

A Quick Change in the Technical Picture

Note, however, how quickly the picture changed on August 8 when transactions ran up to 5,000 shares and the price closed over a point above the closing on any day for many months before. Obviously something had happened to change the technical position of the stock. Demand for it had come into the market and buyers were obliged to raise their bids rapidly to secure it. The upward movement continued with few, brief interruptions and reached 25 in less than a year after the period charted in our illustration – a gain of over 500% from its dormant level.

Omnibus Corporation may seem to offer a rather extreme picture of dormancy, yet it is nevertheless a typical example of a fairly common bottom action in low-priced issues that do not have a large public following. In higher priced and more actively traded stocks such unusually long periods of dormancy seldom appear, but brief intervals of very low activity do often occur at the end of major bear trends.

Relative Dormancy in an Active Stock

In Fig. V.12 we have an example of a Break-out of Dormancy in Consolidated Oil in April, 1933. This stock is one which normally shows good volume and has a good public following, so we should not expect it ever to become so very inactive as Omnibus Corporation. Relatively speaking, therefore, the picture from the beginning of this chart is one of dormancy, within a long and very narrow rectangular

Fig. V.11

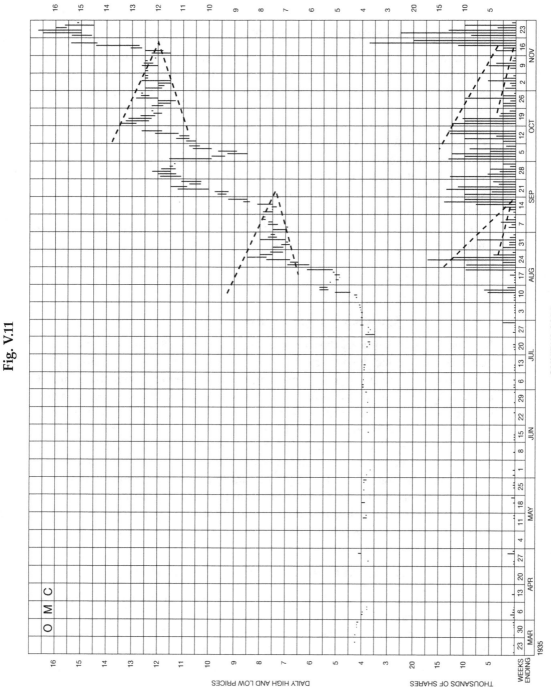

OMNIBUS CORP.

Fig. V.12

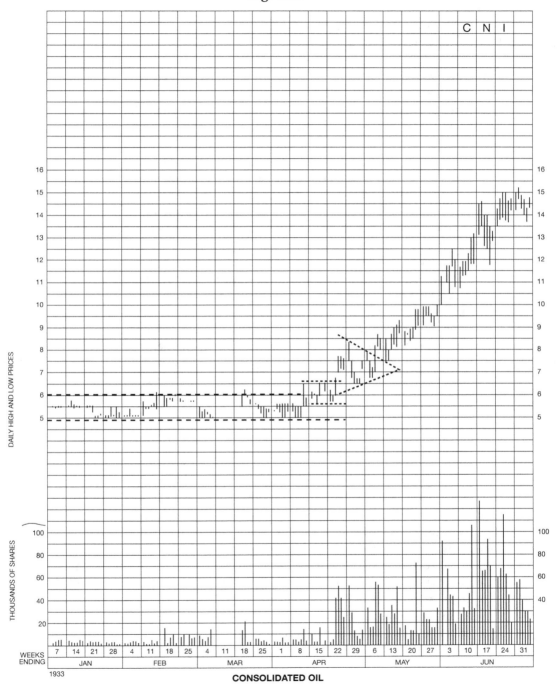

CONSOLIDATED OIL

pattern. The price action which followed is, perhaps, more typical of what may be expected of such patterns than was the price action in Omnibus Corporation. On April 7 there was an attempt to push the price up out of the pattern but the close was back below the level of the top boundary line. For the next ten days prices fluctuated around the upper level – a sign of basic strength, emphasizing the probability of an upward move of profitable proportions to come but offering no dependable indication as to how soon it would come.

A technical trader who chose to take the price movement on the 7th as a bona-fide break-out and bought the stock on the strength of it, might conceivably have had his money tied up in it for weeks or even months before a worthwhile move developed. We know, of course, from our previous discussion of the qualifications for a genuine break-out signal, that this action was not decisive. Nevertheless, it is interesting to note this first tentative stepping up of prices in Consolidated Oil.

On April 19, however, a genuine, emphatic break-out occurred, with high volume and the price closing well out of the pattern at the top of the day's range. A slight reaction a few days later brought the price down (on somewhat lower volume, note) to just above the level of the last minor congestion where it "rested" for a couple of days and then moved up more steadily on strong volume. The technical trader who acted upon the break-out signal had before long a very substantial percentage of profit on his investment.

The step-by-step movement following the break-out of relative dormancy, which we have seen in the Consolidated Oil chart, is a common phenomenon. Often the period of time between each of these steps up is long-extended, which is the reason for our stating that patience is required in trading on this formation in many cases. Progress is none the less sure and eventual profits are nearly always well worth waiting for.

The Island Formation

The last in our study, and undoubtedly the rarest of the reversal formations which have important forecasting value, is the Island. In one respect it certainly takes first rank among all reversal signals and that one respect is the surprising extent and rapidity of the price movements which so often develop out of it, considering the characteristic small size of the formation itself.

In order to define the Island Reversal pattern we shall first have to define another technical phenomenon known as a "price gap". The general subject of gaps will be fully discussed later on in Study VII where we shall learn that the gap has several different manifestations and several different implications depending on its position in relation to the rest of the chart picture.

A First Look at Gaps

For the purpose of our present subject, however, all we need to know is that a gap is an open space occurring on our chart where the bottom of one day's price range comes at a higher level than the top of the preceding day's range – or where one day's top range fails to reach the bottom level of the preceding day. One good example will undoubtedly suffice to make this picture clear, so look now at our next illustration, the Owens-Illinois Glass chart (Fig. V.13), and note the price action in the week ending October 26. On the third day of this week, October 23, the stock's highest price was 111¾ and on the next day the lowest price was 112¾. Between the price range lines of the two days there is an open space, a gap of a full point. This is a good example of a technical price gap.

> *An island is a compact area of price congestion separated by gaps.*

The student will find many charts, especially those of inactive issues and stocks of small floating supply, full of gaps. The charts of other issues which are normally active, and of which a large number of shares are outstanding, may show gaps very rarely. Naturally a gap in a stock of the latter class is presumptively of greater significance than a gap in a stock which habitually makes them more frequently. Presumptively, also, the wider the gap the greater its significance, but here again the past habits of the stock under our observation must be taken into consideration. A gap of a point in a thin and erratic or a high-priced stock might have little or no meaning, whereas a gap of half a point might be highly significant in an actively traded leader or a low-priced issue.

The Island Formation Described

An island is a compact area of price congestion separated by gaps from the preceding and following price movements. If the gaps occur one on the top and the other on the bottom of the congestion area – if, for example, prices "gap into" the congestion from below and then "gap out" of it in an upward movement – we have a continuation pattern of no significance which we need consider here. If, on the other hand, prices gap into the congestion and then gap out again on the same side, with gaps forming at the same level, we have a pattern of great import, the true Island Reversal.

In the above description we have spoken of the Island as a compact area of price congestion but it may be, in fact, and frequently is, completed in a single day, and a One-day Island is a perfectly valid forecasting pattern.

Fig. V.13

OWENS-ILLINOIS GLASS

Gaps Should Form at Same Level

Before we proceed to an analysis of specific examples, we must examine in detail one other point, viz., the requirement that the two gaps at either end of the island occur opposite each other, at the same price level. This does not mean that the two gaps must match exactly in their upper and lower limits but it does mean that at least some part of each gap must come at the same price level. This requirement is important and, in the same connection, it is further required that no part of the Island congestion itself shall extend into, so as to "close" or completely overlap, the gap that occurred at the beginning of the pattern. If, for example, we have a gap on our chart from 29 to 30 and the ensuing price movement works down in a few days to 29 or below, then back up again above 30, and then gaps down from 30 to 29, our gaps form opposite each other, it is true, but the first gap was "closed" by the price action before the second gap occurred, so we do not have a true Island. In brief, some little open price space must extend through the gaps horizontally clear across the chart between the Island and the price track both preceding and following it.

Probably it is not necessary to add that we should have had a fair movement before the first gap, and in the direction of the first gap, before we could expect an Island Reversal of any great import to form.

A Powerful Island Reversal Example

Figure V.13, to which we have already referred, shows the market action of Owens-Illinois Glass for the last half of 1935 and contains an almost perfect example of an Island Reversal of very strong construction. This stock had been in an indecisive but generally downward trend during the Summer of 1935, working down to about 94 in early August, rallying to about 100, dropping again to 95 where the market closed on September 7 at the bottom of that day's range. On Monday, September 9, the next trading day, the price ranged from 93 down to 87, leaving a clear gap of 2 points between 95 and 93 on the chart. Then, for three weeks the stock fluctuated in the general 88–91 zone, never getting up to 93. Between Saturday, September 28 and Monday, September 30, however, another gap occurred, this time in an upward direction, from the Saturday high of $91^3/_8$ to the Monday low of $93^1/_2$. This left a space clear of price action across the chart between 93 and $93^1/_2$ with a compact congestion below it – a perfect island, calling for immediate action. The forecast of this pattern called for not only a reversal of the previous trend but also an unusually powerful movement in the new trend. And the movement which actually followed was not much, if at all, out of proportion to the action we would expect from an Island Reversal of this size and character.

Before leaving the Owens-Illinois Glass chart we will mention again the gap in the last week in October only to state that this is a continuation gap – a type which will be taken up in detail in Study VII.

One-Day Island Forecasts

We had in the example of Island Reversal previously discussed, an island built up of three weeks of price congestion, separated by wide gaps from the preceding and ensuing price track. This gave a forecast of a very important movement. An island of only one day's duration is equally reliable as an indication of reversal in trend but does not, as a rule, lead to so extensive a movement.

The chart of Electric Bond and Share for the last half of 1935, Fig. V.14, shows two good examples of One-Day Island Reversals on August 17 and November 8, respectively, at the tops of intermediate rallies. The gap following the second of these was "closed" or overlapped by the price range on November 14 and again on November 20, but it will be noted that these minor rallies failed to attain the top level of the Island, and the reversal forecast was eventually carried out. An interesting feature of this chart is the Double Bottom formation at the $10^1/2$ level which again reversed the trend following the first Island (see Study IV).

The 1936 American Steel Foundries chart (Fig. V.15), shows a One-Day Island on July 8 that reversed a minor down trend and led to a strong upward movement. The bottom reversal in this stock in early May was built on an Ascending Triangle (see Study III).

Other Island Manifestations

The 1936 chart of Atchison (Fig. V.15), shows two other types of action following the formation of Islands.

On July 7 and 8 an Island formed on the chart following a recession of very small extent. The implication was for an upward movement which in this case was actually a resumption of a previous upward trend that had been only briefly interrupted.

On September 8 another Island, this time a one-day formation, appeared at the top of a two-weeks rally. This was a good reversal signal but some little time elapsed – five weeks, in fact – before a good downward movement got under way. Nevertheless, this Island "worked" and worked very profitably for the technical trader who did not allow himself to be worried out of his position by the two attempts the stock made to rally before succumbing to the indicated technical weakness.

Fig. V.14

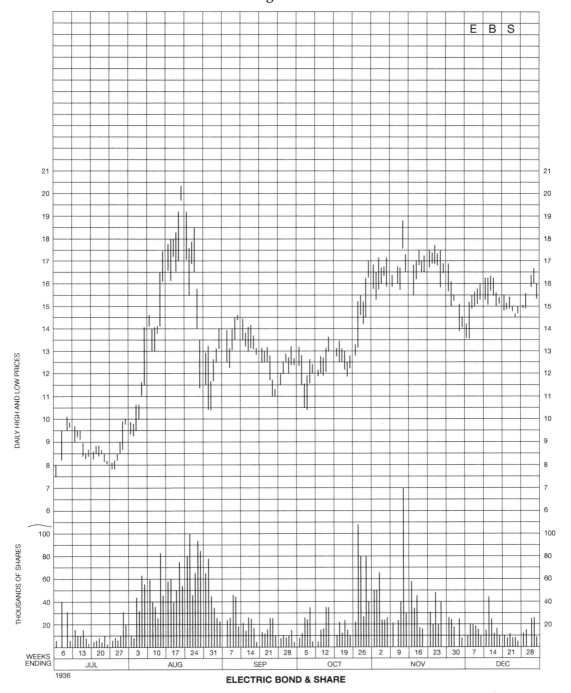

ELECTRIC BOND & SHARE

Fig. V.15

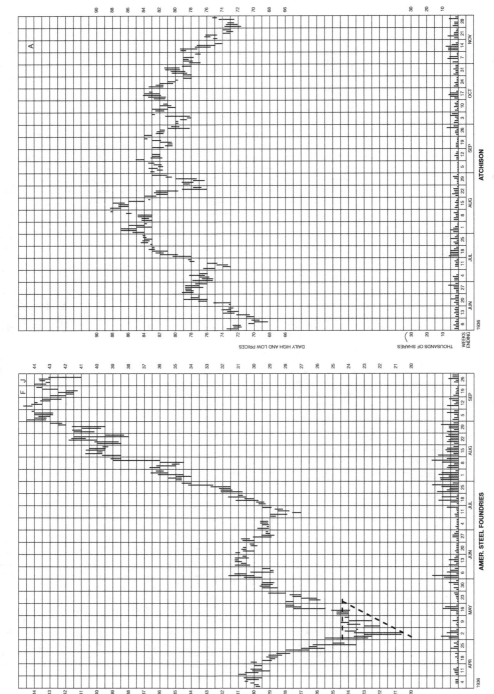

Explanation for Island Formation

In our later study of gaps we shall learn that the first gap into an Island is an "exhaustion" gap which signals a final spurt of activity in a trend and which carries the price into a zone of high resistance. The second gap, out of the Island, is a "break-away" gap which emphasizes the importance of any break-out into a new trend. The strong implications of each of these gaps, when they are combined in one formation as they are in the Island Reversal, account for the rapid and extensive price move-ment in the new trend which the Island forecasts.

Two Interesting and Spectacular Charts

Figure V.16 shows two charts which further illustrate the important moves that may develop out of two of the technical formations we have taken up in this Study.

The weekly chart of Bulova Watch shows a Break-out of Dormancy in 1935, plus a very interesting Symmetrical Triangle developed by the price action during the dormant period. We have noted before how one technical pattern will often appear as a part of another, and how both, as a rule in such cases, forecast the same price action to follow. The very long triangular base in Bulova Watch gave an added clue to the extent of the ensuing upward move.

The Loew's chart shows an excellent Island Reversal which signaled the 1929 top in this stock. Also the reader will see that this Island appeared at the fifth and final reversal of a large Broadening Top pattern which started to form in late January and was completed in March, 1929. In April, 1937, it is interesting to note that Loew's again made an Island top, although not as clean-cut as the 1929 example, and that this 1937 Island formed at the third reversal point of a large Broadening Top pattern which is most easily seen on a weekly chart of that period.

Continuation Formations Next

This Study completes, for the present, our consideration of technical formations which are indicative of a reversal in price trend, although we shall take up later on under the subject of trend line action, etc. other reversal signals which the market may give on occasions. Study VI will take up the subject of formations which indi-cate a continuation or resumption of the previous price trend.

Fig. V.16

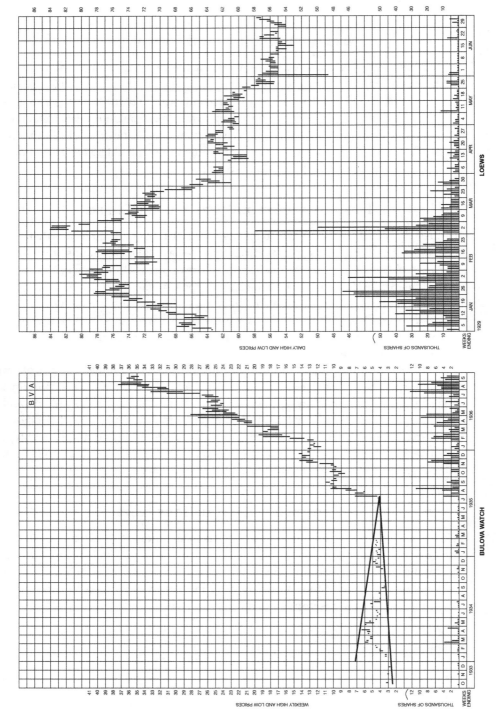

Study VI

MAJOR CONTINUATION FORMATIONS

Definition of the Continuation

The reader is no doubt already sufficiently familiar with the difference between a reversal and a continuation formation to make up his own definition of the latter. The continuation, or intermediate, formation is simply an intermediate pattern which interrupts temporarily the previous major trend, and forecasts continuation of that preceding major trend when the formation has been completed.

The logical explanation for the occurrence of continuation patterns is perhaps not so easily arrived at as for the reversal pictures. In the latter we observed how it was quite natural to expect a period of hesitation – a chart formation, a price area – during the interval when the previous balance between buying and selling was being reversed, with consequent slow reversal of the price trend.

Logic of the Intermediate Area

In the case of the intermediate or continuation formation, which is also in most cases suggestive of an area, there appears this same hesitation, this similar checking of the previous trend, but for different reasons. The most logical explanation of the continuation formation goes back to a basic possibility that it *might* turn out to be a reversal.

When, with the formation of a continuation pattern, the previous major movement is arrested, it is generally because too much resistance is being met, because the preceding movement has been too rapid, because "inside" operators have achieved one phase of their campaign and wish to consolidate that phase, or because they are undecided whether to continue their campaign or to close it, and are waiting for some technical advice on the question from the market itself.

So, when an intermediate formation begins to develop, it is possible that the picture will turn out to be a reversal. It is not long, however, before a technical signal in the market itself appears and indicates, to insiders as well as to the chart student, that all is well for continuation of the previous campaign, that the formation is a continuation rather than a reversal, and that the preceding major movement has been resumed at the end of the formation.

Inside Operations and Intermediate Chart Patterns

Suppose, for instance, that powerful interests with an accumulated line of 10,000 shares of stock, have marked the price up from 50 to 75. At the latter level selling resistance begins to stiffen in opposition to further advance. The bull operators immediately stop their aggressive buying and let the public show its hand for a while. The advance is checked. The interests have a "paper" profit of 25 points on 10,000 shares and while they are waiting to see how strong the technical position is when the stock is left comparatively to itself, they decide to play safe and realize profits on at least a portion of their long line.

Public buying is still good, the resistance which was felt a few days ago dries up, but the operators propose a further test, a further resting period, for more good news to accumulate, for the public to hear and talk about the stock, and so they meet further public buying demand by gradually handing out perhaps 4,000 shares of their line and taking that profit. The result is further irregularity in price, and development of the continuation formation.

The operators have now established the stock in a narrow price range, but they have also determined that the stock is still good for a further markup to around 90, at least. So they begin to buy back some of the stock they sold at the beginning of the formation. They control the price range by selling near the top of this range and buying back near its bottom, meanwhile making a very satisfactory profit turnover and actually strengthening the technical position of the issue.

The public sees that the stock has stopped going up and there is a little public profit-taking, especially if the operators can engineer a sharp shake-out, or false move, at the end of the intermediate formation, and just before they begin the second phase of mark-up. In this way they buy back, at a small net profit, perhaps 3,000 of the 4,000 shares they sold during the formation. They have taken at least 25 points profit on 1,000 shares and clinched that, as well as the intermediate trading profits they made while prices ranged within the pattern.

The Market Writes Its Own Forecast

With a line of 9,000 shares still long, therefore, they are ready to resume their campaign and mark the stock up to the new objective of 90, and the formation which started when they first felt some slight resistance, and which might have turned out to be a reversal formation if that resistance had continued, has now developed into a continuation formation, and the stock continues on up to its higher objective around 90, where the real reversal area is finally formed.

This is merely one rather simplified illustration but it may serve to suggest that intermediate formations have logical bases just as we have seen that reversal formations have. The important point for the chart student, however, is that all of these factors which have influenced the decisions of operators, the balance of buying and selling by the public, the balance of buying and selling by inside interests, or the refusal by the public to either buy or sell – all are

The market writes its own forecast

reflected accurately in the formation of this picture, and they are the factors which go to furnish us with our individual phenomena which differentiate the picture from a reversal formation and set it apart in a class by itself, as a continuation pattern. And it is these continuation formations, and their minor characteristics, which we shall now undertake to analyze in this Study of our Course.

Reviewing the Symmetrical Triangle

In Study III, starting with page 74, we studied the various definitions of the Triangle, or coil, and noted the appearance of the Symmetrical Triangle as a reversal. The continuation Symmetrical Triangle is identical in appearance with the reversal pattern and that is why the formation is a confusing one. We noted also in Study III that while the Symmetrical Triangle, in itself, does not tell us whether it will turn out to be a reversal or a continuation, still it is more often the latter, and that, in any case, there are usually various clues outside the formation itself.

These include the fundamental aspects for the individual stock and the market as a whole, the technical indications in other issues and for the entire market, the volume of trading, and finally, the most important and most reliable factor, the direction of price movement on the break-away.

There is one other factor which cannot always be depended upon but which is nevertheless a recognized aid. That is the length and strength of the movement preceding the formation of the Triangle. If the previous movement has been long, without a nearby halt or intermediate corrections, then the Symmetrical Triangle is more likely to be a reversal. If the preceding move has been only a short and weak one, then the chances are better that the formation will turn out to be a continuation of that previous movement.

Upward Continuation Triangles

Undoubtedly the reader is so familiar by this time with the appearance of the Symmetrical Triangle pattern that he will have no difficulty in detecting any number of examples in his own charts as well as in the Figures in this Course. Frequently a single chart will show three or four good Symmetrical Triangles. They may vary in their size as well as in their angle of convergence into the apex, in almost every imaginable degree, but they all have the same basic meaning for the technical student.

Figure VI.1 the chart of Electric Boat, shows three continuation Triangles of the Symmetrical type which were plain to see as they developed. The first, forming over two months time, with an emphatic break-out in the direction of the preceding upward trend on November 21, gave indication by its size and appearance in general that the upward movement of prices would continue for some distance. The second, which

Fig. VI.1

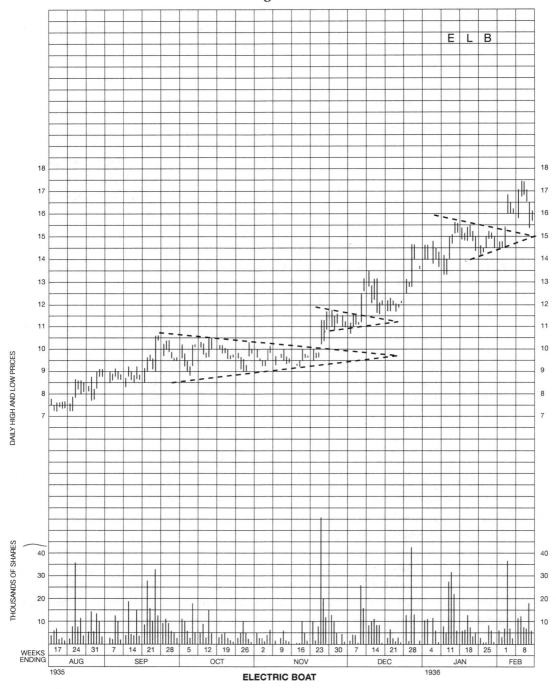

ELECTRIC BOAT

formed immediately thereafter, served only to confirm the forecast of the first. The third is to be seen formed by the price action during the latter part of January, 1936.

Noteworthy in the analysis of this Electric Boat chart is the high volume of activity which accompanied the break-out from each continuation pattern – an indication of the bona-fide nature of the movement, which we shall take up in a later Study under the subject of "false moves". Also noteworthy is the reaction of prices, following the break-out from the second and third Triangles, to the approximate level of these break-outs before proceeding in the upward trend. This reaction to the support level of the break-out is a normal occurrence which may be expected to follow the completion of, perhaps, a quarter of all Symmetrical Triangles. Knowledge of this fact – that such a reaction is normal and has no negative significance – is reassuring to the technical trader who has taken a position on the break-out and who might, otherwise, suspect he had been misled. Also, a reaction of this sort affords a second opportunity to make an additional purchase (sale, if the trend be down) at a profitable level. In this connection it should be noted that these reactions do not always reach the exact level of the break-out; they may carry slightly farther or they may not carry so far.

Examples in Preceding Illustrations

In order to get a comprehensive mental picture of the various forms which a Symmetrical Triangle may take when it occurs as a continuation, we suggest that the reader examine the following examples which appear in the illustrations in preceding Studies, as follows:

Fig. II.1 – Break-out on August 23.

Fig. II.4 – Break-out on February 6.

Fig. III.3 – Break-out on December 24. This shows an almost but not quite horizontal lower boundary line, suggesting a Descending Triangle, but the fact that it followed so shortly after an important reversal pattern made it almost certain that this would be a continuation Triangle.

Fig. III.7 – Break-out on December 7. Note in this case that there were two reactions to the break-out level.

Fig. III.9 – Break-out on June 4 (see discussion of volume action in down-trends later in this study).

Fig. III.10 –Break-out on October 19 (Saturday).

Fig. III.13 –Break-out during the first week of March, 1931. Note that it is impossible to see the volume on a break-out *day* in a *weekly* chart.

Fig. III.15 –Two examples – one in the down-trend (within the Wedge) with break-out April 29, and the other in the up-trend with break-out August 22.

Fig. IV.9 – Break-out on May 15.
Fig. V.10 – Break-out on May 15.
Fig. V.11 – Break-out on September 12. Another breaking out on November 14.
Fig. V.12 – Break-out on May 4.

Volume Action in Continuation Triangles

The reader will have, we trust, examined the volume action as well as the price actions in the examples of continuation Symmetrical Triangles we have cited above. The volume of transactions tends to shrink during the formation of a continuation Triangle just as it does in a Triangle signaling reversal, and the decisive break-out of pattern is almost invariably accompanied by a noticeable pick-up in volume. This increased volume on the break-out is more accentuated in upward movements than in down-trends. In the latter cases prices occasionally have moved some little distance from the theoretical apex before there is a conspicuous increase in activity. The same price tests as to validity of break-outs should be applied to continuation patterns as to reversal break-outs previously studied.

Continuation Triangles in Down-trend

In the examples cited above of continuation Triangles which appeared in Figures illustrating previous Studies, a number occurred in down-trends. The Symmetrical Triangle forms as often as a continuation pattern in a bear market as it does in a bull market, and is equally important and useful in either trend.

Right-angle Continuation Triangles

In our study of the Triangle as a reversal pattern (Study III) we learned to distinguish between the ordinary or Symmetrical Triangle and the Right-angle Triangle. In the latter type one side extends horizontally while the other, the hypotenuse, slants either up toward the apex making an Ascending Triangle and calling for an upward movement of prices, or slants down and calls for a downward price movement. In practice we find many triangular areas which have one side nearly but not quite horizontal and which suggest, therefore, either an Ascending or Descending Triangle. These border-line cases are best regarded as Symmetrical Triangles; it is safest always to assume that the break-out may go in either direction. We have seen in the Goodrich chart (Fig. III.3) an example of a Triangle which suggested the Descending picture; close inspection, however, shows that the bottom boundary does have a slight upward slant, and the break-out actually proceeded in an upward direction. The chart of Holly Sugar (Fig. VI.2) shows the development of an intermediate

Fig. VI.2

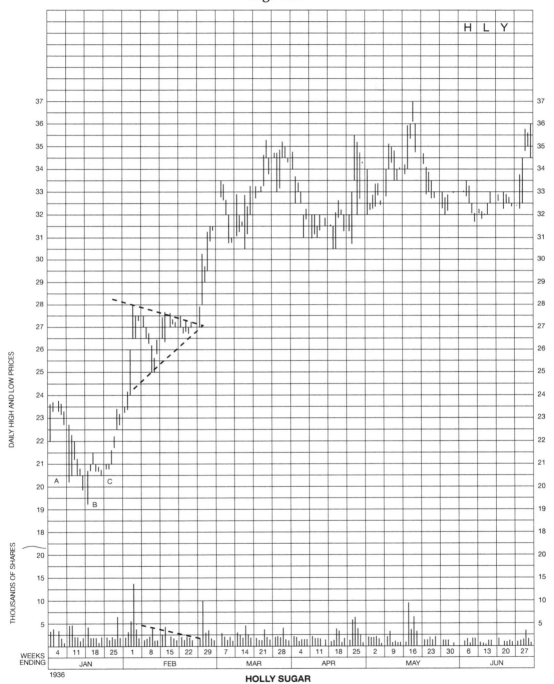

HOLLY SUGAR

pattern in February, 1936, which might be construed as either an Ascending or a Symmetrical Triangle. In this case the break-out in the upward trend did carry out the ascending suggestion but the Triangle might, nevertheless, have turned out to be a reversal as is always possible with Symmetrical Triangles.

True Right-angles Triangles as Continuations

Triangles which show a strictly horizontal top or bottom boundary line – in other words, true. Ascending or Descending Triangles – in the great majority of cases carry out their ascending or descending implication. In our study of reversals we have seen that the appearance of a Descending Triangle in an upward trend forecasts a reversal into a downward trend, and the development of an Ascending Triangle in a down-trend forecasts a reversal into a rising market.

It follows naturally that the opposite conditions will produce an opposite forecast. An Ascending Triangle, for example, developing in an upward trend, forecasts a continuation of the upward movement when the formation is completed. And a Descending Triangle, by the same token, implies continuation when it forms in a down-trend.

The chart of International Nickel for the last half of 1935 (Fig. VI.3), shows a very good example of a small, compact Ascending Triangle which signaled a rapid continuation of the preceding up-trend. This stock had been moving up gradually through the first part of the year and reached a sort of minor buying climax on September 17. It is evident that it met here, at the $31\frac{1}{2}$ level, considerable profit taking which sent the price off rapidly to around 29. A brief rally regained half the previous week's loss and was followed by another dip to the 29 level where good buying again appeared. So far no pattern of clear significance had developed. A technical trader who had carried the stock up from lower levels might have been in doubt at this time as to the advisability of taking his profit; however, his best policy was to wait for some definite sign of reversal even if it meant a loss of a point or two in his "paper" profits.

The rapid turn up from 29 on October 3 was bullish, and from then on a pattern began to appear which made a strong continuation of the up-trend more and more likely. The horizontal top line was very plain to see while, as the volume of trading gradually declined, the tendency of the bottom boundary to lift became increasingly evident. The two boundary lines thus formed an Ascending Triangle out of which we should expect an upward movement. A clear and emphatic break-out occurred on November 1 when prices moved up out of the pattern on high volume and closed at the top of the day's range. Any technical trader keeping this chart had thereby definite advice to buy "Nickel" and could have bought it the following day around $32\frac{1}{2}$, while those who were already long of it could congratulate themselves on not

Fig. VI.3

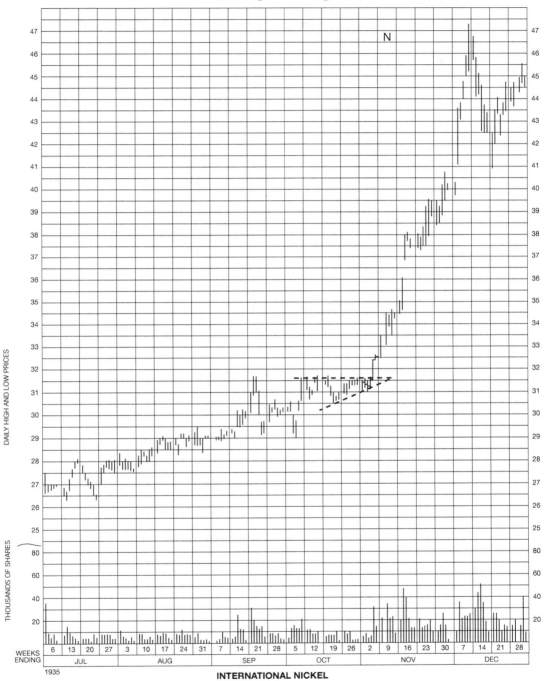

INTERNATIONAL NICKEL

having joined in the flurry of profit taking at 30 to 31 which the chart shows as hav-ing taken place. There is no doubt that many tape-watchers and gossip-followers were shaken out of good positions in "Nickel" at this period because either they did not have a chart history to guide them, or did not realize that no reversal had been indicated on the chart.

A Strong Picture in Anaconda

Another excellent example of an Ascending Triangle in an up-trend, with some very interesting features worthy of detailed study formed in Anaconda Copper at the end of 1935 and beginning of 1936. This is pictured in Fig. VI.4. On December 10, a wave of profit-taking started, sending the price off from 30 to 26¼. Thereafter, for nearly six weeks, Anaconda rallied repeatedly to the 30 level only to meet resistance and turn back again. Each rally was characterized by increasing volume and each set-back by declining volume, an encouraging sign (to be considered in detail later in Study VIII) that the major trend had not changed. During this period, up to January 17, a good Ascending Triangle picture was forming. On Janu-ary 18, however, prices broke down through the hypotenuse. *But* – the close was only a half point out of pattern and the volume was insignificant. On the following two days prices ranged still lower but the volume was even less. At this point our pattern appeared to be spoiled. How-ever, the next day, January 22, told a different story; Anaconda moved up over a point on good volume and closed back above the hypotenuse line. And on the fol-lowing day, volume rose to 60,000 shares and the price broke the top boundary line and closed well away; a definite break-out signal had finally been given, and in the direction which the formation had previously implied. Prices were still reluctant to move away; minor fluctuations held just above the resistance line for two weeks, but it will be noted that there were no closings below the critical level. On February 11 another burst of activity accompanied the beginning of a real mark-up.

> *A false move is usually an indecisive movement out of a pattern on* **low** *volume.*

False Moves Studied Later

In the Anaconda chart which we have just analyzed, the movement of prices Janu-ary 18 to 22 is what is called a "false move", a not uncommon phenomenon which we shall take up in detail in a later study. It will suffice at this time to state that a false move is usually an indecisive movement out of a pattern on *low* volume, whereas a genuine break-out is a strong movement on good volume. A false movement, such as we have seen in the Anaconda chart, once it has returned within the pattern, has

Fig. VI.4

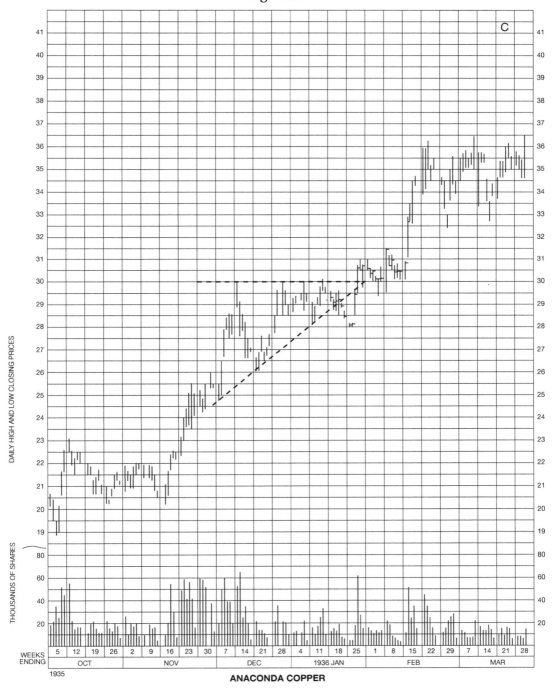

ANACONDA COPPER

no forecasting significance and does not "spoil" the pattern.

A false move differs from an out-of-line move which we discussed in Study III in that the out-of-line movement occurs on fair volume, in the direction which the formation is already suggesting, whereas a false move runs contrary to the implication of the formation and is characterized by low volume.

Descending Triangles in Down-trends

Descending Right-angle Triangles appear as frequently in down-trends as do Ascending Triangles in up-trends, and have the same significance, i.e. a continuation of the previous trend.

A good example of the Descending Right-angle Triangle as a continuation appears in the American Can chart for 1931 (Fig. VI.5). The rapid decline in the price of "Can" was halted early in August, and a Descending Triangle formed with its horizontal side at the 88–89 level. This was broken decisively, with increased volume, on September 14. A subsequent rally carried back up to 88 but failed to penetrate the breakout level.

Examples in Previous Studies

The reader will find several good examples of Right-angle Triangles as continuation formations in Figures illustrating the preceding. Studies of this Course. Refer to the following:

Fig. II.2 –   A descending Triangle following the Head and Shoulders Top in Western Union in 1934. Bottom boundary at the 52–53 level, and break-out with increased volume on April 30.

Fig. III.11 – An Ascending Triangle in Hudson Motor following immediately after the Ascending Triangle Bottom in this stock in 1933. Break-out with high volume on January 15, 1934.

Fig. IV.6 –   An Ascending Triangle at the beginning of the Timken Roller Bearing chart, with break-out February 9.

Inverted Triangles as Continuations

In our discussion of Inverted Triangles as reversals in Study V we noted how hard it is to interpret this formation, as compared with the normal or standard Triangle. Generally speaking, the Inverted Triangles of the symmetrical type seem to present no clue as to what may be their cause. Volume during their formation is usually irregular and apparently meaningless. Break-outs may occur with or without confirming volume. When they break-out with high volume the subsequent move may be of profitable dimensions, but frequently it is quickly halted and reversed. And the chances that they will turn out to be reversals rather than continuation formations is rather greater than is the case with normal patterns.

If it were not for the fact that patterns classifiable only as Inverted Triangles of symmetrical design do appear on the charts with fair frequency, we should be tempted to ignore them altogether. As it is, we feel constrained to warn the beginner not to attempt to trade on them unless other patterns of a more helpful nature appear on the same chart at the same time.

Examples of Inverted Symmetrical Triangles

The chart of Sears Roebuck for the latter part of 1936, Fig. VI.6, shows an Inverted Triangle of symmetrical design formed by the price action during August and early September, best seen if the reader will cover up the chart from September 12 on. Within the formation up to this point there was no dependable indication of what might follow. During the three weeks that followed, however, a small, normal Symmetrical Triangle formed and broke out decisively on the up side, signaling a continuation of the preceding upward movement.

The top boundary line of the large Inverted Triangle was not broken, it will be noted, until October 13, a good ten points above the price level at the origin of the formation. As is the case in a great many Inverted formations, no profitable action could have been taken on the break-out indication given by this formation in itself. Fortunately, trend line action and other more reliable continuation signals would have kept us "long" in Sears during this period.

Almost a Broadening Top

The chart of Standard Oil of NJ for the first part of 1936, Fig. VI.7 shows another example of an Inverted Triangle of symmetrical design, with a break-out accompanied by terrific activity on March 13. The reader will see in this pattern a Broadening Top (Study IV) which was nearly but not quite completed. If the decline from point 5 on March 4 had gone down below 58, the Broadening Top would have been completed, signalling an important reversal of trend. As it was, an important reversal did occur very soon thereafter, bearing out the warning (see Study IV, page 138) that a Broadening Top which fails of completion frequently gives us.

Right-angle Inverted Triangles More Reliable

Inverted Triangles that have one boundary line extended horizontally are somewhat

Fig. VI.5

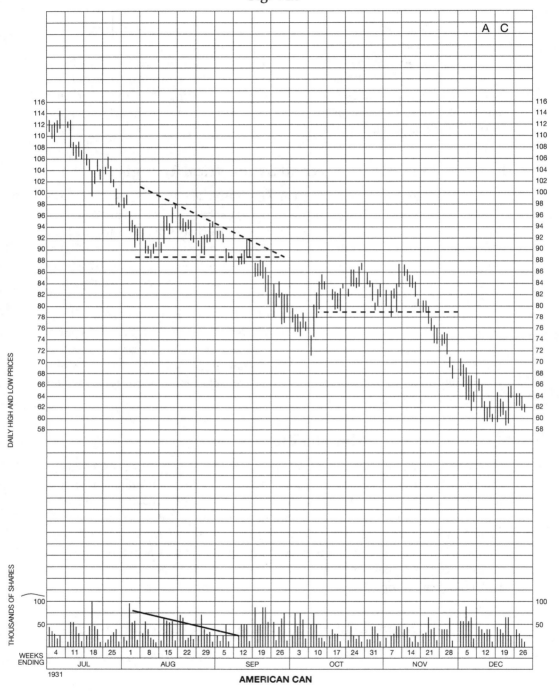

AMERICAN CAN

Fig. VI.6

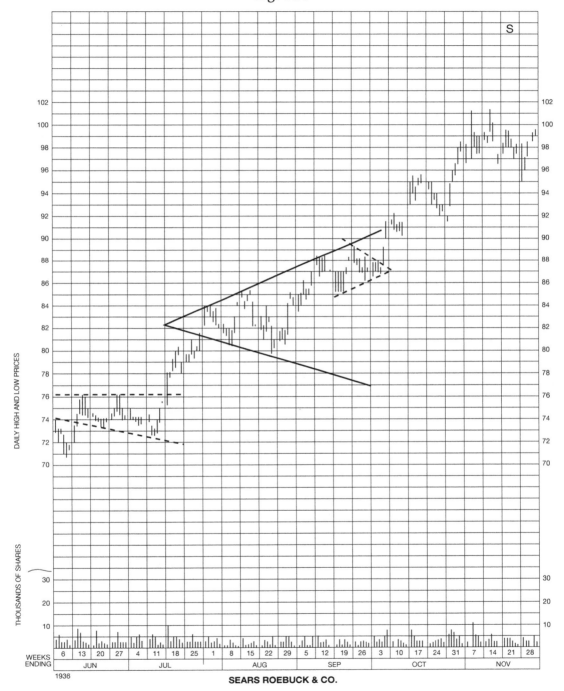

SEARS ROEBUCK & CO.

Fig. VI.7

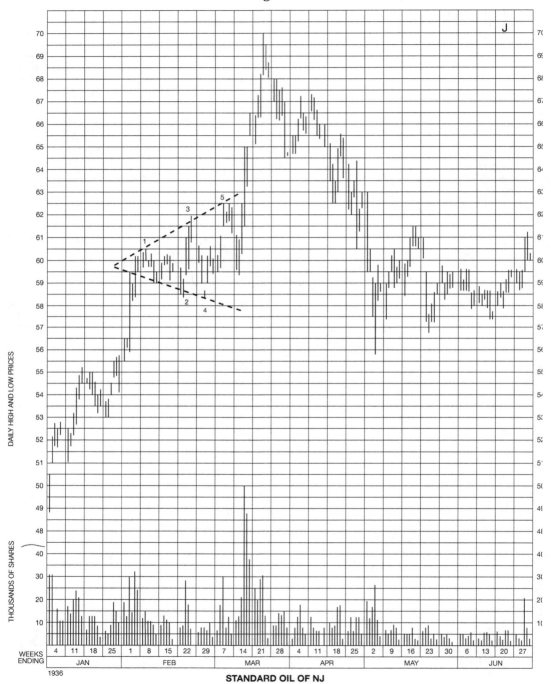

STANDARD OIL OF NJ

more useful to the technical trader than those of symmetrical design. We have in the horizontal side of Inverted Triangles of right-angle design a definite picture of support or resistance as the case may be, a pattern of some apparent logic and, consequently, a pattern that gives dependable breakout signals. The direction pointed by the hypotenuse in these formations seems to have little or no significance, which was also the case, as we have noted in Study V, with Inverted Triangle Reversals of this type. An Inverted Triangle may prove to be a continuation pattern in either an up or down trend regardless of whether the top or the bottom boundary line is the horizontal. In either case, a decisive break-out from a narrow pattern generally signals a worthwhile movement, and from any pattern, wide or narrow, if the break-out proceeds through the horizontal line.

Examples of Profitable Inverted Types

The 1935 chart of Columbia Gas and Electric (Fig. VI.8) shows a long and rather loose formation but recognizable, nevertheless, as an Inverted Triangle with a horizontal bottom and rising hypotenuse. The top boundary was decisively broken on Saturday, August 3, and a good upward movement followed.

The chart of Burroughs Adding Machine (Fig. VI.9) shows an Inverted Triangle with a horizontal top boundary and a downward slanting hypotenuse, which broke out on the up side on Saturday, October 19, continuing the previous upward trend.

Inverted Triangles of this type – with one horizontal boundary – are equally useful as continuation patterns in a down trend.

The Rectangle as a Continuation

In our analysis of the Rectangle as a reversal formation in Study V, pages 156–61, we remarked that this pattern appears also as an intermediate or continuation formation – in fact, more often as a continuation than as a reversal. We commented also on the high degree of reliance that may be placed on any break-out from a rectangular area of price congestion. False movements out of Rectangles are very rare indeed.

It is probably safe to say that Rectangle continuation formations occur more often in the early stages of major or long-term trends than in the later stages. Thus Rectangles appear quite frequently in the first gradual stepping up of prices after a major bottom has formed; as such they represent well organized accumulation in a period of comparatively little public excitement. However, whenever they appear, whether early or late in a major or intermediate market cycle, the direction of their break-out may be depended upon to indicate the direction of the subsequent movement.

The volume characteristics of the Rectangle were also discussed under its rever-

Fig. VI.8

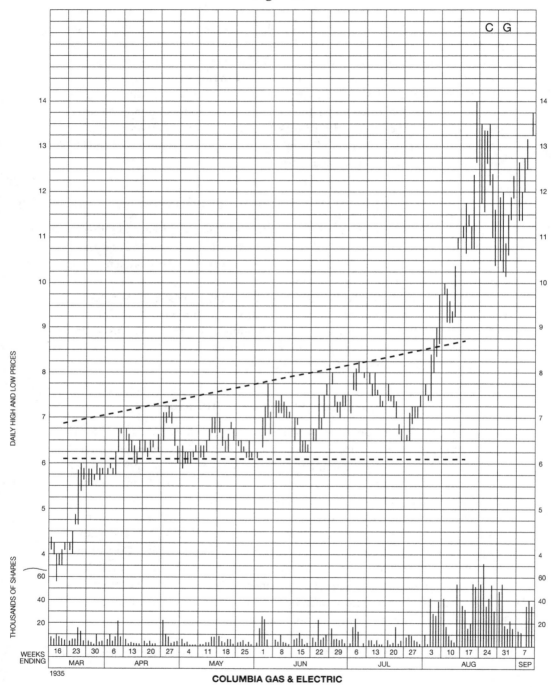

COLUMBIA GAS & ELECTRIC

Fig. VI.9

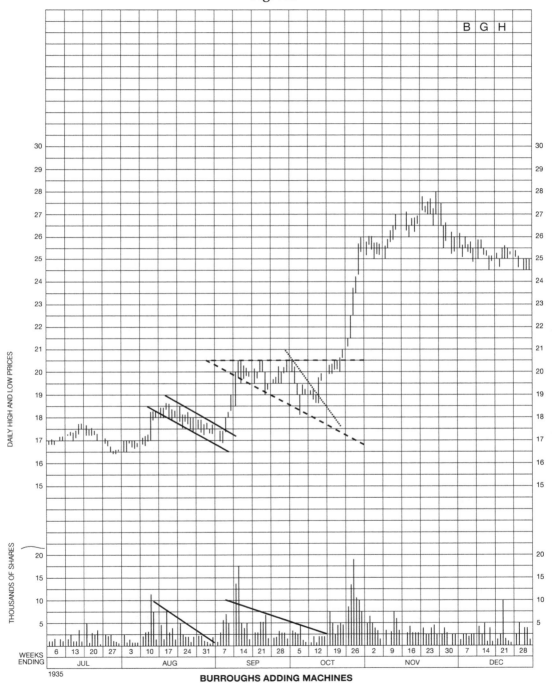

BURROUGHS ADDING MACHINES

sal classification in Study V, and are substantially the same when it appears as a continuation formation.

Examples of Rectangles in an Up-trend

The chart of Transamerica Corporation (Fig. VI.10) shows a Rectangle that presented a nearly ideal pattern and gave the technical trader a clear forecast of a substantial continuation of the up-trend in this stock. The first stages of mark-up met resistance in the second week of August, 1935, either through ill-advised (as it later developed) profit taking or through well organized professional operations, at the 8 level. Thereafter, for ten weeks, the price fluctuated between 7½ and 8, never closing outside of this narrow range. The gradual decline of activity during this period is noticeable. On October 21, however, the stock burst its bonds either professional operators

Rectangles represent well organized accumulation in a period of little public excitement.

were satisfied with the extent of their accumulations and were now ready for the mark-up, or some favorable news brought strong buying from other sources into the picture. So far as we are concerned, the cause does not matter, for the chart told us all we needed to know when we had posted the price and volume action for October 21. We saw then that the price had moved out of pattern up to 8⅜ and closed at the top – a decisive margin of break-out in an eight dollar stock – and the pick-up in volume was conclusive. The chart said, "Buy Transamerica". In five weeks it showed better than 60% profit.

Note that the Transamerica chart is constructed on a ¼ point price scale, which helps to show up any patterns that may develop in a very low-priced issue.

It is not to be assumed that all Rectangles of continuation will lead to price movements of such immediately profitable consequences as did the example we have just studied in the Transamerica chart. It is at least equally possible that the first break-out of a rectangular area will be followed by a reaction back to the level of the top boundary before a mark-up of any considerable extent occurs. Such a set-back is almost invariably accompanied by a shrinkage in volume, and then activity again picks up sharply when the upward movement is resumed.

Rectangles in Chrysler, 1935

Figure VI.11 shows two typical continuation Rectangles which formed during the upward movement of Chrysler in the last half of 1935. This stock is an active trading favorite under normal market conditions and is consequently characterized by high volume. Nevertheless, a general tendency of volume to decline during the

Fig. VI.10

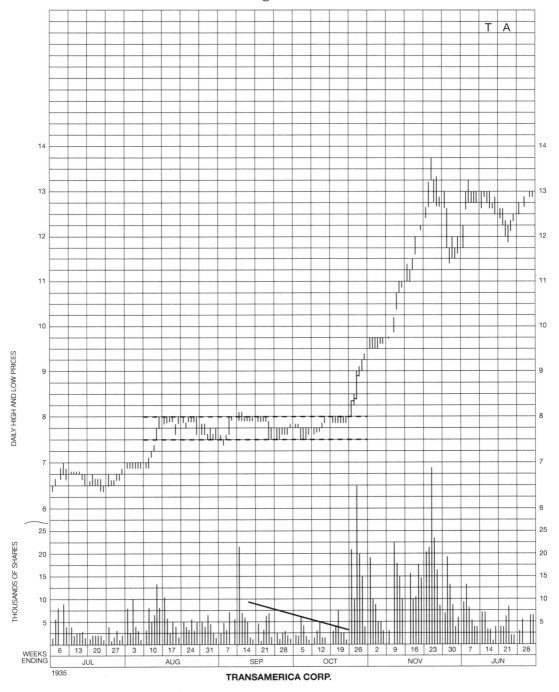

TRANSAMERICA CORP.

Fig. VI.11

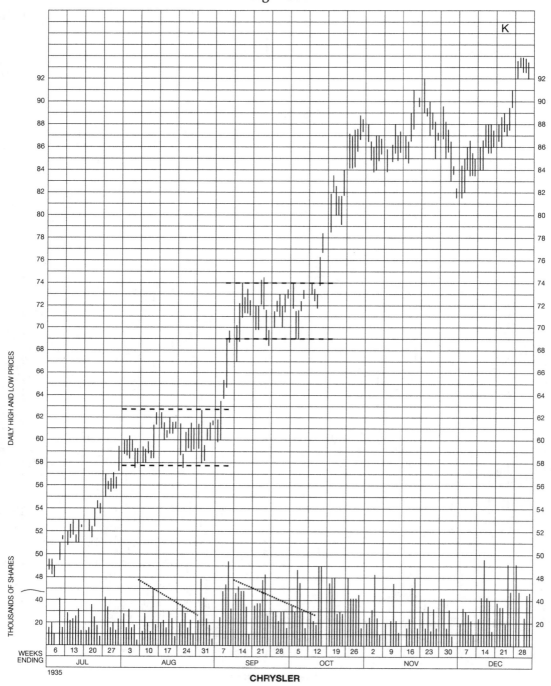

CHRYSLER

formation of the intermediate Rectangles can be seen, and the increase of activity on the break-out days is conspicuous. Any doubts occasioned by the halting of the up-trend of prices at 62 and again at 74, were decisively dispelled by the strong character of the break-outs on September 4 and October 10 respectively.

Rectangle Continuations in Down-trends

The Rectangle appears as a continuation in downward movements somewhat less frequently than in upward, but is equally dependable in either trend. The volume accompanying the initial break out of a downward continuation Rectangle often shows little or no marked pick-up, but we have noted previously in our consideration of Descending Triangle Tops (in Study III) which have, like the Rectangle, a well defined horizontal bottom boundary or support level, that volume confirmation is not required if the price movement is conclusive. In such cases, a conspicuous increase in activity may not show up until the second or third day after the break. The technical trader may depend upon it that any breaking down through, and closing well below, a well-defined support level in a pattern which forms in a down trend or suggests in itself a downward trend, is important even though the volume action is inconclusive.

Examples in the 1931 Bear Market

Reference to the long-term average chart (frontispiece) at the beginning of this Course, shows that one of the important intermediate recoveries in the long decline from the 1929 tops took place in the first three months of 1931, after which the trend was again reversed and prices worked on down to new low levels. A number of stocks developed good Rectangles on their charts in the course of this rapid decline. Two good examples are shown in Figs. VI.12 and VI.13.

In the chart of Electric Auto-Lite (Fig. VI.12) the drop from the top price of 74³/₄ was halted at 61, and for three weeks in April, the price fluctuated between 61 and 66. During this period activity was at a relatively low ebb and generally declining except on one day, April 13, but it is interesting to note that the price range on that one day did not break out of the pattern so the volume on that day had no forecasting significance. On April 17, however, the Rectangle was decisively broken on the down side with even greater volume, forecasting a continuance of the bear movement.

The chart of Ingersoll Rand (Fig. VI.13) is of special interest because it shows a Rectangle formed under unusual circumstances. During August and September in 1931 the price of this stock had fallen rapidly from above 100 in an extremely thin and inactive market. Volume picked up as the first of October was approached,

Fig. VI.12

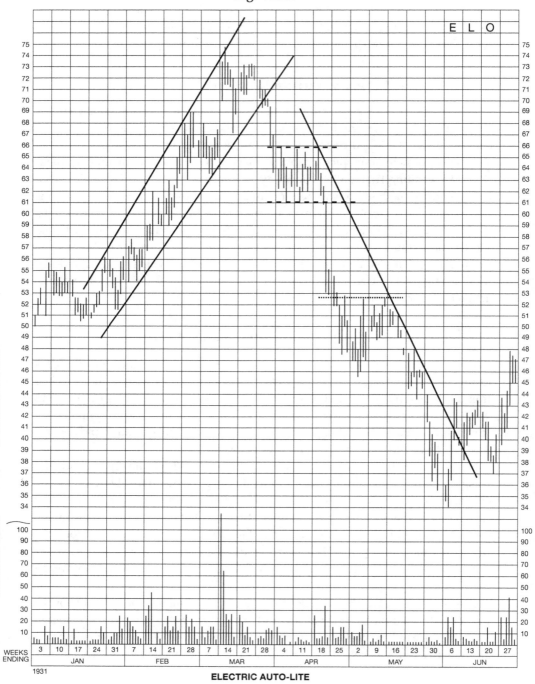

ELECTRIC AUTO-LITE

Fig. VI.13

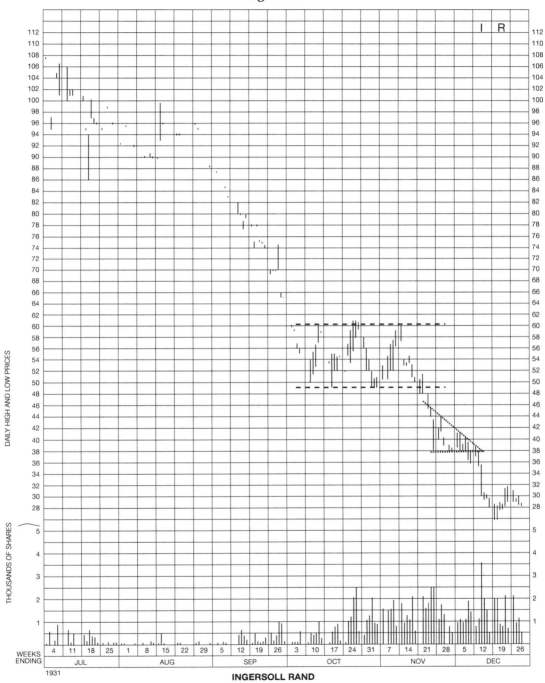

INGERSOLL RAND

however, and the stock now met support for six weeks around the 48–50 level and three times ran up to 60 in sharp rallies during which it later appears that insiders distributed a large amount of the IR stock to the public. The support was withdrawn, or in any event the support level was broken, on November 18; activity was high but no higher, generally speaking, than on many of the preceding days. A conspicuous increase in volume did not show up until the 21st (remember to double the Saturday volume) when the price dropped below 40. This chart illustrates the point regarding volumes not necessarily increasing on breaks through support levels into down trends which we discussed at the top of this page.

Rectangle Continuations in Other Figures

The reader will find a number of other good rectangular patterns of price congestion which signaled continuation of the preceding trend in the Figures throughout this Course. Some are long and shallow and others are short and deep. One which is interesting and worthy of examination is the large Rectangle which formed between the 166 and 175 levels in US Steel following the first drop from the Rounding Top in April, 1930. The break-out on the down side on Saturday, June 7, was confirmed by a notable increase in activity, apparent if we follow the rule of doubling a Saturday's volume. This formation is shown in Fig. III.1.

The price congestion between January 23 and February 9 on the National Power and Light chart (Fig. IV.9) may be construed as a Rectangle continuation with a one-day out-of-line movement on January 27.

Flags and Pennants – Dependable Signals

The continuation patterns which we have taken up so far in this Study – the various types of Triangles and the Rectangle – have one unfortunate characteristic in common, viz., they may signal either a reversal or a continuation of the previous trend and, as a consequence, they oblige us to wait until they are completed and the new movement has already started before we can safely take action. Now, however, we are to study two distinct and easily recognizable formations which do not have reversal implications, and which do signal a resumption of the previous movement at a level which permits the taking of a profitable position.

These two dependable and profitable continuation patterns we call the Flag and Pennant.

These two very dependable and profitable continuation patterns we have chosen to call the Flag and the Pennant because of their obvious pictorial resemblance on the charts to a flag and a pointed pennant, respectively, flying from a mast.

Fundamentally, they are compact and quickly completed areas of "correction" or "consolidation" in a fast mark-up or mark-down state. They may occur either early or late in an intermediate or major trend, but always during a phase when prices are advancing or declining with greater than normal rapidity.

The Flag Flies from a Mast

Thus, the first requirement of the Flag formation is a nearly vertical price movement on the chart, either up or down. This is halted abruptly, usually but not always with a day of high activity, and followed by several days to a few weeks of price congestion within clearly defined parallel bounds. During this period the volume of activity tends to decline noticeably. In most cases, the parallel lines which bound the congestion slope downward if the preceding trend was up, or upward if the preceding trend was down, but they may be horizontal or even be slightly tilted in the same direction as the preceding trend. This, in an up-trend, forms the picture of a rectangular flag flying from a mast, which usually, as we should expect, hangs somewhat downward of its own weight, but is occasionally blown straight out or even slightly upward by a strong breeze. (In a down-trend, the picture is, of course, turned upside down.)

At the end of the Flag, there is a sharp break-out with a marked pick-up in volume, and a resumption of the rapid price movement in the previous trend.

Examples of Flags in Upward Movements

The chart of Deere & Co. for the first half of 1936, shown in Fig. VI.14 formed in February a typical Flag continuation pattern. After breaking out of a Symmetrical Triangle on January 22, the price advanced 17 points to 75 in three weeks – an almost vertical mark-up – a true mast. Then for three weeks the price fluctuated in a range of about $3^{1}/_{2}$ points between two down-slanting parallel lines, forming the Flag. On March 2 the upper boundary was penetrated, but a decisive break-out did not appear until March 5 when volume increased markedly and price closed at 74 (two points out of the Flag pattern). In less than five weeks thereafter the price had advanced to 89. (The student will notice the formation of a pattern at the top of this movement out of which prices "spilled". This is almost too loose in construction to be called a good Wedge but it did carry out the Wedge forecast).

The Flag formation in the Deere chart departs from the ideal in only one respect; the area within the Flag itself is not as closely packed with price movement as is sometimes the case. Nevertheless, this is a good average example.

Fig. VI.14

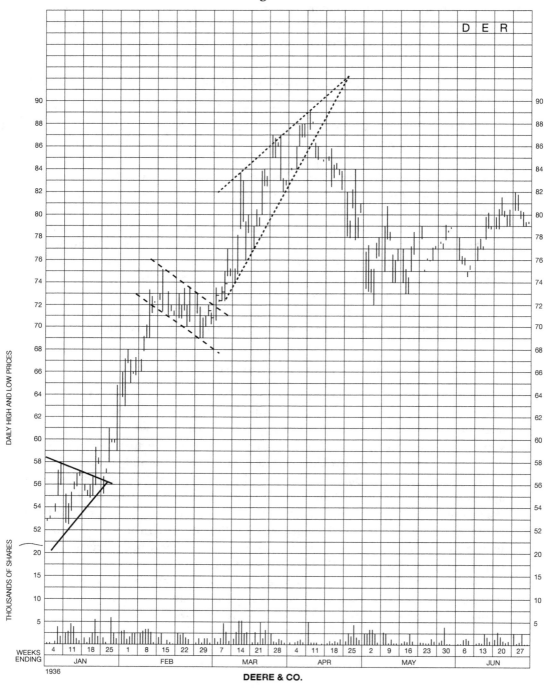

DEERE & CO.

Various Flag Aspects and Interpretations

A narrower and more compact Flag pattern appeared on a very short "mast" in the chart of Burroughs Adding Machine (Fig. VI.9). In this case the compact action within the Flag and the sharp break-out on September 5 were encouraging, but the preceding mast was so short that we could not expect the continuation to carry very far after the completion of the pattern. The subsequent movement was, in fact, quickly halted and another formation (an Inverted Triangle) was required to lay the foundation for a further advance.

Another Flag example appears in the chart of Sharon Steel Hoop, Fig. V.2. Note that the break-out was not confirmed by increased volume until the price closed a full point out of the pattern on February 6.

In long-continued rapid price movements several Flags may appear in quick succession. The chart of Greyhound Corporation (Fig. VI.15) shows several interesting examples in March and April. The reader may to good advantage study in detail the price and volume action throughout this chart.

Upward Flying Flags in Up-trends

The normal Flag picture in an upward price movement is, as we have seen in the preceding examples, somewhat drooping or slanting downward from the mast on which it forms. Less frequently we find continuation patterns in sharp mark-ups (or mark-downs) which slant in the same direction as the preceding trend and must be classified as Flags since they obey the same rules and do not permit of any other construction. A good example of an upward flying flag in as ascending movement appears in the late 1936 chart of International Harvester, (Fig. VI.16). Note the "mast" formed by the rapid advance of prices from September 17 to October 13, the Flag formed by the price action from that date to November 2, with volume declining and the sharp break-out on high volume on November 4, followed by another rapid price advance.

The normal Flag picture in an upward movement is somewhat slanting downward from the mast.

(The price action during the third week of September will be discussed in Study X.)

Flags may also develop between strictly horizontal boundary lines, as was noted in our introduction to this formation. Obviously, such horizontal patterns might be considered Rectangle continuations which happen to be of compact formation and happen to occur in rapid price movements. Whether we construe them as Flags or Rectangles does not matter; the forecast is the same.

Fig. VI.15

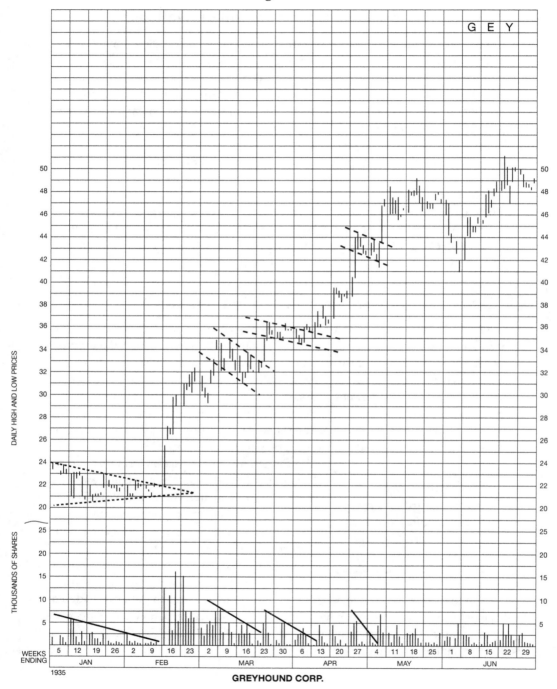

GREYHOUND CORP.

Fig. VI.16

INTERNATIONAL HARVESTER

Flags in Downward Movements

The Flag continuation pattern in a declining price trend is, of course, simply the upside-down development of the pictures we have just analyzed in ascending trends. The mast is formed first by a very rapid price mark-down; the flag is normally tilted slightly upward; volume tends to decline during its formation and then picks up sharply as the price breaks the lower boundary; and then a further rapid decline ensues.

For a typical example, refer to the 1931 chart of Columbian Carbon (Fig. VI.17). After a sharp break from the February high of $111\frac{1}{2}$ down to 93 in two weeks, a wide Flag formed during the first three weeks of March, and broke out into another rapid decline on March 24. It is interesting to note, although it has no special significance, that this Flag developed at the same time as the Rectangle continuation pattern previously illustrated in Electric Auto-Lite (Fig. VI.12).

The Pennant – Cousin to Flag and Wedge

The Pennant is simply a Flag formed within converging rather than parallel boundary lines. With this single exception, it is similar in appearance, duration, volume action, and interpretation to the normal Flag. On an upward pointing mast the Pennant always points down and forecasts a rapid continuation of the upward movement. In a down-trend it presents the opposite picture.

A good example of a Pennant in an up-trend appears in Fig. V.9, the Mack Trucks chart. The break-out from the Rectangle which signaled the bottom reversal in this stock in May, 1936, ran up into a 5-point mast on which a Pennant was "hung" by the price action during the last two weeks of June and first part of July. A sharp break-out on high volume resumed the previous upward movement.

The Columbian Carbon chart (Fig. VI.17) shows a Pennant formed as a continuation pattern in a down-trend during the first two weeks of May, 1931.

Flags and Pennants in Weekly Charts

Just as is the case with most other technical formations, both Flags and Pennants are to be found occasionally in charts of weekly price range, and also rarely in average charts, and their implications are the same as in daily charts of individual issues. Refer, for example, to the two Pennants in 1931 on the weekly chart of Standard Oil of NJ, Fig. III.6.

Fig. VI.17

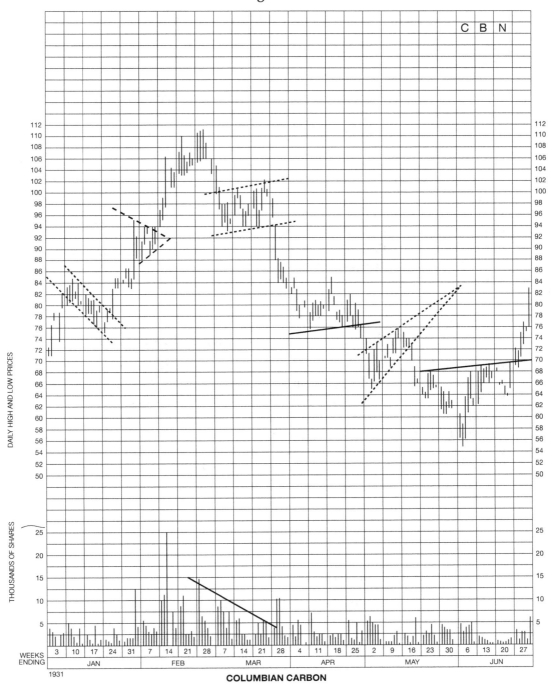

COLUMBIAN CARBON

Relation of Pennant to Wedge Pattern

The reader will have noticed in his study of the Pennant examples cited above a close resemblance to the Wedge formation which we treated as a Reversal in Study III. There is no important distinction between them so far as regards their forecast of a subsequent price movement in the direction opposite to that pointed by the formation itself.

The Wedge Reversal, however, is a formation which usually, though not always, continues within itself the previous price trend, and frequently works out into (and occasionally even somewhat beyond) its theoretical apex before the reversal occurs. The Pennant, on the other hand, forms on a mast of fast price movement and trends for only a comparatively short period of time, in the direction opposite to that of the mast. The Pennant seldom works out into a point or apex before breaking out into a

> *The Pennant is a Flag formed within converging boundary lines.*

continuation of the trend established by the mast (which is, of course, at the same time a reversal of the pattern's own trend).

The "Head and Shoulders" Continuation Pattern

Because the Head and Shoulders Reversal is the first technical formation studied, and because of its distinctive appearance, it is only natural that students should call by that name a certain type of price action which appears with fair frequency in an intermediate relation to the general price trend. This formation is not a true Head and Shoulders for a number of important reasons but we must admit that it is difficult to find a better name for it in view of its superficial resemblance to the Head and Shoulders Reversal. Fortunately, when it is carefully analyzed, the forecast is arrived at in the same way as the forecast from the Head and Shoulders. With the caution, therefore, that the student be careful always to analyze the pattern thoroughly before taking action on it, we shall accept the suggested name and call it the Continuation Head and Shoulders.

An Illustration in Crown Cork and Seal

It will be easier to describe and interpret the Continuation Head and Shoulders if we refer at once to a very plainly pictured example of it, such as appears in the chart of Crown Cork and Seal for the first half of 1936 (Fig. VI.18). The general upward trend in this stock reached a minor climax at 54 on January 15, and was followed by over

Fig. VI.18

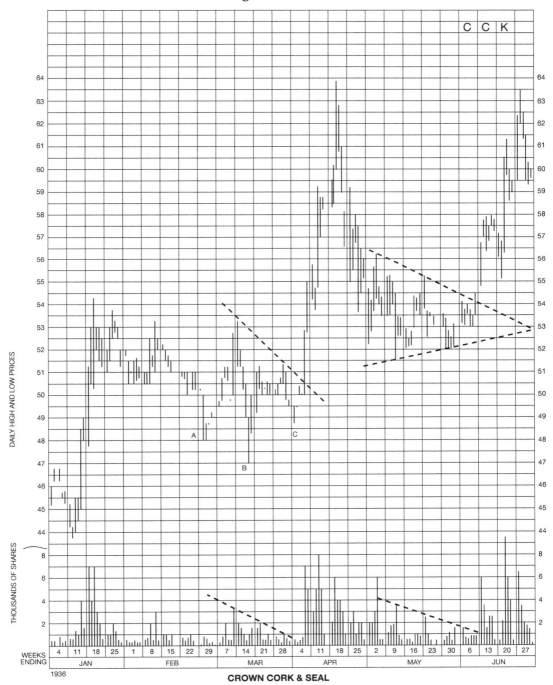

CROWN CORK & SEAL

two months of generally indecisive price action. However, a dip on February 25 and 26 formed (when considered with reference to the subsequent movement) what we may choose to call a left shoulder at A. The next dip on March 13, extending lower, formed a head at B. And the third reaction on March 30 gave us a right shoulder at C, with a neck-base line extended across the peaks made by the rallies on either side of the head, shown by the dotted line on the chart. This was broken with a very marked increase in activity on April 3, and prices thereupon advanced 10 points in three weeks.

Often the Only Helpful Indication

In the example before us it so happens that the price action from March 9 to April 3 could be construed as a Symmetrical Triangle with its top boundary the same as the neck-base line of our Continuation Head and Shoulders, and the bottom boundary drawn across points B and C. However, this is not always so clearly the case with formations of this type, and frequently the appearance of a Continuation Head and Shoulders gives us our only definite clue as to what the subsequent trend will be. It must be emphasized that the neck-base line is just as important a part of the pattern as are the head and shoulders; until the neck-base line is decisively broken the pattern has not been completed and has no forecasting value.

Other examples of Continuation Head and Shoulders patterns may be seen in other Figures in this and preceding Studies. Refer to the following:

Fig. II.2 – Left shoulder at J, head at K, right shoulder at L. Neck-base line broken on April 30.

Fig. II.6 – Left shoulder on November 27, head on December 20, and right shoulder on January 6. Neck-base line broken on January 10.

Fig. IV.15 – Left shoulder April 4, head April 11, right shoulder April 18. Neck-base line broken April 28.

Fig. VI.9 – Left shoulder September 20, head October 3, right shoulder October 9, neck-base line broken October 10. The use of the Continuation Head and Shoulders formula in this case gave an earlier and more profitable forecast than the break through the top of the more easily seen Inverted Triangle.

The reader will note that the above examples include formations in both up and down trends.

Differences from True Head and Shoulders Reversal

One obvious difference between the continuation formation we have been examining and the true Head and Shoulders Reversal which was taken up in Study II, is the fact that the former always appears in the opposite position with respect to the preceding general trend. Another notable difference will appear if we analyze the volume action. It will be recalled that the normal volume accompaniment to the true Head and Shoulders Reversal is comparatively high volume on the left shoulder and head, low volume between the two shoulders and the head, only very moderately increased volume on the right shoulder and, finally, a pick-up in volume when the neck-base line is decisively broken. Reference to our example of Continuation Head and Shoulders in the Crown Cork and Seal chart (Fig. VI.18) shows, however, that in this pattern high volume does not appear on the making of the shoulders or head,

> *The continuation formation always appears in the opposite position to the preceding general trend.*

but rather with the making of the rallies between them. In our later, more detailed consideration of volume action, in Study VIII, we shall see that there is a very good reason for this difference. In the meantime, it will suffice to note and remember this typical volume habit in the continuation form. The only point, in fact, at which the Head and Shoulders Reversal and the Continuation Head and Shoulders

need to agree in their volume charts is the sharp pick-up on the breaking of the neck-base line.

Review of Continuation Patterns

We have concluded in this section of our Course our consideration of clearly defined patterns and areas of price action which may interrupt the movement of prices in an established trend and lead at their completion to a continuation of that trend. It will be advisable at this point to review briefly the continuation formations we have studied and to re-classify them with a view to increasing our practical working knowledge of their uses in trading.

With that in mind, it appears at once that the most important division we can make in these formations is between those that may signal either reversal or continuation, and those that normally signal only a continuation. In doing this, we must remember that no technical formation is 100% dependable; there are exceptions to every rule in technical analysis. For all practical purposes, however, the forecasts are sufficiently established in the great majority of instances to enable us to make the following summary.

1. *Formations Which Lead to Either Reversal or Continuation*
    The Symmetrical Triangle
    The Inverted Triangle – all types
    The Rectangle

2. *Formations Which Forecast Continuation Only*
   a. In an established up-trend
      The Ascending Right-Angle Triangle
      The Flag (usually, but not always, pointing down)
      The Pennant (pointing down)
      The Continuation Head and Shoulders with head hanging down
   b. In an established down-trend
      The Descending Right-Angle Triangle
      The Flag (usually, but not always, pointing up)
      The Pennant (pointing up)
      The Continuation Head and Shoulders with head erect

3. *Special Cases Forecasting Reversal only*
   a. In an established up-trend
      The Descending Right-Angle Triangle
   b. In an established down-trend
      The Ascending Right-Angle Triangle

Their Application in Practical Trading

From the classification we have made above, the technical trader who is already "in" a stock will see that any appearance on his charts of a formation in Group 1 requires vigilant attention since it may turn out to be a reversal and call for his promptly closing out the trade. If, on the other hand, the break-out indicates a contin-uation of the previous trend, then he may relax his vigilance for the moment at least, and ride along with the trend until some other warning signal appears. In certain cases (the Inverted Triangles, for

> *Remember that no technical formation is 100% dependable.*

example) he may be well advised to close his trade without waiting for the break-out especially if other charts are showing him at the same time apparently better profit opportunities.

(In connection with Group 1 we have noted that there are often other factors outside of the formations themselves which may help us to anticipate whether reversal or continuation is the more likely event.)

The appearance of any of the formations in Group 2 need not concern the trader who has already made a commitment in the right trend; they represent only a temporary delay in the increment of profit. Formations in Group 3 (and, of course, all of the true reversal patterns and signals previously studied) call for closing out trades and taking profits at the earliest favorable opportunity.

To the trader who has not already made a commitment in a stock, the appearance of any of the formations in Group 1, or in Groups 2 or 3 according to trend, represents simply an opportunity. He should be prepared to take whatever market action the formation itself or the direction of the break-out indicates.

Formations Which Change Their Nature

We cannot close this discussion, however, without adding our customary word of caution against "jumping the gun". We have noted in the preceding lessons that Right-angle Triangles are ordinarily very reliable forecasters, but even they have their exceptions. Right-angle Triangles occasionally break out in the wrong direction, i.e. through the hypotenuse side. When such break-outs occur, contrary to the expectation of the preceding pattern, one of two things usually happens. One alternative is that prices continue on out to the level of the first reversal point of the pattern and then make a Double Reversal formation – a Double Top in the case of a Descending Triangle after an up-trend, or a Double Bottom in the case of an Ascending Triangle after a down-trend. In such cases the implications of the original Right-angle Triangle are eventually carried out, but not until after a price movement of some consequence in the opposite direction has intervened.

The other, and perhaps more frequent alternative, is that the Right-angle Triangle is turned into a Rectangle. If this Rectangle becomes quite complete and distinctly formed, the break-out from it may go in either direction just as it may out of any Rectangle. For example, the formation in Anaconda (Fig. VI.4) from December 23 to January 23, might be construed as such a Rectangle. In this example, the break-out on January 23 took prices in the direction already forecast by the Ascending Triangle, but if prices had continued to fluctuate "in pattern" between 28 and 30 for, say, another month, a break-out on the down side would have been equally probable.

Study VII

MISCELLANEOUS INTERMEDIATE PATTERNS AND PHENOMENA

In our preceding Studies we have taken up, first, technical formations or patterns which signal reversal of the major or intermediate price trend, and, second, formations which signal continuation of the trend in which they appear. And some of these, we have learned, may indicate either reversal or continuation but give us, in either case, a reliable signal when they break out of pattern.

In this Study we shall take up a number of special formations and phenomena of price action which have rather limited forecasting value in most cases but are, nevertheless an essential part of the technical trader's working knowledge.

The formations we shall consider are:

The Drooping Bottom and Accelerating Top
The Horn
The Inverted Horn
And, following that, we shall take up:
Gaps
Out-of-line Movements
Scallops and other Repeating Phenomena

But First Some General Considerations

In our introduction to the general group of continuation formations we noted that there exist logical reasons for this type of intermediate formation, but that these reasons are based, chiefly, on the fact that the continuation generally starts out as a possible reversal. Even when insiders are perfectly confident that they can push their stock up another 30 points, the mere fact that they themselves may decide on an intermediate period of rest and consolidation of the previous advance, indicates that there is at least a bare possibility that the technical position will have to be reversed and the additional 30 points sacrificed.

Since practically every intermediate formation shows some resistance to the previous straight movement, and since, in truth, the majority are merely stronger developments of what might, under weaker circumstances, be a reversal, it should be easy to see why our cardinal reversal formations do not always work out according to their usual reverse forecast, and why sometimes formations which look, at first, like satisfactory examples of our reversal patterns, may eventually turn out to be merely continuations.

For our more valuable and practical study, however, we may pass on, with this realization, to consideration of a few specific formations which are, as a rule, suggestive of intermediate patterns rather than reversal. Largely for the reasons already considered in the present study and in our previous introduction to the subject of continuations, our group of specific intermediate formations is not as large or important as the group of reversal patterns.

We have already seen the large part which the various aspects of the triangular pattern play in the entire group of continuation pictures. They are, in fact, the most important single picture promising continuation of the previous movement. And the most important of the formations which we shall take up in this section is merely a specially developed aspect of the Right-angle Triangle. In its suggestion of the Descending Triangle it takes the name of the Drooping Bottom. In its suggestion of the Ascending Triangle our new intermediate formation takes the name of the Accelerating Peak.

The Drooping Bottom

The Drooping Bottom is almost any kind of a price formation or congestion which tends to come to a drooping point at the close of its development. The formation need not be long. In fact, there are cases where hardly any area picture is discernible, but the drooping point is always there. The Drooping Bottom is more often found, however, developing as part of, or after, an area picture and most frequently, perhaps, from some form of Triangle pattern. To particularize still further, the Drooping Bottom is most frequent and most dependable as a continuation, when it forms the last portion of a Descending Triangle, and in many instances it suggests almost a special phase of that formation.

An interesting example which may be construed as a special phase of the Descending Triangle, or as a drooping slump out of a Rectangle Reversal, is shown in Fig. VII.I the chart of Chicago Pneumatic Tool for the first half of 1930. From March 15 to April 5 this stock fluctuated between 34 and 37, with volume far above normal levels, forming the suggestion of a Rectangle which, as we have learned in previous studies, might have turned into a reversal or a continuation. By the second week in April, however, the pattern began to suggest the appearance of a Descending Triangle but with a sagging or down-curving bottom line. The bottom of the minor decline at A was a little lower than the preceding minor bottoms, the next bottom B dropped even farther, and C farther yet. Note that there had been up to this point no pick-up in volume to confirm a break-out of any pattern. Nevertheless, the whole picture was one of weakness, apparent to the most casual observer. At C the stock had reached a level where support might have been anticipated for reasons which we shall discuss in detail in Study IX, but the decline to D, continuing the drooping picture, was conclusive.

> *The Drooping Bottom tends to come to a drooping point at the close of its development.*

– 222 –

Fig. VII.1

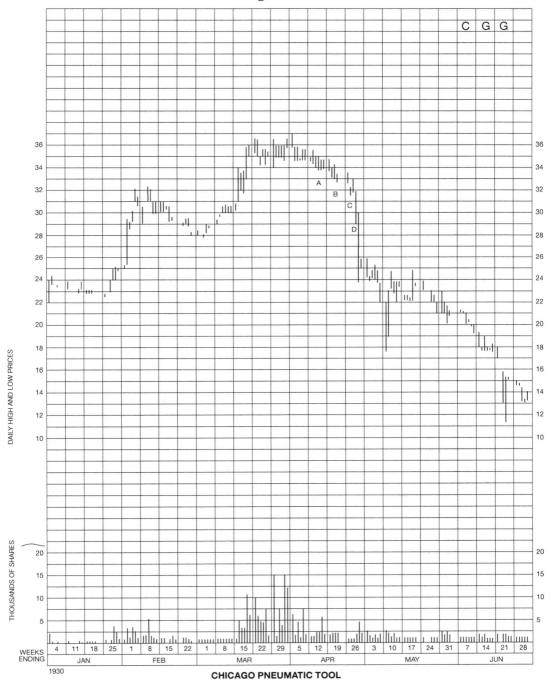

CHICAGO PNEUMATIC TOOL

Continuation Suggestion Always Apparent

The weakness of the Drooping Bottom Formation is always very apparent, as in this case. The stock sags and wilts away under our very eyes, and a child could almost guess that the price would continue on down at an increasing rate.

The Drooping Bottom began to appear in the Chicago Pneumatic Tool chart at B. A bold trader might have "gone short" of the stock at that point, but a more conservative chartist would undoubtedly prefer to wait for a testing of the 31–32 support level before taking a short position and would feel more certain of his forecast at D.

The Drooping Bottom formation implies a continuation of its downhill price movement at a rapidly increasing pace until it reaches a selling climax. The volume during the first stages of the formation tends to decline, and does not pick up until the climax which is accompanied by a sharp burst of activity. Thereafter, a pattern of some sort usually forms and develops a continuation of the downward movement at a more reasonable pace, or, less often, perhaps, reverses the down trend into an intermediate recovery. In the case of Chicago Pneumatic Tool there was an insignificant congestion in the down-trend at the end of April, a sharp drop to $17\frac{1}{2}$ on May 5 followed by an equally sharp recovery to the 22–24 zone, and then a resumption of the downward movement to 12 and below.

Drooping Bottom Offers Quick Profits

The rapidity with which the movement gains headway and reaches its climax makes the Drooping Bottom a very profitable pattern for the technical trader who acts upon its implications promptly. However, he must be prepared to close out his "short" trade with equal promptness for, as we have suggested above, the movement may be reversed after it reaches its climax almost as quickly as it started. An excellent example of such a reversal is shown in the Inland Steel in Fig. VII.2. Without the appearance, before it, of any very definite pattern, a Drooping Bottom began to develop early in April, at points A, B, C and D. From 104, at D, the price dropped precipitately to 92 in two weeks and to 90 in two weeks more, with volume suggesting the climax appearing on April 30 at the 93 level. Here, however, a new pattern – an Inverted Horn which we shall analyze later in this study – began to form, suggesting reversal. After a month, the new up-trend got under way and by the end of August the stock had climbed back to 114, the level from which the Drooping Bottom started.

Fig. VII.2

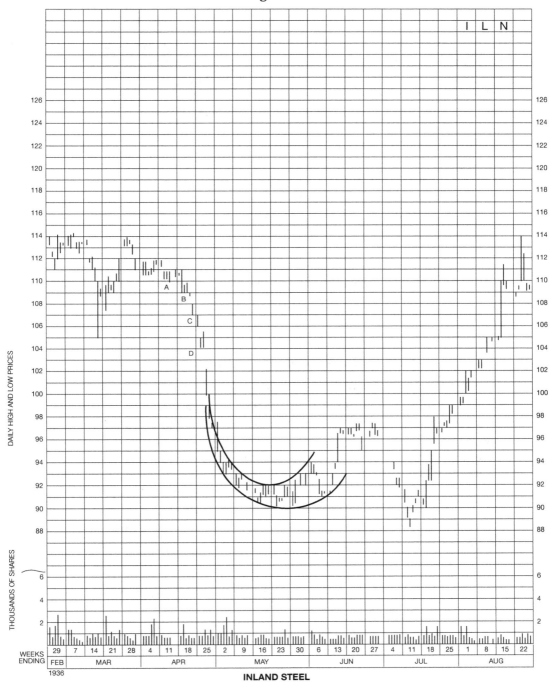

INLAND STEEL

Patterns with an Accelerating Peak

The pattern with an Accelerating Peak should be, of course, simply the upside down image of the pattern with a Drooping Bottom. In practice, however, we almost never find a pattern which must be classified as an Accelerating Peak and nothing else. In other words, although we do sometimes find accelerating movements following bottom formations, the formations themselves are almost invariably completed by a recognizable break-out before the accelerating upward movement or "peak" becomes apparent. Consequently, the peak in those cases cannot be considered a part of the pattern itself but only as serving to emphasize the urgency of the "buy" signal which the bottom formation and break-out had already given us.

And the same holds true of accelerating peaks or upward movements following continuation formations in up-trends. The direction of the movement is almost always signalled by an obvious break-out *before* the movement accelerates into a peak.

The important point to note about formations which are followed, after a good break-out, by an accelerating upward movement, is that the rapid up-curve in the price track indicates a strong continuation to a climax of the upward movement which was already forecast.

Part of the Rounding Bottom Reversal

No doubt it will have occurred to the student that the latter part of almost any Rounding Bottom or Common Bottom Turn might be called an Accelerating Peak, but here again we do not need the Accelerating Peak interpretation except to emphasize or strengthen the implications of a formation which we have already recognized as calling for higher prices. The volume action accompanying the Accelerating Peak part of a Rounding Bottom, as well as that accompanying any accelerating up-curve of prices following other types of bottom patterns, is comparable with the volume action on a Drooping Bottom formation. That is, it is relatively low at first and then picks up as the price movement speeds up, culminating finally in a burst of high activity as the buying nears a climax.

Examples Without Previous Break-outs Very Rare

There is a good and logical reason for the rarity of formations which do not show any ordinary decisive break-out but only a gradually accelerating upward movement out of an otherwise unclassifiable congestion. This reason is expressed in the familiar "street"[1] adage that "prices can fall down of their own weight but have to be *pushed* up". Unlike many old traders' "saws" which are only half true or not true at all, this saying is founded on indisputable fact. The fact is that most top reversals occur when stocks have been distributed out of strong hands into weak and, with strong support removed, very little pressure or volume of offerings is required to start prices down out of an area in which distribution has been completed. This accounts for the phenomenon we have already discussed (in connection with breaks down out of Descending Triangles and Rectangles) of good and valid break-out signals based on only a price movement without volume accompaniment. At bottoms, however, the action is different because it takes buying in large volume, relatively speaking, to push prices up out of congestion and to start the mark-up stage.

An example of the very rare type of pattern which is difficult to classify by any other feature except the Accelerating Peak, is shown in the Atchison chart in Fig. VII.3, at the 1932 bottom in this stock. Volume during the period shown was generally high and irregular except for the first part of July. The acceleration of prices up out of the July bottom became clearly evident toward the end of the month when average daily volume was also increasing notably.

Trading on the Accelerating Patterns

The accelerating upward movements of prices out of bottom congestion (or, for that matter, out of intermediate formations in up-trends) offer the trader the same opportunities for quick profits on prompt action, as do the patterns with a Drooping Bottom in a down-trend. Ordinarily it is good, sound practice to refrain from "chasing" the market. The beginner, at least, had better consider a movement which has already reached the accelerating phase as a train that has left the station, and wait for the next train rather than run after the one he has missed. Nevertheless, the trader who keeps his charts posted up-to-date every day and who may therefore see the accelerating picture developing in its early stages, and who further is in a position to get in quickly and get out just as quickly when the climax appears to indicate a reversal, is reasonably safe in chasing a movement of this type.

Another most important factor to be taken into account, before making a commitment on the strength of an accelerating movement alone, is the past habits of the stock under observation, and especially the probable support or resistance levels that may limit the extent of the movement. These important limiting factors of support and resistance levels are to be taken up in detail in Study IX.

---

[1] i.e. Wall Street

Fig. VII.3

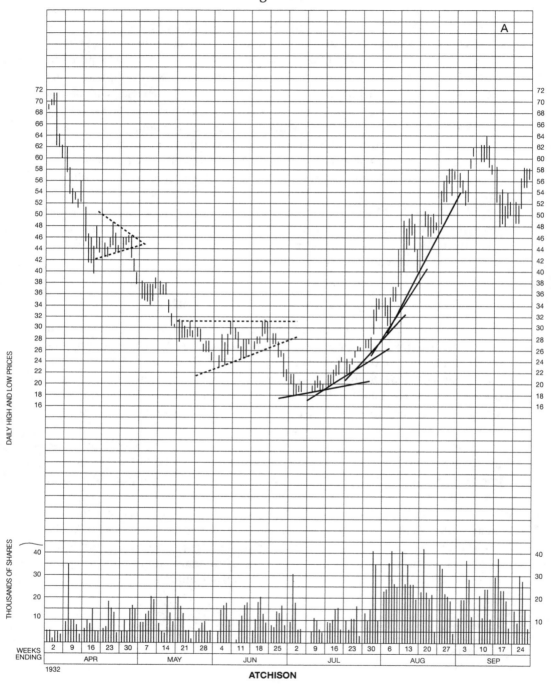

DAILY HIGH AND LOW PRICES

THOUSANDS OF SHARES

WEEKS ENDING																									
2	9	16	23	30	7	14	21	28	4	11	18	25	2	9	16	23	30	6	13	20	27	3	10	17	24
APR					MAY				JUN				JUL					AUG				SEP			

1932

ATCHISON

A

The Horn Formation

Our next intermediate pattern of limited forecasting value is the Horn – a quite definite formation with points of similarity to both the Rounding Turn (Study III) and the accelerating patterns previously discussed. In the converging of the lines which bound the price action it has also a slight resemblance to the Triangle. Its interpretation is almost precisely the same as that of the patterns with Drooping Bottoms or Accelerating Peaks. It calls, that is, for a rapid continuation of price movement in the direction already pointed, to a climax at which there is usually a halt and a congestion before another trend starts.

The Horn may occur at a reversal of intermediate trend, or as a continuation formation. The chart of Certain-Teed Products for the first half of 1936, Fig. VII.4 shows a Horn formation which signaled an intermediate reversal in this stock. Note the "rolling over" of prices during March and April, with the tendency for the price fluctuations to become narrower and the movement more rapid as the top was passed. The Horn pattern came to a climax very quickly in this case, with the development of a price congestion or temporary trading area around the 13 zone,

Chrysler made its "high" for the bull market of the 20s at 140 in October, 1928 – a full year ahead of the market averages.

out of which prices again dropped rapidly the first week in June. The congestion at 13-14 might conceivably have developed a forecasting pattern calling for another reversal, into an up trend, since the Horn itself does not forecast any certain movement much beyond the ensuing climax. In this case, however, no forecasting pattern or "foundation" for an upward move was built, and the downward trend was quickly resumed.

The chart of Standard Oil of California, Fig. VII.5 shows a Horn at the bottom of a minor reversal in the Fall of 1935.

The Horn as a Continuation Formation

The Chrysler chart, Fig. VII.6 shows the price action of this stock during the first half of 1929. (It is interesting to note that Chrysler made its "high" for the bull market of the 20s at 140 in October, 1928 – a full year ahead of the general market averages). In the rapid downward movement of this stock during the period shown, a brief rally in mid-April was quickly halted and turned into a Horn which again pointed prices down.

We refer to the example of a Horn in the Chrysler chart as a continuation, and to that in the Certain-Teed chart as a reversal, because of the relation which the Horn

Fig. VII.4

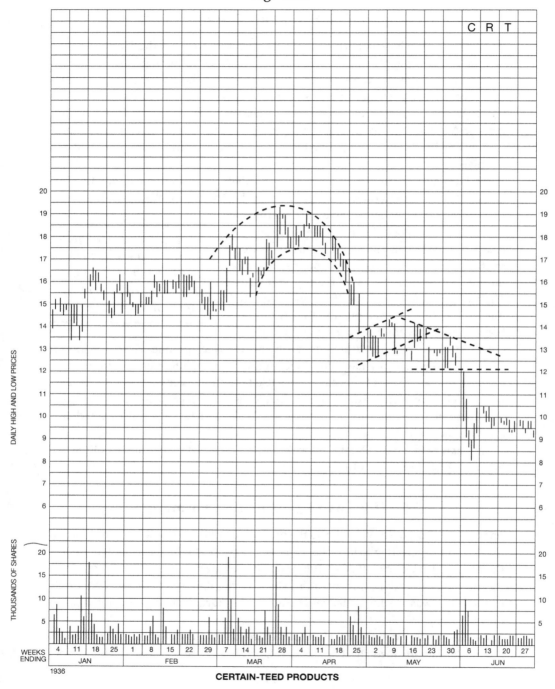

CRT

DAILY HIGH AND LOW PRICES

THOUSANDS OF SHARES

WEEKS ENDING

| 4 | 11 | 18 | 25 | 1 | 8 | 15 | 22 | 29 | 7 | 14 | 21 | 28 | 4 | 11 | 18 | 25 | 2 | 9 | 16 | 23 | 30 | 6 | 13 | 20 | 27 |

JAN   FEB   MAR   APR   MAY   JUN

1936

CERTAIN-TEED PRODUCTS

Fig. VII.5

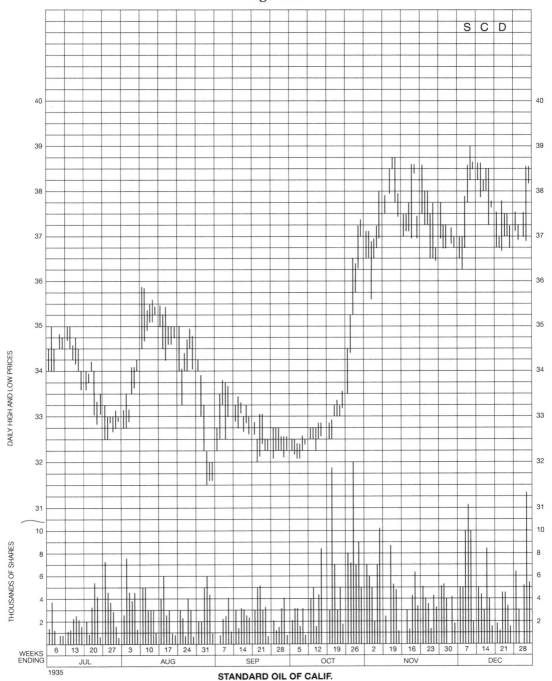

STANDARD OIL OF CALIF.

Fig. VII.6

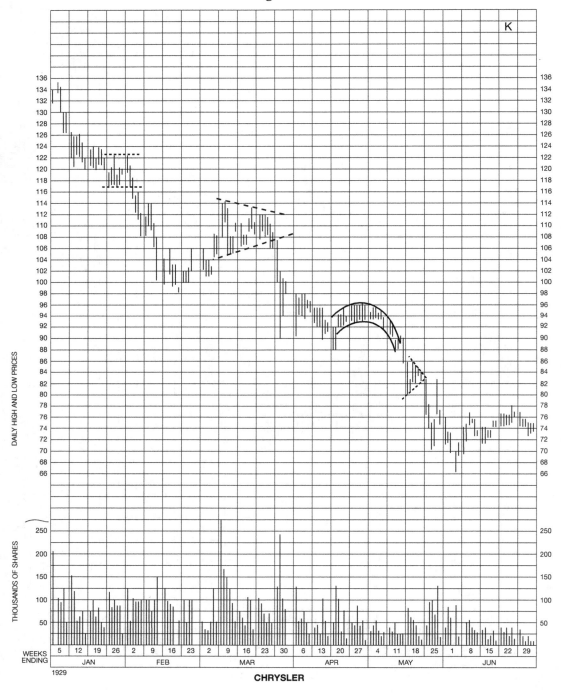

CHRYSLER

pattern bears in each case to the preceding general movement. It is, of course, obvious that the Horn contains within itself a minor reversal; while the narrow, accelerating end of it forecasts a continuation of its own trend to a climax just as do the patterns with Drooping Bottoms or Accelerating Peaks previously studied.

The Inverted Horn

A price pattern shaped like a Horn but with its narrow end forming first, appears much less frequently on the charts than the normal Horn formation. The Inverted Horn also contains within itself a minor reversal of price trend, but the extent of the following movement in the new trend may be quite limited.

A typical Inverted Horn appears in the Inland Steel chart (Fig. VII.2) formed by the price action from the latter part of April to the first part of June.

The forecast of an Inverted Horn may be compared with the forecast of an Inverted Triangle. Both are widening patterns of rather limited usefulness and not very easy to convert to profit.

Concluding the Study of Area Formations

Up to this point, we have been studying formations or area patterns of price action which indicate, either by their own construction or by the break-out which follows them, the direction of the ensuing price movement. We have finished with these and are now ready to take up the study of certain other phenomena of price action which cannot be called formations or patterns but which often have forecasting implications, either by themselves or when considered in connection with accompanying patterns.

The first of these special phenomena is the out-of-line price movement which occurs only in connection with some one of the definite reversal or continuation formations we have previously analyzed, and only after such a formation has already become clearly defined on our charts.

Out-of-line Movements

We had a first, brief look at an "out-of-line" price movement in our detailed examination of the Descending Triangle reversal on the Nash chart, Fig. III.10. A probable explanation for it was suggested in Study. III, page 93.

Out-of-line movements are not common but they appear with sufficient frequency on our charts to warrant our giving them some further consideration. They are found most often in Right-angle Triangles and Rectangles, but may develop also on occasion in any of the other formations we have studied. Or, perhaps, we should say that they develop "out of rather" than "in", because an out-of-line movement is, in fact, a sharp thrust of prices away from an already established pattern. This thrust, however, is quickly reversed and prices return within the pattern.

Most out-of-line movements are completed within a single day and are called, quite naturally, One-day Out-of-lines. Less often the price may stay out of line for two or three days, especially if the basic formation is large. As a rule, the out-of-line price movement is made on high volume as compared with the volume accompanying the nearby price action inside the formation. When the out-of-line movement is completed in a single day, the closing price for that day is usually back within or, at least, very near the previously defined pattern.

> *An out-of-line movement is a sharp thrust of prices away from an established pattern.*

Sometimes Resembles a True Break-out

Although it does not happen often, there are exceptional cases when the out-of-line thrust will take the price quite a distance out of the pattern and result in closing a full point or more away from its boundary. When these thrusts are made on conspicuously high volume they may have all the appearance of, and comply with all the requirements for, a valid break-out. It is this last described out-of-line action which is apt to be confusing to the technical trader, and may well lead him into taking a premature position in a stock. He sees the sharp price thrust confirmed by good volume, and the closing well away from the pattern; he construes it, naturally, as a break-out and places an order with his broker accordingly. And then he sees the stock go back into the pattern and stay there for several days, possibly even for a week or two.

Fortunately, the forecast of an out-of-line movement is for a fairly quick completion of the pattern and then a real break-out in the same direction as the previous out-of-line movement so, except for some little delay and, perhaps, a bit of mental wear and tear, no harm has been done. The stock eventually moves in the "right" direction.

To return, however, to the more normal appearance of the out-of-line movement, it is obvious that when the price does not close out of pattern by a decisive margin, no matter how high the volume, we do not have a good break-out and, consequently, should not be led to act prematurely. Instead we have a very helpful indication, first of the approaching completion of the pattern and, second, of the direction of the ensuing price trend.

Examples of Out-of-line Movement

We have mentioned above the out-of-line movement on the Nash chart in Study III and it is suggested that the student turn back at this point, if he has not already done so, and re-read the description and explanation of it on page 95.

A typical example of the One-Day Out-of-Line appears in Fig. VII.7, the 1934 chart of Johns-Manville. Commencing with the last week of September the price action of this stock began to build what appeared at first as though it might become an Ascending Triangle. Then, when the price dropped to 46 on October 23 and rallied on the next day to the general level of the three preceding minor tops, the pattern began to suggest a Rectangle. In either case a well-defined top boundary line had been established and the decline in volume during the construction of this price area was bearing out the deduction that a pattern of some forecasting consequence was in process of completion.

On October 25, however, the performance of Johns-Manville stock was rather startling. With a conspicuous burst of activity which resulted in a volume greater than on any day for months before, the price was marked up to $50^{1}/_{4}$, a point and a quarter above our pattern's top boundary. If we had been following the tape on that day we should certainly have been led to believe that a decisive break-out was occurring and giving a signal to buy Johns-Manville at once. But if we waited until that night or the following morning when we could post the full day's price and volume action on our chart, we found that the movement had reversed itself during the day, and that the closing price was near the bottom of the range and a point below the critical boundary line. There had been no "break-out", by the tests we have learned to apply. The price track of the stock for the next eight trading days fell within the bounds of the previously suggested Rectangle and it was not until November 5 that a decisive break-out appeared, meeting all the requirements as to penetration, volume and closing. The price action on October 25 was a One-day Out-of-line.

The Interpretation of the Out-of-line Action

It is evident from our analysis of the Johns-Manville chart that a trader who bought the stock on October 25 when it had moved up to 50 would have been sold out on the next day thereafter if he had placed a stop-loss order at, say, $47^{1}/_{2}$. And if he had not placed a stop, he would at best have gained nothing by his hasty action and had over a week to wait before his trade got out of the "red". To the trader who did not act prematurely, however, the one-day out-of-line gave valuable information. It suggested, first, that the pattern of price trend would be up, in the direction of the out-of-line movement.

Fig. VII.7

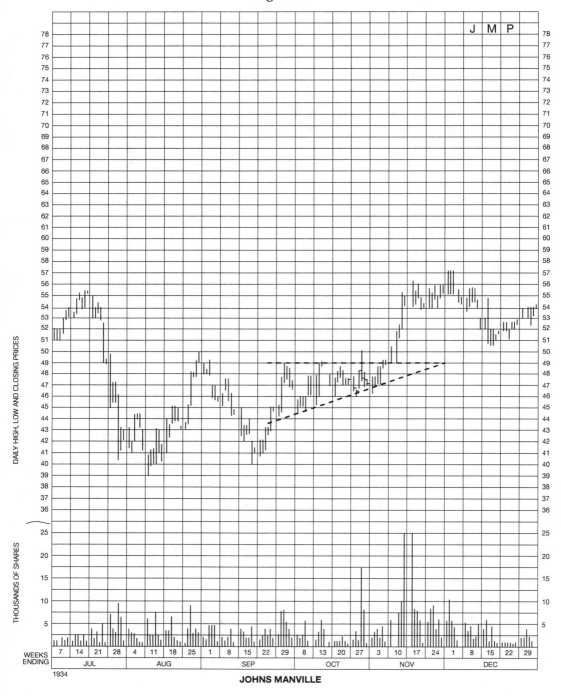

JOHNS MANVILLE

Fig. VII.8

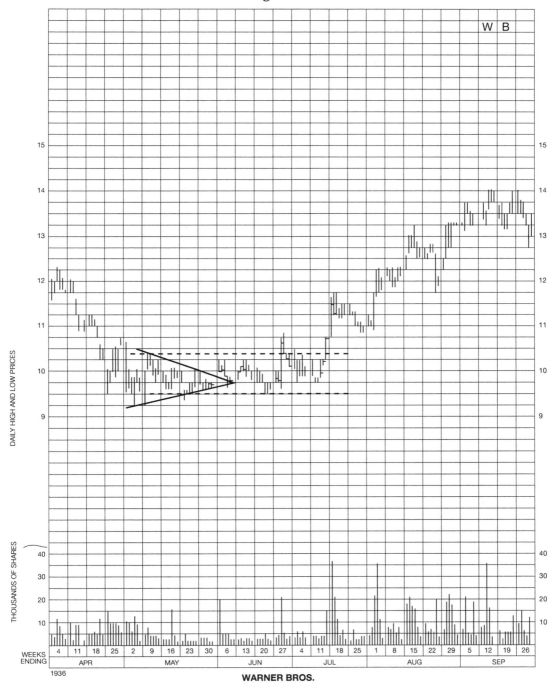

WARNER BROS.

We would not have the student believe that the forecast of an out-of-line movement is infallible for no technical pattern or phenomenon is 100% reliable. It is extremely seldom, however, that a thrust of this character out of and then back within a clearly defined pattern, is not followed by the two results we have named in the last sentence of the preceding paragraph as the out-of-line implications.

Out-of-line for Two Days

Another good example of out-of-line action is illustrated by the 1936 chart of Warner Brothers Pictures, Fig. VII.8. Dropping from $14\frac{1}{2}$ early in the year, the decline was halted the first week in May at 9. Thereafter the price track built a rather loose Symmetrical Triangle out of which there was an attempt to break on June 1; the volume on that day was notable but the price closed at 10, barely out of the pattern, which prevented us from interpreting this as a break-out day. It might, however, be called an out-of-line movement suggesting, certainly, that the technical picture was changing and that a foundation for a reversal of the previous decline was being laid.

After this attempt to break out which failed on June 1, Warner Brothers fluctuated for three weeks in the $9\frac{1}{2}$–$10\frac{1}{2}$ zone, now making the semblance of a Rectangle on the chart. On June 24 another day of high volume appeared and the price moved up to 10, closing at $10\frac{5}{8}$. This time the closing was out of pattern but again not by a decisive margin. On the following day the price was pushed to $10\frac{7}{8}$ but fell back and closed at the Rectangle's top boundary. Here was a very good example of an out-of-line movement which lasted two days. It signaled the near completion of the formation to be followed by a true break-out on the up-side. The break-out, meeting all requirements, came on Saturday, July 11.

The Out-of-line from a Symmetrical Triangle

The student will no doubt have noticed that, whereas the out-of-line movement on June 24 and 25, out of the rectangular pattern, was followed by the normal out-of-line forecast, the out-of-line action on June 1 required the building of a considerably longer pattern before the upward trend was started. There are two reasons for this. The first is that an out-of-line movement through a well-defined horizontal boundary, representing presumably either support or resistance, carries greater weight in technical forecasting than an out-of-line movement out of a Symmetrical Triangle or a Rounding formation. Thus an out-of-line movement down through the bottom of a Descending Triangle, or up through the top of an Ascending Triangle, or through either boundary of a Rectangle, has emphatic significance.

In the case of a Symmetrical Triangle on the other hand, we have to begin with a pattern whose boundaries are less definite; the lines which establish its sides frequently have to be re-drawn several times before the pattern is completed. If an out-of-line movement occurs near the theoretical apex, it may be called a break-out that fails, as in the Warner Brothers chart; when that failure becomes apparent we should quite naturally expect some further foundation to be laid. The sequence of events which we have seen in the Warner Brothers chart is a very common one; first, a narrow Symmetrical Triangle; then, an out-of-line movement which becomes, in turn, a part of a rectangular picture; finally, a break-out of the Rectangle, often preceded by an out-of-line movement of good forecasting value.

Out-of-line Examples in Previous Studies

Beside the movement in Nash cited previously, there are other examples in the charts illustrating our earlier lessons. The rally in Case starting on June 10, 1932, shown in Fig. III.2, may be construed as an out-of-line movement in the Rounding Bottom pattern already becoming evident at that time. The action of prices on November 27, 1933, in the Hudson Motors chart, Fig. III.11, is an out-of-line movement, with the usual consequences. The formation at the bottom of the Chrysler chart in Fig. IV.7 may be interpreted as a Rectangle with an out-of-line movement May 26 to 28.

In our later study of Trend Line action we shall see that out-of-line movements can occur through established trend lines as well as out of patterns.

The Zig-zag Movement

The next phenomenon of price action we have to study is the Zig-Zag. It may be considered as a cousin of the Out-of-Line since it is made up of two movements out of line with the preceding picture, but these two movements protrude in opposite directions. The Zig-Zag is not as common as the simple out-of-line, however, and has only a very limited forecasting value. It may appear at any time or place in the chart picture, though it is usually found in connection with a fairly established trend and almost never in connection with a definite area formation.

The Zig-Zag is a movement which stands out from the rest of the trend and takes the form of a sharp out-of-line movement in one direction, quickly reversed, and then followed very shortly thereafter by just as noticeable a thrust out-of-line in the opposite direction. The first sharp movement may be called the Zig and the second, in the opposite direction, the Zag. The suggested forecast is that, following the completion of the Zag, there will shortly be another break out of the established trend in the direction of the first out-of-line movement, or the Zig. This forecast is fairly reliable but only for a limited movement which may also be quite moderate in rapidity or sharpness.

Examples of the Zig-zag Movement

An excellent example of the Zig-Zag showed up on the Loew's chart for 1936, Fig. VII.9. Note the upward trend of this stock starting in June, within clearly defined parallel bounds. On August 12, however, there was a sharp thrust up out of line, which was reversed and returned within bounds on August 14. This in itself could be construed as an Out-of-line movement and, if nothing had happened to offset it, it would call for another break through on the up-side to follow shortly, and the establishment of a new, possibly "steeper", trend. But something did happen to offset it; the minor reaction from the first out-of-line carried right down into an equally sharp thrust through the lower line on August 21. Then prices came back within the previous trend and, instead of a simple Out-of-line, we now had a Zig-zag, the Zig occurring on August 12 and the Zag on August 21. This called for another limited movement in the direction of the Zig, and it came, right on schedule, so to speak, on September 10.[2]

Note that the Zig-zag is not completed until the second out-of-line movement, the Zag, has reversed and returned within the basic trend or pattern. In brief, each thrust must protrude sharply beyond the established trend or pattern and each must return within it before we have a Zig-zag movement calling for a third movement in the direction of the Zig.

In extent of movement, the example in the Loew's chart might be called a good average example of a Zig-zag. The technical student will occasionally find Zig-zags which protrude much more conspicuously from the basic trend or pattern. The third movement in the direction of the Zig may be expected to proceed at least as far out of line as the Zig and can, of course, go even farther, but the forecast of the Zig-zag by itself is limited.

Recurrent Patterns of Price Action

Every student of the stock charts has noticed many instances of certain issues moving in patterns which repeat themselves over and over again with amazing regularity. We know, of course, that major business cycles produce major up and down trends in securities, which produce a repeating pattern of "hills and valleys" on the charts, but the variance in timing of these major swings is too great to permit us to trade on them by means of the time factor alone. We know, further, that there appear

---

[2] Of special interest to devotees of the Elliott Wave Principle, this section on "Zig-zags" should prove useful in combination with Elliott's writing on the subject.

Fig. VII.9

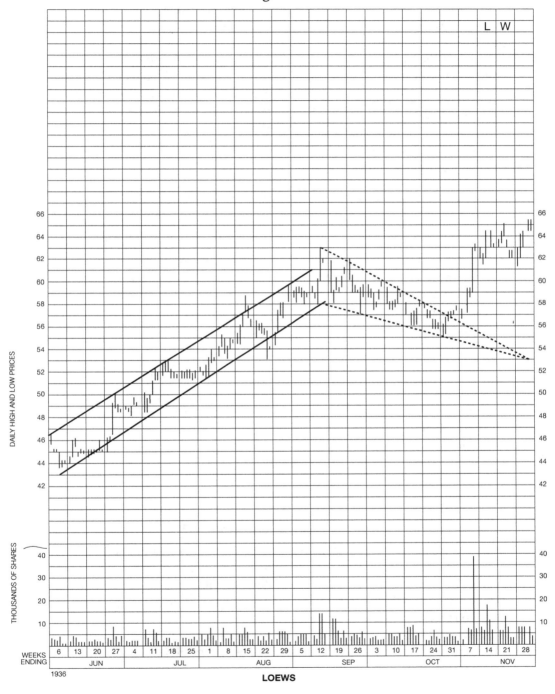

LOEWS

to be seasonal swings in certain individual stocks and in certain industrial groups of stocks, but here again there are so many exceptions, caused by other factors which upset the seasonal cycle, that it is impossible consistently to trade on them with profit.

However, there do appear on occasion in the charts of individual issues repeating patterns or cyclical movements within the major trends, and even within the inter-mediate swings, which seem to have no relation to such fundamentals as seasonal earnings nor any other logical cause. In brief, certain stocks seem at times to develop certain clearly recognizable habits of price action which we may call Recurrent or Repetitive Patterns.

> *Every student has noticed issues moving in patterns which repeat themselves over and over again.*

As a fair illustration of such habit patterns within a major trend we may refer to the weekly charts of Chesapeake & Ohio and Commercial Solvents which are reproduced, side by side, in Fig. VII.10. These show the intermediate declines and recoveries during the greater part of the long bear market following the 1929 tops.

In the Chesapeake & Ohio chart the habit is one of sharp and quickly reversed bottoms alternating with rather heavy and somewhat rounding tops. This picture is "broken" at only one point where the bottom in June, 1930 did not extend down into as sharp a climax as did the other bottoms. Possibly the anticipated 4 for 1 split in the stock accounted for that exception.

In the Commercial Solvents chart, on the other hand, the habit is quite different. The price action is heavier and more rounding at the bottoms, and sharper and more peaked at the tops. These two charts are not shown as perfect examples of recurrent patterns but rather to illustrate the general proposition that different stocks show different habits even in their long-term cyclical movements. However, these long-term habits are not what we are particularly concerned with in this Study; rather we are interested in similar habit pictures which develop in the current movements within the intermediate trends.

The Scallop – an Opportunity and a Warning

One of the recurrent patterns which appears with fair frequency is the Scallop, illus-trated in the chart of Container-A for the first nine months of 1935, Fig. VII.11. Note the regularity of the minor advances and declines within the gradually declining trend of the stock to June and on through the first three months of the upward trend into September. The regularity or periodicity of the minor bottoms is particularly noticeable, each bottom being made about six weeks after the preceding one.

A logical explanation for such pictures as this would be difficult to find but, after

Fig. VII.10

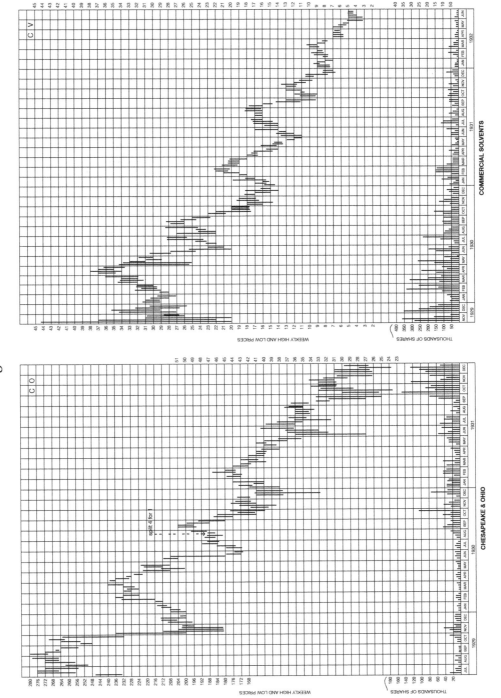

Fig. VII.11

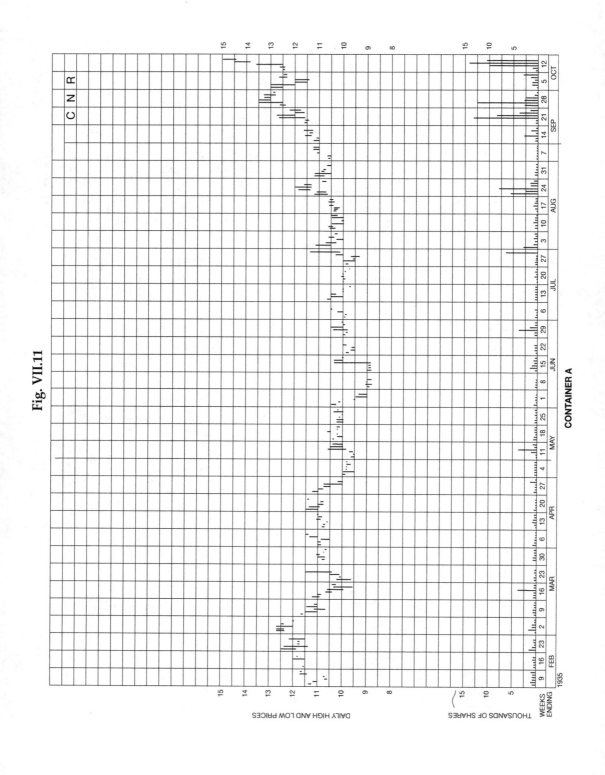

CONTAINER A

all, an explanation is not necessary. All we need to do is to observe the sequence or recurrence of the waves of price action after a few such waves have pictorialized themselves on our chart, to realize that we have a phenomenon of technical value. Such a phenomenon of recurring price action, having once made itself apparent, may be assumed to repeat itself indefinitely until some new factor enters the picture to disturb its rhythm.

In the Chart of Container A the student can see for himself how abruptly the pattern was destroyed the first week in October. The movement immediately thereafter, which does not show on this chart, may be described briefly as a rapid advance in six weeks to 19, a sidewise movement for four weeks, and then another 4-point advance in a single week's time.

Obviously the scallop picture, as soon as it becomes apparent (which in the case of the Container A chart might well have been by the first week in May), offers the technical trader repeated opportunities for quick profits. Any one transaction in the stock may show only a small profit, but the aggregate of all the possible "turns" can certainly become very well worthwhile.

The Warning Given by Recurring Movements

Another type of "scallop" action is illustrated in the 1936 Commercial Solvents chart, Fig. VII.12. Here we have a repetition of movements which might have misled an inexperienced trader into taking a premature position. the upward thrust in each case gave every appearance of starting a profitable movement, but each was stopped short and the price fell off again. A pattern of this sort warns us not to trust any apparent break-out signals until the chart shows that the continuity is broken and the stock has shaken off its "bad habits".

Trading on a recurring price movement, it goes without saying, requires first a thorough study of the stock's chart history and then the ability to act promptly and decisively, plus readiness to abandon a position the minute some unexpected price or volume action indicates a change in the picture.

The Price Gap – an Interesting but Often Puzzling Phenomenon

Out next subject for study – the price gap – is one concerning which much has been written. Many theories have been built around the occurrence of point size gaps and many claims stated as to their forecasting value. Taken at face value, and without careful research and practical testing, these theories might easily lead the student of technical action to believe that gaps were of major importance in forecasting market movements. The Gap does have a a place in technical forecasting, but its value is

Fig. VII.12

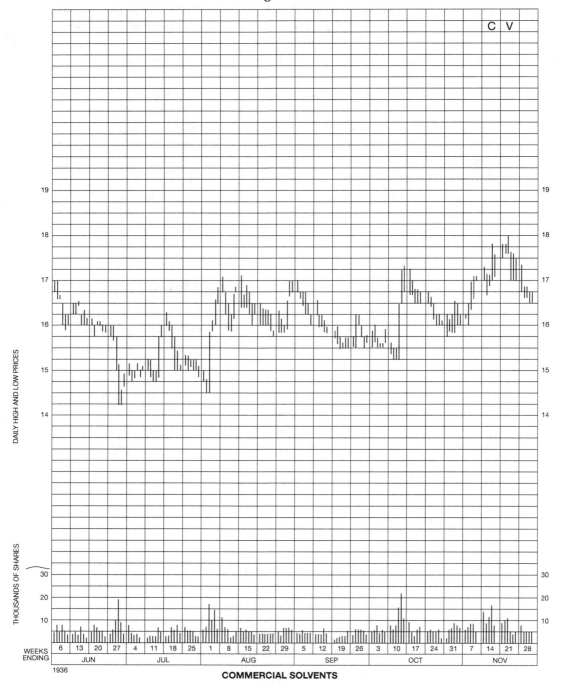

COMMERCIAL SOLVENTS

chiefly confirmatory or modifying in connection with other chart implications, and in many cases, as we shall see, a Gap cannot be classified and given its correct interpretation at the time it is formed. Gaps, therefore, belong not among our important formations and forecasting factors but rather among our secondary chart phenomena of limited usefulness. We must recognize them, appraise them at their true value, and use them when we can.

General Description of the Gap

We have already had a rather superficial introduction to the Gap in our analysis of the Island Reversal formation in Study V (see pages 168–9), but the Gap family is large and worthy of detailed examination. In Study V it was explained that the Gap is a stretch of "open water" between the price range of two successive trading days as pictorialized on our stock charts. In other words, it is merely a failure of the daily price ranges to overlap. On the up-side, a Gap is formed

> *The Gap does have a place in technical forecasting.*

by the low point of one day's range being higher than the high point of the previous day's range; on the down-side, it is formed by the high point of any day's range falling below the low point of the previous day's chart range.

Gaps More Common in Thin Markets

Since the normal movement of prices is generally rather gradual and results in the common or normal overlapping of one day's price range by the next, it stands to reason that failure to overlap and the consequent appearance of a Gap must be the result of an abnormally rapid change in the technical position. This is quite true as regards Gaps formed in the chart of an actively traded stock, but even in such cases the abnormal condition is usually corrected at an early date and the price swings back again into its more normal overlapping habit of fluctuation.

When, however, a stock has a "narrow" market, i.e. when it is inactive, little known, or has only a small number of shares outstanding, the formation of Gaps may be, and usually is, merely the result of this thin market condition. In such cases the appearance of Gaps is not to be considered in any sense an abnormal occurrence. In "thin" stocks the overlapping tends to be spread out over several days or weeks, whereas in active issues we expect it to occur daily.

The chart of Allied Chemical (Fig. VII.13) illustrates the frequent formation of Gaps in a thin stock. It is obvious that these Gaps have no technical importance, being simply the natural result of a narrow market in a relatively "unpopular" stock with a very small floating supply.

Fig. VII.13

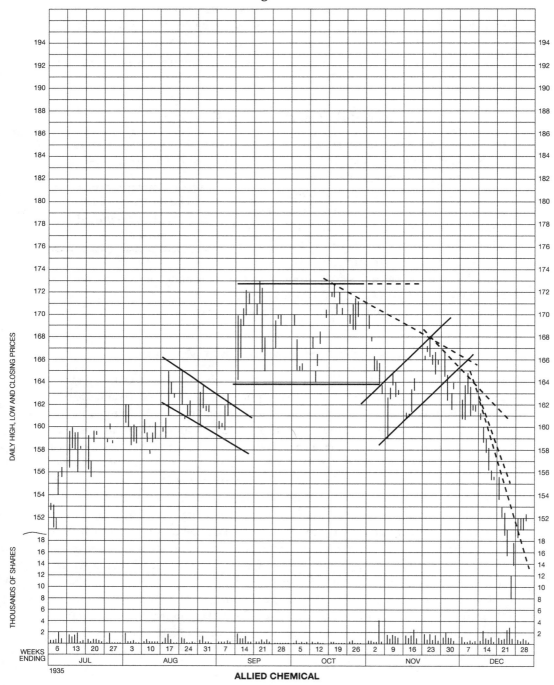

ALLIED CHEMICAL

Stocks of fairly large issue that have ordinarily an active market may at times fall out of popular favor or become temporarily inactive for various reasons, and during these periods will form many Gaps which are of no importance in our study. Note, for example, the many Gaps in the latter half of the chart of Sharon Steel Hoop, Fig. V.2, during a period of inactive trading in this stock.

Gaps Fall Into Four Classifications

Having disposed of the gaps in thin stocks for the present at least, we must return now to the study of their significance in the charts of actively traded issues where, as we have seen, they picture an abnormal technical condition. We shall find that these Gaps may be classified into four groups as follows:

1. The Common Gap
2. The Break-Away Gap
3. The Continuation Gap
4. The Exhaustion Gap

This classification depends on where and how the Gap forms and also, to some extent, as we have already remarked, on what happens afterwards.

The Common Gap – Soon Covered

The Common Gap, in technical terminology is the type of Gap which occurs characteristically in nervous markets, and which is generally "closed" within a few days or within a week or two at the most. A Gap is said to be closed when the price range, on some *future* date, returns to overlap the range immediately preceding the Gap, in which case the "open water" between the ranges disappears. Until this occurs the Gap is said to remain "open".

The Common Gap generally forms during the process of development of some area pattern. The student will find innumerable examples in the charts illustrating our previous studies or, for that matter, in almost any chart he cares to study. In the Johns-Manville chart, Fig. III.12, there are several between points B and F. In the Mack Trucks chart, Fig. V.9 there are seven Gaps inside the Rectangle Bottom formation. There are a number within the Inverted Triangle on the Sears Roebuck chart, Fig. VI.6. The Broadening Tops in Air Reduction and United States Steel, Figs IV.14 and IV.15 respectively, and the Inverted Triangle which almost became a Broadening Top in Standard Oil of NJ, Fig. VI.7 all show Gaps in greater frequency than we should expect during the ordinary trends of these stocks. Note that these occur during active but "nervous" markets. Note also that about the only forecast we can place upon Gaps of this type is that they will soon be covered, and so carry no great significance in technical analysis.

The Break-away Gap

The Break-away type of Gap is, in most respects, just about the opposite of the Common Gap. It appears at the beginning of a movement and generally comes at the completion of some definite area formation. It is seldom covered for some time in the future and, when it proceeds from a strong major bottom formation, it may never be covered, or at least not until the return of prices in the next great cycle some years later. The Break-away Gap is comparatively uncommon and indicates a definite change in the technical picture. It suggests that the technical position of the stock has suddenly become so weak or so strong that the normal balance of buying and selling has been thrown far out of line, as evidenced by the absence of the normal lapping of price ranges. The logical conclusion is, therefore, for a continuation of that lack of balance and a strong movement in the direction toward which the Gap was made.

Examples of Break-away Gaps

If we turn back again to the Johns-Manville chart, Fig. III.12, we can easily and quickly see the difference between the Common and Break-Away types of Gaps. The Break-away Gap appears at J, following the formation of the strong Ascending Triangle with its many nervous Common Gaps.

Other good examples of Break-away Gaps are to be found in the Pullman chart, Fig. IV.13 at the breaking of the neck line of the Complex Bottom; in the Auburn chart, Fig. V.10 at the break-out from the Continuation Triangle in May; in the Electric Boat, chart Fig VI.1 at the break-out of the long Triangle in November; in the Electric Auto-Lite chart, Fig. VI.12, at the break-out from the Continuation Rectangle in April; and in the Columbian Carbon chart, Fig. VI.17, at the break-out from the Flag in March; also in the New York Central chart, Fig. III.14, at the break-out from the Wedge in February. None of these Gaps, it will be noted, occurred inside the pattern; in each case the pattern was already well-defined and the Gap appeared when prices broke away from the pattern.

Apparent Break-away Gaps that Are Later Closed

There are cases, however, in which a Gap is formed at a break-away from a pattern and then prices return to close the Gap and build an addition on the pattern, so to speak, before the real break-out occurs. An example of this action may be seen in the

Republic Steel Chart, Fig. II.1. The price track in this chart from early July to August 8 formed a Symmetrical Triangle out of which prices broke with a Gap on the downside on August 9, and closed near the bottom of the day's range. Except for the fact that there was no appreciable increase of volume, this action appeared to be a valid break-out calling for a decline. Instead, prices on the following day worked back and closed on the lower edge of the Gap, and on the next trading day the Gap was closed and prices went on to build another Triangle out of which a break-out developed on the up-side on August 23. The volume on the day when the Gap was closed was notably higher than on the day it was made. In this case the experienced technical trader would not have been misled because, as we have learned, a break-out from a Symmetrical Triangle should be confirmed by volume before action is taken upon it. (*Note*: a decisive break down out of a formation with a well-defined *horizontal* bottom boundary does not require volume confirmation on the break-out day itself. In many such cases – Right angle Triangles and Rectangles, for example – volume does not show up until the next day or the second day following the break-out. Breaks out of Symmetrical Triangles, on the other hand, should be regarded with suspicion until they are confirmed by volume.)

Difficulty of Immediate Classification

Such apparent exceptions as that in the Republic Steel chart which we have just discussed, occasionally lead the skeptic to object that the differentiation between the Common and the Break-away Gap is merely the definition of two opposite possibilities, one or the other of which must, of necessity, be true. For instance, any Gap which is covered at an early date cannot, by its very definition, be considered a Break-away Gap, while any Gap which leads prices so far away from the previous formation as to keep the Gap from being covered for a long time, is quite naturally indicative of a long move to follow. This is a real objection to our definition of these two types of Gaps, but not necessarily an objection that completely destroys the uses of Gaps in forecasting.

As a matter of fact, it is always difficult and frequently impossible to be certain whether a Gap is of the Common or Break-away variety at the instant that the Gap appears. This is the principal reason why we cannot place too much credence in the various Gap theories and why we must consider Gaps as of only secondary importance in forecasting.

The fact remains that most Gaps which lead decisively out of an established pattern are not closed; they become and remain true Break-away Gaps. And the wider the Gap at a break-out, the less likely it is to be closed.

The Practical Uses of the Break-away Gap

It is apparent, of course, that any Gap which appears when prices break out of a technical formation, makes that break-out all the more conspicuous. The Gap helps to draw our attention to the price action on the chart, so it performs one useful service in this respect no matter how limited its other functions may be.

Further, the formation of the Gap at such a point is prima-facie evidence that a drastic change has taken place in the technical position of the stock. It is logical to assume, therefore, that the ensuing movement will be more rapid, at the start at least, than a movement following an ordinary break-out without a Gap, and this inference is, in fact, borne out in a majority of cases. A further inference that the movement following the Break-away Gap will be more extensive or important because of the sudden change in the technical position, is difficult to prove in practical chart analysis, but there are, as a rule, other factors more helpful and more important technically to guide us in this respect. The size and character of the pattern which forms the foundation of the movement, for example, and the prospective levels where resistance may later be encountered (which we shall take up later in Study IX), are of far greater importance in forecasting than the Break-away Gap alone.

> *The Break-away Gap emphasizes the break-out of prices.*

In brief, the Break-away Gap emphasizes the break-out of prices and indicates a sudden change in the technical picture, but the mere fact that prices have broken decisively out of a technical formation is of greater importance than the Gap. When the evidence of the Gap is added to all the other evidences of a decisive break-out, we are encouraged to act promptly and decisively.

Continuation and Exhaustion Gaps

We have discussed the Common Gap which is a quickly "closed" Gap appearing within a formation or general area of price congestion, and the Break-away Gap which appears at the break of prices out of a formation and is not closed for a long time. There remain two other varieties of Gaps which are hardly likely to be confused with the first two, but may be difficult to distinguish from each other at the time they appear. These are the Continuation and Exhaustion Gaps.

The chart of Woolworth for the latter half of 1936, Fig. VII.14, will help to make clear the appearance of Continuation and Exhaustion Gaps, and contains a number of points which will warrant careful study. Incidentally, it will be of interest to compare this chart with the Woolworth chart for the six months immediately preceding

Fig. VII.14

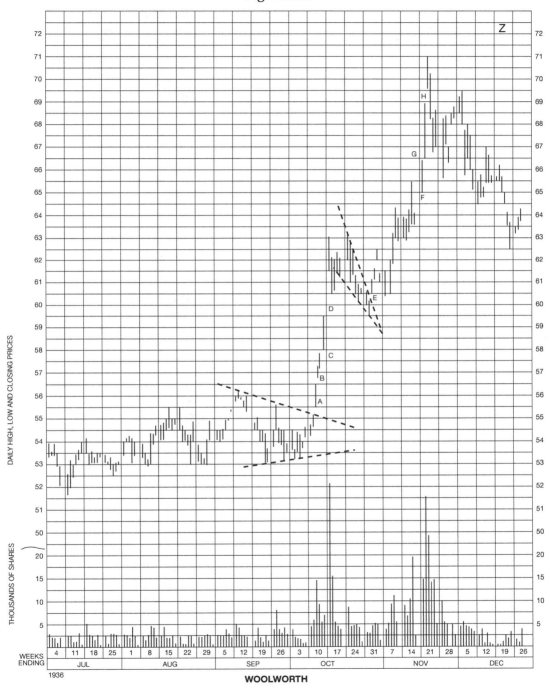

WOOLWORTH

in Fig. II.5 and to note the strong upward drive to 71 which followed the formation of the Head and Shoulders Bottom.

Starting with the second week in October, the Gap in Woolworth marked A must obviously be classified as a Break-away Gap, emphasizing the strong technical position which this stock had developed. This was followed in quick succession by Gaps at B, C and D. Note that these Gaps formed after the price had already moved well away from the preceding congestion, and in the course of a continuous rapid move. They certainly could not be classified as Break-away Gaps, and we should have no reason to suspect, having in mind the previous foundation, that they would be quickly closed and become part of another area pattern. B and C are typical Continuation Gaps, indicating the continuation of the current move at a rapid pace. D presented a somewhat different picture from B and C when it first appeared. We shall return to a more detailed analysis of this Gap at D later but will pass on now to Gaps E, F and G.

Relation of Continuation to Break-away Gaps

The Gap at E, like that at A, is clearly a Break-away Gap occurring as prices broke out of the Pennant formation. The Gap at F is probably also best classified as a Break-away Gap although a break-out from the small congestion resembling an Ascending Triangle had already been signaled on November 13. We may, if we choose, call the price movement on November 13 a One-day Out-of-line, and call the movement on the 16th the real break-out. This, however, is not important. A Continuation Gap may, in fact, be considered as only a specialized form of the Break-away Gap, or vice-versa, since both indicate the rapid continuation of a movement. One occurs at the beginning of the movement and the other after it has started, and neither is covered for some time. The Gap at F in our Woolworth chart may, therefore, be also classified as a Continuation Gap, and such it surely is if we disregard the hesitation in the 63–64 price zone and view our Gap in relation only to the advance from 60 to 71.

The Gap at G is again clearly a Continuation Gap, but at H we have a much wider Gap followed by a reversal day, accompanied by very high volume, and the end of the advance. The Gap at H was an Exhaustion Gap, signalling the last spurt of activity which "exhausts" a movement and foretokens an early correction or intermediate reversal.

Characteristics of the Exhaustion Gap

The Exhaustion Gap is the fourth and last of our important types of Gaps. It is the logical complement of the Gap series. The Common Gap indicates only minor changes, generally within a congestion area; the Break-away denotes the beginning of a strong trend; the Continuation Gap promises the rapid continuation of such a trend; and the Exhaustion Gap suggests the completion of the movement and an early reversal.

It will be seen that the Exhaustion and Continuation Gaps can easily be confused. There is no criterion by which we can positively identify a Gap appearing in a rapid movement as of either the Continuation or Exhaustion variety on the day it shows up on the chart. There are, however, a number of fairly reliable clues which enable us to arrive at a correct appraisal in a majority of cases. First, the Exhaustion Gap appears after an extensive move, a move which has carried out, as nearly as we can judge, all of the forecast of the formation from which it sprung. It occurs usually at the end of a very rapid mark-up or mark-down and is seldom the first Gap in such a movement. The rapid advances or declines which lead to the extreme over-bought or over-sold conditions that produce Exhaustion Gaps, contain as a rule (although not always) one or more other Gaps which are obviously of the Continuation class.

Exhaustion Gaps Made on High Volume

Second, an Exhaustion Gap is almost invariably made by a day of conspicuously high activity. Note the volume on November 17 in the Woolworth chart. In other words, the Exhaustion Gap, representing the climax of a rapid movement, is accompanied by the extremely high volume which we expect to denote climaxes or sudden reversals. Third, the price action on the day following the Gap usually, although not always, shows a One-day Reversal. And, fourth, the price action on the following day or two generally leaves us in no further doubt because the Exhaustion Gap is quickly closed. Finally, the Exhaustion Gap is more often than not wider than Gaps of the Continuation variety.

With these points in mind, let us go back on the Woolworth chart to the series of Gaps at A, B, C and D. The Gap at A, as we have already seen, is quickly identified as a Break-Away. That at B is a Continuation, the only respect in which it departs from what we might consider the ideal for that type being the closing of prices at the bottom of the following day's range (October 8). We should note, however, that this Gap did not occur after a movement commensurate with the preceding pattern and break-out action; also that the volume on October 8 was appreciably less than on the 7th.

An Exhaustion Gap of Only Temporary Effect

The Gap at C is unquestionably a Continuation; the volume on October 10 was high but not extreme and the closing price was at the top of the day's range. D, however, certainly presents a different picture. To begin with it is, for this stock, an extraordinarily wide Gap – two full points – following a very rapid advance of considerable extent. Even more noteworthy is the climactic volume on October 13 and the One-Day Reversal produced by the price action on that day. The Gap at D had all of the "earmarks" of Exhaustion and, perhaps, the only consideration which would have caused us to reserve judgment at this time was the recognition of the extremely important foundation for an extensive upward movement that had been laid during the previous several months.

Nevertheless, the Gap at D did signal a temporary exhaustion of buying power, as quickly became apparent, and the formation of another pattern was required to gather strength, so to speak, for a continuation of the upward trend. This pattern took the form of a Pennant which as we have seen in Study VI, is one of our most dependable continuation formations. The intervention of this strong pattern, plus the fact that it was completed before the preceding Gap was entirely closed, gave ample evidence that the movement was not by any means finished. The Gap at D was, therefore, an Exhaustion Gap of only temporary significance.

The Exhaustion Gap Not Common

The Exhaustion Gap is the least frequently encountered of the four general Gap types, and not all Exhaustion Gaps are as clearly and fully marked by all the usual clues as were those we have analyzed in the Woolworth chart. Another example which may be studied appears in Fig. VI.8. The Gap between August 16 and 17 was an Exhaustion Gap but not clearly indicated as such until closed by the following day's price action. Note, however, the climactic volume on the 17th, following the rule of doubling a Saturday's volume. Note also the Continuation Gap the week before.

The Gap between March 7 and 9 on the Electric Auto-Lite chart (Fig. VI.12) also proved to be an Exhaustion Gap but was not recognizable as such at the time it formed. The volume on March 9 was certainly of climactic proportions but it must be admitted that all the other signals were lacking and that this Gap appeared at first to be a Break-away Gap. Fortunately, such extremely deceptive cases are rare.

Reviewing the Island Formation

It will be of advantage at this point in our study of Gap manifestations, to turn back and review the discussion of the Island Reversal starting on page 168 in Study V. The explanation of the strong reversal implications of the Island was based, it will be recalled, on the rare conjunction of an Exhaustion Gap with a Break-Away Gap, the first indicating an over-running of the previous technical trend and the second a strong movement in a new trend. The first Gap is not always clearly signaled as an

Exhaustion, particularly where the Island takes several days to form, but the second or Break-away removes any doubts. In the case of One-Day Islands, the clues to Exhaustion are usually quite evident. Note, for example, the price action and climactic volume on the formation of the One-Day Islands in the Electric Bond and Share chart (Fig. V.14). Remember to double the volume shown on the chart for Saturday, August 17.

Gaps Forming Continuation Islands

In our study of Island Reversals, brief mention was made of another type of Island pattern formed by Gaps occurring one above and the other below the price congestion, instead of both Gaps forming at the same price level. Such a Continuation Island appears in the 1936 chart of US Industrial Alcohol (Fig. VII.15) being formed during the first part of May. The Gaps C and D make an Island of the Rectangular price congestion between the 49 and 45 levels. We may classify D as a Break-away Gap but, logically, both C and D are Continuation Gaps since, if all the price movement between 49 and 45 occupied only a single day's time, we should have only the normal Continuation Gap picture. Another Continuation Gap appeared at E, and F was an Exhaustion Gap followed by a pattern containing a number of Common Gaps and a reversal of the previous downward trend. The volume on June 11 was not conspicuous except as compared with the preceding week's activity but a definite clue to the classification of this Gap (F), and to the change in the technical position, was given by the failure of prices on June 12 to decline to compensate for the amount of the dividend which the stock went "ex" on that day.

An Abnormal Island Reversal

Another very interesting formation appeared in this Industrial Alcohol chart in early April, following the Gap at A. If we could have disregarded the price action on April 7 which came down just far enough to close the A Gap, the second Gap at B would have given us all the qualifications for an Island Reversal. The closing of the first Gap destroyed this interpretation by strict application of the rules, yet the subsequent price action certainly carried out the Island Reversal forecast. It is, perhaps, only fair at this more advanced stage of our studies to state that such an action is not unique by any means, and that a "broken" pattern of this sort does frequently "work", especially when the first Gap carries the earmarks of Exhaustion. Note the climactic volume on April 2. The measuring implications of the preceding Flag formation, which will be taken up in Study X, gave us another clue in this case.

Another type of formation appears occasionally which does not qualify strictly as an Island Reversal pattern because the Gaps do not form at the same level, yet which

Fig. VII.15

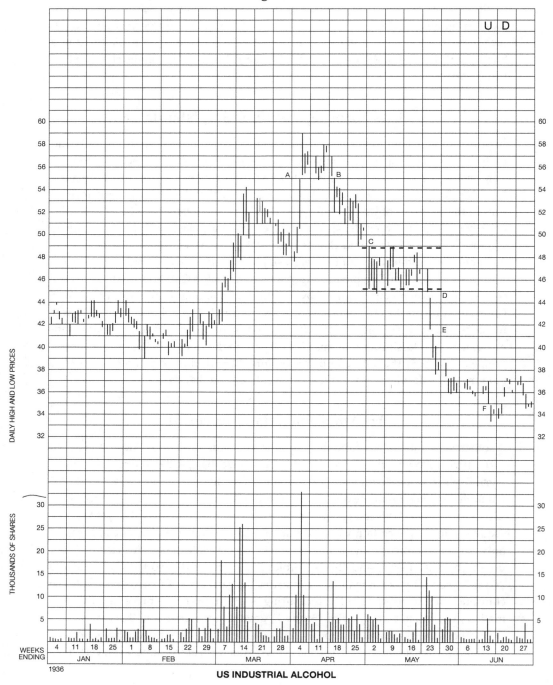

US INDUSTRIAL ALCOHOL

has otherwise all the appearance of an Island. The July bottom in Bethlehem Steel shown on the chart in (Fig. IV.4) is an extreme example of such a formation. Others appear in the C&O chart (Fig. IV.11) in November, and in the Pullman chart (Fig. IV.13) in early December. These pseudo-Islands frequently "work" to a limited extent but the beginner had better not attempt to trade on them unless other more certain technical considerations lend them confirmation, and certainly never without close "stop loss" protection. Some indication of the probable extent of the ensuing move may be deduced from the relative levels at which the two Gaps form. This point may be quickly studied if the student will draw a line across the chart through the two Gaps in each of the examples cited and compare its slant with the following price movement. Again, however, we must put in a word of caution against too great a dependence on Islands which do not conform strictly to rule.

Limited Forecast of Islands Within Patterns

Another type of Island formation which the novice is often inclined to take too seriously is a small Island developed after a very short preceding price movement, frequently within the bounds of a large pattern. Such Islands have an extremely limited forecast, roughly approximating the extent of the movement which led to them. This limitation applies as well, of course, in the majority of cases to the typical Island Reversals formed outside of previously established pattern levels, but in those cases the ensuing movement is naturally of more profitable extent.

Examples of small Islands formed within congestion zones appear in the Woolworth chart, Fig. VII.14. The student, is, quite possibly, tired of looking at this chart but we shall beg his indulgence and ask him to refer to it once more in this connection. The Gaps between the 4th and 5th and the 12th and 14th of September, with the intervening price action, built an Island which reversed a minor rally and carried prices back to the approximate level from which the rally started. Quick action on this Island would have yielded at most a gross profit of less than two points, hardly worth the risk and expense involved. Another example appeared in the action between October 29 and 31; the decline of a point on the next day carried out the full forecast to be expected from this One-Day Island. Still another Island appeared in the last week of November; it should be noted that the subsequent decline was more logically predicated on the reversal signal already given by the exhaustion of the rapid advance to 71, than on this Island which could be taken only as reversing the rally of about two points immediately preceding.

Gaps Which Defy Classification

Although the majority of Gaps which appear in the charts of active stocks may be assigned, some at once and some after the lapse of only a few days, to one of the four classes which we have analyzed in this study, there will be many Gaps which do not comply with the rules and cannot be surely classified. Seldom if ever, however, do such unidentifiable Gaps upset the general picture or lead to an incorrect interpretation. Any Gap forecast must, as we have seen, be based on its relation to the whole chart picture which precedes its formation. A Gap which has no apparent connection with, or basis in, the previous price action should be regarded with suspicion only, and may be disregarded entirely as a forecasting factor (except as a possible support or resistance point for which see Study IX later) if the subsequent price action does not seem to give it any importance.

Gaps on Ex-dividend and Ex-rights Days

Mention was made in Study I (page 19) of the advisability of noting Ex-dividend days on the charts. Theoretically, prices should decline by the amount of the dividend on the first day that the stock sells on the Exchange without carrying the right to receive a dividend previously declared. These days when the dividend "goes off", or the stock goes "ex", are always indicated in the newspapers which publish complete financial reports by their adding the symbol "x d" or some other recognized notation after the name of the issue.

If the stock goes ex-dividend by an amount of, say, $2.00, the price range on the "x d" day should, theoretically, fall two points below the range for the preceding day on the chart. We should expect a Gap to appear in that case between the "x d" day and the day before; especially if the stock is fluctuating at the time in a narrow range. It is obvious that a Gap commensurate with the amount of the dividend, on such an occasion, has no technical significance. If, however, the gap exceeds by an appreciable margin the amount of the dividend it does have a limited significance depending on that margin. If the chartist has difficulty in visualizing the effect of ex-dividend action, he can make it plain on his chart by extending the price range on the "x d" day upward by the amount of the dividend, using a dotted or a colored line. This device helps in appraising the Gap action, if any.

Disregard Break-outs Caused by Ex-dividends

In practical charting, technical patterns are seldom thrown out of line by a stock's going "ex" a small dividend payment. Large regular dividends and year-end specials of unusual amount may occasionally "go off" when a stock is fluctuating within a narrow pattern and the resulting ex-dividend drop or correction may, in those cases, produce an apparent break-out or, at least, a movement which spoils the pattern. Break-outs which are obviously the result of only a normal ex-dividend correction should, of course, be disregarded, and the subsequent price action watched to determine the true technical trend.

The same considerations apply to the interpretation of Gaps and price action occasioned by a stock's going "ex-rights", except that the value of the rights is frequently difficult to appraise with exactitude.

Summary of the Gap Study

Briefly summarized, we have learned that the Common Gap is the least significant of the four recognizable types, forecasting at best only a return at an early date to the normal price range. The Break-away type also has little significance beyond its emphasis of a break-out from a technical pattern, and its suggestion of a rapid movement to follow. The Continuation Gap, like the Break-away, is useful chiefly as emphasizing the strength and rapidity of the price movement. In which it develops. The most important of the four types is the Exhaustion Gap which, it may be hoped, we shall be able to recognize in the majority of cases, not only by the extent of the preceding movement but also by the usual accompaniment of high volume and the immediately ensuing reversal indications.

In general, we have learned that Gaps must be analyzed with respect to the whole preceding and accompanying chart picture. They should be regarded, at best, as of secondary or confirmatory value.

Finally, they, like other technical phenomena and patterns, are not infallible. Gaps, in particular, may be indefinite and misleading if an attempt is made at too hasty analysis. Nevertheless, when viewed as minor indicators in conjunction with the rest of the chart picture, they offer decided assistance in weighing all the technical factors and arriving at a reasonable forecast of the future trend.

Gap Implications to be Studied Later

We have referred in passing to the support or resistance uses of Gaps which will be taken up later in our general consideration of support and resistance levels in Study IX. There is one other application of the phenomenon of Gap action to the forecasting of price movement which will also be deferred to a later study. Certain theories as to the measurement of the extent of price movements based on Gaps have been advanced and are of considerable interest if not entirely dependable. These theories will be fully discussed under the general subject of measuring formulas in Study X.

Before leaving the present discussion of Gaps, it should be added that some chartists apply the various rules to occasions where no true Gap appears but where the price ranges on two successive days simply fail to overlap, or where there is an appreciable Gap between the closing price, considered by itself, of one day and the next day's price range. There is some logic for this, particularly in the latter case, but it stands to reason that true Gaps, representing a greater and more plainly evident departure from the normal, must carry greater weight in technical analysis. Where the Gap action is not definite the usual Gap implications must be at least proportionately discounted.

Study VIII

TREND LINE ACTION

We have completed in the preceding Studies our detailed examination of the various individual chart formations and phenomena which occur at intervals within trends or at trend reversals. We are ready now to take up the broader aspects of price trend and volume action. These subjects are, perhaps, less definite than our basic forecasting patterns but they are none the less important, especially in the appraisal of major cycles and major reversals. They lead to long-term vistas of the stock market, but we shall see that this long-term point of view can be helpful constantly in our trading operations on the immediate movements. The correlation of the broader trend implications with the basic individual formations gives us a more complete grasp of technical price action.

The Trend Line – Working Definition

The first of our general subjects for study is the trend line, a subject which is probably already somewhat familiar to the student since it was undoubtedly the first of the technical manifestations of the market to be discovered, and much has already been written about it. The fact that stocks, individually and as a whole, move in fairly definite trends has long been recognized and studied by economists as well as practical traders. The Dow Theory, which we shall discuss later, is based on general trend action. The striking uniformity and definition of the major trends is one of the first points noted in a superficial study of long-term charts, both of individual issues and of the averages.

A trend line is a straight line drawn on the chart through or across the significant limits of any price range to define the trend of market movement.

Trend lines may be of practically any length, defining a major, intermediate or minor trend or the boundary of an area formation. The longer they extend the more valuable and important they become in technical forecasting. They are usually drawn across two or more tops or bottoms, but they are permissibly drawn slightly inside the extremes of a few individual ranges if such construction extends them through a greater number of tops or bottoms, as the case may be, in the general trend. This slight deviation from the strict construction across extremities is permitted because it is also true that the greater the number of extremes touched by the trend line, the more dependable is that line.

Examples of Long-term Trend Lines

It will help us in arriving at a clearer and more complete definition of the trend line, and how it is drawn, if we pause here to examine two samples of trend line action in long-term charts. The monthly price range of the Dow-Jones Industrial Stocks Average from 1924 through 1936 is shown in Fig. VIII.1. The monthly chart of Bethlehem Steel for the same period is reproduced in Fig. VIII.2. The solid diagonal lines drawn on these charts are major trend lines; the dotted lines are secondary or subsidiary trend lines which will be discussed later.

Undoubtedly, the most impressive feature in each of these monthly charts is the extraordinary accuracy with which the trend line of the 1929–1932 bear market (in each case, E-F) defines the upper limits of every intermediate rally within this major trend. Before we comment further on these pictures, however, one point should be noted. The primary trend lines are drawn across tops in downward trends, and across bottoms in upward trends. The reason for this is that experience has shown such lines to be more important and more accurate than the lines bounding the other sides of the trends. This rule may also be stated by saying that primary trend lines are drawn along the right-hand limits of diagonal price trends.

> *The greater number of extremes touched by the trend line, the more dependable is that line.*

The Theory of Trend Lines

The usefulness of trend lines depends on our basic theorem that a technical position, or price movement, once established, will be continued until something happens to change the technical situation. This, at first glance, may seem to offer little comfort, for we know that a technical situation may change at any time. However, stocks do move in trends, definitely, as a cursory glance at almost any chart will clearly show. The more powerful the causes that produce a price movement, as evidenced by the chart pictures, the more clearly defined the trend will be and the longer continued and more profitable to the trader. Once a trend becomes fairly delineated the odds strongly favor continuation.

In a general sense, therefore, trend lines are most serviceable in calling the chart student's attention to the main price trend. They are of little use during the process of any area formation with little continued progress either up or down, but attain their greatest importance when prices are pursuing a fairly regular upward or downward movement. The most profitable trend lines, therefore, are those drawn at an angle or, in other words, diagonally across the chart.

Practical Uses of Trend Lines

More specifically, trend lines are of great practical value in determining the proba-

Fig. VIII.1

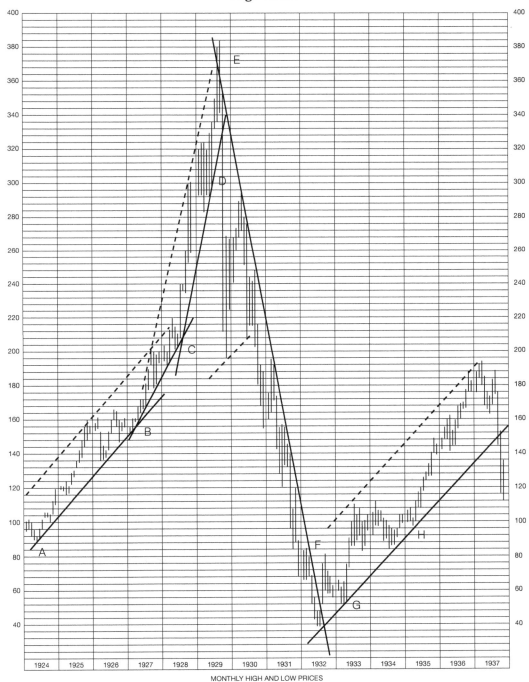

MONTHLY HIGH AND LOW PRICES
DOW JONES INDUSTRIAL AVERAGE

Fig. VIII.2

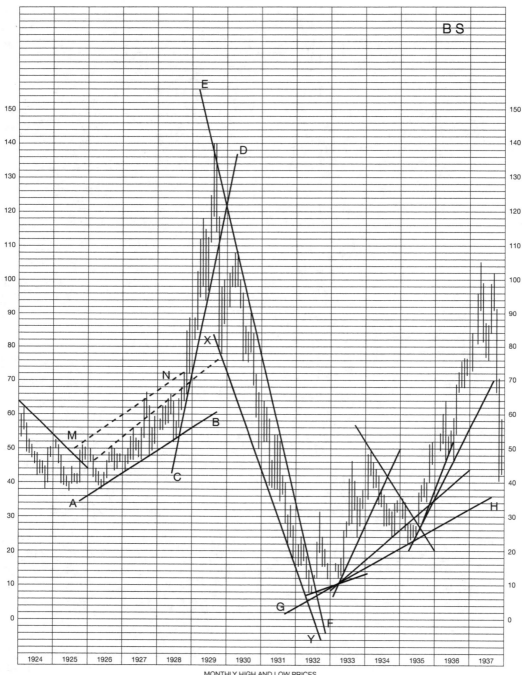

MONTHLY HIGH AND LOW PRICES

BETHLEHEM STEEL

ble limits of intermediate declines and recoveries within established major trends, or of minor rallies and reactions within established major trend, no matter how definite, will almost always be subject to intermediate reversals but, so long as no major reversal appears, the price movement tends to come back to the previously established trend. And the same holds true for minor fluctuations within the intermediate trends. By outlining these trends, the trend lines give us our theoretical limits of price swing, and aid us in forecasting the probable extreme objective of the next reversal within any given trend.

Trend lines are also of great service, in the opposite or negative sense, when they are broken. Trend lines must of necessity be broken some time since the stock market never pursues a single direction forever. They are broken as soon as there is an important reversal in technical movement, and they become valuable then in calling our attention to such reversals while they are still in their incipient stage. We need not curse trend lines, therefore, when they are broken, especially if they have already proven long, dependable and profitable. Rather we should bless them for having been thus profitable and for now notifying us that a change is probable.

So trend lines serve a double purpose. While they last they define the line of continuation in a movement, and when they are broken they serve notice of a probable reversal and advise us to forget the old lines and start searching for new ones to define the new trend.

Trial and Error Method in Establishing Lines

Trend lines are not, in themselves, a rose-strewn path to definite market forecast and profit, however. They are fallible, just as are all the other chart phenomena we have studied. And dependable trend lines are not always easy and quick to define. The determination and use of trends is to a considerable extent a matter of good sense, familiarity and experience. Moreover, the drawing, or placing, of trend lines is open to considerable trial and error even on the part of the experienced professional.

No one can take a chart, immediately draw trend lines on it and be certain that they are the proper, or even the best, trend lines that could have been inserted for continuation of the current movement. That is just as impossible as is the absolutely certain forecast of definite future prices by any finite individual.

On the contrary, the more experienced the chart student, the more humble will he be in his current or previous view, the more ready and willing will he be to desert his previously drawn trend lines and try another line, or another set of lines, if action of the price chart indicates the wisdom of such revision.

Proper Angles for Trend Lines

In particular, there is much room for alteration of angles in a trend line. What looks at first like a major movement may start out very sharply and steeply. The analyst is quite justified in drawing the proper trend lines to define that original angle of movement, but the experienced analyst will keep his mental reservation that the angle of advance or decline is much steeper than usual for this stock and that the line will probably have to be changed later on.

He will therefore know what degree of faith to place in the trend lines which are called for by the movement thus far. If subsequent movements reduce the angle of his first too-steep trend line, he will be more thankful than annoyed, for the more natural angle gives greater promise of reliability and permanence.

On the other hand, the experienced analyst will know about how small an angle it is safe to have in his particular stock without suggesting actual reversal. If the previous steep movement is leveled off a few times he draws his new trend lines gladly. But if subsequent movements reduce the angle of the previous trend so far below the usual or normal angle of trend, then he will begin to grow suspicious of that previous trend, and begin looking for signs of an important reversal in the opposite trend.

Practicing on the Chart

We may put to test the theoretical discussion of trend line drawing in the preceding paragraphs, and gain a more practical idea of trend action, by analyzing Fig. VIII.3. This chart shows the price and volume action of Baltimore and Ohio during the last six months of 1935.

On July 22, following a formation which does not show in its entirety on this chart, there was a break-out indicating a strong advance in this stock. The first minor setback after this break-out gave us our first two points (the bottoms on July 22 and 26) across which to draw a trend line – the line indicated by A. This line, however, was obviously too steep to last; it was broken on August 8 after which we had a new and better line – B. This second trend was broken on August 27; the volume action on this minor reaction (which will be discussed later on in this Study) indicated that the up-trend had not yet been reversed. A third trend line – C – was now established, which was not broken until September 20. The subsequent decline was reversed on October 3; in the meantime, however, we had a down-trend line – D – established across the tops on September 19 and September 30. Note that this line is drawn across the outer peak on the 19th and not from the top of the movement on the 11th; the down-trend did not start until the 19th.

Fig. VIII.3

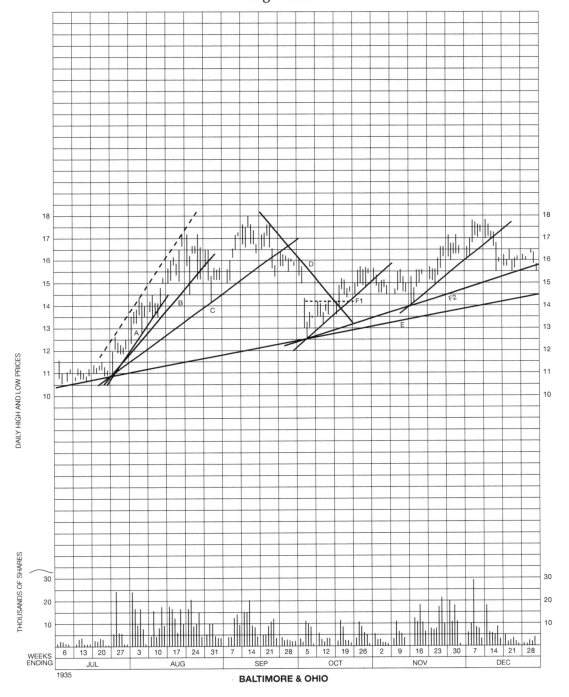

BALTIMORE & OHIO

A Tentative Long-term Line Appears

Following the reversal day on October 3, the price action built the semblance of an Ascending Triangle with a break-out on the up-side on October 15 (note volume action during this interval). We were now able to draw a trend line – E – across the July and October bottoms. The slope of this line indicated that it might well define an important and long-continued upward movement. Note that the down-trend line D was broken by the same price action which signaled the break-out from the Ascending Triangle on October 15.

This reversal in trend gave us again, in F-1, a first minor up-trend line which was too steep to hold, but the second minor trend line, F-2, held to the end of this chart.

Before we leave this six-months chart to follow the subsequent action shown in the next Figure, the student is requested to note for future reference the fact that the first minor advance in August was not reversed until a third minor up-trend line (C) had been drawn, and this third line was broken (on September 20) when the minor trend had reversed. Note also that once the trend lines B and C were broken, the ensuing rallies were unable to get back through them. This particular phenomenon will be discussed under the subject of resistance in Study IX.

Following Through the Next Six Months

Look now to Fig. VIII.4 where the next six months of price and volume action in Baltimore and Ohio have been added to the six months we have just examined, giving us now a full year's chart of this stock from July 1, 1935 to June 27, 1936. On this chart we have dropped the lines A, B, C, D, and F-1 which are no longer of any use to us, but have continued the significant lines F-2 and E.

The first thing we notice is the continuation of the trend above the line F-2 for nearly seven months. This line, which we drew across the bottoms on October 2 and November 12, was barely pierced on December 28 but the closing on that day was back above it. It was "ticked", or at least very closely approached, many times – on December 19, January 21, March 13, 23 and 30. It was not definitely broken by a decisive margin until April 21.

Patterns Appearing Within Trends

Here we may well interrupt our discussion of trend lines to consider for a moment the other more familiar chart patterns which the student has doubtless already noticed.

No clearly defined technical price formation appeared in the course of the F-2

Fig. VIII.4

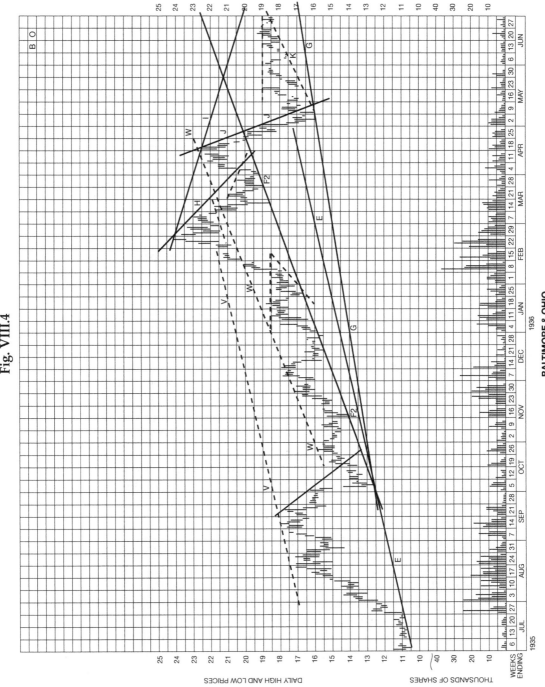

BALTIMORE & OHIO

trend until the end of January when a fair Ascending Triangle developed, with a break-out on February 4 accompanied by notable volume, and was followed by a fast mark-up to 24¼ on February 21. This rally was reversed by another Triangle which broke down on March 9, and was followed by a quick decline to our trend line. Again a Triangle formed with a break-out, on the up-side this time, on April 2, which break-out also broke the minor down-trend line H. The ensuing advance was comparatively weak, however.

The Right-angle Triangle which formed with high volume accompaniment at the top in February was the largest and most significant looking formation yet to appear, and indicated a decline of greater proportions than the reaction to the F-2 line. This line was, in fact, broken late in April by a rapid drop in prices to 16, which broke also our tentative long-term line E, giving us, in the meantime, a minor down-trend line J, and a more important line I.

A New Long-term Trend Line Defined

The steep down-trend J was broken on May 5 and thereafter, with activity at a low ebb, the price action built a long and rather loose Ascending Triangle approaching an apex at the end of this chart, with its bottom boundary defined by the minor trend line K.

Connecting the bottom on April 30 with the old October bottom now gave us a new long-term trend line, G.

At this point the student is perhaps becoming a little impatient with our detailed account of the trend line phenomena in the Baltimore and Ohio chart, and wishes to get on to a more practical consideration of forecasting conclusions. With the promise, however, that there are many helpful conclusions which will be drawn when all the returns are in, let us draw a deep breath and study first another six months of B & O chart history. Figure VIII.5 shows the price and volume action for the full year of 1936, adding another six months to the last six months shown in Fig. VIII.4.

Completing the Picture in Baltimore and Ohio

The first point of interest which the student will note upon comparing this new chart with Fig. VIII.4 is the price action during the first two weeks of July. The Ascending Triangle, calling for higher prices, which was in process of formation during June, did not produce a normal break-out. Instead, prices slumped out of it near the apex and declined nearly a point and a half, almost to the new long-term trend line G. Volume, however, was conspicuously absent on this abnormal move, giving us an important clue; this was a "False Move" and a fairly typical example of this phe-

Fig. VIII.5

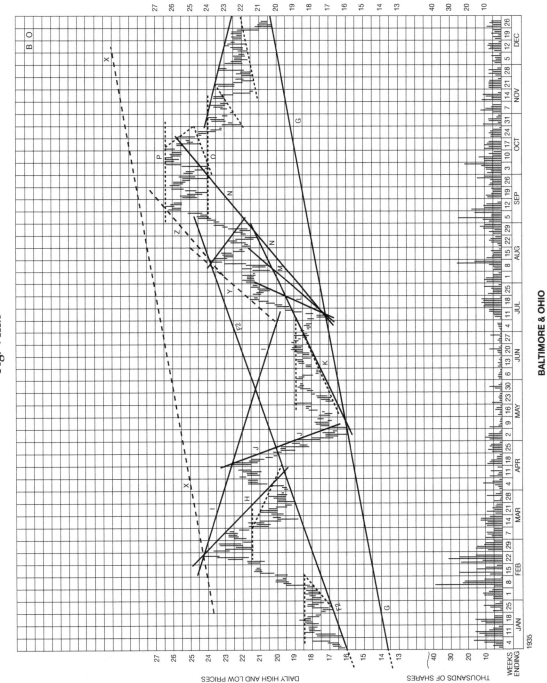

BALTIMORE & OHIO

1935

nomenon which will be discussed in detail in Study X.

Volume picked up during the second week of July and the price also advanced rapidly, carrying out the Ascending Triangle forecast. The down-trend line I was broken on July 14. Thereafter, the first minor up-trend line, L, was quickly broken; it was obviously too steep to hold. A second line, M, was broken by the reaction on August 21 and 22, which in turn gave us a third line, N. This third line was pierced on October 1 but was not decisively broken until October 15. Here again, as in August, 1935, the breaking of the third minor up-trend line signaled a reversal of trend, and again the subsequent rally failed to get back through the trend line. By the end of the year the price of B & O had fallen nearly to our last long-term trend line, G.

Figure VIII.6 carries B & O on through November, 1937. The most interesting feature on this chart is the continuation of the long-term up-trend line G, to which the price returned in June after the Spring decline of 1937, and which was finally decisively broken (with a gap) on August 26. The continuation of the decline from that point established a new major trend – a down-trend – and a new major trend line, S.

The student will notice various price patterns, besides those we have mentioned, in this series of B & O charts covering over two years, and other trend lines of an experimental, or at least very temporary nature. We have noted, however, every line which an experienced chart analyst would consider as having significance at the time it became defined.

The secondary trend lines, or parallels, drawn in dashes (see V, W, X, etc.) will be discussed later in this study.

Trading on the Simple Primary Trend Line

The reader may possibly be more disappointed in the temporary and unreliable quality of trend lines as exemplified in the Baltimore and Ohio charts than he is impressed with their advantages. Yet, purely on a basis of a fair interpretation of the trend lines, there were many opportunities for quick trades in this stock during the eighteen months we have followed its action. If we were trading only on the long side of the market, for example, we might have bought on July 24, 1935 at around $12^1/_4$ and sold on September 23, when line C had been broken, at around 16. We would have bought again on October 15 at around 15 and sold on March 9, 1936 at around 21. A third purchase was indicated on April 2 at around 21 and this trade would have been closed out at a loss at around $19^1/_2$ when the F-2 line was broken on April 20. The next purchase was indicated on July 13, when line I was penetrated and would have cost around 20; the next sale, on October 15 at around 25.

Note that three of these four trades showed a good profit and the fourth a small loss-a very satisfactory average. Note also that, in making these trades, we did not

Fig. VIII.6

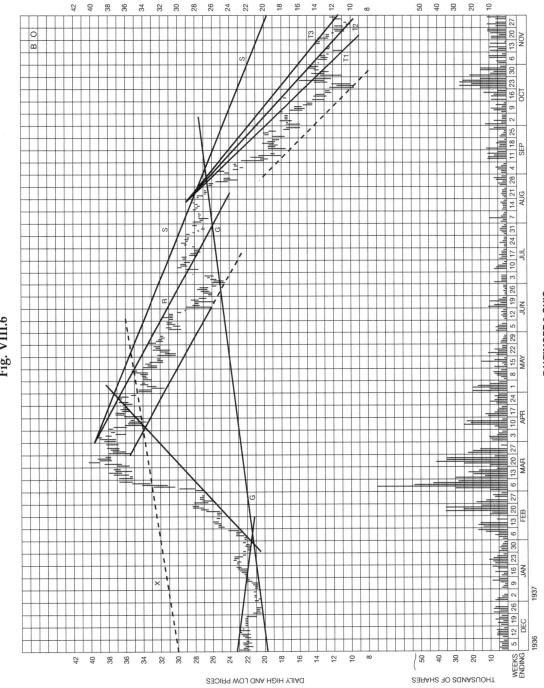

BALTIMORE & OHIO

take fully into account the strength of the implications of the Right Angle Triangle top in February-March, 1936 nor the Ascending Triangle in May-June. The former should have deterred us from making the third trade which proved unprofitable, and the latter would have put us into the fourth trade at around $18\frac{1}{2}$ instead of 20, increasing our gross profit by $1\frac{1}{2}$ points.

Thus we see that, while the single trend line is not infallible, it offers very profitable trading help, especially when it is considered in conjunction with any of our previously studied formations and other chart phenomena that may appear.

The Double Trend Line or Trend Channel

We have considered so far only the single or primary trend line. The double trend line is a set of two single trend lines bounding both the upper and lower limits of a trend. One is the primary trend line we have already examined at some length in the three Baltimore and Ohio charts; the other is a secondary line parallel to it, defining the opposite limits. The double trend lines do not have to be exactly parallel but, unless they are nearly so, they are of very little value in forecasting.

As might be expected, parallel trend lines are much less common than plain single or primary lines, but when found they are much more reliable. And when they appear in connection with long-term major movements, they provide outstanding profit opportunities. A practiced glance at almost any stock chart will tell the experienced student whether there is a chance for parallel trend lines. As in the case of single primary lines, some latitude is permissible in drawing them.

Establishing Parallel Trend Lines

Normally it takes at least three terminal range points to give us a basis for drawing tentative parallel trend lines. Two points are required, of course, to define the primary line, and the opposite limit of price movement between these points gives us the third point through which a secondary line may be drawn parallel to the primary line. The more points available through which the parallel trend lines pass, of course, the more reliable and important is the trend thus defined.

Established parallel trend lines form a trend channel within which the price action fluctuates back and forth just as a stream meanders from side to side within the limits of its valley floor. When the parallel lines define a major trend – when, in other words, the trend channel is a wide one – the trader is able to reverse his position each time the price approaches one of its trend limits and get worthwhile profits alternately from the long and short side of the market, that is by alternately buying and taking profits and then selling short and covering.

Trial and Error in Establishing Parallel Lines

For practice in finding reliable parallel trend lines we may turn back again to Fig. VIII.4. Our first opportunity to test the parallel line principle came when we drew the tentative long-term primary line E across the July and October bottoms. Drawing a line – the dotted line marked V – through the September top and parallel to E, gave us a purely tentative trend channel. Both of these lines were broken by the next intermediate movements and so had to be abandoned.

Another opportunity arose when the primary line F-2 was established. The secondary line W drawn parallel to F-2 across the top of the intervening rally in the last week of October "worked" quite well for over three months.

It should be noted that parallel trend lines cannot be considered reliable for trading purposes until they have been at least once tested and "proved" by subsequent price action. If, for example, the price of B & O on February 19 had declined from instead of

> *The more points available through which the parallel trend lines pass the more reliable the trend.*

rising through the V line, we should have been justified in believing that we had established a dependable trend channel, and might have sold the stock in the expectation of covering when it had continued in its decline to the neighborhood of line E again. It is interesting to note that the advance through V was, in fact, quickly reversed, but the line nevertheless had been violated and a new definition of the major trend was required for conservative trading operations.

Playing the Major Trend

In the meantime, however, the parallel lines F-2 and W had formed a good trend channel, but a relatively narrow one. We may use this as an illustration of an important corollary to the general principle of trading on parallel trend lines. That corollary is that it is much safer and much more profitable to play the intermediate movements that run in the direction of the basic major trend, rather than the minor corrections that run counter to it.

This same principle is also expressed in the old trader's axiom, "In a bull market use the dips for buying; in a bear market sell on the rallies". The point is that the minor movements which run in the direction opposite to the general trend do not carry as far in terms of points or dollars as those which run with the trend. The application of this principle in trading practice depends, of course, on the narrowness of the channel and the degree of slope of the trend. If the trend slants sharply, either up or down, and the channel is narrow, the counter-trend or "correctional" movements will offer little or no scope for profit. If, on the other hand, the channel is wide and the trend slopes very gently, the counter-trend movements will run farther in terms of points and may be turned to profit.

Relative Profits With and Against Major Trend

This point was brought up by our reference to the W-F-2 trend in the B & O chart, but it is more clearly illustrated by the Industrial Rayon chart Fig. VIII.7. After the "April drop" in this stock in 1936, a bottom was made on June 6, and a top by the ensuing rally on June 17. The next bottom gave us a trend line extending into the six months pictured on our present illustration and indicated by A-1. The secondary parallel line, A-2, was cut by the advance in September but, in the meantime, another trend had been established, indicated by the lines B-1 and B-2.

Purchase of Industrial Rayon had been indicated early in June. Sale was indicated by the application of the trend channel theory when the price approached the A-2 line on August 18, and re-purchase when the A-1 line was touched on August 21. Now in the steeper B trend, however, note how little profit there would have been in selling after the successive advances to the top of the trend channel; a sale, for example, was indicated on October 6 at around 38 but the subsequent decline extended only to 37, leaving practically no margin for profit on the "short side". Obviously, the trader who bought Industrial Rayon in June was better off if he stayed "long" of the stock through all of its minor fluctuations within the upward trend until the line B-1 was broken (with a typical Break-away Gap) on November 23.

Incidentally, the student will note that the lines B-1 and B-2 are not exactly parallel. However, they are nearly so, near enough to comply with the requirements made for a valid trend channel, and they are perfectly defined by those tops and bottoms from which they originate.

Trend Lines Help to "Let Profits Run"

Such narrow and steep trend channels as the one we have just examined in Industrial Rayon serve, therefore, a very useful purpose in keeping us "long" if the trend be up, or "short" if the trend be down, until the intermediate trend is actually reversed. The same purpose is, in fact, frequently served by single or primary trend lines in those cases where it does not seem possible to establish a definite secondary line or trend channel. Note, in this connection the trend line action on the Sears Roebuck chart for the last half of 1936, as pictured in Fig. VIII.8. The use of the single trend line would certainly, in this case, have prevented us from taking profits prematurely, had we owned the stock in July.

Fig. VIII.7

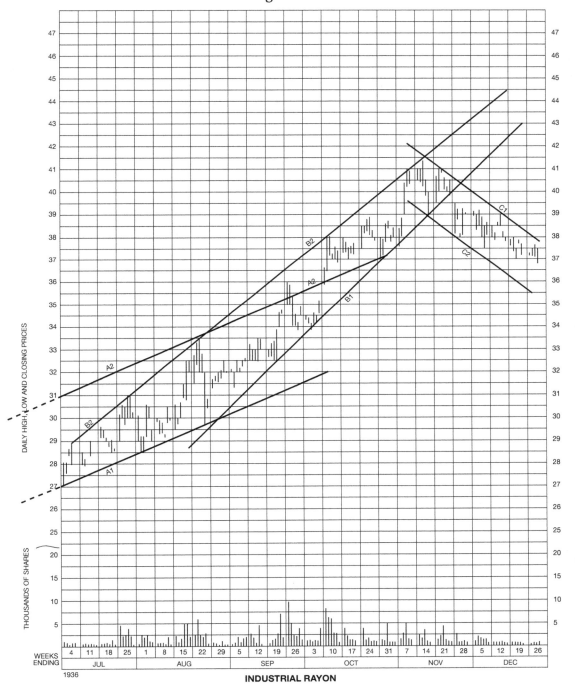

INDUSTRIAL RAYON

Fig. VIII.8

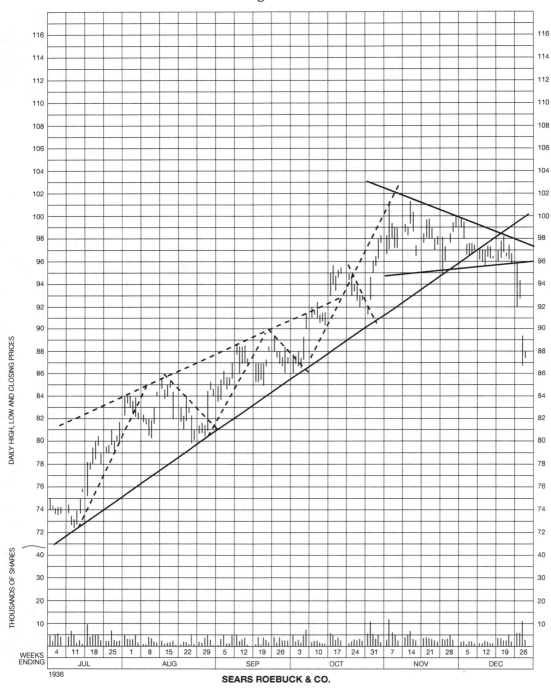

SEARS ROEBUCK & CO.

This point leads us into the consideration of a general principle of trading tactics, the principle of cutting losses and letting profits run. The experienced trader knows how important this is. The value of it may be less obvious to the beginner. We shall discuss this principle later under the general subject of market tactics; in the meantime, suffice it to say that one of the most common mistakes made by the "green" trader is to let his losses run while he cuts his profits by grabbing a few points too quickly.

In the matter of preventing premature commitments, trend lines are of even greater use to the long-term trader or investor on the major cycles. Note, for example how the major down-trend line E-F on the Bethlehem Steel chart shown in Fig. VIII.2. would have warned against the purchase of this stock for a long-term position until the line was decisively broken in August, 1932.

Trend Lines Often Give Early Reversal Signals

Another useful service frequently performed by trend lines is the forecasting of a reversal, before the reversal signal is given by the completion of one of the technical formations we have taken up in our earlier studies. This also is illustrated by the Sears Roebuck chart (Fig. VIII.8). Note that the trend line suggested a reversal the second week of December, permitting a sale in the 97–98 zone, whereas the Symmetrical Triangle which was in process of formation at the same time did not break out until December 21 by which time the price had dropped to 92.

The Baltimore and Ohio chart (Fig. VIII.5) shows a similar situation in October 1936, when the trend line N was broken on October 15, while the large Rectangle formation did not break out on the down side until October 22, a point and a half lower down in price.

In other cases, a technical formation of sufficient size and strength to indicate an important reversal may be completed and give us our trading signal before the trend line is broken. A case in point is the Symmetrical Triangle top in February-March, 1936, on the B & O chart.

Horizontal Trading Areas

In our discussion so far of parallel trend lines or trend channels we have given all of our attention to diagonal trends, slanting up or down. And we have seen that the sharper the slope of the trend, the farther it departs from the horizontal, the less profitable it is to trade both ways of the market within the trend channel. At the opposite extreme we find occasionally well defined trend channels which are practically horizontal. If these channels are broad, affording several points of swing between the top and bottom lines, they give profitable opportunities for taking alternate long and short positions in the market. When these channels are narrow, the opportunities are still there but the profits are more limited and greater agility is required of the trader to capture them.

An example of a horizontal trend channel is shown in the chart of American Radiator and Standard Sanitary for the last half of 1936, Fig. VIII.9. This channel is only about two points wide; nevertheless, the student will see that it had potentialities for profit for the nimble trader who grasped its implications promptly. The close relation between this picture and our old friend the Rectangle is, of course, easy to see. The volume action within these parallel trends, however, does not as a rule show the gradual but noticeable decline which we expect to accompany the formation of a Rectangle. The resemblance to the Rectangle does not show up so plainly in the wider and "looser" horizontal trend channels. Note, for example, the US Smelting chart, Fig. VIII.9

The Trend Line as a Reversal Indicator

We have made frequent reference in this study of trend lines to the forecasting significance of any price action which "breaks" them. When a trend line is first broken, the question always arises as to whether or not a reversal of trend has been signaled. Before we proceed to a thorough discussion of this admittedly troublesome question, let us first consider what may be called a significant break.

To begin with it is obvious that the longer the line on our chart the greater the chance of a slight error in the angle at which we draw it. The farther we extend the line from the points which originally determined it, the more exaggerated becomes any slight departure from the true trend. Consequently, the longer our line has run from its origin the more critical we must be of any price action which apparently breaks the line, and the more conservative in taking action on it. A point or two is not important in appraising the price action of a stock in its long-term cyclical trends, nor is a fraction of a point a decisive movement in several weeks of intermediate trend action. With this basic principle ever in mind, of allowing for probability of error and for natural variations of no technical significance, we may turn our attention to certain more specific rules.

What Constitutes a Significant Break

In general, we should follow the same rules in appraising the significance of a price break through a trend line that we apply to a break-out from one of our familiar pattern formations. In other words, we must take into consideration the extent of the price movement, the closing price on the day the line is penetrated, and finally the volume, although volume, as we shall see, is not a necessary accompaniment to a decisive break in a trend line.

Fig. VIII.9

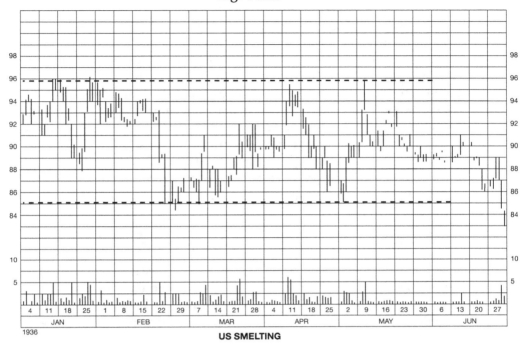

DAILY HIGH AND LOW PRICES

1936

US SMELTING

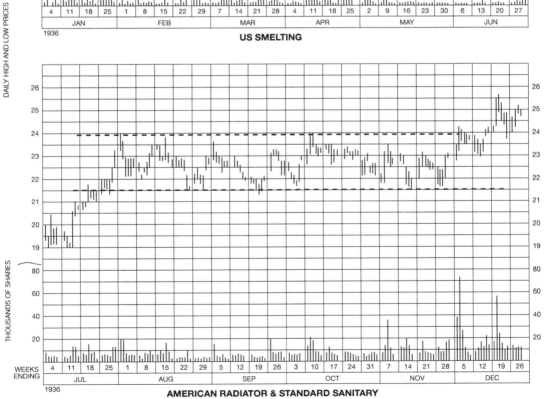

THOUSANDS OF SHARES

WEEKS ENDING

1936

AMERICAN RADIATOR & STANDARD SANITARY

The first and most important consideration is the extent of the penetration. A price movement which penetrates a well-established intermediate trend line by less than a full point in a stock selling under 50, may have little or no technical significance beyond occasioning later, perhaps, a slight correction in the drawing of the line itself. In a stock selling between, say, 25 and 50 we should require a full point of penetration, and proportionately greater penetration in stocks selling at higher levels. A short minor trend, on the other hand, may be invalidated by a smaller penetration.

Along with the extent of price movement, the closing price level must be taken into account. If the price ranges through a trend line on any given day but returns and closes within the trend we are seldom warranted in considering the trend violated although such action is frequently followed shortly by a valid penetration. As a rule we must look for the price to move through and close by a decisive margin beyond the trend line before we may call the trend broken.

Volume Action on the Break of a Trend Line

Although an increase in activity often accompanies a decisive penetration of a trend line, especially when the penetration is on the up-side, we cannot depend on it. The most we can say is that increased volume accompanying a penetration emphasizes the significance of that penetration. When the price breaks the trend and by the same action breaks out of a pattern formation, the significance of the trend break is measurably increased.

Gaps frequently appear when an important trend line is penetrated; such gaps are Break-away Gaps with the same significance as those which appear at the break-out from area formations, and may be construed as a decisive penetration.

The student may well review at this point our detailed analysis of the four Baltimore and Ohio charts (Figs. VIII.3, VIII.4, VIII.5 and VIII.6) with special reference to breaks which proved significant. Note also that there were several instances of indecisive penetration which could be disregarded – the price action during the first week of December, 1935, for example, and again on the 28th of that month. Another good example of price action which could not be considered conclusive in extent occurred in the first week of October, 1936.

Fanning Trend Lines and Flattening Trends

Having studied the qualifications for a decisive break of a trend line, we may now revert to the broader question of the forecasting significance of such a break. The most important question is always, "Has a reversal taken place? Are prices which have been going up now going to go down, or are prices which have been in a declining trend now going to advance"? There are, unfortunately, no simple and sure tests we can apply to give us a quick answer. Trial and error, constant study, and practical experience, bring eventually a high degree of ability in interpreting the breaking of trend lines to the technical student. Trend line action is no more infallible than are our other technical formations and chart phenomena, but when the whole chart picture is studied, there will usually be found many helpful guides to a correct forecast.

The steepness of the trend is, as we have seen in our analysis of the Baltimore and Ohio charts, frequently a reliable clue to the probability of a reversal. When a trend starts out at a steep pitch we should expect it to be broken and corrected to a more moderate angle before any actual reversal into a movement in the opposite direction. Such corrections in trend may be described as a fanning out of trend lines since the successive lines spread out or diverge from their common point of origin as do the ribs of a lady's fan. As a rule – more often than not, that is – when this fanning action occurs, the breaking of the third line signals a reversal of at least minor consequence. We have seen two good examples of this in B & O – the first in August and September, 1935, when A, B, and C were broken, and the second in the July–October trend in 1936 when L, M and N were broken.

Flattening Trends Related to Rounding Turns

Another trend line action which is somewhat analogous to the fanning phenomenon and which is also comparable to the formation we have studied previously under the name of Common or Rounding Turn, is called the flattening trend. This action might, in fact, be described as a very large, very gradual, and rather irregular Rounding Turn (without, however, the characteristic volume action by which we test the reliability of Rounding Turn price action). We may refer to the 1929–1932 weekly chart of Atlantic Refining (Fig. VIII.10) for an example of this phenomenon of flattening trends. No detailed analysis or special comment is required to call our attention to the evident imminence of a reversal as the trend approached the horizontal in 1932.

Patterns Help in Interpretation of Trend Lines

The formation of a pattern of forecasting significance at the time a trend line is broken often aids greatly in determining whether the break signals an important reversal or only a correction in trend angle. Naturally, of course, if we recognize such a pattern as one of great technical importance we do not need the trend line action to give us our reversal clue. Most reversals of major and intermediate trends are, in fact, forecast by pattern formations or other individual phenomena which we stud-

Fig. VIII.10

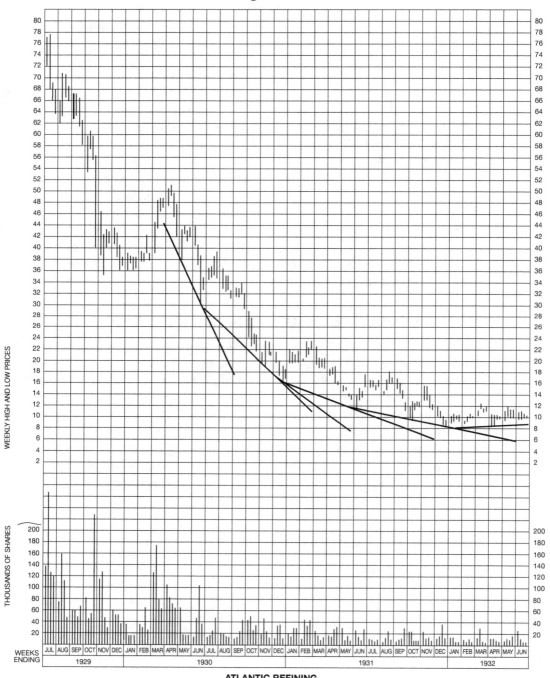

ATLANTIC REFINING

ied, and often by both, as well as by the breaking of trend lines. The point for the student to remember is to use all of his "tools" all the time, qualifying his pattern forecasts by the trend line action, and appraising the importance of trend phenomena in the light of any patterns which may appear on his charts. Note how several familiar patterns aided and confirmed our interpretation of the trend lines in the B & O charts.

The Throw-back After Trend Breaks

In connection with the breaking of trend lines on reversals there is one very practical and helpful price action which occurs with sufficient frequency to warrant our giving it at this point a careful study. We call this the "throw-back." It is the strong tendency of prices to return to the trend line shortly after they have broken through it, a tendency manifested in, probably, as many as two out of three ordinary breaks out of trend.

There are several good examples of the throw-back in the Baltimore and Ohio charts. In Fig. VIII.3, for example, note the rally of prices in the first week of September to the trend line B which had been broken on August 27, and the rally on September 23 to the C line which had been broken on the 20th. In Fig. VIII.4, note the decline on February 17 nearly to the level of the W line after it had been broken on the upside the preceding week. In Fig. VIII.5, a throw-back

> *The "throw-back" is the tendency of prices to return to the trend line.*

appears on October 19 after the penetration of the N trend line. The student will find other examples in these charts as well as in the other charts illustrating this Study, and for that matter in almost any chart he may care to analyze.

Practical Use of the Throw-back

It is difficult to arrive at a logical explanation of the throw-back phenomenon, but its practical application in trading is quite apparent. We cannot count on its occurring after every penetration, unfortunately, and the throw-back does not always extend all the way to the old trend line – it may touch the line, it may "bump" along it for several days and rarely even penetrate it for a fraction of a point, or it may fail to reach it by an appreciable margin.

Bearing all these chances and variations in mind, however, the experienced trader may well try for such an obliging throw-back movement by taking only a portion of his position when the first signal is given by the breaking of the trend line. But the average beginner had best be sure of getting his trade made without taking a chance on the stock's kindly obliging him with a throw-back.

It should be noted that a throw-back can seldom be expected when a Break-away Gap appears as the trend line is broken.

Estimating Extent of Probable Move by Trend Lines

We have mentioned briefly at the beginning of this Study the usefulness of trend lines in arriving at an estimate of the probable objective of any price movement arising out of an area formation. Now that we have inspected the trend line action in several charts we may well give this very practical matter some further study. It is an important point to be considered whenever we are called upon to decide whether or not to trade on the implications of any continuation pattern, and especially when we have to decide which of two or more such patterns on different charts offers the greatest potential profit. It arises also in connection with reversal formations in minor or intermediate trends.

As working examples, note how the price movement following the break-out from the Right Angle Triangle top in March, 1936 in the B & O chart (Fig. VIII.4) was halted at the F-2 line, and a minor correction required before a further decline carried the price on down. Then note how the downward movement was finally stopped in the neighborhood of the longer term line, E. Note also that the advance in July out of the previous strong Ascending Triangle (Fig. VIII.5) was halted in the neighborhood of the new long-term line, X, drawn parallel to G.

Trend Lines on Logarithmic Scale

Before leaving the subject of parallel trend lines it may be advisable to consider them in relation to the type of scale used in plotting the chart. There are three principal types of scales used for stock charts: the straight or arithmetic scale, the logarithmic or ratio scale, and the square-root scale. Each has its advocates although the square-root scale is least used and appears to have no important advantages. The reader is probably familiar with the difference but, in short, the ratio or logarithmic scale shows a smaller space vertically for each full point in price as the price moves upward, giving equal space to equal percentage of movement. The distance from 10 to 20 on the ratio price scale, for example, is the same as the distance from 20 to 40, and that again is the same as the distance from 40 to 80, and so on. The arithmetic scale, on the other hand, allows equal spaces for each full point, no matter how high or low the price may go. The arithmetic scale is the one we have used on all the charts up to this point in this Course.

The square root scale may be described as a semi-ratio scale, coming between the arithmetic and logarithmic types. For those who are mathematically minded, it may be added that the trend line formed by a stock that advanced one full point in price each day over a given period would be a straight line on an arithmetic chart. On a logarithmic chart the trend line would be a logarithmic curve, and on the square root chart a true parabola, the former flattening out more rapidly than the latter.

The advantages claimed for the ratio scale are based chiefly on the fact that the higher stocks go in price the wider the fluctuations tend to become, measured in points of movements. The logarithmic scale is supposed to compensate for this tendency by plotting actual distances on a percentage basis.

Logarithmic vs. Arithmetic Scale

In our experience, however, we have found that the arithmetic scale is easier to use, and the distortion of patterns is much less than on the logarithmic scale. Ratio plotting tends to compress the patterns at high price levels almost to insignificance, and to exaggerate the patterns formed at low levels out of all proportion to their technical importance, making their correct interpretation extremely difficult.

As to trend lines, logarithmic charts, with one possible exception, do not ordinarily give us straight lines which can be turned to profit in trading. The one possible exception is the long-term bull market trend which tends to accelerate or curve upward on an arithmetic chart. This phenomenon appears most plainly and consistently on the monthly charts of the averages and certain of the more substantial leading stocks which follow the general market closely. Note, for example, the upward acceleration of the 1924–1929 bull market trend on the arithmetic monthly chart of the Dow-Jones Industrial Average in Fig VIII.11 Plotted on a logarithmic scale the line A-B-C-D would be practically a straight line instead of an upward curve, and its breaking in October, 1929, signalled the end of the major movement. A similar straight line drawn

> *Logarithmic vs. Arithmetic Scale. The arithmetic scale is easier to use.*

across the 1932 and 1933 bottoms on a logarithmic scale was broken in March, 1937.

On the other hand, logarithmic charts are of no assistance in major downtrends, nor in either up or down intermediate trends. In brief, we believe that the average trader need not trouble with logarithmic charts, unless he wishes, just as a matter of general interest, to keep a weekly or monthly average chart on a logarithmic scale.

GENERAL REVIEW OF VOLUME

In all our studies of price patterns and phenomena so far we have discussed with them the characteristic volume accompaniment, and the student has, we trust, come to recognize the fact that volume is an extremely important part of the science of technical analysis. It may not be absolutely correct to say that, "Volume is half the

Fig. VIII.11

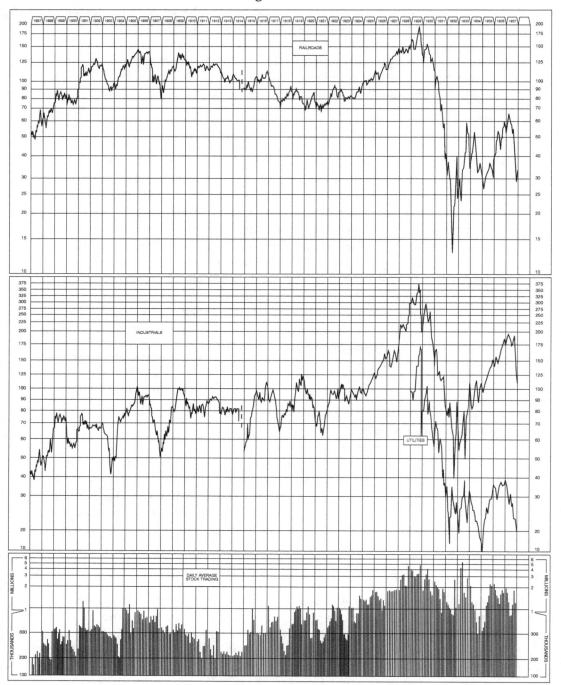

THE DOW-JONES INDUSTRIAL, RAIL & UTILITIES AVERAGES ON A SEMI-LOGARITHMIC SCALE
Refer to discussion of trend lines on logarithmic charts on page 290, Study VIII, and compare with Frontispiece.

picture", but this saying is helpful, nevertheless, in emphasizing the importance of always considering *both* price action and volume in forecasting from our charts.

It is in order, therefore, to review the principles of volume action which we have touched upon in our studies to date, and to bring them together into a brief general survey.

Volume is the measure of buying and selling taking place in a given stock within any stated period. Every transaction involves both a buyer and seller. One of them is willing (or obliged) to buy the stock and the other to sell it at a certain price. As prospective traders in that stock, it is our desire to interpret the transactions in terms of their probable effect on the price trend. Generally speaking, we have no means of knowing positively who is buying and who is selling, or why. We do not know from the mere fact that a transaction or a certain number of transactions has taken place, whether the buyers are smarter than the sellers, or vice versa. If, however, the volume of these transactions can be related to price movement, and can be compared with the past history of volume in our stock, we are frequently able to deduce its significance in the technical picture.

Past History Important in Study of Volume

The most important consideration, then, in the technical interpretation of volume is its relation, first, to the volume habit for the preceding period, and, second, to the price movement or lack of movement which accompanied it. In other words, it is not the number of shares traded on a certain day that has significance but the comparison of that number with the number traded on the several days preceding and, to a lesser degree, during the previous weeks and months. Before we can draw any helpful conclusions from the volume chart we must have a fair amount of back history as a basis for comparison. In all our discussion of volume, therefore, it must be understood that by high volume we mean volume greater than normal in the specific issue and at the time under consideration.

And, while we are stating general principles, it bears repeating that no technical factor or phenomenon is infallible. This applies to volume as well as price.

Volume Characteristics Previously Discussed

In our previous Studies we have had occasion to make specific mention of volume or relative activity in the following connections:

1. The general principle of high volumes at reversals in trend. This point requires further analysis and considerable qualification in the light of our now more

advanced understanding of technical forecasting, and we shall discuss it farther on in detail.

2. The characteristic decline of daily volume during the formation of area patterns such as the Triangles, Flags and Rectangles, especially as these patterns
approach completion, and also during the formation of the rounding patterns
until they pass "dead center."

3. The notable pick-up in volume which usually accompanies the break-out of
prices from an area pattern, or in certain cases follows within a day or two.

4. The high volume which signals the climax of a rapid movement out of an accelerating (or "drooping") price pattern.

5. The high volume which accompanies the formation of an Exhaustion Gap.

Volume as an Indication of Reversal

At this stage of our studies it will be evident to the reader that the volume phenomena mentioned under 4 and 5 above are closely related. In each case we have a very
sharp mark-up or mark-down resulting in either an over-bought or over-sold condition signaled by a conspicuous burst of volume. And these types of climactic or
exhaustion volume are apparently related to the more general condition of increased
volume at reversals. When we come to analyze the characteristic volume action on
reversals, however, we find that climactic or exhaustion volume plays a part but
only a part in the entire picture. We find also an interesting and frequently helpful
distinction between the typical volume action on top and bottom reversals.

Typical Volume Action on Reversals

The typical volume chart during a period of trend reversal shows two up-thrusts or
increases, the first of which accompanies the last strong movement in prices in the
old trend and the second the break-away into the new trend. The first is climax or
exhaustion activity, and the second is related to the volume increase which we have
already discussed in some detail as characteristic of break-out movements from
technical formations. Although the chart picture is not always clear, and although
there are many exceptions to the general rule, most charts of reversals will show,
when carefully analyzed, both climax and break-away volume, even when no very
definite technical area pattern or formation appears.

In the case of Head and Shoulders reversals in which the head extends only a
short distance beyond the level of the left shoulder, the climax volume usually
appears with the formation of the left shoulder, and a lesser climax or volume
upthrust attends the head. The break-away volume appears when, or very soon
after, the neck-base line is broken. When the head extends well beyond the left

shoulder level, the real climactic volume usually accompanies the drive that makes the head. In the case of the Triangle reversals, the climax volume appears at the beginning of the formation, on the last thrust of prices in the old trend before the price action begins to show the triangular convergence. This, of course, is usually the point at which prices reach their far-thest extent in the old trend.

Most charts of reversals will show both climax and break-away volume.

In the case of Rectangle reversals the volume action is typically the same as in Triangles. With the Rounding and Complex rever-sal patterns, however, the picture is slightly different. In the case of the typical Rounding or Common Turn, the climax volume appears just before the price track begins to flatten out, and the break-away volume appears after prices have started to turn into the new trend. The volume chart on Complex reversals is usually rather confused; in general, the volume action may resemble that on a Common Turn, or that on a Head and Shoulders, or a combination of the two.

Differences in Volume Charts at Tops and Bottoms

The characteristic distinction between the volume action on tops and on bottoms appears when we compare their relative climax and break-away volume. Speaking very generally, for there are many exceptions, at a top the climax volume is greater than the break-away volume, while at a bottom the break-away volume tends to run higher than the climax volume. This difference is due, no doubt, to the same basic factor which finds expression in the old street adage, "Prices can fall down but have to be pushed up".

In addition to this usual, though not invariable, difference between top and bot-tom volume patterns, there is also a tendency for the volume between the climax peak and break-away peak to run duller at bottoms than at tops.

Volume Action at Temporary Halts in Trends

From our detailed examination of various charts and charts formations in previous Studies, the student will probably have already discovered that the volume pattern developed at intermediate halts in trends is much the same as that developed at reversals. Since such halts do, as a rule, result in some slight retreat or correction, they are comparable in a sense with reversals. In each case we have a stemming of the technical tide which may show climactic volume action, and in each case, after a more or less indeterminate price trend, we have a break-away which is usually accompanied by break-out volume. The difference between the reversal volume pat-tern and the intermediate congestion volume pattern is more a matter of degree than kind. The important distinction between the two is found in the direction of price movement on the break-out rather than in the volume action. The experienced technical trader, nevertheless, is able to develop a sense of volume which helps him to arrive at a reasonable guess as to whether or not reversal or continuation is likely.

Declining Volume During Pattern Formation

Another characteristic of volume action which has been quite fully discussed in our previous Studies, is the tendency for volume to decline during the period of formation of a technical area pattern. This shrinkage in activity is especially conspicuous, as a rule, as the formation nears completion, just before a break-out occurs. Knowledge of this rule is useful to the technical trader because it helps him to decide whether or not a certain price pattern is classifiable as a dependable forecasting formation. Where the price action presents a well-defined area picture the volume action is confirmatory but not critical; where the price action presents a poorly defined pattern, the volume action frequently "casts the deciding vote". It is a common error of beginners to see technical formations where none exist; the application of the volume test to those situations will help them to avoid incorrect conclusions and profitless trades.

Volume as an Indication of Continuation

We have, of course, in the common phenomenon of increased volume attending break-outs from technical formations, one specific example of the use of the volume chart in forecasting continuation. We have seen how a pick-up in volume almost invariably accompanies a price break-out in an upward direction and usually, but not always, accompanies a price break-out downward. Where higher volume does not attend the initial break downward, it usually picks up notably within a day or two as the movement progresses. When volume does not pick up, a "false move" (which we shall take up in Study X) is to be suspected. There is no need to discuss break-out volume further except to say that any conspicuous

> *It is common to see technical formations where none exist; application of the volume test will help.*

increase in activity when prices move out of an area of congestion, regardless of its pattern, is an indication of continuation. It should also be noted that an increase in volume attending the penetration of a trend line has somewhat the same significance as the increase attending a break-out from a pattern, and confirms the importance of the trend penetration.

And, once more, in this connection, let us recall the rule of doubling the actual volume of a Saturday's trading in order to bring it into fair comparison for technical purposes with the volume of trading on other days of the week.

Relation of Volume to Price Movement

There is another aspect of volume study which we have not mentioned heretofore, the relation of volume to progress in price movement. This has been the subject of considerable research, with rather disappointing results in so far as our being able to discover any dependable trading rules. The most that can be said is that, so long as prices continue to move in apparent proportion to the volume of activity, the forecast is continuation. When, however, several days of high volume are attended by no price movement the suggestion is that important resistance has been encountered, and that some correctional movement will follow. This general principle is subject to much leeway in its application to specific situations, and judgment must be used in appraising its importance with relation to other factors appearing on the same chart.

Relation of Volume Action to Basic Trend

Finally, there is one more general rule of volume action which is often of use to the technical trader when other elements of the chart picture fail to give a definite clue. This rule may be expressed in simple terms as follows: volume tends to run higher when prices are moving in the direction of the basic trend, and lower when prices are moving contrary to the basic trend. It should be noted that this rule holds true in only a general sense; it should not be applied to a single day's volume action for there are frequent exceptions. Taking into account the chart picture for a reasonable period, however, it works out with a high degree of dependability.

Good examples are plentiful – will be found, in fact, in almost any chart which we may care to examine. The student will recall that we made use of this rule in our analysis of the Inverted Triangle which formed at the 1929 top in General American Transportation (Fig V.1) and again in the analysis of the Ascending Triangle in Anaconda Copper (Fig. VI.4). It comes into play in the analysis of the Out-of-line movements which we took up in Study VII, and is a great help in the detection of false moves which we will take up later in Study X. And, finally, it is of decided assistance in appraising the significance of the set-backs which frequently follow after break-

Volume tends to run higher when prices are moving in the direction of the basic trend.

outs from area patterns, a phenomenon which we have referred to on several occasions, particularly on page 183 in Study VI.

Most Useful in Intermediate Trend Trading

This general rule which we are discussing applies also to the broad pictures of major or cyclical trends presented by weekly charts, but is of little practical use in long term trading since too great a time must always elapse before the volume relation becomes clearly developed. It is, however, of great practical value in trading on the intermediate movements, both in the continuation and reversal phases of those movements.

Specifically, it is most useful in deciding whether a reaction in an upward trend is the beginning of a reversal into a downward trend, or simply a minor fluctuation which will soon run out and be followed by a resumption of the upward movement. Or, in a downward trend, whether a rally is initiating a reversal or simply correcting a temporarily over sold condition.

The student will understand that this rule is merely one more tool in the kit. By itself it is of limited usefulness, but considered in connection with all of our other technical guides – patterns, gaps, trend lines, etc. – it helps us in arriving at a reasonable forecast of the future price action.

THE DOW THEORY

This is a good place in our studies to give some brief attention to the Dow Theory since that theory is based primarily on general trend and volume considerations, with practically no reference to the many specific formations and phenomena which we have been studying in this Course.[1]

It is noteworthy that Charles H Dow, the man who first set forth the principles which have been developed into what is now known as the Dow Theory, applied these principles himself only to the "averages" and apparently only, or at least chiefly, as a means of judging the basic business and financial trends, rather than as an aid to speculation. His followers have been more attentive to the speculative application of the principles, and the public at large has come to conceive of the Dow Theory as a complete guide to successful stock trading which is very far from the fact as well as from the original purpose of its author.

---

[1]. For further information on the highly respected tenets and practical applications of the Dow Theory's well-grounded usage for market analytics, plus the several profit-proved improvements to it by Samuel Moment, the next work in this Series of Market Classics is recommended; "New Blueprints for Gains in Stocks and Grains" combined with "One-Way Formula", both by William Dunnigan.

The Two Averages Used by Dow

The Dow Theory depends upon the simultaneous study and interpretation of two averages – the Dow-Jones Industrial Average (of which a long-term chart is shown in the Frontispiece of this Course) and the Dow-Jones Railroad Average. In the days when Mr Dow first promulgated his basic principles of market action, the railroads collectively constituted an extremely important part of the American financial picture. The capital invested in railroads represented a very large share of the corporate wealth of the country. Moreover, virtually every movement of goods, whether raw materials or finished products, went by rail. Consequently, every change in business activity was reflected promptly and directly in railroad income. This condition, which no longer maintains, accounts for the great importance which Mr Dow attached to the movements of the Rail Average. Many present-day students of the averages now discount the importance of the Rails. Certainly the movements of the railroad averages have been difficult to apply in the Dow Theory, and frequently downright misleading, in the interpretation of the market as a whole since 1932.

The Major Tenets of the Dow Theory

The leading contemporary exponent of the Dow Theory is, without doubt, Mr Robert Rhea, from whose work "The Dow Theory" the following brief summary of six of the principal tenets of the theory are quoted.

1. Dow's three movements: "There are three movements of the averages, all of which may be in progress at one and the same time. The first, and most important, is the primary trend; the broad upward or downward movements known as bull or bear markets, which may be of several years' duration. The second, and most deceptive movement, is the secondary reaction: an important decline in a primary bull market or a rally in a primary bear market. These reactions usually last from three weeks to as many months. The third, and usually unimportant, movement is the daily fluctuation."

2. Both averages must confirm: "The movements of both the railroad and industrial stock averages should always be considered together. The movement of one price average must be confirmed by the other before reliable inferences may be drawn. Conclusions based upon the movement of one average, unconfirmed by the other, are almost certain to prove misleading."

3. Determining the trend: "Successive rallies penetrating preceding high points, with ensuing declines terminating above preceding low points, offer a bullish indication. Conversely, failure of the rallies to penetrate previous high points, with ensu-

ing declines carrying below former low points, is bearish. Inferences so drawn are useful in appraising secondary reactions and are of major importance in forecasting the resumption, continuation, or change of the primary trend. For the purpose of this discussion, a rally or a decline is defined as one or more daily movements resulting in a net reversal of direction exceeding three per cent of the price of either average. Such movements have but little authority unless confirmed in direction by both averages, but the confirmation need not occur on the same day."

4. Lines: "A 'line' is a price movement extending two to three weeks or longer, during which period the price variation of both averages moves within a range of approximately five per cent. Such a movement indicates either accumulation or distribution. Simultaneous advances above the limits of the 'line' indicate accumulation and predict higher prices; conversely, simultaneous declines below the 'line' imply distribution and lower prices are sure to follow. Conclusions drawn from the movement of one average, not confirmed by the other, generally prove to be incorrect."

5. The Relation of volume to price movements: "A market which has been overbought becomes dull on rallies and develops activity on declines; conversely, when a market is oversold, the tendency is to become dull on declines and active on rallies. Bull markets terminate in a period of excessive activity and begin with comparatively light transactions."

6. Individual stocks: "All active and well distributed stocks of great American corporations generally rally and decline with the averages, but any individual stock may reflect conditions not applicable to the average price of any diversified list of stocks."

Application to Stock Trading

The student who wishes to investigate the Dow Theory at length will find all of its principles fully expounded in the works of Mr Robert Rhea. As a broad, basic study of the general market trend it is of unquestioned authority, but as an aid to successful trading in individual stocks our experience indicates that it is of extremely limited value. One cannot buy or sell the "average", and individual stocks do not make their tops or bottoms at the same time as the averages, nor move at the same rate. More often than not, by the time a "signal" has been given by the averages important profits or opportunities for profit have been lost.

Study IX

SUPPORT AND RESISTANCE LEVELS

In our last Study we learned that one of the uses of trend lines is in estimating the probable objective of an intermediate price movement. The existence of a well defined trend, suggesting that any movement of prices will be turned back as it reaches the trend line, gives us a basis for measuring the probable immediate profits to be gained in a prospective trade, and for comparing the potential profits in one stock with another. This restrictive action of trend lines may be called a phenomenon of resistance – one of the many which the technical trader finds it profitable to know and put to use. The general subject of support and resistance levels is one of the most interesting, and most practical as well, of our Course in Technical Analysis. We shall devote the greater part of this Section to it.

The Importance of Reversal Levels

We gave our first attention in this Course to the various formations or patterns which forecast a reversal of price trend. Most certainly, indications of reversals are of prime importance in practical trading, because we may assume continuation of the previous or current trend until signs of reversal appear. Reversals are our signals that the technical position is undergoing change and that it is necessary to take action, to adjust our trading policy to the changing technical trend or forecast.

If we can get advance information by some means or other, regarding the probable point at which a reversal of the trend may occur, we have a great advantage in planning our practical market operations. We shall be forewarned, if we decide to take a position in a certain stock, to scrutinize with particular care its action as depicted on the chart when it approaches that point or level. And we shall be prepared all the more quickly to accept and act upon any evidences of reversal that show up there. So, any information as to the levels at which strong resistance to further movement may be expected is of practical help, first, in determining whether or not it will be profitable to take a position in a stock, and, second, in determining when it may be wise to take profits.

Deciding Upon Our Terminology

Resistance levels, generally speaking, are those price ranges at or within which increased offers (or bids) are met, resulting in a stemming of the technical tide, and either a reversal of trend or, at least, a temporary halt and "congestion". It will make our study easier, however, if we abandon the broad use of the term "resistance", confining its application to those levels at which *upward* or advancing price movements are halted, and use instead the term "support" to describe those levels where *down-ward* or declining trends are arrested.

A resistance level, then, is an approximate level, or fairly well defined price range, where a previously advancing stock meets resistance in the form of strong selling. A support level is an approximate level or price range where a preceding decline meets support. In the form of strong buying. A resistance level may, therefore, be called also a "supply area" – an area, that is, in which an increased supply of the stock for sale is encountered. And, by the same token, a support level may be called a "demand area."

Methods of Forecasting Resistance Levels

We have seen in our previously mentioned trend line action one method of fore-casting probable support and resistance points. There are, in fact, a great many nearby and temporary supports and resistances set up by the various patterns of price action which we have studied in the preceding sections of this Course, and we shall take these all up later in the course of this Study. First and foremost among support and resistance levels in practical trading importance, however, are those which occur at price ranges which have been marked and identified by the appear-ance of area formations or price congestions at those same ranges at some preceding period in the trading history of the stock. Such future developments of support and resistance are, obviously, the repetition, at a later date, of support or resistance pre-viously manifested at the same levels, since we know that any price congestion or formation, whether reversal or continuation, reflects in itself some measure of sup-port or resistance.

Resistance Levels Become Future Support Levels

It is important to note at this point, however, that an area formation built by resis-tance will, if later penetrated, manifest itself as a support level. And, in the same manner, a support level will, when broken through, show up as a resistance point in future price movement. Each may repeat in its original role but more often they exchange roles. In other words, an area formation, whether originally one of resis-tance or support, may repeat later on in the same or the opposite position, tending to check whatever movement happens to approach its level from either above or below.

Logical Explanation for Reversal Levels

Any logical explanation for support and resistance levels must take into account various natural as well as artificial causes. One natural explanation lies in the fact that the public, and all trading elements, tend to remember previous area levels and thus make them important. While a stock is changing its price level rapidly, day after day, the public will be buying and selling at widely divergent levels and there will be no unanimity, or strong memory impression, in such changing prices.

But if the stock has formed an area, has held within a fairly narrow range for some time, then public purchases and sales tend to bunch up on that range and the public remembers that particular price level. The longer the time which the stock spent in that range, therefore, and the greater the total volume of transactions which took place therein, the greater becomes the importance of that range for future technical consideration.

> *The public and trading elements tend to remember previous area levels and thus make them important.*

If a stock advances very rapidly, for instance, from 75 to 100 there is not enough time spent at any particular price range for it to become significant. But if the stock now meets resistance and fluctuates for a month between 95 and 100, then the public will be much more likely to remember that particular price range in connection with that stock and to be governed thereby at a later date. And, obviously, this range will have been especially impressed on the many who bought or sold within it.

Now suppose that the stock again advances on up in a fairly straight and rapid movement and then forms another long area range around 125. The 125 range now assumes much greater importance than any of the prices between 100 and 125. At those two levels, at 100 and at 125, we have now had formed area formations and thus resistance or support points.

The Memory Factor Comes into Play

Let the stock whose theoretical movements we followed in the preceding paragraphs now begin to react from 125 back toward 100. There will not be nearly as much public interest in its successively declining price levels on the way down as there will be when the price again strikes that previous area range at around 100. When that price is reached, however, people will begin to buy who recall seeing the price there before and who, meanwhile, have wished they had bought at that earlier level. Now they see a second opportunity to buy there and many of them do.

Or there may be many traders who went short of the stock the first time it hesitated at 100, who foolishly failed to protect themselves with stop-loss orders, and who worried about their paper losses while the stock went up to 125, and are now glad to be able to cover their short sales by repurchase without loss, as the stock gets back again to the 100 level. Thus from various natural tendencies, there is built up greater buying or demand which becomes technical support at the 100 level, which was formerly a resistance point.

If we assume that this support level around 100 reverses the price trend once more, then the stock will meet resistance to further advance when it again approaches that former resistance level of around 125. At that level, many who wished they had sold out the first time the stock hit 125 and before it started back down to 100, now find they have a second opportunity to sell at 125 and do so. Short traders, who, while the stock was going down to 100, wished they had sold short at the 125 level, now find that they, too, have another opportunity to sell short at that price. Thus there is clear logic to the importance of resistance and support levels, simply from rather natural considerations.

Artificial Factors Also Occasionally Effective

Other reasons may be found, however, in a consideration of more artificial movements, such as may be produced by the plans of professional operators. Inside groups work not only with such natural ideas in view as those we have just noted, but they also have usually very definite ideas of the price levels at which they wish to accumulate most of their stock and where they wish to distribute it. Such a campaign assumes advance formulation of a definite and organized plan to buy a large block of stock at around a certain price level and sell it around another price level.

If the operators buy most of their line of stock around 100 and decide to sell it out at around 125 they are hardly likely to sell it all the first time the stock hits 125. It is more likely that they will be able to sell perhaps only two-thirds of their holdings the first time the price reaches that goal. Exhausting the buying power at 125, temporarily, they will let the stock drift lower of its own accord, unless it is weaker than they thought and gets within striking distance of 100 again. In that case their best procedure might well be to buy back some of the stock they sold at 125, thus check the decline at 100, and start the issue back up again. But when the new advance approaches 125 once more, they will begin to sell the rest of their holdings, in accordance with the original plan of buying around 100 and selling around 125.

Thus we see how support and resistance levels, once established, may well continue to exercise important and dependable influence on future movements.

Degree of Reliability of Supply and Demand Levels

In any case, we shall find that such support and resistance levels are quite reliable. Once more, they are not infallible, as we know, but they are probably more important and more reliable than the average of the various patterns and rules which we have been studying. Sometimes the probable levels of resistance or support forecast by the back history do not hold but they are still valuable for the chart student. They may hold only temporarily but as soon as it is fairly established that the previously noted levels are not holding, then they become useful in a negative way at least, because they attest to the decisive force of the current movement, label it as a strong and powerful one, and suggest most emphatically that the movement will then continue on until it meets the next probable level of resistance or support.

Quite naturally, the question of how long old support or resistance levels remain effective, enters into any appraisal of their dependability in practical trading. Before we discuss this point, however, it will make our study easier if we first analyze some examples of support and resistance action as it is manifested in major trends.

Old Bottoms Become Future Tops

For an almost perfect exemplification of the general principle that support levels once penetrated become resistance points in future advances, and vice-versa, the student may refer to the monthly chart of the Dow Jones Industrial Average, Fig. VIII.1. Let us follow first the long bull market action from 1924 to 1929 and note the levels at which resistance was encountered. The first such level showed up at 120–124 where the advance was halted for five months. The next appeared in the 160–164 range (each line represents four points on this chart) where prices struggled for over a year before again pushing upward. Resistance that took six months to break, developed again at the 200 level. There was a little difficulty getting through 216–220, and then an almost "vertical" advance to 320–324 where five months' resistance was encountered before the final drive pushed through to the 1929 top.

Now follow the price action during the great 29–32 bear market. The first panic collapse took prices down in two months to 212 and then to 196, meeting support and rallying from a zone that had formerly manifested itself as a resistance level, and which we noted as such in the preceding paragraph. The catastrophic nature of the 1929 collapse is indicated by the ease with which it smashed through the support level which we should have expected normally to develop around 320.

After this first panic drive, however, a more normal sequence of swings appeared. The rally from 196 was a strong one, taking the average price back up again to 296 in April, 1930. Note that the resistance point here was at the same general level as the support under the first six months of price action during 1929. In other words, an old bottom here became a new top.

And Old Tops Become New Bottoms

The next decline in the bear market was halted briefly around 216, encountering support where resistance had formerly appeared in early 1928 advance. An old top had become a new bottom. The next sharp decline met support around 160, a level the importance of which had been demonstrated by the chart from October, 1925 to March, 1927. Here again an old resistance level manifested itself later as a support level. The rally in early 1931 met resistance and was turned back at 196, at the same level where the first 1929 panic decline had met support. The ensuing drop was stopped at 120, now appearing as a support level whereas it had been a resistance level in late 1924 – early 1925.

The action of prices through the first stages of the bull market that started in 1932 is not so directly comparable in its early stages, but it will be noted that the first advance was reversed in the general level of the last bear market congestion. Also the 160 level which appeared first as resistance in 1925–1927, then as support in 1930, and then as resistance in 1931, appeared again as a resistance point in April, 1936. The decline in June 1931 met support at 120 and rally in November met resistance at the same 120 level. The top of the September, 1932 advance furnished support throughout 1933 and 1934.

Value of Weekly Charts in Forecasting

The student of the market cannot fail to be impressed by the extraordinary influence exerted by these old tops and bottoms even after a lapse of months and years. Their importance in forecasting the probable nearby objectives of current movements is plain to see, even from our quick survey of the twelve years' action of the Dow-Jones Industrial Average. In applying this support and resistance study to individual issues however, the weekly charts give more exact and detailed information than the monthly charts. They show much more plainly the levels at which congestions of significant duration appeared and the levels through which prices moved rapidly without developing support or resistance patterns. The weekly charts also picture the volume at different price levels, a factor which becomes useful in determining the probable future importance of such levels.

The weekly chart of almost any actively traded issue will show, when carefully analyzed, a number of good examples of the influence of old support and resistance levels on later price action. Let us study, for example, the trading history of General Electric, starting in July, 1929, as depicted on the weekly charts of this stock. The price and volume action up to July, 1932 is shown in Fig. IX.1. The figures along the left-hand margin give the price of the stock before it was split 4 for 1 in January, 1930, and those along the right-hand margin the price after the split; only the latter figures are needed in our study.

Weekly charts show much more plainly the levels at which congestions of significant duration appeared.

Fig. IX.1

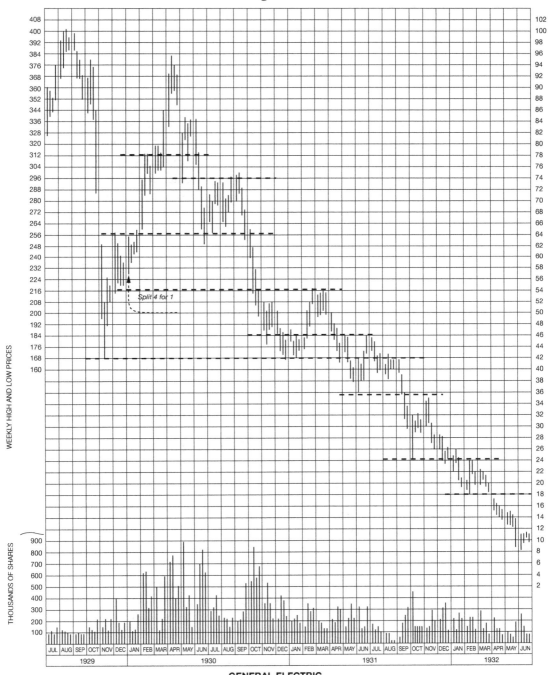

WEEKLY HIGH AND LOW PRICES

THOUSANDS OF SHARES

Split 4 for 1

GENERAL ELECTRIC

Volume a Factor in Estimating Future Influence

Dropping precipitately from its top around 400, the price of General Electric fell in November, 1929 to 168. These prices were equivalent to 100 and 42 respectively in terms of the stock after it was split, and 42 thus became a level to be noted for future reference. The ensuing "post-panic" recovery carried the price up to 64–65 where two months' resistance was encountered, with a reaction back to 54–55, before the advance was continued. The next drive met resistance for a month and a half at about 78–79, then pushed on and was finally reversed around 94–96. Now starting down, a first sharp drop penetrated the 78–79 level (a distinctly bearish performance) but met support around 74; the high volume registered on this movement (last week of April and first week of May, 1930) suggested that this support level would have great future significance. Incidentally, in studying the volume depicted on this chart, bear in mind that the volume before the 4-for-1 split should be multiplied by four to bring it into fair comparison with the subsequent volume.

The next mark-down in the bear market met support in the 64–65 zone which had been a resistance zone in late 1929. A recovery now encountered resistance in the 74 zone, a level which we have noted previously as likely to be important. The three months price action between 64–65 and 74, approximately, gave these levels further emphasis for future consideration.

Levels Established During the Bear Market

Without going into tedious detail we may now follow the price action of General Electric on down through the bear market to the 1932 bottom and note briefly the levels at which support and resistance appeared.

Support appeared around 46–47 in November, and at 42 in December, 1930, the latter having been noted as a support level in 1929. Next, we met resistance around 54 (cf. December, 1929), support around 36, resistance near 46, and then what appeared to be important support, volume considered, around 24–25. The subsequent recovery, however, fell short of 36 where we might have expected it to reach (cf. June, 1931) and was reversed around 34–35. The next support level appeared around 18, and 24 appeared as we might have anticipated as a resistance point in February, 1932.

Before we leave this chart it is suggested that the student review the foregoing analysis and note how the dotted lines are drawn on the chart to define the apparently significant boundaries of the price movements and congestions. A sort of an optical method of averaging is employed in arriving at these levels, having in mind that later price movements may either slightly penetrate or not quite reach lines set too exactly. Study also the volume, because it is logical, obviously, to suppose that the greater the aggregate volume attending the establishment of a support or resistance level, the longer that level is likely to have effect on future price action.

Levels Repeating in the Opposite Trend

Having defined the price levels or zones which appeared to be important in our support and resistance study during the bear market in General Electric, we may now test their actual effect on the progress of prices in the opposite trend. Turn to Fig. IX.2 which traces the trading history from July, 1932 through December, 1936, showing the weekly high and low price range and volume. On this chart the levels marked on the preceding chart have been extended by means of dotted lines to facilitate our study of their continuing influence.

We note first that the 18 level was penetrated by the first sharp rally, although we might have expected resistance there; Nevertheless, following along through 1933 and 1934, this level did have continued significance, briefly as resistance in November, 1932, and afterwards as support for many reactions.

Excepting for the sharp penetration in the summer of 1933, the 24–25 level, which we marked down in 1931 as likely to be important, became a wall of resistance that was not finally breached until June, 1935. The 42 level which first appeared as support for the panic drop in 1929, demonstrated its importance in 1936 where it became a resistance and an intermediate reversal point. In fact, the effect of this began to show up at 41 in November, 1935. The apparent influence of the next three old support and resistance levels above 42 is shown even more plainly on the daily chart of General Electric for the last half of 1936, Fig. IX.3.

Forecasting the Next Steps in General Electric

We have seen in the foregoing study how long old levels of support and resistance may retain their potency in subsequent markets. And, we have had some noteworthy examples of old support levels or bottoms becoming resistance points or tops in later movements when prices approach these levels from below. Studying the back history in General Electric we might logically forecast, as this is written, that the stock would meet resistance to further advance around 54–55 (cf. December, 1929 and February, 1931) and that once this level was passed, there would be a fairly free movement to around 64–65 (cf. June-August, 1930).

Resistance and Support Levels in Intermediate Trends

Up to this point in our study we have been concentrating on the major support and

Fig. IX.2

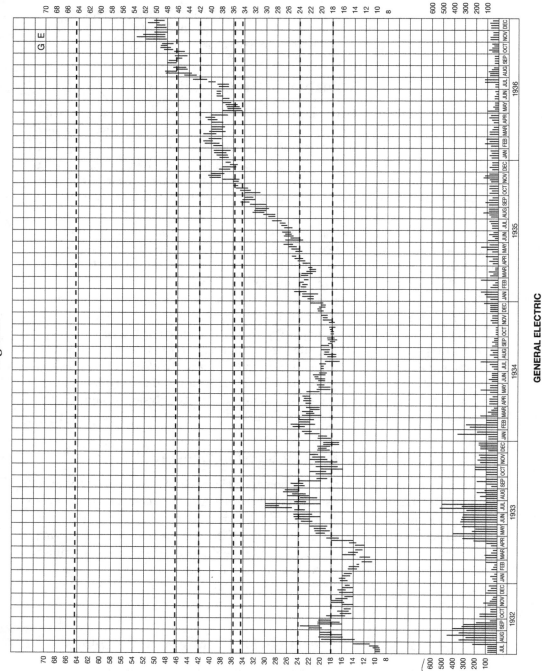

GENERAL ELECTRIC

Fig. IX.3

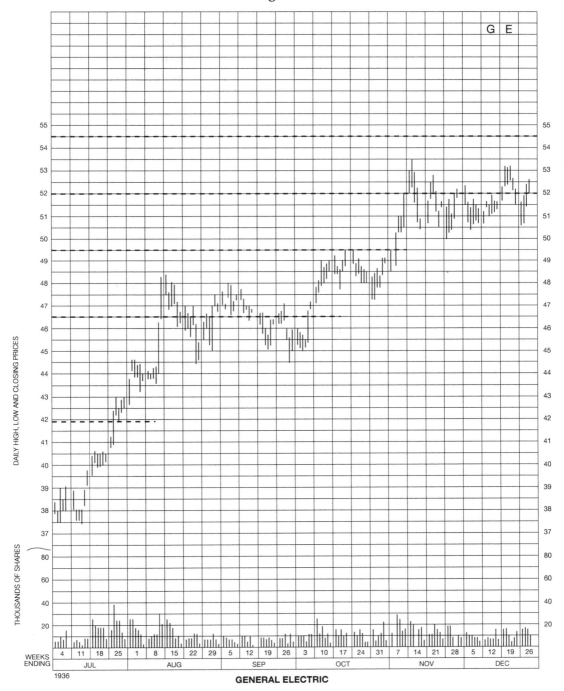

GENERAL ELECTRIC

resistance zones depicted on the long-range charts and defined in general by the limits of the intermediate price movements. Naturally these are the most important levels for the technical trader to determine in advance if possible, and we have seen how, in general, they are most readily forecast from the past trading history shown on weekly charts. We have seen also that these levels cannot be set exactly by any mathematical process, and that a certain amount of judgment, and optical appraisal of the price and volume action, is required to estimate their future potency. Despite this lack of absolute precision, however, it is quite obvious that important support and resistance levels, or demand and supply areas, can be very closely approximated.

If we turn now to a study of the minor fluctuations within an intermediate price trend we find that exactly the same phenomena of support and resistance are manifested therein that we found in major trends. These minor fluctuations cannot be seen on weekly charts but may be found on the daily chart of almost any stock in an active movement. A number of good support examples appear in the chart of Snider Packing, Fig. IX.4.

Minor Tops Later Become Minor Bottoms

Snider Packing in July and August, 1935 encountered resistance to price advance at the 19 level, which was finally broken through on August 29 (note the volume). The ensuing rally "made a top" around 21 and the price then re-acted to 19, meeting support at that former resistance level. After advancing from there to around $23\frac{1}{2}$, the next reaction was stopped at around 21; again a previous top had become a new minor bottom. And so on – each minor reaction was supported and reversed at the approximate level of a previous minor top, with only one exception, that exception being the decline on October 22 which did not carry all the way down to the preceding top at $24\frac{1}{2}$.

When an intermediate reversal appeared in November the first sharp drop was halted at the approximate level of the late October minor top, and the next drop encountered support in the neighborhood of the top level made on relatively high volume the last week of September.

Negative Usefulness of Minor Support Levels

The technical trader quickly develops a practical sense of what levels are most likely to afford support or resistance, as the case may be, to future price movements. Naturally, such manifestations of minor supports as were shown in the August to November advance in Snider Packing, are of importance to the intermediate trend trader only when they are broken. Reactions to the levels of preceding tops in an

Fig. IX.4

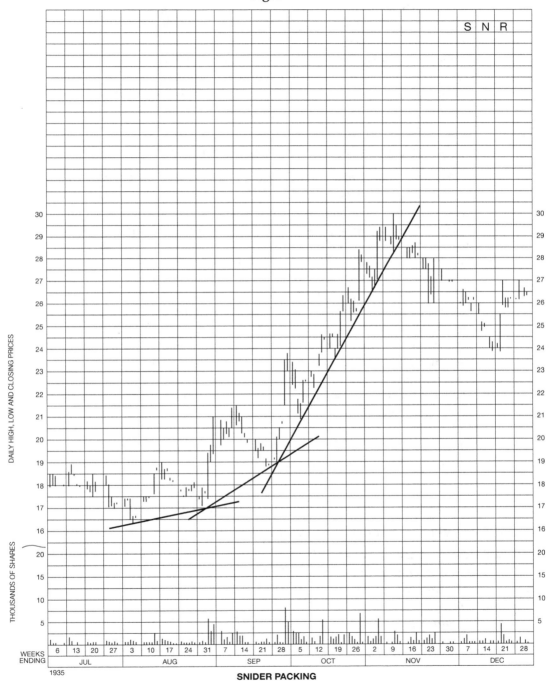

SNIDER PACKING

intermediate advance are a normal expectation and do not carry any unfavorable implication. The breaking of what should be a good support level for a minor reaction, however, suggests a more important change in the technical picture and the strong possibility of an intermediate reversal of trend.

The student may find many good examples of minor support and resistance in the charts illustrating our previous studies in this Course. The levels are clearly defined in the Mack Trucks chart (Fig. V.9) and the Electric Boat chart (Fig. VI.1); also in both trends on the Columbian Carbon chart (Fig. VI.17).

Resistances Set Up by Patterns and Trend Lines

We have learned the importance in technical forecasting of support and resistance levels established in previous trading history, and we have observed how such levels may function interchangeably as either resistance or support depending on the direction from which prices approach them. We have noted in our preliminary discussion of resistance that there are various possible reasons for this repetitive action, including the factor of memory. Once established these levels do not change with the passage of time although they may eventually lose their effectiveness; in other words, the resistance at a certain level may become exhausted and disappear but it does not change its level. And we have noticed how long they last, especially if made originally on high volume.

Now, however, we come to a different type of resistance which does not arise from previous manifestations of support or resistance, repeating always at the same general level, but which is created instead by a price trend or pattern or one of our well-defined area formations. The support or resistance so created may be encountered at different levels depending on the time element; this week it may be expected at a certain price level but next week it will be met at a higher or a lower level. In other words, the line of support or resistance to price movement set up by many trend and area patterns is a diagonal rather than a horizontal line.

Trend Lines Defining Support and Resistance

In Study VIII we discussed the tendency of prices to move in waves within fairly regular trends which frequently can be defined with great precision by a single trend line, and occasionally by a set of more or less parallel lines along either side of the trend channel. In an upward price trend the primary and most dependable line is drawn across the bottoms of successive reactions. This line becomes in effect a sort of moving support

The line of support or resistance to price movement is a diagonal rather than a horizontal line.

level tending to halt and reverse price declines whenever they approach it. In a downward price movement the primary trend line is drawn across the tops of successive rallies and becomes a moving resistance level. Where the trend channel is sufficiently regular to permit the construction of parallel trend lines, the upper line functions as a moving resistance level and the lower as a moving support level.

Perhaps this attempt to relate ordinary trend action to support and resistance phenomena is not founded on any true and fundamental connection between the two, except in the very broad sense that we should naturally expect resistance to develop against any great departure from a trend dictated by major, basic conditions. But when we come to a consideration of the price action that follows characteristically after a trend line is broken, we have a "horse of a different color". We find that the old trend line still resists any movement of prices back through it. We had occasion to refer to this phenomenon in our study of trend lines in the preceding section of this Course, under the subject of the "throwback" (see page 289).

Broken Trend Lines Soon Lose their Technical Significance

This continuing effectiveness of trend lines after they have been broken disappears rapidly, however. Once a new trend becomes clearly defined outside the old trend boundaries, the old trend lines seldom appear to have any technical significance. In fact, the resistance (or support) to a throw-back usually appears only once; a second price movement back toward the old trend is likely to meet little or no opposition at the old line. The longer the lapse of time after a trend line is broken before a throwback movement occurs, the less potent the line becomes as support or resistance to that movement.

The Cradle – a Strong Resistance Point

Knowing that a single trend line has important support and resistance functions, even after it has been broken for at least a limited time, we should naturally expect that any point where two trend lines come together would be doubly difficult for prices to penetrate. This is, in fact, the case and suggests the name "cradle" for such a point.

The cradle appears where any two converging trend lines cross. Its appearance in a rapid upward trend is illustrated by the Anaconda chart (Fig. IX.5), where the two lines, A and B, intersect at the 30 level during the first week of May, 1936. Note the reaction of prices to this point. Prices do not always return to a cradle, but it is notable that they do return in many cases, and that the movement almost invariably is stopped there and reversed. Later on, well beyond the cradle, one or both of the trend lines may be broken.

Fig. IX.5

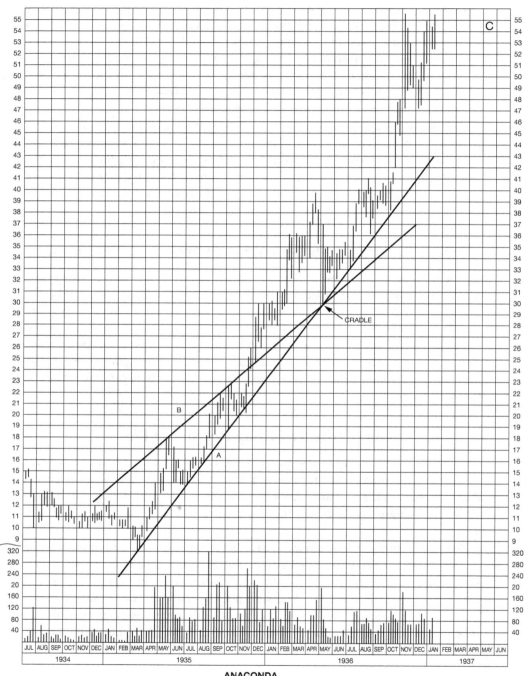

ANACONDA

Resistance and Support at Head and Shoulders Reversals

The various reversal and continuation formations studied in the first part of this Course also have characteristic support and resistance lines which, like trend lines, function strongly for a certain length of time after prices have left the formation. In the case of the Head and Shoulders Pattern, the neck-base line extended beyond the point where it is "broken", becomes a critical line on the chart. After this line is first broken, giving the signal of a reversal in trend, prices may return to it but very seldom are able to get back through the line by any decisive margin. Where the neck-base line is a horizontal one, the support or resistance which it sets up is easily explained by our general rules brought out in the first portion of this Study. Where the neck-base line slopes up or down, however, its function as a support or resistance is comparable only with the similar action of trend lines.

> *Any point where two trend lines come together would be doubly difficult for prices to penetrate.*

A good example of resistance at the extended neck-base line of a normal Head and Shoulders top can be seen in the week of October 24 on the chart of Union Carbide and Carbon (Fig. IX.6). The functioning of a sloping neck-base line as a support is shown on the chart of the Head and Shoulders top in Union Pacific on the same page (see weeks ending October 12 and 19).

Like the minor support and resistance levels which we studied on the daily chart of Snider Packing (Fig. IX.4), the support and resistance function of a neck-base line is, for the intermediate trend trader, more to be "honored in the breach than in the observance." The return of prices to that line is not to be considered abnormal, nor does it contradict the forecast of the Head and Shoulders formation. So long as the neck-base line "holds" (as it nearly always does) against any attempt of prices to move back through it again, the original forecast is still in force.

Support and Resistance Lines on Multiple Formations

In our analysis of the Double Top and Double Bottom, and the related multiple formations (in Study IV) we observed that a Double Top is not completed technically until prices have declined from the second top down through the level of the "valley" between the two tops. We can now relate this observation to our study of support and resistance phenomena. The "valley" indicated a support level and, until this support was penetrated, we could not conclude that a reversal of trend had occurred. Of course, once this support level is penetrated it becomes a resistance

Fig. IX.6

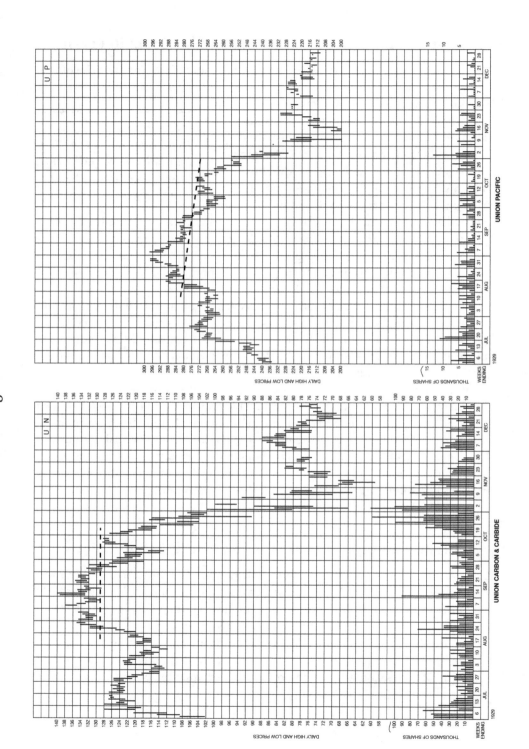

level to any subsequent advance. The same principle applies in the analysis of the other varieties of multiple tops and bottoms.

Applying the Rules to the Rectangles and Right-angle Triangles

A similar support and resistance interpretation applies to the action of prices within and after they leave a Rectangle. Obviously, the upper and lower boundary lines of this familiar and dependable forecasting pattern are resistance and support levels. When a break-out occurs, penetrating one of these levels, that level changes its role at once; if the price advances, breaking the upper or resistance level, that level thereupon becomes a support. Prices may continue to advance for a few days or even for a week or two following the break-out and then react to the level of the top of the old pattern, and get support there, before a strong up-trend develops. When prices break down out of a Rectangle, the bottom or support boundary becomes a resistance level to which a subsequent rally may return, but seldom penetrates.

In the same manner, the upper or horizontal boundary of an Ascending Triangle becomes a support level after a break-out; and the lower boundary of a Descending Triangle becomes a resistance level. The support action was demonstrated in the movement of prices after the break-out from the Ascending Triangle in Anaconda Copper which we examined in Study VI (page 188). An excellent example of the resistance function of a Descending Triangle appeared in the American Can chart in Fig. VI.5; and the same rules apply, of course, to any pattern with a horizontal boundary line.

Support and Resistance Set Up by Symmetrical Triangles

When we come to analyze the points at which evidences of support or resistance appear after a break-out from a Symmetrical Triangle, we find a quite different type of action. The pattern of support and resistance lines which form around the latter part of a Symmetrical Triangle is an interesting one and might almost be compared to a "magnetic field."

The first line of defense against any return movement of prices following a decisive break-out, depends on how far from the apex the break-out occurs. If the break-out takes place before the pattern is completed – say, only half or two-thirds of the distance from the beginning of the formation toward its theoretical apex – and prices thereafter do not move very far away before a reaction occurs, we may expect that reaction to be halted at or near the extended boundary line of the formation. In other words, if prices break out on the up-side and then the advance is halted very quickly and reversed, the upper boundary of the original pattern becomes a support line, in

Fig. IX.7

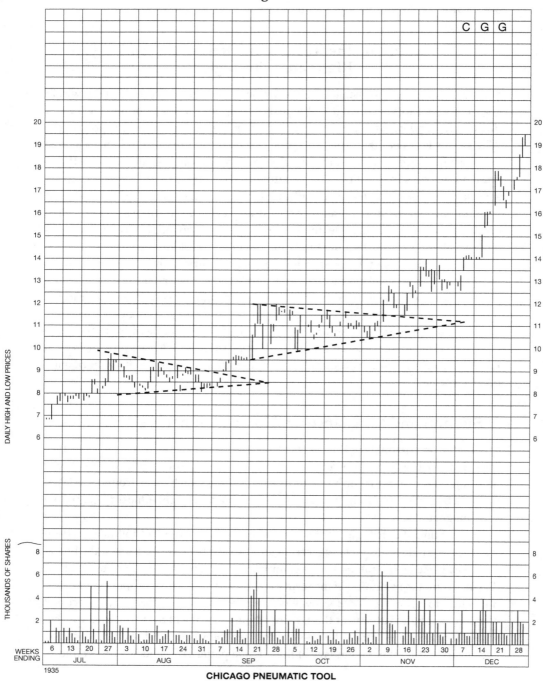

CHICAGO PNEUMATIC TOOL

much the same fashion as a trend line after the latter has been penetrated. If the break-out occurs on the down-side, the lower boundary of the Triangle becomes a resistance line to any immediate rally.

A good example of support at the boundary of a Symmetrical Triangle appears in the chart of Chicago Pneumatic Tool for the last half of 1935, reproduced in Fig. IX.7. The price pattern which started to build in the third week of September broke out with a decisive advance, attended by a conspicuous burst of volume, on November 4. This advance, however, was continued for only one more day of trading and then prices dropped back (with volume characteristically diminishing). On November 12 the price range touched the extended top boundary of the Symmetrical Triangle and "bounced" away again. Of course, we should not expect that support will always make itself evident so precisely at the exact line as it did in this example; a fraction of a point either way in a stock selling in this range would be an equally good manifestation of support.

The Apex Level Becomes Significant

Now suppose that our Symmetrical Triangle formation does not break out until near its apex, and a reaction ensues before prices have moved very far away from the break-out level. In that case the normal expectation is that the return movement of prices will meet resistance at the approximate level of the Triangle's apex. An illustration of this may be seen on the 1931 chart of US Industrial Alcohol in Fig. II.3. Within the large Head and Shoulders top that formed in February and March in this stock there was a good Symmetrical Triangle bounded by the heavy dotted lines. This was broken on the down-side, near its apex, on March 12 but no great pressure of liquidation developed on the first break-out and a short rally ensued. Note how this rally was halted for three days, however, at the apex level, and the downward movement then got under way in earnest.

The potency of the apex level for support or resistance seems to extend for some distance beyond the apex itself and the chart student is sure to find in the course of his charting operations many examples of reactions to this level following an initial break-out from a Symmetrical Triangle formation. So long as this level resists the return of prices back through it the forecast given by the break-out may be considered to be still in effect.

The Symmetrical Triangle Forms a Cradle

The intersection of the two sides of a Symmetrical Triangle forms a cradle, just as does the intersection of converging trend lines previously discussed. And, just as we might expect, this cradle point puts up a very strong resistance to any attempt of

Fig. IX.8

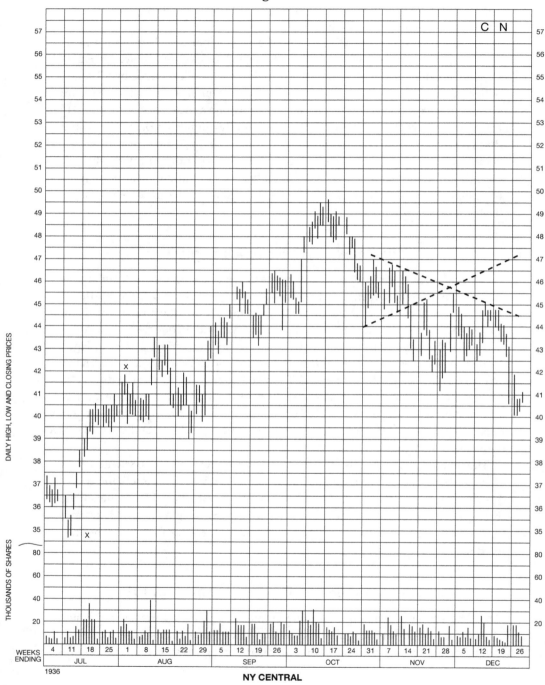

NY CENTRAL

prices to move through it, and such an attempt is usually reversed very quickly. An example of resistance at a cradle point appears in the late 1936 chart of New York Central in Fig. IX.8. Following the top in this stock in mid-October, a broad Symmetrical Triangle was built by the price action from October 26 to November 12. After the break-out on the down-side, the price rallied, on November 17, to the bottom boundary of the Triangle and met resistance there as we might have anticipated. The ensuing decline extended to 41¼ where another minor reversal occurred, taking the stock back up to 45½ on November 28. There it met resistance at the cradle formed by the extended sides of the Triangle. A later rally, in the second week of December, was turned back below the apex level, at the extended top boundary of the Triangle which thus functioned in much the same manner as any trend line. The sides of a Symmetrical Triangle may, in fact, be considered minor trend lines.

The Symmetrical Triangle in the New York Central chart was actually a part of the larger Complex Top which the student has no doubt recognized; its price action was quite well defined but the volume during its formation was irregular. The pattern of resistance levels following its break-out, however, was exactly what might have been anticipated, and the fact that resistance was encountered at these levels on three strong rallies, tended only to confirm the Triangle forecast calling for a further decline.

A Third Significant Level

We have considered in the preceding paragraphs the levels where support or resistance may be anticipated when a minor reversal occurs shortly after a breakout from a Symmetrical Triangle and before prices have moved very far away from the pattern. In a majority of cases, however, a decisive break-out carries prices quite a distance before the movement is halted or "corrected." In such cases we should not expect a return all the way back to the apex level, at least not without some fairly definite indication of a change in the technical trend. In the normal sequence of price movement we find, in fact, that once we have gotten well away from the Triangle any minor reversal or "correction" is usually stopped at the approximate level of the extreme top (or bottom) of the Triangle, made at the beginning of its formation. In other words, we have now left the "magnetic field" of the Triangle itself, and may look for the more common support and resistance action which was exemplified in the Snider Packing chart in Fig. IX.4.

A small-scale but perfectly typical illustration of this action appears in the Electric Boat chart (Fig. VI.1). Note that the reaction following the breakout from the small Triangle on December 5, met support at 11¾ the level of the top of the Triangle. The Auburn chart (Fig. III.7) shows two good examples of this type of support – on November 15 at the top level of the preceding Triangle Bottom, and on December 20 at the top level of the preceding Continuation Triangle. The latter level still held as a support, in fact, on the next reaction in the second week of January.

Refer also to the weekly chart of Texas Corporation (Fig. III.13) for an example of resistance at the bottom extremity of a Symmetrical Triangle. Compare the Triangle which formed December, 1930 to February, 1931 with the advance in August, 1931.

Judgment Required in Forecasting Support Levels

We have seen in the foregoing study of Symmetrical Triangles that the levels at which support or resistance may normally be expected to develop, depend on the extent of the price movement following the break-out and the time when the reverse movement occurs. It is impossible to lay down any exact arithmetical rule by which the chart student may determine just where and when one level has been passed and another reached. Experience as well as study is required to gain a sound judgment of what constitute critical levels at any stage of price movement. The beginner need not be unduly alarmed, however; if he studies his charts carefully and analyzes every action and reaction with respect to the patterns preceding it, he will quickly acquire a "feeling" for support and resistance phenomena and, incidentally, a great respect for this very interesting subject.

Support and Resistance at Gaps

One more phenomenon requires some brief consideration in connection with our pattern studies and that is the effect of Gaps on support and resistance levels. When a Gap appears as prices break out of a technical formation, we have learned that such a Gap is seldom "closed". It would follow naturally that the abnormal technical condition which produced the Break-away Gap, might well set up at the same time a support or resistance level which would stop any attempt of prices to return to the old pattern. A reaction which follows shortly after an upward Break-away Gap is, in fact, usually supported at or near the level of the top of the Gap. Note for example the price action on June 19 on the Johns-Manville chart in Fig. III.12. And downward Gaps set up similar resistance levels.

> *Experience is required to gain a sound judgment of what constitute critical levels of price movement.*

Continuation Gaps sometimes function in the same way. A good example of support at the level of an upward Continuation Gap appears in the Timken Roller Bearing chart (Fig. IV.6). Note the Gap formed during the second week of February at the 52 level and the reaction to that level the first week of March. Generally speaking, if the Gap is a wide one, we may expect some support at its top level; if that fails to hold, support may appear within the Gap or at its bottom level; if those fail, the suggestion is that the price movement will continue eventually to the next support level.

Practical Uses of Pattern Resistance Study

We have given considerable time and space in this chapter of our technical studies to the analysis of the various support and resistance levels which are normally developed by the principal continuation and reversal formations. It would be natural to ask why we need to pay so much attention to them. One reason – and the most important one – is that an understanding of the normal habits of price movements saves us from undue worry. We shall not become too concerned if we have bought a stock when its chart showed a decisive break-up out from an Ascending Triangle, for example, and then see the price react right back to the level of the Triangle. So long as the normal support appears at that level, we may retain our confidence in our original forecast and expect the worthwhile upward movement predicted by the Triangle to come in due time.

A Second Opportunity to Buy or Sell

A second, very practical reason for studying support and resistance phenomena in connection with forecasting formations, is that we are often enabled thereby to make a commitment at a profitable level which we missed making when it was first signalled on the chart. For one reason or another, we may not have bought a stock when it first broke out of a pattern in an ascending movement; if a reaction back to the support level of the pattern ensues, however, we have another good opportunity to buy before the movement gets away from us.

The most favorable buying (or selling) opportunity comes as soon as the break-out shows up on the chart.

Many experienced technical traders, in fact, buy only a part of their "line" on the break-out, figuring on buying the rest when and if a reaction to support takes place, even placing an order in advance to buy at the anticipated support level. There is much to be said in favor of this policy but the beginner should keep in mind the fact that such reactions do not always occur – or if there is a quick reaction it does not always carry back to the support level. A rapid review of the illustrations of typical formations throughout this Course will show that in the great majority of cases the most favorable buying (or selling) opportunity comes as soon as the break-out shows up on the chart.

How Long Are Previous Levels Valid

The question arises frequently in technical chart analysis as to how long a previous support or resistance level retains its power and importance. It is admittedly difficult to arrive at a definite answer. Some clues may be gleaned from our study of the possible explanations of these levels at the beginning of this chapter; we have noted also that volume is a factor to be considered.

Speaking very generally, the support and resistance levels established by minor fluctuations such as we saw in the Snider Packing chart (Fig. IX.4), lose their importance after two or three months. On the other hand, the support and resistance levels established by the tops or bottoms of important intermediate movements in a major trend (such as we saw in the weekly chart of General Electric in (Fig. IX.1) may still be effective after a lapse of years when the next major trend brings prices back to those levels. We have, then, the general rule that the greater the movement which produces it, the longer the potency of any level in future market action.

Then, in the next major trend we may, of course, have new levels develop – as well as the old ones that repeat – and these new levels may become significant in turn in another later trend. For example, note on the daily chart of General Electric in Fig. IX.3 the resistance that showed up at 44$\frac{1}{2}$ the week ending August 1. This 44$\frac{1}{2}$ level became support for the reactions August 21 and September 25. The general 44$\frac{1}{2}$ level may show up again as support or resistance months later, perhaps taking the place of the old 46$\frac{1}{2}$ level as an important level in future trading. So far as we can see on this chart, however, it is to be regarded only as one of our minor levels which may soon lose its value.

> *The support and resistance levels established by the tops or bottoms of intermediate movements in a major trend may still be effective after a lapse of years.*

Another factor seems to have some bearing on our question of longevity and that is the sharpness of the price movement to and away from the original reversal level. A gently rounding top following a slow rise in prices, usually has less effectiveness as a support level after a lapse of time, than does a sharp peak formed by a rapid advance of prices and then a rapid retreat. In this connection note the long lasting importance of the 42 level in the General Electric charts (Figs IX.1 and IX.2) first established by the sharp drop to that level in the Fall of 1929 and the fast subsequent rally away from it.

Fifty and One Hundred as Critical Levels

Every follower of the stock market has noticed at one time or another how price movements are halted and congestions developed around the even fifty and hundred levels. There is no doubt but what prices have difficulty in many cases in "working through" these levels. The reason is, probably, simply a reflection of the tendency we all have to think in round numbers. How often we hear the casual comment on a stock selling at say, 42, that it "ought to go to 50". Traders are apt to place buy or sell orders at these round number levels, and what started as a purely artificial resistance becomes reinforced by public covering or profit-taking taking, as a consequence of which the influence of these levels on future market action is further strengthened. Moreover, in former days, 100 was the par value of most leading stocks and "par" was naturally an important and significant level, tending to stop any movement of prices through it from either direction. Such very artificial support and resistance levels, however, are not as powerful as those more natural levels previously discussed; the back history of trading, after all, is our best and safest guide.

The Half-way Intermediate Movement Theory

Although it is not; perhaps, related technically to our study of support and resistance, this seems to be a logical place to take up briefly a general theory of price action which has, at one time or another, been given considerable attention by market analysts. This theory states that when a major movement is interrupted by a reversal, this interruption is to be regarded as only an intermediate movement so long as it retraces half or less than half of the ground covered by the previous major move. If the assumed intermediate movement carries on and retraces more than half the ground covered by the previous move in the direction of the major trend, then the suggestion is that a reversal in the basic trend may be in the making. What we assumed at first to be only an intermediate correction may now very likely become instead the first true movement in a new major trend.

Examination of a great many charts over a period of years shows that this theory has some foundation in fact, but is not an altogether reliable trading rule. The majority of intermediate corrections do not retrace much over a half of the previous movement in the direction of the major trend, but some retrace two-thirds of the distance and occasionally a correction will take prices almost all the way back, without the basic trend being reversed. Two-thirds is, perhaps, a safer limit to set: an intermediate movement then which retraces two-thirds of the distance covered by the previous major movement would certainly be subject to suspicion as indicating a possible major reversal.

The "Bounce" Away from Support or Resistance

One more point remains to be discussed in connection with the practical application of our support and resistance study, and that is the action of prices when they approach such a level. A quick inspection of the various chart examples we have used to help our understanding of these phenomena, indicates that prices may do one of two things – they may either halt and build a pattern of congestion lasting for some time before the level is finally penetrated, or they may "bounce" back into a reversal movement of more or less importance.

There seems to be no dependable guide to forecasting which type of price action will follow the attainment of a critical support or resistance level. (In fact, we have seen that occasionally there will be no halt of any consequence in the current movement, but that is the exception rather then the rule). We must take into account other chart factors, such as volume, the extent and sharpness of the preceding movement, the character and size of the pattern from which it arose, the appearance of the charts of other stocks, and the market as a whole, as well as the potential strength of the anticipated support or resistance. And then we must watch to see what sort of pattern develops on the individual chart of the stock which has reached this critical level.

A Good Place to Take Profits

In the final analysis, it is a pretty safe rule to withdraw from the stock when it nears what looks as though it might be a strong support or resistance zone, depending upon your position, and wait to see what develops before again entering the market. If, for example, we had bought General Electric in 1935 and had carried it up into February, 1936 (see Fig. IX.2), we should have been well advised to sell it and take our profit when it approached the 42 level which previous trading history had indicated would likely be a "tough" resistance point. Then we might wait to see whether GE could work through that level before we bought it again, or watch for the building of some strong ascending pattern to indicate that the advance was ready to continue. Such a pattern did, in fact, develop (on the daily chart of the period) in May, 1936.

The natural corollary of this sound trading rule suggests that it is not good practice to buy a stock – that is, take a new long position in it – when the price is close under a strong resistance level. We may have a break-out from what appears to be a powerful pattern just two or three points under a resistance level; judging by the pattern alone we might be tempted to buy, but we know that the resistance is there and may overcome completely the technical strength of our pattern. In such cases, the conservative trader waits to see whether the resistance will "hold." If the resistance level is decisively broken then he can confidently count on a worthwhile movement.

Use of Support and Resistance Levels in Short Selling

We have already noted, on page 307, the failure of even the best nearby support levels to hold in the panic phase of a bear market. At these times prices drop precipitately, under pressure of accumulative margin calls and forced selling, until weak holdings and the public generally have been thoroughly shaken out. With this exception, however, bear market tactics differ in no respect from the bull market tactics discussed in the paragraphs above.

It is not advisable to sell a stock short when its price has dropped to, or is nearing, a good support level. The safest level at which to go short is after a rally to the vicinity of a resistance point, or right after a decisive break down through support. Then as the next support level is approached the short sale should be covered and the stock given a chance to rally before again selling it short.

Study X

MEASURING RULES AND FORMATIONS

The trader in stocks has three questions to decide before he takes a position in any particular issue. They are:

1. When has a movement started?
2. In which direction will prices move – up or down?
3. How far can the movement carry before it is reversed, or halted in a long and unprofitable congestion?

The first two of these questions are answered directly and with a high degree of dependability for the technical student, by the patterns and formations we have analyzed in the first seven chapters of this Course. The third question, however, is certainly of equal importance, for with all the market to choose from, we naturally want to use our trading capital to best advantage at all times. We want to buy or sell only those stocks which promise the most worthwhile movements percentage-wise. So it behooves us in interpreting our charts, constantly to compare one opportunity with another and to estimate as well as we can which offers the greater profit.

Back History of Support and Resistance

In our study of Support and Resistance (Study IX) we saw how useful those levels, established in the previous trading history of a stock, became in forecasting its future market action. Especially in the longer range analysis of major and intermediate trends as pictured on the weekly charts, the influence of old support and resistance points was clearly evident even after the lapse of years. From those levels we derive our first and best aid in estimating the probable objective of a price movement once it has gotten under way. Suppose we find amongst the number of issues we are charting, two stocks in about the same price class which have developed formations of apparently equal strength, both breaking out at the same time in what would seem to promise a profitable upward movement. But suppose the back history of one, as shown on its long-range weekly chart, indicates a probable resistance zone only a few points above the current price level, while in the case of the other there is nothing in the back history to suggest any resistance for 20 or 30 points above the break-out. Obviously, other things being equal, the second stock has a better chance of making a worthwhile advance than the first. The first may conceivably, if its technical action is very strong, plow right through its old resistance level and move on up for many points without a halt, but the odds are against it; the more likely consequence is at least a long and patience-trying delay at the old resistance level, with the possibility even of a reaction and the building of another pattern before the resistance is finally penetrated.

Noting Significant Price Levels on Current Charts

A thorough and painstaking analysis of the trading history of any stock whose market action we may wish to chart for trading purposes, is therefore well worth the time and trouble it entails. That trading history is most easily studied and the probable levels of support and resistance determined through the medium of the weekly charts. And our study should carry back at least to the beginning of the preceding major trend. In other words, if we are charting a stock during a long-term bull market movement we should examine its trading history all the way back to the top from which the preceding bear market started. If we are following a stock in a bear market we should analyze its action back to the bottoms from which the preceding bull market started, in order to determine its probable support levels.

If we wish to be particularly thorough we may carry our studies even farther back into history by means of monthly charts, with a view to establishing the most important levels which tend to repeat as supply or demand areas. Monthly charts may, in fact, be used instead of the weeklies in analyzing the trend immediately preceding the current one, but some of the significant levels as well as the volume action tend to become obscured on the monthly charts; the weekly record if available is much more helpful. Once we have determined as well as we can through our study of past trading history the levels where resistance or support are most likely to be encountered by our stock in its current trend, we can note these levels on our current daily charts. We may even mark these levels according to their anticipated importance, by means of some convenient code. By transferring our notations from one sheet to the next when it becomes necessary to start a new sheet, we can thus keep before us constantly a valuable gauge to our stock's potential movements while we watch its daily action to determine when to trade in it, and save ourselves the time and labor of digging out the back history every time the stock moves.

Trend Lines as Measuring Indications

In Study VIII we studied trend lines and trend action, and we learned that once a definite trend has been established we can place a reasonable degree of reliance upon its continuance, at least until strong signs of reversal appear. In trend action, therefore, we have another gauge as to the probable objective of a current minor or intermediate movement; the odds favor its being halted and reversed in the vicinity of the trend line toward which it is moving. The exact price level at which this reversal occurs will depend, however, on the "angle" of the movement – that is, on the time it takes prices to get to the trend line. If the trend channel slopes at a steep angle, any minor price movement within it in the direction opposite to, or across, the basic trend may be extremely limited in terms of actual price change. This important consideration was illustrated very well in our analysis of the trend line action in Industrial Rayon (Fig. VIII.7 and pages 280–1).

Primary Trend Lines More Dependable

Generally speaking, we find trend lines most helpful in our measuring forecasts when we apply them to the "corrective" movements which run contrary to the general trend. Trend lines work best, for example, in defining the probable limits of intermediate advances within a major bear market, or the minor advances within an intermediate downward trend, and vice-versa in bull movements. In these cases we are, of course, working with the single or primary trend lines which, as we have learned, define the tops in a declining trend, or the bottoms in an advancing trend. Only occasionally can we draw good workable parallel or secondary trend lines; when we can, they are very useful in suggesting the probable objectives of price movements in both directions within the trend channel.

Measuring Implications of Patterns Themselves

The student will see that both of the preceding methods of estimating the probable extent of a price movement depend on our recognizing in advance certain conditions which tend to set a limit to that movement, something which that movement will meet and by which it will presumably be stopped or reversed. But there are, of course, many cases where the back trading history gives us no clues as to resistance or support levels, and where no well established trend appears on the charts. In such cases we are obliged to make our estimate of the probable extent of movement by reference to its origin; we look to the pattern from which it sprang, or to signs that develop within the movement itself, to determine how strong it is and how far it is likely to go.

> *We find trend lines most helpful when we apply them to the "corrective" movements contrary to the general trend.*

In our earlier Studies, we learned that in a very general sense the larger and clearer the pattern, whether it be a reversal or a continuation formation, the more extensive the movement of prices we may expect to follow its completion. We made note also of the fact that the direction of the basic trend must be taken into account in appraising the importance of a pattern. Prices tend to move more easily in the direction of the fundamental market trend. Consequently, in a general bull market comparatively small bottom patterns may produce surprisingly extensive upward movements, while very large and impressive top formations may be followed by quite insignificant declines. In a general bear market we are apt to have just the opposite, of course, with top patterns producing long and extensive declines, and bottom patterns comparatively small rallies. This consideration of the basic trend, however, need not concern us when we are comparing the patterns appearing simultaneously in two different stocks both of which are evidently working in the same trend.

Measuring Implications of Head and Shoulders

The first reversal formation which we studied in this Course, was the Head and Shoulders. In our analysis of this pattern we made brief mention (on page 63) of one fairly reliable measuring formula that may be applied to it. This formula may be simply expressed as follows: the price movement will proceed at least as far (in terms of points or dollars) after the breaking of the neck-base line, as the vertical distance in points from the level of the head to the neck-base line, before it is halted. The halt at that point may be only a very brief one, followed by a resumption of the movement, or it may develop into a minor and temporary reversal, sending prices back in the opposite trend to the level of the old neck-base line before the movement originally forecast by the Head and Shoulders is resumed. Or a complete technical change may develop at that point canceling and reversing the Head and Shoulders forecast.

Testing the Head and Shoulders Measuring Formula

We may apply this rule to the various Head and Shoulders formations pictured on the charts in our preceding lessons and check its accuracy. Starting with the Head and Shoulder top in Republic Steel (Fig. II.1) if we draw the neck-base line across points C and I, the vertical distance from that line to the top of the head is about 28 points. The neck-base line was broken at the 112 level by the price action of the last week of October. Applying our measuring rule, we should expect a halt in the downward movement to show up on the chart 28 points lower, or around the 84 level. The movement was not, in fact, halted until it had reached 73, where a minor rally sent prices back up to 89.

In the Head and Shoulder top in Western Union (Fig. II.2), our rule worked out with surprising accuracy, but in the case of the US. Industrial Alcohol top, (Fig. II.3) the rule called for a halt around the 56 level and the movement shot right through this level and showed no signs of stopping until it reached 38. The rule worked on the Borden chart (Fig. II.4), and in connection with Head and Shoulders bottoms, on the Montgomery Ward chart (Fig. II.6), also on the Du Pont chart (Fig. II.7). On the Woolworth chart (Fig. II.5), on the other hand, the measurement of the small Head and Shoulder bottom called for a first advance to about 52 before a halt; instead a minor reversal occurred at G at 50½. The formula applied to the larger, outer, Head and Shoulder called for an advance to 56, and this also failed by a slight margin.

Reliability of Head and Shoulders Measuring Rule

Inspection of the examples cited in the preceding paragraphs gives us a very good idea of the degree of dependability we can place in our rule, although it is suggested that the student check all the other Head and Shoulder formations he has available, including Figs. II.9, III.5, IV.10, and IX.8. It is interesting to note in the case of the last, the New York Central chart (Fig. IX.8), that our rule calls for a halt at about 40 whereas a minor reversal occurred at 41¼. Evidently, this measuring formula works fairly well but with many exceptions. It is hardly necessary for us to lay down any practical trading rule based on it. It may prove useful occasionally as suggesting a good point to take profits for a quick turn, provided another more interesting opportunity is in the meantime showing up on another chart.

Measuring Implications of Triangles

Students of the technical action of stocks have, from time to time, attempted to discover dependable measuring rules that can be applied to price movements arising from Triangle formations. It is our conclusion based on a critical examination of many hundreds of examples that no reliance can be placed in any of the theories that have been suggested. The most interesting of these theories states that prices will move about the same distance (in points) from the break-out level to the next halt or reversal, as they moved from the last preceding congestion to the first reversal point which started the Triangle. We refer to this theory as interesting because it does seem, to work out in many cases. One such case appears in the Holly Sugar chart (Fig. VI.2) and several fairly close examples in the Omnibus Corporation chart (Fig. V.11) and the Electric Boat chart (Fig. VI.1). A quick look at the many other Triangles pictured in this Course will shown, however, that the formula does not work out in the great majority of cases. Obviously, also, it cannot be applied at all to Reversal Triangles.

A more conservative measuring formula applied to Triangles states that the movement on the break-out will proceed at least as far as the extent of the price range at the open end of the Triangle or, in other words, the greatest depth of the pattern itself. It would appear that this Triangle measuring rule does work out with considerable dependability, but that we can account for the movement more reasonably on the basis of either trend or support and resistance action, usually the former.

Flags and Pennants as Measuring Patterns

Although, as we have seen, little practical trading dependence can be placed in any measuring implications of Triangles, we find an entirely different situation when we come to examine the price action which follows the completion of those closely related patterns, the flags and Pennants. These two very interesting and reliable continuation formations give us, in fact, some of our most accurate measuring forecasts.

The Flag we have learned (Study VI) forms on a mast – a nearly vertical price movement, either up or down. The length of the mast (in points) from the preceding congestion to the point where the Flag begins to form, will be found to indicate in by far the great majority of cases the extent of the rapid price movement which proceeds from the last reversal point in the Flag. Refer for example to the Flag shown on the Deere & Co. chart (Fig. VI.14). The mast on this chart ran up 18 points, from about 57 to 75 at which level the Flag began to develop. Note that this measurement is taken to the top of the Flag. Now the bottom of the Flag from which prices resumed their rapid advance, formed at the 69 level; adding 18 points to 69 gave us 87 as the probable immediate objective of the movement, exceeded in fact by only two points.

Measurement Applies Only to the Mast Itself

The same rule applies with equal dependability to all types of Flags as well as to Pennants. A clear cut example of its accuracy in connection with an upward flying Flag in an up-trend appears on the International Harvester chart (Fig. VI.16), the comparable points in this case being 79 to 91 and 89 to 101. Note, however, that in determining our measurement we take only the length of the mast itself from the last preceding congestion or minor reversal point, disregarding any previous price movement. In the case of the first Flag formed early in March on the Greyhound chart (Fig. VI.15) we should measure only the mast from the minor reversal at 30; and in the case of the third Flag formed at the end of April we should measure only from the week's congestion at the 39 level.

The Flag Rule Does Not Forecast A Reversal

The Greyhound chart (Fig. VI.15) will serve also to illustrate another point in connection with our Flag measuring formula. This formula gives us the probable immediate objective of the price movement but does not call for a reversal of trend or even a long halt when that objective is attained. We may, in fact, have only a very brief halt at that level and then a rapid continuation of the previous trend, which was the case in Greyhound in the Spring of 1935. The masts on that chart, it will be noted, were quite short and the Flags relatively large. When a mast is long (in terms of points), however, and its Flag relatively small, we should naturally expect the movement to be pretty well exhausted when its indicated objective is reached. In brief, we should apply the same judgment in our practical trading use of this measuring formula that we know it is necessary to apply in trading on any technical patterns or theories. If the movement seems to have carried prices as far as we might reasonably expect, then the Flag "yard-stick" indicates a very good level at which to take profits, step aside, and watch for further chart developments.

The "Half-mast" Congestion Pattern

Flags (and Pennants) are apparently created by quick profit-taking in unusually rapid price movements, but it is difficult to explain by any logical reasoning just why they should appear in most cases so close to the half-way point in the course of such movements. Of course, the fact that they do is what we are chiefly interested in in this study, rather than in the possible reasons for it. Whatever the reasons may be, these same causes apparently are to be credited with producing another measuring pattern which carries the same forecast as the true Flag.

This closely related measuring pattern we have called the Half-mast Congestion. It can hardly be classified as a pattern at all in the sense in which we have used the word throughout this Course, for it does not take any single definite form. It is simply a very compact price congestion which forms on a "mast" and extends for five days up to three weeks, its duration depending roughly on the length of the mast. This congestion may take on the appearance of a very small "solid" Triangle or Rectangle, with volume tending to shrink as it forms, just as we expect volume to act toward the completion of any true continuation formation. In some cases it cannot be related visually to any of our recognized patterns but it is, in all cases, notably solid or compact and it should not show any tendency for prices to "give way", or for the price range to broaden out. It forecasts a rapid continuation of prices in the same direction and about the distance as the mast which preceded it, and more often than not suggests a good level at which to take profits.

Examples of Half-mast Congestions

An almost perfect example of this extremely helpful measuring formation is shown on the chart of Western Union for the last half of 1935 (Fig. X.1). After struggling for two months, the 51–52 resistance level was penetrated with a terrific burst of

Fig. X.1

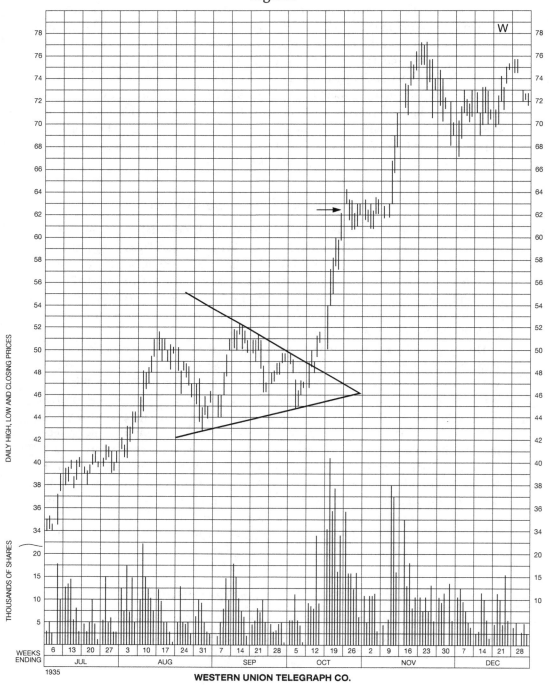

WESTERN UNION TELEGRAPH CO.

activity on October 14 and a nearly vertical advance to 64 ensued. There the movement was halted, and the price action built a very compact congestion pattern with volume declining until November 7 when another burst of volume appeared and the price moved up in less than two weeks to 77. Measuring from the break-out level at 52 to the top of the first mast at 64 gave us our measurement of 12 points for the probable extent of the next move; note how accurately this forecast was borne out. This particular Half-mast Congestion bears a slight optical resemblance to, but cannot be strictly defined as, a Triangle; it is, however, a very compact congestion with no semblance of "give" to it. If we were not already "long" of Western Union at this time we might well have bought the stock when we saw its price and volume action on our chart through the week ending November 2.

A Less Distinct Example

The chart of US Rubber for the first half of 1936 (Fig X.2), contains another good example of a Half-mast Congestion formed during the week ending March 21. In this case, prices advanced in a "mast" from $19\frac{1}{2}$ to 27 and then built a compact congestion around the 26 level for a week during which volume declined. A rapid continuation to about 34 was indicated and did in fact get started on March 24 (note the volume) but in this case the movement was quickly halted around 30 where it had carried out only half of its indicated advance. Two weeks of indecisive action ensued and our Half-mast pattern at this time appeared to have been thrown overboard by the sharp reversal in the general market trend which was then occurring. Nevertheless, on April 8 another burst of activity appeared and the price was marked up to its predicted goal.

Reliability of the Half-mast Pattern

The two examples of Half-mast Congestions which we have shown worked out so accurately that it is, perhaps, necessary to pause here and repeat once again our words of caution against an utter and blind dependence on any technical pattern or other forecasting indication. There are no such words as "always" or "never" in the technical analysis of stock charts. The Half-mast congestion and the Flags are very dependable patterns as technical formations go, but they may and do occasionally violate all the rules and disappoint us by failing to work. The trader who buys or sells on their implications must be ready to change his mind and abandon his position when the "exception that proves the rule" does appear.

Like the Flags and Pennants, the Half-mast Congestion appears in down as well as up trends, and carries the same forecast in either direction.

Fig. X.2

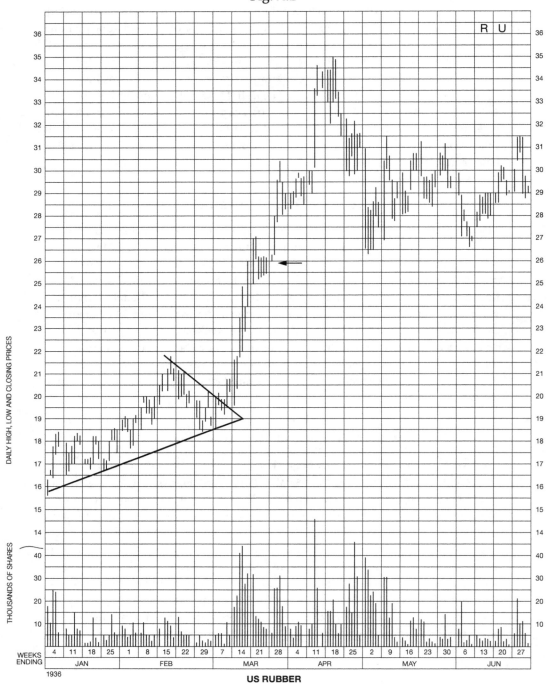

US RUBBER

Measuring Theories Applied to Gaps

Still another set of measuring theories has been based on the appearance of price Gaps. In fact, Continuation Gaps have been called Measuring Gaps by some students because of their reputed measuring value. There may be logic in the belief that Gaps should be relatable in some way to extent of price movement. Gaps are evidence of an abnormal condition in the technical picture and should, therefore, lend themselves to a measurement of technical strength or weakness, which in turn should be expressed in the subsequent price advance or decline. Logical or not, however, we have found that none of the various Gap rules or theories works out with sufficient accuracy to make it a thoroughly dependable guide in trading. Nevertheless. It will pay us to examine two of these theories because they do express, however inaccurately, a measurement of price movements in which Gaps appear contrary to the habits of the stock under observation.

> *There are no such words as "always" or "never" in the technical analysis of stock charts.*

The Single Gap Measuring Theory

One measuring formula which is applied to a chart in which a Continuation Gap (see pages 252–4) appears following a normal break-out and a more or less rapid price movement, states that the movement will continue from one to one and a half times as far beyond the Gap as the distance from the break-out to the Gap. In other words, the first Continuation Gap in a rapid advance or decline (provided it was not preceded by a Break Away Gap) comes when the movement is about 40% to 50% completed. In applying this rule, we must of course, bear in mind that Gaps in a thin stock which shows Gaps frequently, have little or no technical significance.

An application of the Single Gap Measuring Theory may be made to the chart of US Steel Fig. X.3. No Gaps appeared in the price action of this stock through January, 1936. At the end of that month prices broke out of a small Symmetrical Triangle on the up-side with a good increase of volume but with no apparent disposition to "run away". The movement gathered strength on February 10, however, advancing nearly four points on that day and closing near the top of the day's range at $55\frac{1}{2}$. The strong upward push continued on the following day, taking the price to $58\frac{1}{2}$ and leaving a Gap of nearly a full point behind it. Considering the habitual close overlapping of daily price ranges in "Steel", this was a noteworthy performance and gave us an opportunity to test our measuring theory. The movement from the break-out at 49 to the Gap at 56 (disregarding fractions) covered 7 points, and the forecast

Fig. X.3

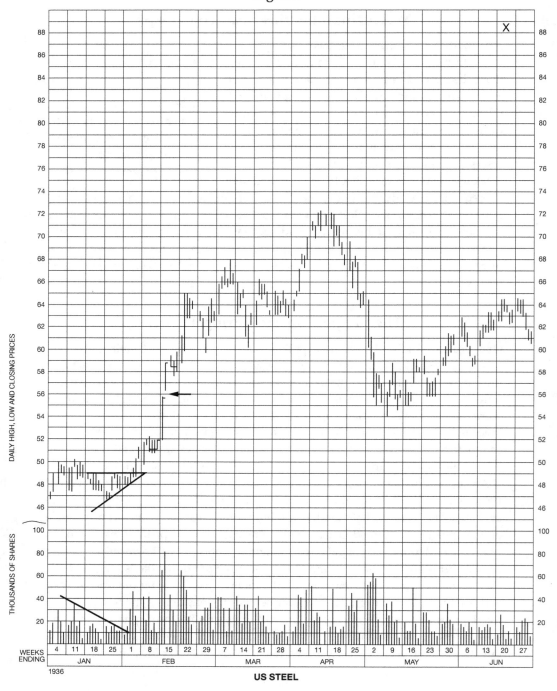

US STEEL

of the Gap called, consequently, for a further rapid advance of from 7 to 10 points. This would take the stock to somewhere between 63 and 66 before we should expect a halt or a reversal to develop. "Steel" did, in fact, move right up to 65, thus carrying out the forecast most generously.

Wide Variance in Movements Following Gaps

Now, it is only fair to state that the student with plenty of chart history available can find a goodly number of examples to prove almost any measuring formula within reason which he may choose to demonstrate. It is easy to find them, that is, after the movement is completed. But, in the practical application of the Single Measuring Gap Rule, at the time a Gap appears on our chart, we are often faced with the difficulty of deciding just what price level we should take as the origin of the movement and from which our measurement should start. Also we are not always able to decide positively and immediately whether we are faced with a Continuation Gap or an Exhaustion Gap. Finally, even when the origin of the movement is well defined and the Gap is obviously of the Continuation class, the subsequent movement may fall far short of the suggested limits or extend far beyond it.

Single Gaps in rapid price movements appear in the chart of General Theatres Equipment (Fig. IV.12) and the chart of Standard Oil of NJ (Fig. V.5). In the former a Gap came between April 22 and 23 in the down trend following a Head and Multiple Shoulders top reversal. The theoretical neck-base line of the top pattern (drawn across the bottoms of January 29 and March 13) was broken at the $10^1/_2$ level by the price action during the week ending April 11. The Gap appeared at $7^3/_4$. Applying our rule, a further rapid decline of from 3 to $4^1/_2$ points was suggested. The actual decline carried prices down 4 points, and was almost completed in a single day.

A Less Easily Interpreted Example

In the Standard Oil of NJ chart (Fig. V.5) a conspicuous Gap which was quite evidently of the Continuation class, appeared between March 24 and 25. Before we could apply our measuring rule we had first to determine our starting point. The safest – certainly the most conservative – level from which to measure was the small and rather indefinite price congestion at 67 next below the Gap, and that measurement did work out very well in forecasting the next minor congestion. Taking a longer view of the chart, however, it was apparent that a more important "break" had occurred at the 64 level where a down-sloping intermediate trend line across the January–February tops had been penetrated with a significant increase in volume. Measuring from 64, a movement to between 77 and 80 was called for. But, looking still farther back, we saw that the rapid upward trend in which our Gap appeared had really started out of the small bottom congestion at 61 (note volume) and, from that base, our Gap might forecast a continuation of the advance to somewhere between 79 and 84 before reversal. Either of these interpretations, as it happened, would have worked out fairly well since the first reversal came at the 80 level.

The student should refer also to the following examples which appear on the plates in previous lessons, some "worked" and others didn't.

Fig. I.3 –   The quarter-point Gap at 131 following the breaking of the trend line on July 28.
Fig. II.1 – The large Gap at 118 in late August.
Fig. II.3 – The small Gap at 58 in late March.
Fig. V.13 – The Gap at 112.
Fig. VI.8 – The Gap at $10^1/_2$ the week ending August 10.

Probably it is not necessary to add to our discussion of the Single Gap Rule the caution that a Gap should be disregarded as a basis for measuring if it is quickly covered.

The Multiple Gap Theory

In the preceding paragraphs we have studied the measuring formula applied to a single Gap of the Continuation type appearing in an otherwise normal price movement. If, however, a movement starts with a Break-away Gap and then shows a Continuation Gap, the logical supposition is that we have to deal with a more drastic technical change and may expect a more extensive move to follow.

This is expressed in the Multiple Gap Measuring Rule which states that the movement will continue about two times as far beyond the second Gap as the distance (in points) between the first and second Gap.

A good, clear-cut opportunity to apply this rule appeared in the US Industrial Alcohol chart (Fig. VII.15). Prices broke out of the Continuation Rectangle on the down-side with a Break-Away Gap (D) on May 19. This was followed immediately by a Continuation Gap (E). The first Gap appeared at the 45 level and the second at $41^1/_2$, a difference in points of $3^1/_2$. Two times that was 7. The forecast, then, was that the movement would continue on down 7 points from $41^1/_2$, or to somewhere around $34^1/_2$. The down trend was, in fact, halted at $33^1/_2$.

May Be Applied Also to Two Continuation Gaps

The same measuring formula is applied to the appearance of two Continuation Gaps in a rapid price movement, as well as to the combination of a Break-away and a Continuation Gap, and may be carried on indefinitely, in theory at least, so long as Continuation Gaps continue to show up in the movement. Of course, common sense warns that any abnormally rapid price movement must run into trouble eventually; an over-bought or over-sold condition is apt to develop very quickly. Consequently, we should not place too much reliance in any measuring rule based on them. There is always the danger that one of our Gaps will turn out to be of the Exhaustion variety.

A Working Example of Measuring Gap Analysis

For the application of the Multiple Gap Rule to Continuation Gaps we may turn back to our old friend, the Woolworth chart (Fig VII.14). The first opportunity to test the rule came when the Continuation Gap B appeared immediately after the Break-away Gap A. These two Gaps were approximately $1\frac{1}{2}$ points apart so their forecast was for a further advance of about 3 points which, added to the $56\frac{1}{2}$ level of the second Gap, gave $59\frac{1}{2}$ as the probable objective. Gap B was followed immediately by C, however, giving us a new base from which to measure. Skipping the arithmetic details, which the student can easily work out for himself, we now had a new forecast calling for a further advance to somewhere in the 60 range, a forecast which was carried out very nicely in short order.

The next opportunity to test the rule came when the Break-away Gap at E was followed by another Gap in three days at the 62 level. This combination called for continuation to 65. Instead, a small Island Reversal developed and prices dropped back to the support level of the Gap at E before the advance was resumed. The forecast, as it happens was carried out later but, in the mean time, the rule had failed. Still another test came in the final rally when Gap F was followed by G, forecasting continuation by our formula to about $71\frac{1}{2}$. This, as can be seen, was not quite carried out. The volume at this stage, however, made the Gap at H appear too suspiciously like an Exhaustion Gap to lead us to expect much more of the movement and, when the Gap was closed the next day, its exhaustion character was established.

Dependability of Multiple Gap Rule

The Woolworth chart gives us a very fair test of the Multiple Gap Measuring Theory and confirms the necessity for exercising caution as a movement extends farther and farther from any good foundation pattern. It demonstrates the inadvisability of relying too stubbornly on the measuring rule. The chart should be watched closely and constantly for other technical suggestions, and the measuring forecast should be abandoned promptly as soon as any upsetting factor appears. The difficulty which we noted in Study VII of distinguishing positively between Continuation and

Exhaustion Gaps, further emphasizes the risk attending a blind dependence on the Multiple Gap Theory.

The Chrysler chart (Fig. IV.7) may also be studied with reference to the application of the Multiple Gap Rule in a case where the two Gaps occur at a considerable distance apart – about as far apart, in fact, as we should expect to find them useful for measuring purposes. Generally speaking, the closer together the two Gaps, the more dependable their measuring forecast.

The Time Element in Measuring

Before we leave the subject of measuring rules, it may well be stated again that we have never found a time cycle theory that could be depended on in practical trading. The study of time theories is fascinating; it has intrigued analysts into the most exhaustive research; yet not one single reliable rule of time has ever been discovered.

FALSE MOVES AND SHAKE-OUTS

Various allusions have been made from time to time in previous chapters to the matter of False Moves and Shake-outs but up to the present we have offered no adequate explanation for this phenomenon. These movements do occur; however infrequently, and are sufficiently misleading (at least to the neophyte) to warrant the following detailed observations.

In so far as their chart interpretation is concerned there is really very little difference in the implications of the two terms. "False Move" and "Shake-out" – in fact many students use them indiscriminately to describe identical situations and we have but little quarrel with this alternate usage.

Specifically, though, the term "False Move" is more commonly used to designate a somewhat longer price movement than the "Shake-out" – the latter usually consuming but a day or two (similar to the One-day Reversal or One-day-out-of-line) while the False Move is less sharp and may extend over a week or more. The Shakeout may occur at almost any time, inside or outside a formation, while the False Move is usually considered as applying to those puzzling, rather indecisive, but comparatively limited price movements which proceed out of definite formations in the wrong direction, i.e. – opposite to the subsequent true or more extensive movement. The assumption is that the Shake-out is definitely engineered by operators in order to "cross up" the public, and catch stop-loss orders before starting their mark-up or mark-down campaign, while the False Move proper is rather the result of temporary market indecision or withdrawal of professional activity.

The Chart's Most Confusing Enemy

In any event, we are not so much concerned with their causes as we are with their results. For the purposes of this study we may use the one term "False Movement" to describe all price movements which give, or appear to give, a wrong forecast. If they proceed far enough (in terms of price movement) and are accompanied by increased volume they become the most dangerous and troublesome of all price formations in chart analysis, and practical market trading. They may simulate a genuine and valid break-out, leading us to take a position in a stock, which the subsequent movement proves to be wrong. In such cases actual loss as well as worry and mental confusion may result.

Even when they do not carry out all the requirements of a valid break-out, they are confusing and upsetting, throwing into doubt, temporarily at least, the entire theory of practical trading on chart patterns. Suppose, for instance, that a strong and highly dependable downward reversal formation has finally been completed, with every positive indication pointing to the early beginning of a long and profitable decline in a stock. But just as the stock looks weakest and perfectly prepared for commencing that major decline, the price suddenly jumps several points in a few days. This movement would be exactly contrary to the dictates of our technical analysis. But we have learned by constant precept, if not yet by practical experience, that no chart formation is infallible, that they all go wrong at times, and that when they do, the ensuing major movement is usually in exactly the opposite direction from what was anticipated. It is easy to see, therefore, that such a sudden advance, even though small, when we expected a major decline, can upset all carefully laid plans, and can lead to mental and personal confusion on the part of the practical chart student or trader.

Such a false move can so upset the average trader that he decides his chart has failed, his analysis has proven false, and that he should switch his forecast from a long downward to a major upward, movement. Consider then the further chaos of analytical judgment when, just as he has reversed his original analysis, the false move comes to an end, the stock drops off again, and then proceeds to embark on that long, powerful and profitable major downward movement which the observer had been correct in predicting from his original analysis of the downward reversal pattern.

Misleading False Moves Fortunately Rare

The False Movement may appear in almost any situation whose chart formation is susceptible to definite and dependable analysis, which means that it may appear in connection with practically any formation which our studies have taught us to recognize and credit with forecasting value. Fortunately, the majority of False Movements should not lead to our actually trading on their misleading implications provided we apply to them the "acid tests" for a valid break-out which we have previously studied. Nevertheless, we should give some attention to the kind that ought not to mislead us into taking an incorrect position, as well as to those rarer examples which are our chief concern because they do definitely give an incorrect forecast. We must learn to recognize them and to defend ourselves against them, not only with a view to cutting possible losses but also for the sake of perfecting our knowledge of how stock prices can act, and avoiding loss of confidence in our forecasting methods.

Triangles Most Susceptible to False Moves

We have already seen that the Triangle may be either a reversal or continuation pattern, though it appears more often as a continuation. Its double entendre results in the necessity, in most instances, of withholding our forecast for the direction of the next important movement until the Triangle is completed and the movement signaled by the break-away. This makes the triangular pattern especially susceptible to the confusing influence of false movements. Also, from a purely logical and natural standpoint, we might expect False Moves to occur in connection with Triangles, especially at the apex, because as that apex is neared, activity is so low and the price range so narrow that it takes only a very small over-balancing of the technical status quo to bring about an erratic and temporarily false price movement. In these same circumstances it is evident also how easy it is for professional operators to engineer a False Move. We do not wish to imply that all False Moves are purposely engineered by insiders but some of them certainly are.

False Movements should not lead to our actually trading on their misleading implications.

The Ordinary Symmetrical Triangle False Move

A good example of the False Move out of a Symmetrical Triangle appears in the chart of General Motors for 1936, (Fig. X.4). This shows what might be called the more "normal" type of False Move, and one that should not have led to a wrong forecast. Note the Symmetrical Triangle formed by the price action from April 30 to June 1, with volume declining as the pattern approached its apex. The Triangle had become so narrow by June 1 that any ordinary price range would almost inevitably have to penetrate one of its sides. The lower side was, in fact, penetrated on June 2

Fig. X.4

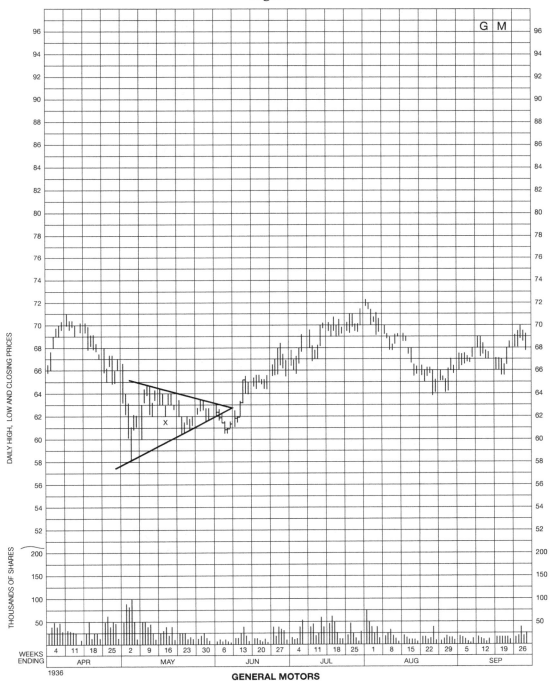

GENERAL MOTORS

and prices ranged indecisively downward for three days, closing on the 4th and 5th at 61, a full point below the penetration. Then the trend was reversed, indecisively again, until June 10 when prices rose a point and a half, closing above the Triangle's apex level, and a good advance ensued. Now note carefully the volume action attending this performance. During the entire week in which prices ranged below the Triangle, activity was at an extremely low ebb – lower than during any of the preceding weeks on this chart – but, when prices started to advance, volume picked up, with a notable increase on the day that the apex level was penetrated on the up-side.

Most False Moves Attended by Low Volume

This example, as stated, shows the more normal and less deceptive type of False Move in which volume remains at a low ebb during the movement of prices in the wrong direction, and increases when the true trend gets under way. We can see that in this case the False Move did not give a valid break-out signal; the price movement was indecisive and there was no pick-up in volume such as we expect to accompany a good break-out from a Symmetrical Triangle. Consequently, if we were following General Motors at this time we might have been somewhat concerned by the price action during the week ending June 6 but should not have been led to forecast a downward movement. Watching the volume closely, we should have suspected a False Move and, when the volume picked up the following week, that would have confirmed our suspicions and led us to the correct forecast for a price advance.

Volume increases when the true trend gets under way.

The Exceptional False Move with High Volume

A more unusual and much more deceptive type of False Move out of a Symmetrical Triangle is shown on the chart of Hiram Walker (Fig. X.5). In this case the Triangle was completed by August 5 but no break-out developed; prices continued in an indecisive side-wise trend until the end of the week when, on Saturday, volume picked up and prices started to fall. By the following Tuesday, August 11, price and volume action both indicated a valid break-out on the down-side and called for a further decline. On the next day, however, despite even greater volume, the price held firm. Two days later it advanced and closed above the apex level, and on Saturday it gained over a point and a half, with terrific volume, leaving behind it a full point Break-away Gap.

The subsequent action in Hiram Walker requires no comment. The price movement from August 8 to 12 was a False Move of the most dangerously confusing sort,

Fig. X.5

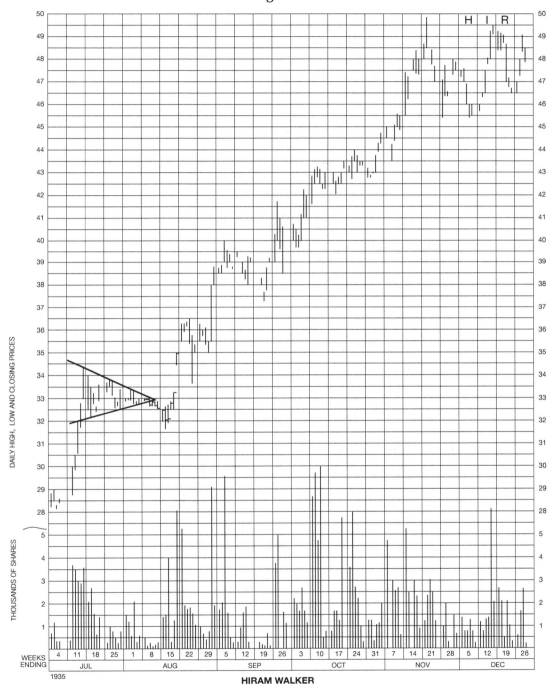

HIRAM WALKER

1935

displaying no clue whatever as to its real character. There was nothing for the trader who acted upon it to do but reverse his position quickly when the true movement developed, and take a small loss for the sake of the much greater gain to be anticipated from the true move. This False Move bears every evidence, as we examine the completed chart, of having been definitely engineered by insiders for the purpose of shaking out stock in weak hands, to add to their "line" before they started to mark it up. It is, in brief, the type of movement we might term specifically a Shake-out and it is fortunate, indeed, for the technical trader that such movements are extremely rare in today's markets and cannot be accomplished without the signals for the true move being all the more quickly and conspicuously given. We shall refer to this point later on in this study when we consider the bright side of the Shake-out picture.

False Moves from Right Angle Triangles

The two examples of False Moves previously shown have arisen out of Symmetrical Triangles and it is noteworthy that in each case they occurred after the formation had been completed into its apex. False Moves develop also out of Right-angle Triangles under the same circumstances but, quite naturally, are not so apt to mislead us since any price movement contrary to the trend suggested by the pattern itself would be subject to distinct suspicion. We have had occasion to refer briefly to one such False Move in our preceding lessons, in connection with the Ascending Triangle in Anaconda Copper (Fig. VI.4) and it is suggested that the student refer back to that chart and the comments on page 188 regarding the False Move. The pattern in Anaconda Copper suggested definitely by its ascending nature an eventual break-out on the up-side. Consequently, the movement January 17 to 21 ran contrary to the forecast of the pattern itself, and when we considered also the low volume attending it, we ought not to have been misled into relinquishing a profitable long position, much less into selling short, until more definite indications appeared on the chart. It should be emphasized that False Moves of this sort out of Ascending or Descending Triangles seldom "spoil" the pattern or occasion the re-drawing of boundary lines.

False Moves out of Rectangles

We have come to regard the Rectangle as an especially dependable forecasting pattern; any False Move arising out of a rectangular formation should therefore be most deceptive and this is, in fact, the case. It is encouraging to know that False Moves occur with extreme rarity in connection with Rectangles, but that only makes the exceptional break-out that turns out to be false all the more liable to misinterpretation.

An example of this abnormality is shown in the American Machine and Foundry chart, Fig. X.6. The price action in this stock from July 8 to August 25, 1935, built a Rectangle with volume diminishing notably during the last week of this period, suggesting an imminent break-out. On August 27, prices broke down through the lower boundary line, at the 23 level and closed at $22^{1/4}$ at the bottom of the day's range, with a goodly increase in volume. This had every appearance of a valid break-out, lacking only a small fraction of a point of carrying out the full price movement we like to have for a decisive break in a stock selling at this price level. The next day's action failed to carry the movement any farther, however, and then volume ran low again for nearly a week with prices showing no decision. On September 9 a strong upward movement started, producing a valid breakout with high volume, on the 11th, and a good advance ensued.

The False Move vs. the Out-of-line Move

What makes a False Move out of a Rectangle even more treacherous when it is attended by increased volume is the quite natural assumption on the part of the technical trader that he is dealing with an Out-of-line movement. When, for example, prices closed back on September 6 within the bounds of the Rectangle on the American Machine and Foundry chart, it was logical to consider the preceding downward break as an Out-of-line movement forecasting the eventual true trend. The break-out in the opposite direction comes therefore as an entirely unexpected and highly disturbing development.

False Moves Following Head and Shoulders

Another rare type of False Move, also highly deceptive, appears when prices break the neck-base line of a Head and Shoulders formation and then refuse to carry on in the trend which this action forecasts. An example of this phenomenon appears in the New York Central chart (Fig. IX.8). Note the Head and Shoulder pattern formed by the price action from July 23 to August 21, with the left shoulder formed July 28, the head August 6, and the right shoulder August 19. The neck-base line of this pattern slanted upward slightly and was broken on August 21 when, on increased volume, prices declined to 39 and closed nearly at the bottom of the day's range. This was approximately a full point penetration – virtually enough, considering also the volume and closing level, to call it a valid breakout. On the next day, however, prices ranged back up and closed at the neck-base line, and did not close below the line again. On August 27, with volume again increased, a strong upward move got under way.

Fig. X.6

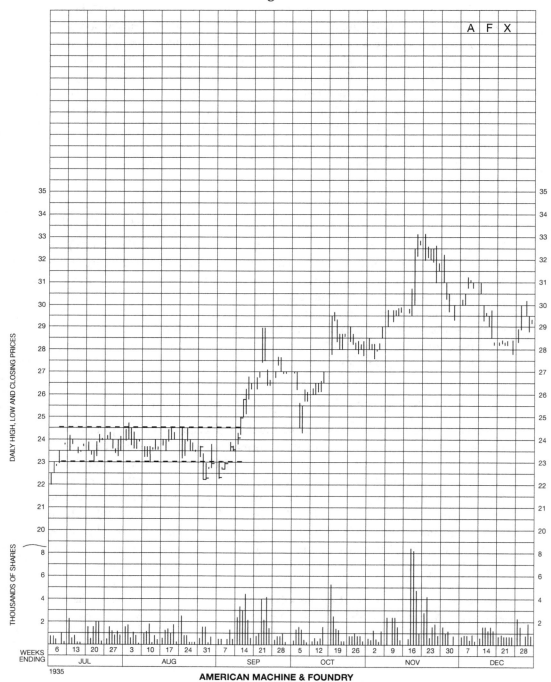

AMERICAN MACHINE & FOUNDRY

Defense against False Movements

The student may well ask, after reading the foregoing and examining the chart illustrations, if we are constantly at the mercy of these misleading phenomena. To a certain degree the answer must be, frankly, that there is no adequate or infallible defense against the most extreme type of False Move. But the extreme type is not common and against the more common, normal type of False Move we do have various helpful safeguards.

One such defense, as we have already noted, consists in a close observation of volume. In most cases, if the volume tends to increase on a move out of a pattern, or through a critical chart line, then the move is more likely to be genuine. If volume is low, or tends to diminish on the move, then it is more likely to be a False Move. This is logical because when insiders are ready to move a stock on a long major swing, they have cleaned up most of the shares available around its current levels, and it does not take much volume at that stage to produce a move. If the operators now wish to force a False Move, they will try not to lose any more than is absolutely necessary of their now-precious position. And if, as is quite possibly the case, their engineered False Move meets public action tending to reduce their position instead of increasing it as was intended, then they will certainly cut short their deceptive tactics. If, on the contrary, the move out of pattern is genuine, then insiders know they must act boldly and quickly to complete their position before their move attracts other traders to that side of the market.

The Shake-out on High Volume

There is one notable exception to the rule that low volume indicates a False Move and high volume a true trend. That is the One-day Reversal or turnover day. Such a day is marked by high volume almost all day, but with the price starting in one direction in the morning, reversing itself on volume, and coming right back again in the afternoon to the early morning level. When such a One-day Reversal breaks out of a pattern it is more characteristic of the Shake-out. In any case, it is easily distinguished by the reversal which takes place during the day, indicating that the early move was a false one and that at least the nearby trend will probably be in the opposite direction. It will be readily seen, of course, that such brief Shake-outs seldom take prices far enough out of pattern to constitute a dependable break-out signal, especially if we demand, as we should, that prices not only move but also *close* out of the pattern by a decisive margin.

Strict Construction of Break-out Rules

To sum up, our best defense against the commoner manifestations of the False Move lies in taking a very strict and conservative attitude toward all break-outs, both as to volume and extent of price movement, as well as closing level. If, in addition to meeting all of these requirements, the break-out is accompanied by a Break-away Gap (in a stock where Gaps are infrequent) we may, of course, feel doubly confident of a true movement.

In this connection it should be noted again that any break down out of a pattern occurring on or within a day or two following an ex-dividend or ex-rights day should be disregarded unless subsequent price and volume action confirm the break as due to more permanent and basic factors. This is particularly true if the break is accompanied by only ordinary volume and the amount of the price drop is closely comparable to the amount by which the stock is "ex." An example of a False Move attributable to ex-dividend action appeared in the International Harvester chart (Fig. VI.16), in the week ending September 19.

The Use of Stop-loss Orders Against False Moves

We already know from experience, or shall soon learn (later on in this study), the practical advantages of using stop-loss orders in most of our market trades. As a defense against that rare and most deceptive type of False Move which gives every price and volume indication of a genuine and valid break-out, the correct placing of stop-loss orders is most important. Unfortunately, one of the often cited drawbacks to the employment of stop-loss orders is the danger of their being caught by just such extreme cases of False Move or Shake-Out as we have been examining. Admitting this danger, especially if the stop-loss is injudiciously placed, we hold nevertheless that its habitual use is indicated.

Stop-loss orders should be so placed as to reduce the chances of their being caught by anything but a true movement. That means that they must be set far enough away to reduce to a practical minimum the probability of their being "touched off" by a Shake-Out. An experienced eye and seasoned judgment, as well as an understanding of the basic principles of placing stop-loss orders deserves a more extended consideration than we can give it here parenthetically in our False Move Study. We shall take it up in detail later in this lesson, starting on page 363 and that section should be studied with the possibility of False Moves always in mind.

False Moves Have Their Bright Side

Once we have watched the development of a False Move on our charts, and have clearly identified it as such, there is one very cheerful conclusion we may draw. There is very rarely more than one False Move out of a pattern. We are warranted, therefore, in feeling reasonably certain that we will encounter no False Move in the opposite direction. For that reason, many technical traders actually welcome False Moves because of the decisive action of prices to be expected in the opposite trend once the False Move has been completed and the true movement started. Thus a False Move, though perplexing at the time it is occurring, becomes really a friend in disguise, giving us confidence to maintain our position when prices have started to move conclusively in their true trend.

To sum up, False Movements are to be expected from time to time on our charts, and we should be constantly on our guard against them. Although they may occur from almost any type of pattern, they seem to appear more frequently near the apexes of Triangles and are usually suggested by attendant light volume and indeterminate price action. The wide-swinging shake-out type, against which there is little-protection, other than replacing our original position when warranted by later technical action, is very rare. All in all, false moves are not so much to be feared as to be recognized for what they are and turned to all possible useful advantage.

There is very rarely more than one False Move out of a pattern.

The "End Run" – Not a False Move

A phenomenon of price action which occasionally shows up on the charts and which might appear upon superficial analysis, to be related to the False Moves we have just been studying, is the "End Run." This occurs when the price movement proceeding from a perfectly valid break-out, out of a very strong pattern, fails to carry as far as the strength of the pattern forecasts, but is instead quickly reversed into a considerable movement, in the opposite direction. A good example of this End Run action appeared in the chart of Kennecott Copper for the first half of 1936 (Fig. X.7). A strong Ascending Continuation Triangle developed in this stock during the period from February 19 to April 4 with a strictly defined top or resistance boundary at 39. Prices broke decisively out of this formation on April 6 and every chart indication called for an extensive advance. Instead, the movement was quickly reversed around $41\frac{1}{2}$ and a rapid decline ensued, right down through the natural support level formed by the top of the previous Ascending Triangle, and on to $33\frac{1}{2}$, for an 8

Fig. X.7

KENNECOTT COPPER

point or 20% loss. This setback in Kennecott, a market leader, occurred at the time of, and was undoubtedly caused by, the substantial intermediate reaction in the general market which had already started and which carried some of the averages down as much as 30%. Kennecott was ready to go up and made an attempt to do so, but could not long withstand the general liquidation then taking place. The strength of this stock was evidenced, nevertheless, and the implications of its strong February–March formation fully carried out later, by Kennecott's rapid recovery and subsequent advance, reaching 63 in November.

> *The "End Run" occurs when the price movement fails to carry as far as the strength forecasts, but is quickly reversed.*

End Runs are also occasionally traceable to previously indicated strong resistance (or support) zones close to the break-out level. In those cases our study of the back history will usually forewarn us and prevent us from relying too heavily on the implications of the pattern alone. In the Kennecott chart the back history showed that strong resistance would probably be encountered in the 41–42 zone, and that the upward trend might in consequence be halted there for a time, but the extent of the reaction to $33^{1}/_{2}$ could not be explained on that basis.

Where the End Run is caused by general market conditions, or by unexpected developments of an important basic nature affecting a whole industrial group, the breaking of what should be a strong support or resistance level set up by the pattern, is a definite warning to step aside with as small a loss as possible and wait for the situation to clear up. In the case of Kennecott the price and volume action from April 20 to 23 was conclusive; the decline might well have extended much farther than it did if the fundamental situation in this stock, reflected by its previous technical pattern, had not been so strong.

Like False Moves, End Runs are not common but it is important to recognize them for what they are and be prepared to act promptly on their appearance.

STOP-LOSS ORDERS

We have referred briefly in our study of False Moves to the defensive use of stop-loss orders, but that is only one quite limited consideration in their employment. Their first purpose – to minimize losses – is suggested by their name, but they can also play an important part in the protection of any profits already accrued on a successful trade in the event of a sudden or unpredictable reversal of trend. In general, they serve the broad and most important function of almost automatically enforcing the observation of one of the cardinal principles of successful trading, the principle expressed in the old market adage, "Cut your losses but let your profits ride."

It is "unfortunately" quite normal and human for inexperienced traders to be too readily satisfied with small profits while they let their losses on their unsuccessful commitments run on and on to serious proportions. This misguided policy accounts for a fact which brokers frequently comment on, that the majority of the individual transactions made by their clients show a profit yet a distressingly large percentage of their accounts show net losses on balance at the end of any considerable period. A few needlessly large losses have more than outweighed many small profits. The constant, habitual use of stop-loss orders on every commitment, long or short, will correct this tendency. Stops, properly placed, will hold to moderate limits any loss on your original capital – will protect your entire capital plus the expenses incident to your commitment as soon as it begins to run in your favor – and will subsequently and progressively insure the capture of a large share of your paper profits as they accrue.

The Mechanics of the Stop-loss Order

A stop-loss order, or more strictly just a "stop" order in the technical language of the exchanges, is an order placed with your broker to buy (or sell) a definite number of shares of a particular stock only when and if a transaction in that stock has been recorded at or beyond a specified price. The stop order is not executed until after the stock has been traded at (or beyond) the price it specifies. Suppose, for example, you have bought 100 shares of US Steel at 50 but do not wish to keep it if its price falls to 48 or lower because its decline to that level would change the technical picture and indicate still lower prices to follow. You can ensure your stock is sold promptly in that event by placing a stop order with your broker at 48, "good until canceled." The order remains on his books unexecuted until you cancel it or until Steel sells on the exchange at 48 or below. A decline to $48^1/_2$ will not affect it, but as soon as a transaction at 48 or lower takes place your stop order becomes in effect a regular market order and your broker immediately sells your 100 shares of Steel at the best obtainable bid.

If your stop order calls for the sale of an "odd lot" (anything less than 100 shares in the cases of most stocks) your order is executed at $^1/_8$ point beyond the first full lot transaction occurring after your stop price has been reached.

Stop-loss orders in actively traded issues are usually executed quite close to the "stop" price specified in the order, but in the case of infrequently traded ("thin") issues, and on opening transactions affected by important unexpected news, stop orders may be executed several points away. This occasional and, naturally, most distressing execution (some points beyond your stop limits) should not, however, deter you from continuing without fail to employ stop orders in your trading activities. Seldom will the eventual outcome fail to justify the wisdom of the stop-loss order.

When to Place Stop-loss Orders

One question in connection with our consideration of stop-loss orders can be answered quickly and definitely, and that is the question of when to place the stop order. It should be placed at the same time you make your original commitment or, at the very latest, just as soon as you have notice from your broker that your regular order had been executed. There is no occasion for any exception to this rule. Your judgment in the placement of stop orders will be far better at the time you make your commitment than later on, after you are committed, under stress of puzzling market action, perhaps, or news releases, or the fear of "taking a loss."

When you see strong technical evidence – a valid break-out, for example, from a definite reversal or continuation pattern – which warrants the purchase or sale of a security, you should at the same time examine the picture and decide at what level a price movement in the opposite direction would indicate that your forecast had gone wrong, or beyond which you would not care to hold your position. Then place your stop-loss order at that level at the same time you instruct your broker to buy (or sell) the stock for you.

Shifting the Stop-loss Order

Once your stop-loss order is placed it should never be shifted except to some level farther along in the direction of the trend that shows you a profit – the trend which you anticipated in making your commitment. If your forecast works out you can and should move your stop order along, but remember that your first stop-loss order is placed to hold any possible loss to a minimum. It should not be moved except to conserve profits. If you have bought and have placed a stop order at a price below your commitment it may be moved higher but should never be moved lower. And, conversely, if you have sold short and have placed your stop-loss order above your commitment, shift it to lower levels as profits develop, but never move it higher.

Where to Place Stop Orders

There are many arbitrary formulas for the placing of stop-loss orders. While we may grant readily that any formula – even a rigid arithmetic rule – is better than none, the correct placing of stops should be governed primarily by the technical pictures we have studied in this Course. The principles, after all, are quite simple. Stops are used to relieve us quickly and automatically of "bad trades" if the forecasts upon which we based those commitments turn out to be mistaken, or if there is an unexpected change in trend. They should be placed, therefore, so that they will be caught by any price movement which reverses our original forecast or indicates that a trend which has been working in our favor now has turned against us. At the same time they should be so placed that they will not be "touched off" by any minor movement which does not upset or reverse our basic forecast.

The application of these principles is not difficult. We can study them most easily by reference to a specific chart example. Let us take a "long" commitment first and see where stop orders should be placed to protect it. Suppose, for instance, we had been attracted to the possibilities for profit on an advance in US Rubber common stock in the Fall of 1936. During August and September this stock made a Symmetrical Triangle which is shown in Fig. X.8. On September 23 the price advanced out of the pattern with a conspicuous increase in volume, which, although the closing price was hardly out by a decisive margin, strongly suggested the advisability of an immediate purchase, especially in view of the fact that the general market at that time was in a major cyclical up-trend.

Applying the Principles to a Long Commitment

In making this purchase, we were firmly convinced that a strong upward movement in US Rubber was ready to start but we had to take into account the possibility of either a False Move or an Out-of-line Move. If we were dealing with an Out-of-line Move, our purchase would eventually show a profit and should be held, but in the meantime the price would drop back into pattern again. In that event it should not drop by any considerable margin below the bottom of the last dip or minor reversal in the pattern made during the week ending September 19, at 30. But we have to make some allowance for a sharp shake-out; experience has indicated that a fair allowance is about 5% of the value of the stock. In the case of US Rubber, which at this bottom was around 30, 5% would be about a point and a half; so our stop-loss order should be placed $1\frac{1}{2}$ points below 30, or at $28\frac{1}{2}$. With this determined, we would proceed to give our broker an order on September 24, to buy US Rubber at the market and, at the same time, a stop-loss order to sell it at $28\frac{1}{2}$ Stop. On September 25 the price did drop back into the pattern slightly but turned up again on the following day and moved rapidly away, leaving our $28\frac{1}{2}$ stop unexecuted.

Before we follow our trade in US Rubber further, perhaps it would be a good idea to give a little more thought to the 5% allowance suggested in the preceding paragraph. On a stock selling in the $10 range this would be half a point; in the $50 range, two and one half points; in the $80 range, four points, etc. This, of course, is an arbitrary figure and, consequently, like all of the other arbitrary rules for break-outs and measurements which we have studied in this Course, it is subject to judgment and qualification. If the stock in which we are dealing moves habitually within a narrow

Fig. X.8

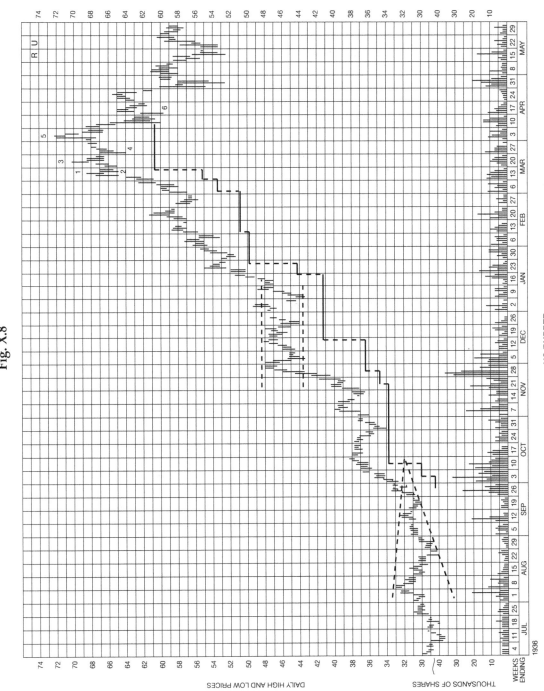

US RUBBER

range – a stock such as General Motors, for example – we might decrease our allowance somewhat below 5%. If, on the other hand, we are dealing in a wide swinging issue like Vanadium Steel, we should allow it a little more margin, say 8%. A study of the past performance of the stock will generally suggest what deviation, if any, from the normal may be expected and allowed for.

The First Shift in the Stop-loss Level

Now we can go back to our US Rubber trade and consider the next step in stop-loss tactics. After prices have moved away from a good forecasting pattern such as we had in this case, there will occur minor set-backs, gaps, continuation patterns, and "congestions" or indeterminate sideways movements which, as we have learned, establish new minor support points and give us a basis for the placing of new stop orders. In "Rubber" we have already had one such – the set-back on September 25, to 31½ – and after prices moved up and well away from the pattern, we could place a new stop-loss order at 30, 5% under the bottom of this minor dip, or better at 29⅞ since it is good practice to put stops slightly below the round figures such as 25, 30, 50, etc. Shake-outs tend to be stopped at those points.

How soon is it safe to move a stop order?

But here we have another question; how soon is it safe to move a stop order? Again we shall have to lay down a rather arbitrary rule for our general guidance with the understanding that it may be qualified by our study of the habits of the stock. Our rule is to wait until the price ranges of two days are entirely beyond the price range of the day that establishes the new stop-loss level. If we are working in an up-trend, as in our US Rubber example, we wait until the low prices on two days are higher than the highest price during the bottom day of the dip. In this example, the high range of the bottom day, September 25, was 32¾. The first two days to range entirely above this were September 29 and 30. On October 1, then, we could cancel our original stop-loss order placed at 28½ when we bought the stock, and put in our new stop order at 29⅞.

This "two days away" rule (with such modification as the individual situation and good judgment may occasionally suggest) applies in either up or down trends and to gaps and the other chart patterns on which we base stop orders as well as minor reversals. We will apply it as we follow along our trade in "Rubber".

Remember always to cancel a previous stop-order at the same time you place a new one. Otherwise, both will remain open on your broker's books and both may be executed at some later date. Your broker will not cancel the previous stop unless you so instruct; he is, in fact, bound to execute it so long as it remains uncancelled.

A Gap Provides a New Basing Point

After the minor set-back of September 25, the price of US Rubber moved up steadily without giving us any new technical indication for a further shift in our Stop Loss order until October 3. The price action of that date produced a half-point gap from $35\frac{1}{2}$ to 36. Continuation Gaps, as we know, set up minor support and resistance levels which are not as a rule broken decisively except by a change in trend. Before shifting our stop order from $29\frac{7}{8}$, however, we should again apply the "two days away" rule. The high range of the gap was 36 and it was not until October 7 that two days ranged entirely above that level. On October 8 we could cancel our stop order at $29\frac{7}{8}$ and place a new stop at $33\frac{3}{4}$, 5% below the bottom of the gap at $35\frac{1}{2}$.

Following this there was some little further advance and then a set-back on October 23 to $35\frac{1}{4}$. For the moment this looked like a minor turning point but it was followed on the 26th by another decline to 34. That, however, finished the minor reaction and prices again moved up, leaving our $33\frac{3}{4}$ stop untouched. Note that we would not shift our stop on account of the new minor bottom at 34, since that would have meant placing it lower down and the rule is never to move a stop order except in the direction of profit.

Completing the Trade in US Rubber

Our next opportunity to move up the stop order came on November 18, when we were "two days away" from the minor bottom of November 14 at $36\frac{1}{2}$, and could shift the stop to 5% below that point. We could move it up again on November 24 to $36\frac{1}{2}$, about 5% under the November 20 bottom. We did not get "two days away" from the bottom of the reaction which came in the first week of December until December 10, but then we could move our stop to 5% below it, placing it at $41\frac{1}{4}$. Over a month then elapsed before we found any development that warranted another shift. During this period a Rectangle developed with a conclusive break-out coming on the up-side on January 15, following the five-day congestion – almost a Flag – from January 8 to 14, and the bottom of this congestion could then be used as a new base point, bringing the stop up to $44\frac{1}{2}$.

The gap made by the January 20 price movement enabled us again to move our stop, this time to $49\frac{7}{8}$ (avoiding the even 50). Another shift to $50\frac{7}{8}$, 5% under the February 5 reaction was called for on February 9. The side-wise congestion of February 9 to 15 gave us a fair basing point for a shift to $54\frac{1}{4}$ but the more conservative policy was to wait for a clearer development which did not appear until we had the reaction to 56 during the last week of February. On March 2, "two days away" from that bottom day range, we could transfer our stop order to 53½. On March 8 we could move it up again to 55¼, basing it on the reaction to 58 on March 4.

Our Stop Finally Executed

The next basing point for a stop order was provided by the large gap which appeared on March 10. We did not get two days ranging entirely above this Gap until March 13; then we could transfer our stop order up to 60¾. And that was our last shift for we were given no new base on which to work higher. The reaction of March 22 held above our stop level but the sharp drop on April 7 took us out; when the price declined to 60¾ on that day our stop order became a market order to sell and our broker accordingly sold our stock. We had carried the stock up from around 33 to above 60, taking a gross profit of about 27 points.

Now, after we were sold out on our stop order, the price rallied, worked back in fact nearly to 66 before the end of the month, but this rally certainly did not suggest a new purchase. On the contrary, the very decline which "touched off" our stop order completed an important reversal pattern, a clean-cut (1-2-3-4-5-6). Broadening Top (see Study IV, page 132), and the rally to 66 barely carried out that 50% recovery of the last move of the pattern which we have learned to expect in many cases but which does not always develop. We were well out of US Rubber; six months later it had dropped to 20.

The Stop Loss Order in Short Selling

The intermediate trend advance we have been following in US Rubber pictures clearly the helpfulness of properly placed stop orders in keeping a trader in his position in the direction of an established trend, and saving him from the worry and mental confusion of the "tape watcher" or "hunch player" who is so often shaken out in the early stages of a move. But if stop orders are useful in long trading they are practically indispensible in short selling operations. When a trader buys long, the price cannot possibly go against him more than the purchase price of the stock, whereas when he sells short he runs the risk, theoretically, of an almost infinite advance. Practically every well-informed economist holds that short selling is justified on its own merits, but it is certainly not justified from a practical trading standpoint unless definite stop orders are used on every short commitment.

Placement of the Initial Stop on a Short Commitment

The techniques which we employed in placing stop orders to protect a long position in our hypothetical trade in US Rubber apply as well, of course, in short trading. The student, if he has followed closely our discussion and watched the application of our stop order principles on the US Rubber chart, may need no further explanation of stop loss technique, but an examination of its use in connection with a short sale will surely do no harm if we make it reasonably brief.

Let us follow a hypothetical trade in US Steel through the down trend which started in August, 1937. Figure X.9 shows the daily price and volume action of this leading stock for the last half of the year. Steel came down from its March top at 127 to a low of 91 in June, 1937, and then in July rallied quickly, almost back to its previous high. There was fair volume during the first part of this movement but as the advance tended to slow up in August the volume dwindled away to smaller and smaller proportions. During the third week of August prices began to drop with volume increasing. By August 26 a Rounding Top was evident and Steel was obviously a good "short."

There were other evidences in this chart, taken in connection with the preceding daily chart and the weekly chart, to suggest liquidation of Steel in late July and early August, but we are concerned now with a conservative short position that would not be taken until after the change in trend was fully apparent. Such a change was conclusively indicated, of course, by the development of the Rounding Top which we have learned (in Study III) is one of the most important reversal formations. Moreover, it is a formation that appears characteristically at the tops of bear market rallies and signals, consequently, declines of considerable extent. Its development in so many leading stocks in August of 1937 was one of the strongest possible confirmations of a major bear trend. (Refer to pages 68 and 70 in Study III.)

Stop-loss Orders in Short Trading are Buy Orders

To return to our example, let us assume that we decide to sell Steel short after posting the chart for August 26. Before giving our broker an order to sell it, however, we must first determine where to place a stop-loss order to take us out of our commitment promptly should our forecast of a decline prove incorrect. Examining the chart, we find the top of the congestion at 117 on August 23 to be our nearest valid basing point, so our first stop may well be placed 5% of the price above this level, at 122¾. Note that in this example we are selling short so our stop orders will be orders to buy, and will be placed above rather than below the current price. Early on August 27 then, we instruct our broker to sell, say, 100 shares of Steel short at the market and, at the same time, give him an order to buy 100 shares at "122¾ Stop."

Now here is a case where our rule requires the stop to be placed a considerable distance away from the current price, about 15 points in fact. In such cases, most traders would feel, quite reasonably, that they would not care to risk so great a possible loss no matter how confident they might be in the correctness of their inter-

Fig. X.9

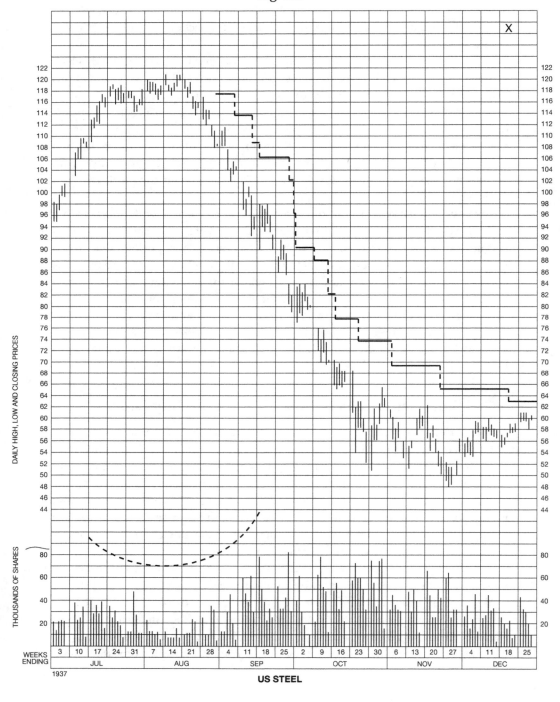

US STEEL

pretation of the technical picture. Good judgment here would dictate some departure from the strict rule, bringing the stop-loss order down to, say, 117½, slightly above the minor bottom made on August 11. As a matter of fact, within a day after our commitment was made we were "two days away" from the small gap made at 113 and could justify by the technical action a stop at 117½.

The down gap on the following Wednesday, September 1, with increased volume, gave gratifying confirmation of our forecast, and when the following two days ranged well below this gap, we could shift our stop order down to 5% above it, to 113½. On September 7 another gap appeared, even larger than the preceding and with volume still greater; hence on the 9th a new stop order could be based on this development, bringing our stop level down to 109¼. The next opportunity to drop our stop-order down came on September 13 when we could shift it to 106⅛. After September 23 when prices had dropped "two days away" from the top day's range of the preceding week's rally; our stop at 106⅛ could be cancelled and a new order entered to buy at "103 Stop."

For the next four weeks our short commitment in Steel showed rapidly growing profits as prices continued to tumble. During this period there were several good technical indications calling for a change in the stop order level. We need only list them briefly and the student can check them with the chart and discover for himself in each case the basis for action.

Here are the indicated shifts:

After	September	25 –	to 96¾
"	September	27 –	to 90¼
"	October	4 –	to 88¼
"	October	7 –	to 82
"	October	11 –	to 77¾
"	October	20 –	to 73½

By late October the down trend showed signs of slowing up but no evidence of reversal had appeared as we come to the end of our six months chart. Two more opportunities to move the stop level in the direction of profit, i.e. down, were however, presented during November. After the action of November 3 the stop order could be transferred to 69½, and after November 19 to 65¼, in each case placing it 5% above the top of the preceding rally. Again, after December 14 it could be dropped to 63.

The Use of "Mental" Stops

For one reason or another, many traders dislike to use stop orders, preferring to keep "mental stops", as they say, on their commitments, and to give their own market orders, to buy or sell as the case may be, when their mental stop levels are reached. Most of the objections to the use of regular stop orders, placed in advance with one's broker, are in our opinion of little or no validity in present day markets. One objection, frequently expressed, is that just at the time stops are caught the market reverses and moves away again the direction originally expected, with the result that the trader takes an unnecessary loss and "loses his position." Obviously, this unfortunate experience is due not to the employment of a stop-loss order but rather in most cases to its improper placement.

Other traders hesitate to annoy their brokers with stop orders, because their accounts are small or because their broker has spoken scornfully of the practice. To accept and execute stop orders is a part of your broker's duty; you are entitled to courteous and efficient service from him in this matter and should insist upon it. Good brokers encourage the use of stop-loss orders as a wise and conservative measure for the protection of their clients' principle and profits.

Theoretically, there is no reason why a "mental" stop should not serve the purpose just as well as a regular stop-loss order entered with the broker, provided of course that the trader is constantly in touch with his market and knows at once when his mental stop level is reached. Practically, however, the temptation is always present to delay action at the critical moment, to "give it another chance," to shift the order mentally, and as a consequence take eventually a much greater loss than necessary. In the long run, the experienced trader finds carefully placed stop-loss order an essential part of the successful trading practice, and by placing them in advance, "in cold blood" so to speak, he avoids the mental confusion and tendency to procrastinate which unexpected turns in the market always create.

Stop-loss Orders of Little Help within Patterns

In the examples of intermediate up and down trends which we have used in this Study to illustrate the placing of stop-loss orders, note that commitments were not made until they had been indicated by the completion of important forecasting formations. It is on such relatively safe technical positions that stop orders are most effective. Some traders like to play for short profits on the minor movements within patterns, Such as the wide-swinging trading areas which the market developed during the months following the October, 1937 "panic." Trading within these areas or wide patterns is precarious at best and, unfortunately, the use of stop orders does not make it any safer since they can seldom be placed close enough to turn the odds in favor of the profit side without undue risk of loss. The use of stop orders on commitments made within area patterns cannot be recommended.

Do Not Neglect Other Chart Indications

By dwelling so much in this Study on the importance of employing stop-loss orders, we certainly do not wish to convey the impression that the student should invariably wait for his stops to be "touched off" before closing out his commitments. In the great majority of trades the student will, if he follows his charts closely, see some sign of reversal or exhaustion which will enable him to take his profit and get out at a much better level than his current stop orders. Measuring formulas, resistance levels, climax volume, exhaustion gaps – all of the various technical phenomena which we have studied in this Course – should be watched for and used to secure the most profitable close-out prices.

Other Minor Uses for Stop Orders

Stop orders may also be used to put a trader into a new commitment as well as to take him out of an old one, or to reverse his position in the market in case of a sudden change of trend. If we buy 100 shares of stock, for example, and put in a stop-loss order below our commitment for twice that number of shares, a change in trend will not only sell us out of our long position but will also put us short 100 shares at the same time. This type of stop order is known as a doubling stop or switching stop. Some traders will anticipate a break-out from a formation, such as a Rectangle, by putting a stop order in above the pattern at a level that should be reached by a valid breakout. Thus when and if a break-out develops they are immediately put long of the stock. These applications of stop orders may on occasion be used by the well-financed trader but we do not feel that they have any special advantages and do not recommend them for the average technical student.

Stop-loss orders, after all, are best employed as insurance, as necessary in the business of stock trading as other forms of insurance are in other businesses.

Study XI

USE OF LONG-TERM CHARTS, AVERAGES AND GROUPS

Reviewing the Ground-work

In all of our preceding studies we have been taking up one individual aspect of technical chart theory after another, studying each one more or less separately, and attempting to discover its relative merits and importance. This progressive study of individual phenomena has, it may be hoped, given us a broad fundamental basis upon which to build and round off our hoped-for education in the entire field of complete chart analysis.

One by one, we have taken up and studied the tools which shall constitute our aids in the practical work to come. One by one, we have examined these separate tools, have observed their individual uses, their importance and their place in the picture with regard to individual reliability. Having thus completed our apprentice-ship, it remains only to fit these tools into actual use in the more important task of practical chart analysis, gradually getting the experience that comes from following larger pictorial records of trading, deciding for ourselves which tools, which indicators, which formations, to use on each point as it arises, and thus co-ordinating our individual guides and rules into one compact catalogue of knowledge for success-ful analysis of any and all types of stock charts, to arrive at our ideal goal of accurate market forecasting.

The Monthly Chart

In general, we have studied the shorter and more frequent formations developing on daily charts, but such patterns can be of almost infinite duration, growing stronger as they grow wider and longer. When these formations drag out for more than a few months they begin to be more easily discernible on weekly or monthly charts than on daily ones.

Weekly charts have great usefulness at such times. They have also the important advantage of requiring much less labor and attention in practical construction. Moreover, they often call our attention to formations which might not be so clear or might not show at all on a small daily chart. It should be plain to the reader by now that the theories and formations which we have studied are applicable not merely to daily charts, but to charts made up on almost any consistant basis of time or scale. Likewise, since such theories are merely the resultant phenomena of open-market trading, they are applicable also to commodity movements, to cotton, wheat and corn prices, for example, or to the pictorial record of just about any commodity whose price fluctuations result from supply and demand in an open and free bar-gaining market. We shall have something to say about commodity charts later, but let us first study the patterns which may appear on a monthly stock chart.

Formations Develop on Monthly Charts

The monthly charts of General Motors and Liggett & Myers Tobacco-B reproduced in Fig. XI.1 show 13 years of price action in these stocks. The vertical lines on these charts represent the high and low range of prices for each month from January, 1924 to December, 1936, inclusive. The volume does not appear.

The General Motors chart is complicated at first glance by the several split-ups in this stock, and the 50% stock dividend effected in September, 1926. However, we need not be disturbed by these changes in the capital set-up from time to time since the price scale has been adjusted with every change so that the continuity of price action has been preserved on the chart. The prices along the right-hand margin represent the price per share as this is written.

Starting in 1924, the first pattern suggested on this chart is a small Symmetrical Triangle indicated by the price action from November, 1925 to June, 1926, large Triangle indicated by the price action from November, 1925 to June, 1926, followed by another rapid advance. We have the Accelerating Peak suggested in the first months of 1927, and then a very good Ascending Triangle at the end of that year which led in March, 1928 to an advance from 140 to 199 in a single month. At the top we find a Complex pattern – a Shoulders and Double Head of huge proportions which took a year and a half for its completion. The ensuing drop took prices down to 34 and then the price action for nearly two years built the suggestion of an enormous Descending Triangle leading to a further decline to 8 in 1932. Turning into an uptrend we find a fair representation of a Flag formed from August, 1932 to March, 1933. The pattern from July, 1933 to March, 1935 looked as though it might be completed as a Head and Shoulders Reversal but the neck-base line was never broken and the price action continued on into June, 1933 to build a large continuation Triangle which broke out into a further rapid advance. No definite formation appears as we approach the end of the chart but the student will readily see the possibilities for the development of several interesting patterns.

The monthly chart of Liggett & Myers Tobacco-B may be similarly analyzed. From 1924 to 1927 we find a well-defined upward trend with a suggestion of the Accelerating Peak in March–July, 1926. A Triangle Reversal appears at the top in 1927. From July, 1928 to the end of 1930 we find a fair Inverted Triangle of great size – or this whole 3 years' pattern might be called a Continuation Head and Shoulders. Another large Head and Shoulders Reversal formed the 1931–1933 bottom in this stock, and the right shoulder of this formation was also a good Flag Continuation. The price action from November, 1934 to August, 1936 suggests the possibility of a Head and Shoulders Top which, however, would not be completed. unless the neck-base line were broken. The action throughout 1936 suggests the a Symmetrical Triangle which

Fig. XI.1

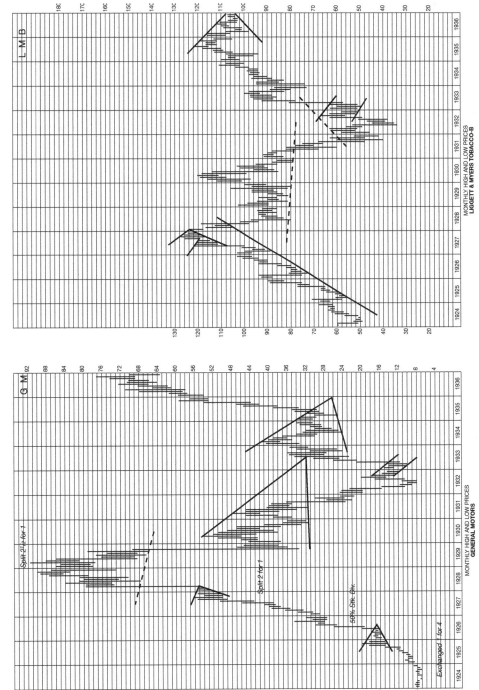

MONTHLY HIGH AND LOW PRICES
GENERAL MOTORS

MONTHLY HIGH AND LOW PRICES
LIGGETT & MYERS TOBACCO-B

might, of course, signal either continuation or reversal depending on the direction of the break-out.

Monthly Charts Not Useful in Trading

The student may well be impressed by the power of some of the patterns suggested by these monthly charts and by the extensive price movements proceeding from them, but he should recall the many months, and in some cases years, required for the building of patterns and the long periods during which no patterns appear at at all. From our brief inspection of these, it is obvious that it is seldom possible for a trader to make a dependable forecast from the patterns on the monthly charts in time to profit by them. For ordinary trading certainly the daily and weekly charts are much more useful and dependable. In the consideration of long-term investment policies, however, the monthly charts become of use as well as interest, and occasionally they suggest the possibility of important developments which can be checked on the daily or weekly charts and converted into trading profits.

The Uses of the Average Charts

We have had occasion to refer at various times in our previous Studies to the averages and the average charts. We have noted that an average is merely a composite of a certain number of selected individual stocks, and the average chart might be called a sort of composite photograph of the charts of all those individual issues. These average charts are subject, within limits, to the same sort of technical analysis which we apply to individual stock charts. And, because we are dealing with a composite representing more or less the general market, any technical formations we may discover in the averages should be more important in forecasting for the whole market itself than the formations appearing in only one or a few individual stocks. It is easy to see, in other words, that if enough individual stocks act in sufficient graphic unison to develop a composite chart formation, then the forecast indications are just that much stronger.

However, we know that it is possible for certain stocks or whole groups of stocks in a general market average to be in a major down trend at the same time that the others are trending upward. Even on an important turn in "the market" some issues reach their reversal points weeks or months before others. (Compare in this respect the two monthly charts in Fig. XI.1.) For the trader with a limited portfolio, therefore, who wishes naturally to employ his capital constantly to the best advan-

Average charts are subject to the technical analysis which we apply to individual stock charts.

tage, the charts of his individual stocks are of far greater practical value than any of the averages.

On the other hand, we know that most stocks do follow sooner or later the major swings of the market. Consequently, for the long-swing investor with a large portfolio, who is not so much concerned with switching for trading profits from one individual issue to another as he is with major investment policies or with income, the averages are of prime importance. The student will find it interesting, as well as instructive, to apply for himself the various patterns which we have studied to the daily chart of the New York Herald Tribune's average of industrial stocks, shown in Fig. XI.2.

The Uses of Group Charts

In a general way our remarks regarding the broad market averages in the preceding paragraphs, apply as well to the group averages – the oils, foods, steels, rails, utilities, etc. The student who wishes to buy from time to time or maintain his own charts of certain industrial group averages will find much of interest in them but relatively little of practical trading value. Just as whole groups of stocks may, and do frequently, move in a trend opposite to the apparent trend of the general market averages, so do individual stocks within a certain group move contrary at times to the trend of the group average. It is perhaps safe to say that as a general rule it is more profitable to buy stocks whose group shows a strong technical picture rather than those whose groups shows a weak picture, and vice-versa, yet there are many exceptional situations.

A comparison of the price action of two different group a verages is afforded by the charts in Fig. XI.3. These charts show the price range and volume on a weekly basis of the *New York Herald Tribune*'s weighted averages of five food stocks and seven copper stocks, respectively, from July, 1934 to the end of 1936. During the greater part of this period the average price of the copper group advanced rapidly and steadily, with set-backs or corrections of relatively insignificant proportions, while the average price of the food group swung up and down without making much net progress. On a long-term basis this difference is striking, but it can be seen that the food group offered just as good trading profits (assuming for the sake of argument that one could buy or sell the "group") in shorter term operations. In fact, more money could have been made trading on both sides of the market in the foods than in the coppers. Forecasting patterns appear occasionally on the group charts, just as we have seen that they do in the general average charts, but not nearly so often as on the charts of individual issues.

Fig. XI.2

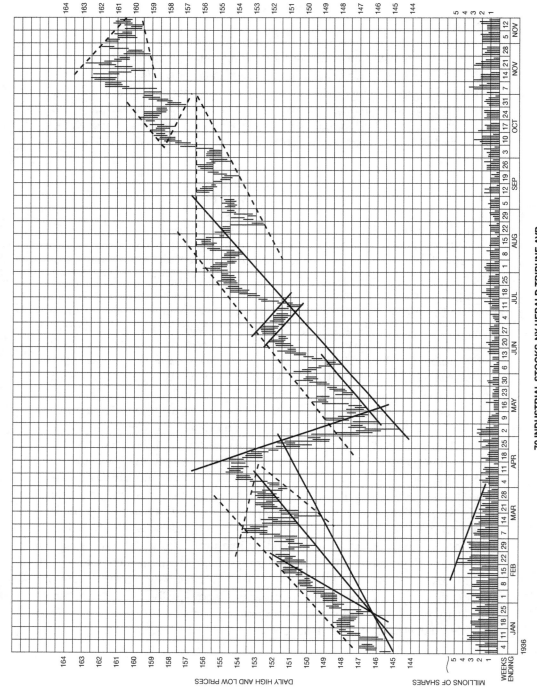

70 INDUSTRIAL STOCKS-NY HERALD TRIBUNE AVR.

Fig. XI.3

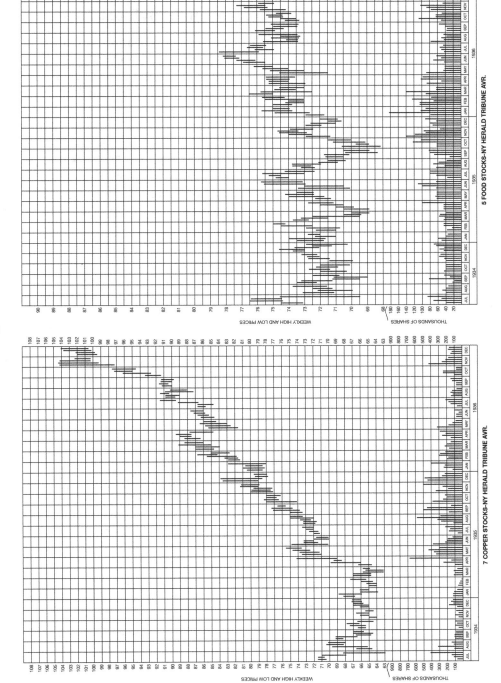

Time More Profitably Spent on Individual Charts

The student will have to decide for himself just how much time and attention he cares to devote to maintaining and analyzing general market and group average charts. If he is charting a diversified list of 40 or 50 individual issues, his individual charts will, as a rule tell him all he needs to know about "the market". He must remember that when a forecasting pattern, no matter how strong, shows up on the Dow-Jones Industrial Average chart, for example, he cannot order his broker to "buy 100 shares of the Dow-Jones Industrial Average". If a Head and Shoulders top develops on the chart of the Theatre stocks average, he cannot sell 50 shares of "Amusement" at the market. He must, in brief, do his trading in specific issues, which may or may not be moving in the same direction or at the same rate as their group or "the market" at the time. Only their own individual charts can tell him which to buy or sell.

Lessons in Long-term Analysis

As we complete these analytical studies of the long-swing price movements in single issues, in groups and the general averages, we may pause to consider any general lessons which their observation might suggest. For one thing we may repeat that successful practical trading from chart action comes not from following with blind and dogmatic confidence every technical suggestion that may appear, but rather by keeping always an open mind, and using the many individual chart factors merely as an aid to general analysis.

We may also observe the advantages of playing the major trend, once it is definitely confirmed, and letting one's intermediate market position always favor that major trend when there is any doubt about intermediate movements.

And this leads to still another rule, that in almost all cases the trader should compromise with his own opinions, with the chart forecast, with any and all ordinary and normal future indications, preferring to take the middle of the road rather than veering impetuously to one extreme or the other. The corollary of that general theory is that, in purely long-range operation, both accumulation and distribution should be accomplished on a scale policy. In other words, sell out gradually when it appears that the end of a bull movement is approaching and buy gradually when it appears that the end of a long bear trend is approaching. This rule applies primarily, of course, only to cyclical or semi-investment operations, rather

Successful practical trading from chart action comes from using the many individual chart factors merely as an aid.

than to the ordinary trading in which it is presumed that most students of this Course are interested.

SHORTER TIME INTERVALS IN CHARTING

Another general aspect of chart science upon which we may well touch in rounding out our technical education, is the application of chart formations and principles to practically any time range interval which we may choose in pictorializing the original trading record. The major portion of our studies has been conducted upon the basis of daily ranges, since the daily charting interval has proved to be by far the most practical and most useful for ordinary operations and for ordinary technical analysis.

We have seen, however, that this daily interval may be expanded to give weekly, monthly, or even yearly charts, each of which may have certain advantages. We may also observe that on the other side of the daily charting interval we may break down the time element to almost infinitely small proportions, to include hourly charts, fractions of the full hours, and even down to the extreme of charting every transaction in a stock or group of stocks, the latter being termed the transaction, or ticker, chart.

Breaking up the Daily Time Interval

The first practical break-down of the daily charting interval is naturally the hourly chart. In such a chart the only difference in technique is that the separate intervals of the pictorial trading record charted are the hour instead of the day. In other words, the hourly chart shows both a price and volume line for each hour of trading instead of for each separate day of trading.

In theory at least, the patterns which form on an hourly chart have the same significance as they would have on a daily chart, except that we should, of course, expect the movements arising therefrom to be small in extent in proportion to the size of the patterns. One phenomenon of price action – the Gap – which has its distinct uses in forecasting from daily charts, may safely be assumed to have little or no forecasting value when it appears between the price ranges of two hours within the same trading day. Occurring at that particular time, which we have selected arbitrarily for charting purposes, it could have no more and no less significance, obviously, than a sudden price change coming any time inside any hourly period, in which event it would not show as a Gap on our chart. An over-night price Gap, appearing on a daily or an hourly chart, has a psychological influence, besides representing an accumulation of technical strength or weakness during the interval when the market is closed, but the Gaps which may show up on an hourly chart within a day's session have no such psychological or accumulative influence.

However, we need not devote any more space to a consideration of hourly charts. It must be quite apparent to the student that they offer little or nothing of value to the average trader. The scalper or quick-turn artist, who is interested primarily in capturing small profits on the minor fluctuations within the day, might find an hourly chart of some assistance but he would have to watch both the tape and the clock all day, noting every transaction in his list of stocks and making his entries at the end of every hour.

The Ticker or Transaction Chart

The extreme break-down of the time interval is naturally the transaction or ticker chart, in which the transactions are really not grouped according to time at all but in which each transaction, with price and volume, is charted on a space of its own. In between the hourly chart and the ticker chart, are the half-hour interval, the fifteen minute interval, or any time interval we may desire to use, the only important requirement being that the time interval be consistent throughout each individual chart. A corruption of the ticker chart is the 200-share transaction chart, in which the 100 share transactions are ignored and only those charted which involve more than this basic unit of trading. This results in considerable saving of time, space and energy but does not appear theoretically to be as precise or valuable as the basic ticker chart.

It is easy to see that these break-downs of the daily time interval involve much additional labor, especially as we progress down to the transaction, or ticker, chart, which records every individual transaction, with price and volume. A graphic record of every transaction in a stock has its points of interest perhaps to the specialist, and to the theorist in research, but certainly can be of little value to the practical trader.

The Minor-Move Chart

Another alternative of the ticker chart is one which may well be called the Minor Move chart since it has certain practical advantages in affording a good picture of minor intra-day movements without requiring the patience and detail of the ticker chart. It is made by drawing a vertical line on the price chart to show the extent of each minor move in either direction until the price, as recorded on the ticker, reverses this direction by moving a certain set distance back and away from the extreme price of the previous direction. Any basis of reversal may be selected, the usual ones being from a half point to three points. When the previous minor movement is thus reversed, a horizontal line is drawn from the extreme of the preceding movement, to the right and on to the next vertical space. Then the new minor move in the reversed direction is noted by another vertical line extending in the opposite direction, until that new movement is, in turn, reversed, when the process of charting is repeated.

In other words, if we decide on a minor move basis of one full point, and our stock opens the day at 50 and proceeds down to 49, we draw a vertical line from 50 to 49. If it goes back up to 49⅞ we take no action on the chart because the reverse movement has been less so far than our selected unit of one full point from the extreme of the previous movement. But, if it then goes down to 48⅛ we continue our original vertical line down to that price level. If the stock now recovers to 49⅛, however, our minor move has reversed. From the extreme of 48⅛, we draw a short horizontal line across to the next vertical space, and then draw our new minor move line from 48⅛ to 49⅛, and so on. This type of Minor Move chart gives a fairly accurate picture of intra-day movements, but it does not lend itself easily to the notation of the time element, and precludes the charting of volume.

The Minor Trend Line Chart

One variant of the Minor Move Chart, which also takes into account only price movements of pre-determined extent, differs only in the method employed in drawing the lines denoting the significant price changes and may be called the Minor Trend chart. Using the same data, for example, which we used in the previous paragraph to explain the Minor Move chart, we would start our chart at 50 and draw a diagonal line down to the 48⅛ level on the next vertical cross-section line to the right, then draw a diagonal line from that point to the 49⅛ level on the next vertical cross-section line, and so on.

Both the Minor Move and Minor Trend chart have the same limited use and the same decided disadvantages for the practical trader, besides making it necessary to keep or buy every day an accurate record of all the transactions in every stock charted.

Point and Figure Charts

One other corruption of the ticker chart is quite similar to the Minor Move chart except that symbols or the actual price figures are written into the chart itself instead of drawing short vertical and horizontal lines. This type of chart has many names but it is usually known as the Figure chart or the Point chart. The general scheme is open to varying details of personal taste and policy, but if we accept the previous example of noting only one-point moves, as in the case of the Minor Move chart, then we should write in any consistent symbol or, more generally, the exact figure,

Fig. XI.4

PERCENTAGE CHANGES IN 683 COMMON STOCK PRICES
DECEMBER 31, 1935 TO DECEMBER 31, 1936

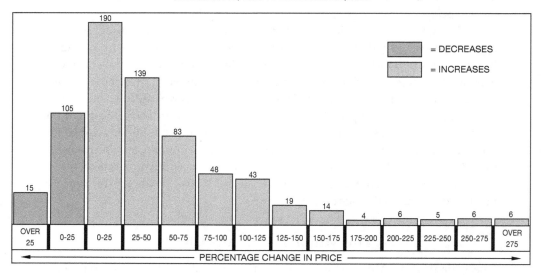

The total market value of all common stocks listed on the New York Stock Exchange advanced from the beginning of 1936 to the end of it by 29.4 per cent. But there were many issues which declined in price. Of the more active common stocks listed on the Exchange 683 issues were traded throughout 1936, after eliminating all of those in which the number of shares was affected by consequential stock dividends, "split-ups," "split-downs," or reorganizations. From the beginning of 1936 to the end of it 563 of these issues advanced in price, but 120 of them declined.

The range of price change was great. Some issues fell to prices which at the end of the year were as little as one-seventh of those at the beginning of the year; and other issues advanced to prices something more than four times those at the beginning of the year. There were as many issues which advanced more than 28.5 per cent as there were which either declined or advanced less than 28.5 per cent. A quarter of the issues advanced 66.7 per cent or more, and a quarter of them advanced

less than 7.7 per cent or else declined. The data enforce the observation that the stock market is not one market but many markets with widely diverse price trends. The range of individual price change is large compared with the average change in prices as a whole. That the change in the market value of particular holdings will parallel that of all stocks combined accordingly cannot be assumed.

In the diagram the height of the bars shows the number of issues, the price changes in which were within the percentage limits indicated at the bottom of the chart. There were, for example, 15 issues which decreased more than 25 per cent in price. There were 105 issues where the decreases in prices ranged between zero and 25 per cent. On the other hand, there were 6 issues that advanced more than 275 per cent, and 6 issues which advanced between 250 and 275 per cent. There were more issues in which prices advanced from zero to 25 per cent than in any other of the designated 25 per cent intervals.

50, in our first vertical column and on a level with that price on the horizontal price scale. As the stock declined to 49 we should write that figure, 49, in at its proper level just under the 50 figure.

Following the same data, however, we should not enter the 48 symbol in this same vertical column because the decline was reversed at 48$\frac{1}{8}$ before it reached the 48 level. When this reversal did occur we would simply begin a new column in the next vertical space, starting with the base figure of 49 and continuing to build up through each whole number of the advance until the next reversal was reached.

Point, or Figure, charts may be constructed for any scale of minor movement we care to select, using half-point, point, 3-point, or 5-point moves as our minimum unit, for example, but here again the picture does not lend itself to volume or time notations. Over a sufficient time interval some of our familiar technical formations will develop quite satisfactorily on such charts, and are susceptible to the usual analysis and forecasting deductions except that, as we have noted, we are deprived of the extremely important aid of the volume factor. Gaps also are not shown. Certain specialized measuring formulae are sometime applied to Point or Figure charts for use in short-swing forecasting but these measuring formulae seem to work out in practice somewhat less accurately than the general measuring rules which we have previously studied in connection with vertical line charts.

Limitations of Point or Figure Charts

Like the other types of Minor Move and Minor Time interval charts which we have examined in the foregoing paragraphs, the Point or Figure chart requires taking from the tape a complete record of every transaction in the stocks charted, or the daily purchase of this data from statistical organizations who make a business of supplying it. Since Point or Figure charts show only those price movements which equal or exceed the pre-determined minimum which is used as the basis for charting, they do not, naturally, show all of the daily price ranges in most cases. If a Figure chart is being constructed on a 3-point basis, for example, the price may range as much as 2$\frac{7}{8}$ beyond the last recorded point on the chart, without this excess movement's ever being noted thereon. On a single point chart a movement of $\frac{7}{8}$ of a point may be disregarded in the same way. It may be argued that price movements less in extent than the movement which is originally taken as the basis for figure charting should have no significance in interpreting the market, but we have found that this is by no means always the case. Small movements may be highly significant, especially when they are considered with relation to the attendant volume.

After a very considerable study and application of Point or Figure charts, we have been obliged to conclude that they offer the practical trader no advantages over the ordinary vertical line chart. In extremely rare cases they have signalled a quick reversal following a rapid, almost "vertical" advance of unusual extent which occurred without developing much of a pattern, except perhaps exhaustion volume, on the daily vertical line chart. But, even in those exceptional cases, it would have been necessary for the trader to sit at the ticker and post his chart as each transaction came over the tape in order to get the reversal signal in time to profit by it. Moreover, movements such as these, spectacular though they may be, during the few days in which they occur, are rather dangerous playthings for the ordinary trader. When they occur in a stock in which the trader already has a long position the judicious moving up of stop loss orders during the advance affords ample protection for profits. On the other hand, many significant phenomena of forecasting value appear constantly on the vertical line charts which never show at all on Figure charts.

Only Specialized Value for Intra-day Charts

Although we do not recommend these various types of intra-day and special Minor Move chart to the average technical student, it is only part of his thorough education to know what they are and how they are constructed. It is easy to see, first, that their operation requires not only a tremendous amount of additional labor, but also the chartist's presence in the brokerage board-room, hanging over the ticker throughout the entire day's trading, or at least poring over the transaction records after the close to glean the material for his ultra-detailed chart.

In the second place, we know from experience that the average student or trader does not get a great deal out of such charts, and certainly fails to get value commensurate with the additional time and other disadvantages involved. In specialized cases the intra-day chart can prove important and valuable for very short-term forecasting or scalping operations but for the average chart trader they can be almost as confusing as useful – almost as misleading, in overly magnifying the importance of very short intermediate moves, as the previously condemned practice of watching the ticker itself.

Wherever they are used, however, it is highly important that the intra-day charts be used merely as an accessory to the daily chart, for the latter continues to be the fundamental basis for our practical analysis of technical movements, and really the only basis required, in fact, in ordinary trading operations.

Other Special Lines of Chart Research

For many years, as the reader may well imagine, the stock market has been the subject of intensive study and research which has extended into every conceivable graphic and mathematical method of interpreting its action. The student who wishes can find almost endless fields for further exploration. Moving averages, oscillators, ratio calculations, breadth of market factors, etc. – all have their protagonists. Their study is interesting, even fascinating, for one who has the time to devote to it, but their practical value is, to say the least, very questionable in actual trading operations. It is our experience that they nearly always lead to confusion and indecision rather than to profitable action.

In this Course we have concentrated on those practical, well demonstrated and easily applied methods of interpreting the technical action of the market which, if conscientiously employed with common sense and judgment, will bring reasonable profits with safety. We have avoided the untested and the purely academic – the "interesting if true" theories – the more or less esoteric studies which do not permit of practical forecasting conclusions in time to permit of profitable trading action. The methods of technical analysis taught herein do not entail subscribing to any continuing "service" for data or analysis. They demand of the trader only a reasonable amount of time and thought – such as he should devote to any serious business involving the same amount of capital risk and opportunity for profit.

THE CHARTING OF OTHER TRADING MEDIUMS

At the very beginning of our course we noted that most of our rules of technical action, while applied directly to the study in hand, may also be applied to other fields, insofar as such rules spring from varying aspects of a universal type of action resulting from the two opposing factors of supply and demand.

While the stock market is probably the most specialized, practical and profitable field for charting and chart theory, still its general logic may consistently be applied to all other markets where the price movements we wish to study are a result of free and open trading, allowing full sway to the conflicting forces.

The Bond Market

The bond market, for instance, presents itself as a fairly satisfactory medium for charts and chart theory, even though the limitation of trading, lack of speculative operations and professional campaigns as well as the comparative absence of short selling, reduce the efficacy of chart theories to a substantial minimum. Such factors operate not only to present too simple pictures and too few patterns, but they tend also to limit the swings of bond price and to keep trading at a lower volume than in stocks, both results being disadvantageous for chart operation. Furthermore, of course, the greater investment stability inherent in the bond itself is a restraining factor in wide price swings and thus in potential market profits.

The bond market does not lend itself, therefore, to the application of technical chart action nearly so well or profitably as does the stock market, but the underlying principles apply none the less, and bond charts are not only practicable but fairly common and often highly useful to the interested trader, as well as to the bond dealer and investor. The technical patterns on bond charts are developed more plainly, and the charts thereby rendered more useful, if the price scale is made larger than would ordinarily be practicable on the chart of a stock selling at the same level. The larger scale compensates for the normally narrow price swings in the bond market.

The bond market presents itself as a fairly satisfactory medium for charts and chart theory.

An Example of Bond Chart Action

A chart of the price movements in a typical high-grade railroad bond is pictured in Fig. XI.5. This shows the price and volume action in New York Central's Refunding $4^1/2$% bonds of 2013, for the last half of 1936, arranged on a scale which depicts most clearly the patterns which developed therein. Starting on July 9, the price advanced in a "mast" from 87 to $89^1/2$ around which level a compact pattern of congestion was built with volume tending to decline in the process, giving us a Half-mast formation that called for a further advance to around 92. This forecast was, in fact, carried out in less than three weeks and at least partial profit-taking was suggested at that level by the Half-mast implications. The first minor trend line was broken by the decline on August 21, but the price action on the 24th left behind it an Island, forecasting a renewal of the up-trend, and a new purchase if we had closed out our previous long position. The price action from September 8 to 16 suggested a Flag, although the break-out on the up side on the 17th was not accompanied by an increase in volume. The ensuing advance gave validity to the Flag, however, and called for another halt (by the application again of our measuring rules) to around $95^1/2$, at which point profit-taking, at least on a part of our commitment, was again in order.

In the meantime the August 22 bottom gave us a new point across which to construct a trend line, with a parallel secondary line across the previous tops. The recession which formed the Flag touched the trend line on September 16 but did not violate it, and the price range on September 23 reached the upper line and was followed by a reaction as we might have anticipated on the basis of trend action alone. On October 17, however, the trend line was penetrated slightly and prices moved sidewise until the 21st when a further recession indicated that the trend had been decisively broken.

A third trend line was drawn across the October 26 bottom and when it was violated, a coming reversal in the major trend was strongly suggested. This indication was further confirmed by the fact that the December rally did not succeed in getting back above the third "fan" of the trend line by a decisive margin.

Fig. XI.5

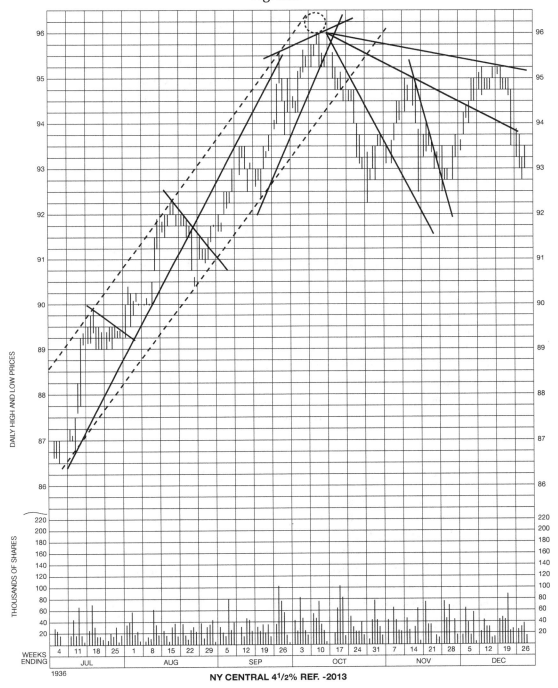

NY CENTRAL 4¹/²% REF. -2013

Charting the Commodity Markets

The freer commodity markets are much more fertile fields than the bond market for the additional application of charts and technical forecasting theories. These markets come much closer to our ideal state of free and open speculative trading centers. They present the necessary interplay of conflicting forces resulting in faster price movement. They offer a much wider sphere of speculative interest, are open to purely professional operations and speculative campaigns, generally allow short selling with operation consequently possible on both sides of the market, and are characterized by much wider and more profitable swings than the bond market.

Wheat, corn, rye, oats, cotton, wool, sugar, copper, rubber, coffee, cocoa – in short the entire list of open-market trading commodities – are more or less favorable fields for chart operation. But it is not the individual commodity itself which determines the practicability of chart application. It is rather the nature of the market for that specific commodity, the kind of trading, the activity, the availability of necessary data, the characteristic extent of major swings, and other fairly apparent considerations, which determine the theoretical value which the application of charts might offer. And it may be generally observed that the closer such characteristics approximate to the almost ideal standards present in stock market trading, the more accurate and profitable will chart application be found in each individual market.

The wheat and cotton markets are perhaps the ones most commonly studied and interpreted by means of charts, due largely to their superiority in many of the points just mentioned. Both are large, important and profitable markets. They include free and open trading, heavy volume of activity, short selling, the opportunity for speculative campaigns, and, finally, are generally characterized by wide and profitable price swings.

Charts Interrupted by Exploration of Different Options

One complication that arises in the charting of wheat and cotton, as well as certain other commodities, results from the conflict or spread between the various future delivery dates, which come and go as almost separate markets. In Wheat, for example, it is possible on any given date to trade in three different "options". In November one may buy or sell Wheat for the December, May or July delivery, on the Chicago, Winnipeg or Kansas City markets. When the May option is closed, i.e. when trading ceases in Wheat for May delivery, the December option is opened and trading commences in Wheat for delivery the following December. When the July option is closed, the market for delivery in May of the next year is opened. On any given date September Wheat may be selling for five cents a bushel more or less than

July Wheat. In the case of Cotton, trading is carried on simultaneously in eleven different options or future delivery dates.

(It must be assumed that the student will take steps to acquaint himself – if he is not already informed – on the mechanics of the commodity markets, and the nature of the contracts to deliver or take delivery which are the actual basis of trading, before he undertakes to make use of charts in commodity market operations. He will have to learn about spreads, squeezes, switching, etc. This knowledge, however, is not essential to our present discussion of charting and chart analysis.)

Different Methods of Charting Options

As a consequence of this simultaneous trading activity in different future deliveries, the chartist is faced with a problem which does not arise in the charting of securities. The simplest, and often the most practical, method of chart operation is to treat each developing option as a separate and distinct market. Each of his charts on Wheat then will run for only seven to ten months depending on the option, and he has the choice of maintaining one, two, or three different charts at any given time, and may regard each as a different trading medium just as he would regard the charts of three different stocks. This procedure, however, has the disadvantage of failing to provide the long-range continuity which we have found so valuable in the analysis of stock charts.

A first step in providing this continuity and broader view of the general market in a commodity like Wheat is accomplished by charting all the different open and active future options on one large sheet, using different colored inks or crayons to distinguish the different options. Green, for example, may be used for May, red for July, blue for September, and black for December. As each old or spot option passes out of the picture, the new future, and most distant, option is added to the chart. Owing to mechanical limitation on the use of color in reproducing these lessons, we are unable to show a chart of this type, but the method is, we trust, perfectly understandable.

Another, somewhat less complete and useful but much simpler expedient is to chart only one option at a time, usually the nearest future delivery, dropping each old option on or before the first day of its delivery month and carrying right on from that point with the next option. The December delivery, for example, in Wheat may be charted through November 30, then the May delivery through April 30, and so on. A chart prepared on this plan for about eight months from June 6, 1936 through January 30, 1937, is reproduced in Fig. XI.6 showing price and volume of transactions on the Chicago Board of Trade. The spreads between the prices of the two different options at the time that the change is made from one to the other on the chart will occasionally confuse or break the continuity of the picture to some extent, but

Fig. XI.6

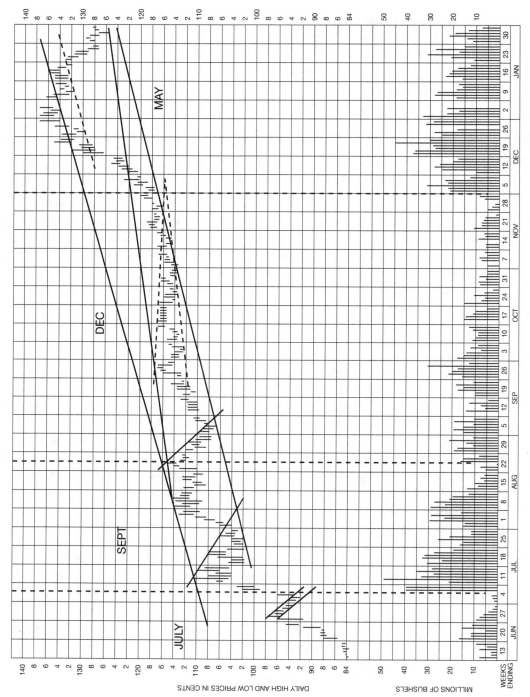

WHEAT TRADING

normally this spread is small, the switching operations of traders as well as the natural laws of supply and demand tending to produce a close conformance.

Averaging All Active Options

Perhaps the soundest of all methods for those who have the time and the facilities, as well as the desire to study the market intensively, is to carry along one master chart of the price movements of all open and active future options averaged together. This master control chart offers the desirable continuity for practical study and longer-term operations, and may be used as a valuable guide not only in evaluating the general market but also in connection with the smaller and shorter charts on the individual options, which are maintained at the same time so long as each remains extant.

The preparation and upkeep of such a master chart requires more calculation and labor than the average stock chart for it must consist in somewhat of a running average of all options. As each old, or spot, option expires the new future option is added into the average to replace it, and thus a satisfactory and continuous average of the general market is made possible and practical.

Charting the Different Markets or Exchanges

In addition to the complications introduced by the concurrent trading in different future delivery options, the trader in Wheat is also faced with the problem of deciding how many and which of the great grain markets he should follow. Wheat futures are traded on the open markets of Chicago, Minneapolis, Duluth and Kansas City, for example, in this country. Of these the Chicago market (Board of Trade) is the largest and most important. Kansas City is generally considered to rank next in importance, especially as a cash market. The Winnipeg market in Canada is large and active, subject to fewer restrictions and consequently more sensitive to world wide influences than any of our domestic exchanges. Liverpool is the premier Wheat market of the world. Most traders carry on their active operations on only one of these exchanges but find it advisable to follow one or more of the others. Official volume figures are ordinarily obtainable only on the Chicago market.

Close Relation Between Prices of Different Grains

Just as different stocks may be affected and carried up or down together by general financial and industrial tides, so, different grains are influenced to some extent by the same set of general conditions. Moreover, if Wheat, for example, goes up in price, Corn may be purchased and used in its place for many purposes. A dearth of one kind of grain is reflected in an increased demand for other kinds. Thus the Corn market affects the Wheat market and vice-versa, and both may affect the Rye and Oats market in so far as one may be consumed in place of the other. Consequently, the active trader in Wheat usually finds it advisable to chart and watch the action of corn and the other grains, applying the developments on those charts in his analysis and forecasts of the Wheat charts.

Formations Appearing on the Wheat Chart

Returning now to the Wheat chart in Fig. XI.6, we may observe some of the familiar patterns which appear thereon. Note first that our chart is based to begin with on the trading in the July option to the end of June, then the September option to August 19, then the December option to December 28, and then the May option to January 30. The volume of trading in each option tends normally to decline as the delivery month is approached, and this normal habit must be taken into account when interpreting the volume record. Our chart has been transferred to the next option in each case as trading in the nearby delivery became relatively inactive.

We have first, from June 23 to June 30, a good Flag pattern formed on a mast which extended from around 85 to 97, and was followed by another rapid advance from 94 to around 110. The price action from July 13 to July 27 gave us a minor down-trend line which was broken on the up-side on July 29, with a marked increase in volume. There was also the suggestion of a Symmetrical Triangle at that point. The recession on August 11 met support at the level of the July 16 top. The recession at the end of August carried prices back down to the support level of the late July break-out before it was reversed and the upward trend resumed, carrying the price to 117 on September 24.

A Continuation Triangle and a Measuring Gap

From that date to November 14 we have a long, thin Symmetrical Triangle, with a decisive break-out on the up-side on November 16. Note the increased volume attending the break-out, also the subsequent minor reaction on shrinking volume to the support level of the extended top side of the Triangle, which formed a cradle with the long-term trend line at that point. The Continuation Gap between December 12 and 14 permitted the application of our Measuring Gap formula which called for a further advance to the 133–137 zone. The reaction from the top around 137 early in January, and the failure of the subsequent rally to reach the previous high, gave us a Head and Shoulders formation with an upward slanting neck-base line which was broken with an increase in volume on January 19. The ensuing decline was halted, however, at the logical support level of the top of the Gap made in mid-December.

The long major-up-trend line drawn across the bottoms of July 18 and September 2 had not been broken at the time of this chart's completion. Subsequently, Wheat made a small Head and Shoulders bottom at the trend line; the neck-base line of this pattern was broken with increased volume on February 3, with a Break-Away Gap at the 128 level; and the price had advanced to around 138 at the time this Study went to press.

Basic Formations and Interpretations Unchanged

We would not have the reader believe that the Wheat chart we have just analyzed is the ideal type of chart upon which to undertake operations on the Chicago Board of Trade. But it has no doubt served to demonstrate the fact that the same formations whose forecasting value we have learned to recognize on stock charts are developed on grain market charts as well, and have the same significance, being produced by the same free interplay of the forces of supply and demand. The factors which produce technical changes in the market for stocks operate similarly in the grain markets and create similar pictures on the charts. And just as is the case with stocks, the grain charts present a composite picture of the net result of all the opinions, hopes, fears and knowledge (published and unpublished) pertaining to supply and demand which govern the trend of prices. If we can translate the chart picture into a reasonable forecast of the likely future trend we do not need to concern ourselves with the basic causes; the chart has weighed and evaluated them for us.

Charting the Cotton Market

In general the methods and principles we have discussed in connection with the Wheat market apply as well to the technical analysis of the Cotton market. Contracts for the future delivery of cotton are traded in this country on the New York and New Orleans Cotton Exchanges and, in smaller volume, on the Chicago Board of Trade. The Liverpool Exchange is the principal foreign market. The average American trader will find it necessary to chart only one market – either the New York or New Orleans, depending on his location and personal preference. Official volume of transactions is not recorded or published on any of the exchanges so we are obliged to get along without this very useful aid in interpreting the price action.

Cotton may be purchased or sold for future delivery any month of the year, the market for January of the following year being opened as soon as the spot market for January of the current year is closed. Thus each individual option remains open for eleven months. Not all of the different months' options are actively traded, however. The January, March, May, July, October and December deliveries are normally the most important in speculative and hedging operations and are, as a rule, the only ones on which complete price reports are published in the daily papers. Final delivery date on futures contracts is the seventh business day before the end of the month, and trading is closed on the notice date which is five business days (excluding Saturdays) before delivery date.

An Example of Cotton Market Charting

The various methods of charting the general market which were suggested in connection with Wheat, may be applied also to Cotton. The chart in Fig. XI.7 shows the price action of the 1937 March, July and January Cotton deliveries during the last half of 1936 on the New York Exchange. The March delivery is charted at the top of the page, July in the middle, and January at the bottom, each on its own scale. The chart is too short to give us any indication of long-term trends, but minor trends appear quite plainly defined. The student will find upon close examination Islands, Triangles and other of our familiar technical patterns.

The close conformance of the trends in the three options on this chart, comparing one with the other, is most conspicuous. This should be expected, of course, since the only respect in which they differ is in the date of delivery. Any tendency on the part of one option to depart from conformity with the other active options in price action, should be regarded with suspicion; in other words, until a certain break-out of formation or reversal in trend in one option is confirmed by a similar break-out or reversal in one or more other options, it should not be made the basis for a forecast or a commitment. For example, note in our chart of the July option the Triangle formed by the price ranges from September 8 to October 13, with a break-out on the up-side on October 16. We had no volume to guide us in appraising the reliability of this break-out but certainly it had all the other earmarks of a true movement calling for higher prices. Comparing the July with the March and January option charts, however, we could see that no advance in prices had been signalled on either of the latter. The logical assumption then was that the break-out on the July chart should be regarded as a false move, at least until such time as the other options confirmed it. This example emphasizes the advantages of maintaining either a control charge of the average of all the open options in a single commodity, or else individual concurrent charts of at least several of the active open options.

Commodity Trading Has its Own Problems

Our discussion and illustrations of the application of technical chart analysis to commodity trading have been designed to bring out the general principle that chart

Fig. XI.7

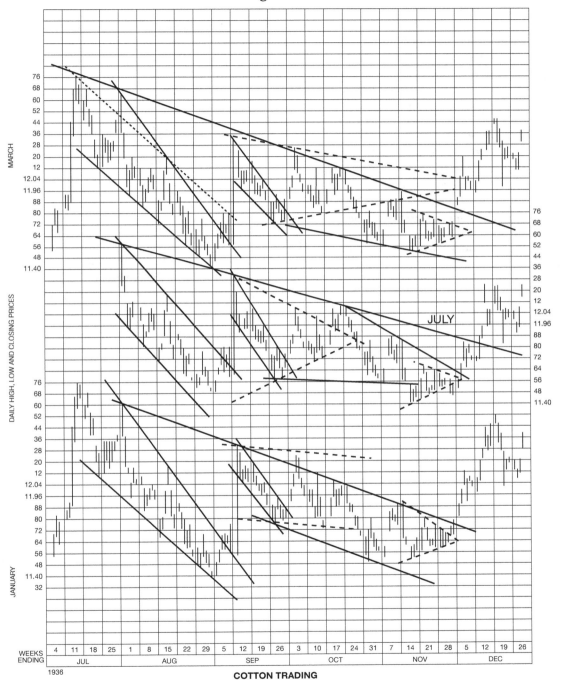

MARCH

DAILY HIGH, LOW AND CLOSING PRICES

JANUARY

JULY

WEEKS ENDING	4	11	18	25	1	8	15	22	29	5	12	19	26	3	10	17	24	31	7	14	21	28	5	12	19	26
	JUL				AUG					SEP				OCT					NOV				DEC			

1936

COTTON TRADING

action is subject to much the same interpretation wherever the factors of supply and demand are allowed free play. No attempt has been made to detail the many practical points of difference between trading in stocks and commodities. It is hoped, however, that out brief consideration of commodity charting will serve as an introduction and a guide to further productive research and study along technical lines for those who wish to engage actively in commodity operations.

One point of difference between stock and commodity price movements, which is, of course, reflected in the charts, may be mentioned briefly. The production of agricultural commodities such as Wheat and Cotton is directly affected by the weather and other more or less unpredictable factors influencing the crop. Commodity prices are much more sensitive to news than stock prices. A sudden news break may produce a wild flurry in the stock market but this lasts as a rule for only a day or two and then the previous trend is resumed, or else a period of congestion ensues and a technical pattern is built which gives us a forecast of the next trend. In the commodity markets, on the other hand, many minor reversals occur as a result of news, which are not forecast by any area formations.

> *Commodity trading chart action is subject to the same interpretation wherever supply and demand are allowed free play.*

Study XII

TRADING TACTICS

Practical Trading on Chart Formations

Through the application of our individual patterns of longer-term pictures we have progressed in our study of technical market science from the separate observation of fundamental pictures, theories, and rules, toward our ideal objective of a broad background for successful analysis of the constantly unfolding pictorial record and for more advanced application of our knowledge in practical market trading.

Having mastered these fundamentals, completion of the student's education in technical forecasting and scientific trading lies largely within the scope of his own continued initiative and interest and in the experience which comes only from his own conscientious application, observation and study of additional chart records for himself.

Some Aids In Practical Trading

As we prepare to leave the reader to his own devices, however, we may take a little further time to observe some of the more important and more profitable rules and theories which apply directly to the practical use of our chart knowledge in actual market trading.

We have already stated one of the most important of these practical trading rules with regard to both long-swing and short-turn trading with the charts as a broad background. For the trader, the rule is to trade mostly along with the confirmed major trend, rather than switching his position to try for every suggested intermediate movement contrary to that trend. Its corollary is to give always the balance of doubt to the side of the major move, and to resist mentally the temptation to anticipate one's wishes for a major turn. The trader is always justified in taking small profits and in playing in and out of the market but the point is that in such short-turn trading he must never lose sight of the direction of the major movement, for in that direction lie his best chances for profit.

For the long-swing investor, the rule is compromise and gradual shifting of one's line. Here, too, it is even more definitely advisable, of course, to play along in the direction of the major trend rather than to try to take advantage of intermediate corrective movements. But the most important point is gradual accumulation and distribution on a scale down or up, and at least some respect for the theory that neither accumulation or distribution need ever be 100 percent completed for the long pull.

> *Trade mostly along with the confirmed major trend, resist the temptation to anticipate a major turn.*

Selection of Operating Stocks

Selection of the best individual stocks to buy and sell will come gradually, as a rule, from experience and practical observation. The student will find that he accumulates certain "pet" issues for various reasons, perhaps because they constitute his longest chart records, perhaps because they offer more perfect patterns, perhaps because he has always been interested in the stock, or perhaps because his forecasts have worked out more profitably in such stocks than in others he has tried.

Such an accumulation of a "pet" list is quite logical and proper, provided it does not lead into stubbornness, into overtrading, into lack of proper diversification or into a narrow point of view which fails to retain an open mind and a keen inquisitiveness into all other charts, or which keeps one from watching for more favorable developments elsewhere.

Having pet stocks is all right, therefore, if it is not carried to an extreme either in time duration or trading volume. If this tendency is carried to an extreme, the student will not only fail to see other better opportunities and find his capital tied up in profitless situations, but he will gradually find himself going stale on his "pet" stocks, with resultant false analysis and loss. Why this "staleness" should result is hard to explain yet every veteran trader has experienced it. Obviously, the proper course then is to drop the "pet" stocks from active trading, turn the attention to a broader list and concentrate on other issues for a while at least.

Diversification of Risk

Diversification of risk is also an important factor in practical chart trading. It is hoped that the reader is by this time not merely convinced of the usefulness of chart patterns but is also quite conscious of their fallibility and sudden reversal. One proper and practical means of turning these two opposing truths to profit is the diversification and limiting of individual risk. The average trader, almost without exception, might better trade in 25-share lots of four different stocks, even though commissions and taxes are higher, rather than confine his operations to 100 shares of only a single stock. And still better if his four stocks are selected from four different groups. The wisdom of this course is perfectly obvious, yet it is strangely uncommon in practice. The trader must constantly fight any inclination to overtrade in single stocks, as well as in the general market. At the opposite extreme, and equally to be avoided, of course, is the dilution of one's trading capital and attention among too many different issues.

Comparative Swing Power of Stocks

One very useful factor to keep in mind when making up a list of stocks to chart with a view to trading in them, is the relative "swing" habits of different groups and of the individual issues in each group. That certain stocks tend habitually to swing both up and down in greater movements, percentage-wise, than others, is a fact well known to experienced traders. Certain issues are notoriously sluggish and disappointing in their price movements, year after year, while others are most spectacular in their ups and downs. Few traders, however, appreciate how remarkably consistent stocks are in their swing habits, and how accurately their relative swing power can be computed from a study of their market history over a term of years.

Careful analysis of the swing habits of a large number of stocks often produces some rather surprising results. It develops, for example, that certain stocks popularly regarded as having characteristically wide and rapid movements, actually offer less profitable opportunities on a percentage basis than others which do not ordinarily attract much public attention. And others, commonly regarded as "doggy", really present excellent percentage movements. The swing power of a stock depends on a number of factors, most important of which is the nature of the industry. Certain industries are little affected, comparatively speaking, by general business conditions. Others fall into the "feast or famine" class, profiting enormously in times of general prosperity and suffering equally conspicuous deficits when business is depressed. Certain companies, by virtue of a more elastic organization, abler management or lower fixed overhead charges, are better able to adapt themselves to changing business conditions than others. Seasonal business trends produce marked ups and downs in the profits of some corporations and this condition is reflected in the wide swings of their stocks.

Capitalization and Leverage Factors

Stocks of which a comparatively small number of shares are outstanding move faster as a rule than those of larger issues. And this condition is further affected by the floating supply – the number of shares, that is, which are ordinarily available for purchase or sale in the market. The leverage factor is also of importance. The common shares of a corporation which has no outstanding bonds or preferred stock, appreciate or depreciate theoretically in exact proportion as the earning power of the company increases or decreases. If, on the other hand, a company has a large funded debt and preferred stock on which it must pay interest and dividends at a fixed rate before the common stock receives any share of the profits, the leverage factor comes markedly into play and the common stock advances or declines at a faster rate than the total profits of the company.

Study the Habits of your Stocks

But over and above the natural and more or less predictable factors affecting stock price movements, there are differences in swing power between individual issues which are attributable only to intangible trading habits. The student will learn in time, if he studies carefully the characteristic movements of his stocks, in terms of percent rather than points or dollars, which of them can be depended upon to return him the greater profits on a given investment.

Consistency of Swing Habits Illustrated

The relative swing power of two different stocks in the same industrial group is graphically portrayed in Fig. XII.1. The two stocks whose gains and losses have been charted thereon are Otis Steel and United States Steel, and their action compared with the concurrent average action of their group of 17 steel stocks. The successive important price advances and declines of US Steel from June, 1932 to June, 1936, are indicated by the solid vertical lines. The advances and declines of Otis Steel at the same time are indicated by the dotted vertical lines.

The zero line on this chart represents the price level from which the group average started each up or down market movement during the period covered. The upper 100 line represents in each case the price level to which the group average attained on the advances, and the lower 100 line the price level to which the group average fell on each decline. In other words, each movement of the average is taken as 100% and the relative movements of the two individual issues are thus compared with the action of the group as a whole on a straight percentage basis.

For example, the first advance of the group after June, 1932, took their average price up 155% above their level at the start. This, for the sake of comparison, is considered 100 on the graph. At the same time, US Steel advanced from 21 to 45, an increase of 114% from its starting level; but Otis Steel advanced 192% from its starting level. As compared with the group action, therefore, 124%. Consequently, the solid line representing US Steel extends up only to 73, while the dotted line representing Otis Steel extends to 124.

The same method has been used in extending the lines for each ensuing decline and advance. It will be noted that the percentage movement of Otis Steel in every case but one (the first intermediate decline) was greater than US Steel; also that it was in all but four out of 34 movements better than the average for the group. US Steel in every case moved less percentage-wise than the group average. The consis-

Fig. XII.1

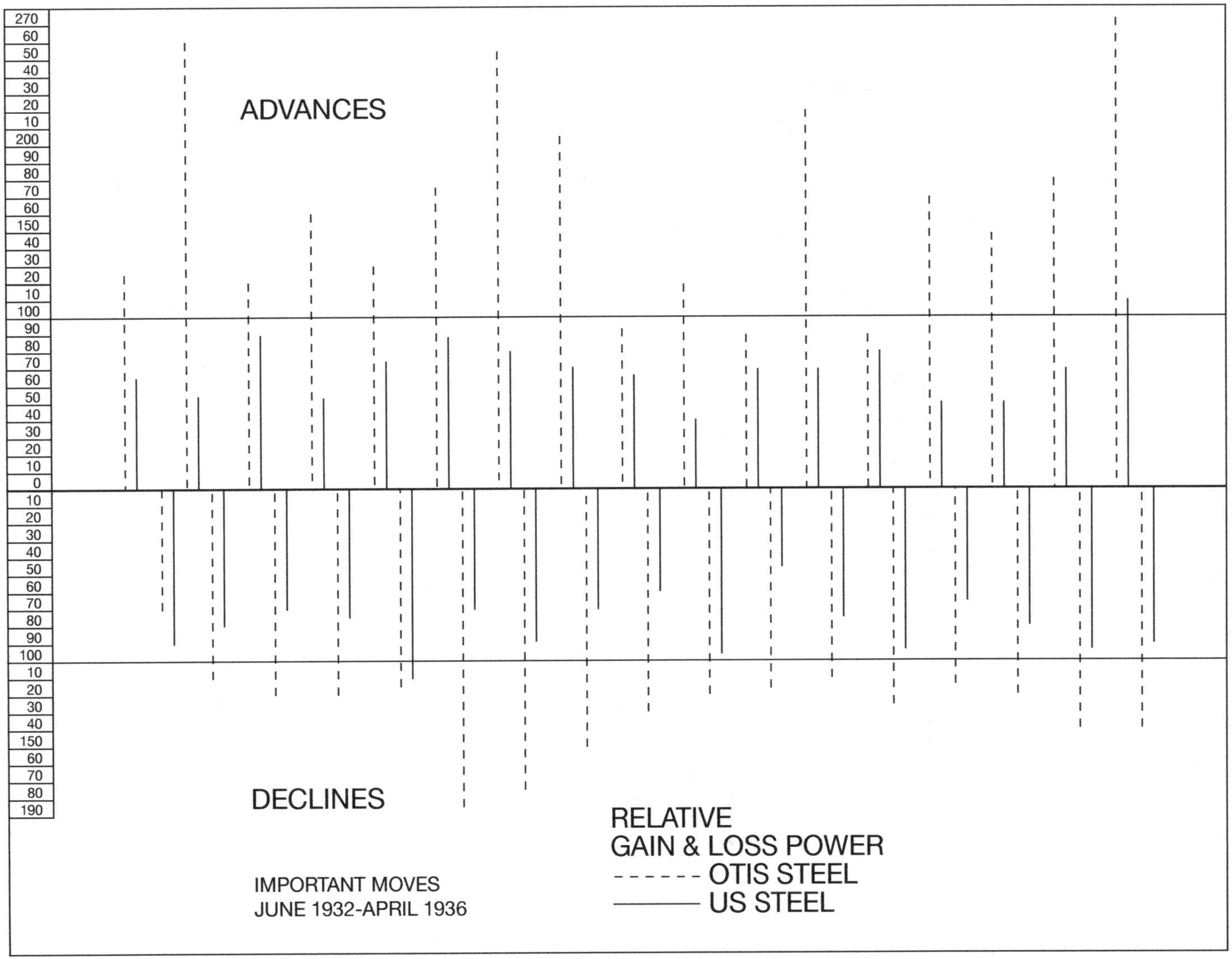

ADVANCES

DECLINES

RELATIVE
GAIN & LOSS POWER
- - - - - OTIS STEEL
———— US STEEL

IMPORTANT MOVES
JUNE 1932–APRIL 1936

tency of these performances through 34 price advances and declines over a period of four years may surprise the student but it is, in no sense, extraordinary. Similar results appear in a study of almost all stocks that have been listed long enough to give a statistical base for computation.

Obviously, the comparison of the relative gain and loss power of US Steel and Otis Steel, suggests that the trader would find it more profitable to chart and to trade in the latter.

Relative Swing Power of Two Rail Stocks

Generally speaking, there seems to be a correlation between price level and swing power. Stocks which sell at high price levels tend to move within a narrower range in terms of percent than do stocks selling at low prices. This is not always apparent to the casual observer who sees Case, for example, go up or down 6 to 10 points in a few days but does not convert this price change into percentage movement. There are plenty of exceptions to the rule, however. One such is illustrated by Fig. XII.2, which shows the movements of Southern Railway and Canadian Pacific as compared with the average movements of their group – the Railroads. The important advances and declines of the average price of 28 railroad stocks from June, 1932 to June, 1936 is taken in each case as 100, and the advances and declines which Southern Railway and Canadian Pacific made at the same time are expressed graphically as percentages of the group movement. Southern Railway is represented by the dotted line and Canadian Pacific by the solid line. In this example it will be seen that the higher-priced stock, Southern Railway, shows consistently greater swing power.

Poor Stocks to Chart

Charting experience will also teach the careful student which stocks do not make good patterns with sufficient frequency to lend safe guidance in trading. Generally speaking, "thin" issues with a small floating supply or an inactive market, do not make distinct patterns and are more easily manipulated by inside operators contrary to chart indications. Also very high-priced issues are apt to make less profitable movements in terms of percentage, as we have stated above in our discussion of swing power. On the other hand, very low-priced issues are apt to make big moves, percentage-wise, in a single day and then move sidewise for a long and patience-trying period – a habit which renders them poor subjects for chart trading. Other things being equal, stocks in the middle price ranges give the most satisfactory chart results.

Fig. XII.2

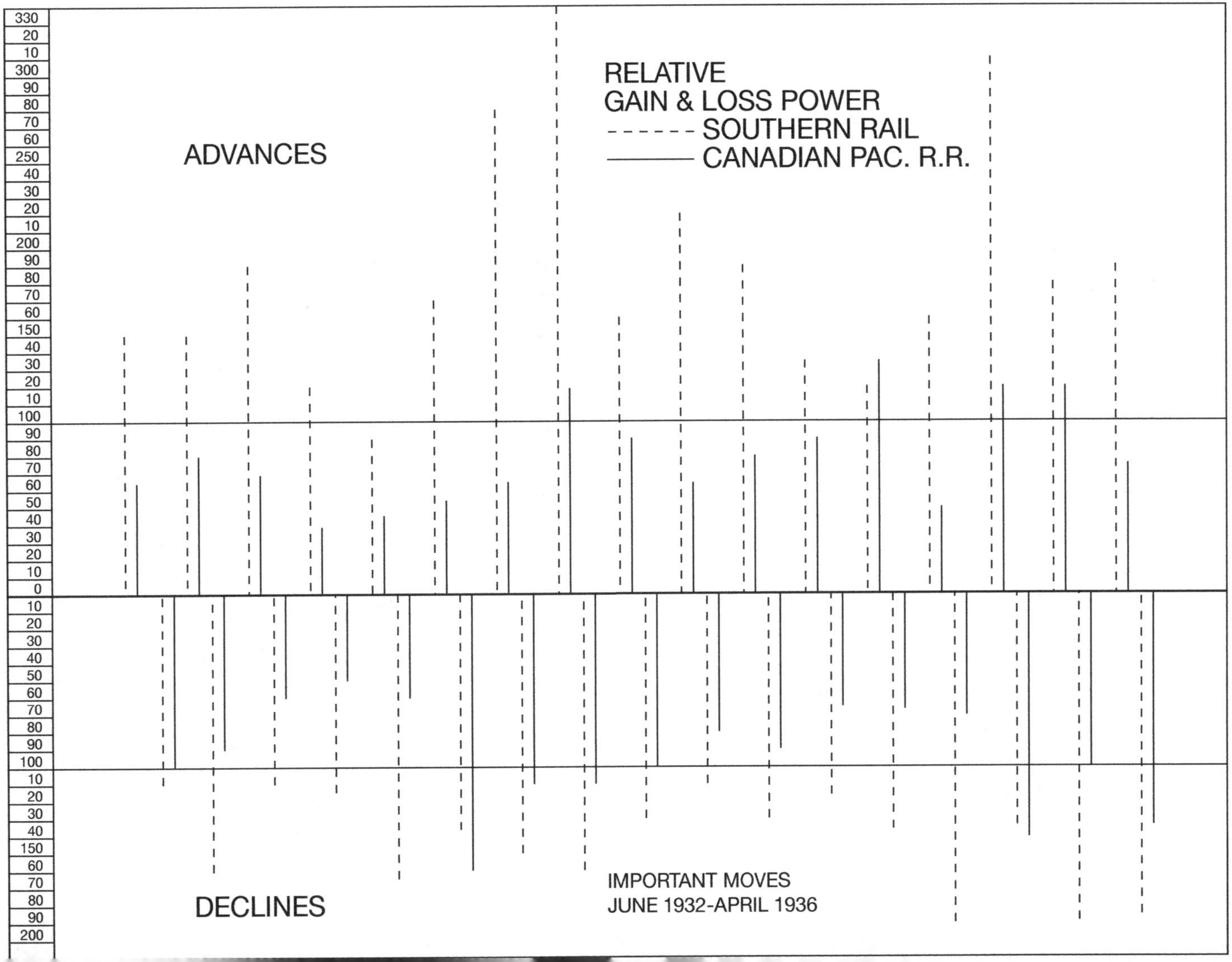

RELATIVE
GAIN & LOSS POWER
----- SOUTHERN RAIL
———— CANADIAN PAC. R.R.

ADVANCES

DECLINES

IMPORTANT MOVES
JUNE 1932–APRIL 1936

Don't Force Chart Pictures

Having selected and charted a number of stocks for a few months, and sometimes even for only a few weeks, the beginner is apt to be led by his enthusiasm for the subject into seeing technical patterns where none in fact exist. This brings up another important rule of practical chart trading: never force the picture. There are constant temptations to read somewhat fantastic analyses into very irregular and imperfect formations. The student will recall that we have sometimes used considerable imagination in suggesting various indefinite patterns in our previous observations on particular charts, especially the monthly charts in this chapter, but that is quite different from risking actual cash upon such suggestions.

Stocks in the middle price ranges give the most satisfactory chart results.

If the indefinite patterns simply confirm the forecast of a definite one, then trading commitments are justified, but the student is never justified in actually trading on the basis of what slightly resembles a specific formation. Chart trading is by no means infallible even on nearly perfect patterns, without adding the risk which arises from careless or wishful analysis through the aid of an active imagination.

Wait for the Ideal Situation

Exercise of the imagination is quite logical in theoretical analysis but when practical trading commitments are at stake let the student wait for the ideal situation. For instance, the practical student will find days, weeks, even months, passing by, in certain individual cases, without a chart presenting any sort of a pattern or formation definite enough to justify an actual trading commitment. His patience will thus be sorely tried at times but it is almost self-evident that patience is a prime requisite and that it is far better to wait for the ideal situation than to rush into actual cash commitments merely through a desire for action when the situation is not strong enough or definite enough to warrant it.

Practical profits are often possible during the process of building formations, but by far the more certain and larger profits are made in the rapid moves in the direction of the major trend which come between these area formations or preparation periods. It is much better to be patient, to restrain one's ambition for profits, and to stay out of the market entirely when no perfect patterns appear for a time, rather than to become impatient and rush in enthusiastically on less than ideal situations. Too hasty action often leads to eventual loss of profits, capital and confidence.

Remember the old traders' adage: "There are three rules for making money in the stock market. They are (1) Patience, (2) Patience, and (3) More Patience.

Too Close Contact with Market Inadvisable

In our occasional references up to now to actual market action taken on technical forecasts, it has been inferred that all trades were to be executed at the opening on the morning following the completed chart picture, or the trading decision. For the normal and average student trader this is unquestionably the best procedure. In all our chart study we have taken the attitude that the student is not watching the ticker, is not in a brokerage office or board-room, is not even in direct touch with his broker. The professional trader, the quick-turn artist, the scalper, may watch the minor moves of the market during the day's trading and may derive benefit

> *Three rules for making money in the stock market are (1) Patience, (2) Patience, and (3) More Patience.*

therefrom in the form of better opportunities for catching sharp swings during the day when they are just getting under way. But the average chart student will seldom if ever lose very much by holding himself aloof from constant communication with the ticker and, indeed, he is much more likely to benefit by divorcing himself from the excitement, the conversation, the gossip, the impetuosities, and the nerve strain, which emanate from watching the erratic fluctuations within the day's market from the dubious vantage point of the board-room. Many professional operators are past masters in the art of so splitting or bunching their orders as to make the tape produce the effect they desire at a certain time of the day on the crowds who are watching it in the board-room.

The ideal aim of the chart student is to let the action of the market speak for itself in forecasting its own technical position, and it is exceedingly difficult to assume the calm open-mindedness necessary for such an ideal, while exposed to the psychological tides of board-room gossip, news, hopes and fears.

Regular Time for Daily Chart Consideration

We have previously noted (in Study I) that it is well for the student to have one certain, regular and habitual time each day for making up his charts, preferably after the close in the evening. He can then evaluate the day's movements at his leisure, bestowing as much or little time as seems necessary from the importance of the shifting scene, and if he is not in close touch with his broker, he can make out his orders in calm and unhurried serenity and mail them the same evening, to reach his broker early the next morning.

Limited vs. Market Orders

In our practical trading examples we have also assumed that orders are entered "at the market" rather than at limit prices. We hold to no dogmatic theory or rule on this point. There are plenty of occasions when it is more advisable to place limit orders and to take the smaller chance of missing out on execution and possibly even on a profitable move, rather than to take the larger chance of being caught by an overnight spread, or a wide opening. Limit orders are generally advisable, of course, in excited trading, where spreads are probable, or on important news breaking after the close. They are also useful where the habitual, or probable, daily range is wide, and where it seems logical that some time during the following day will see the price temporarily at a more favorable level than is probable at the opening.

With such not so very common exceptions, however, it would seem to be the better policy to trade at the market instead of with limit orders. The disappointments and losses and errors of judgment which result from the failure of execution on limit orders more than outweigh, in the long run, the small advantages which may accrue. In the majority of cases the trader is not justified in trading at all unless he can see the probability of a worthwhile move of at least four or five points.

It is manifestly foolish and illogical, therefore, for the trader to take a chance on missing out entirely on this profitable move of many points merely on the chance that he may save from a fraction to a point or so by placing a limit order instead of a market order.

Intestinal Fortitude – a Word to the Naturally Conservative

In concluding our discussion of various practical suggestions for using our basic chart knowledge: in actual trading, a word about "nerve" or intestinal fortitude may not be out of place. We hesitate to address this portion of our observations to the general mass of average readers because in most cases we find that the average student is more apt to need words of caution and of restraint rather than encouragement to action. But there is most certainly a definite type of individual who is so conservative as to need a word or two on decision and initiative and action. Whether fortunately or unfortunately, this class of personality is in the minority, but it may frankly be stated that it is this class, also, which makes the most consistent success in technical chart trading.

The student who has the innate character most favorable to profitable chart trading is the individual who will naturally attain to a conservative and skeptical attitude toward all of our chart rules, and will therefore fear to tread where others, less capable perhaps, rush in blindly and over-confidently to their ultimate loss. Though those of careful and skeptical temperament are probably in the minority, they are the successful minority, and our constant reiteration of caution, conservatism and mistrust of all technical rule and theory has probably struck in them a more responsive chord than in the larger group for whom such admonitions are intended. This small, conservative class of souls may therefore need to pay special attention to our final advice of this study, which is the gospel of decisive action when conscientious study has led to definite and sincerely grounded conclusions.

The Too Conservative Student

The conservative student will err on that side of his nature. He may, for that reason, be more successful in the long run. But, contrary as it may seem, he must guard against over-conservatism, against over-caution, against too much doubt and timidity. The chief stumbling block for this type is his hesitation. He reasons out a perfectly clear and correct case for a certain type of direct and definite action. Then he weighs the opposite possibilities too carefully, and decides to wait.

His market movement gets away from him. His judgment was correct but the longer he procrastinates, the more hesitant he becomes, the more psychologically uncertain, and the less likely to make profit from his correct analysis. The result of such procrastination is not only a possible psychological upset but, in not uncommon cases, the tendency finally to force himself to rush in without the usual careful analysis and sound sense, at a time when the movement which was forecast with proper logic some time ago, is just about over with, or is about to reverse itself for a technical correction at least.

The Conservative vs. the Overconfident Type

The reader must decide for himself in which class he belongs, and he should have no great difficulty in properly determining whether this advice is for him or for an entirely different dispostion. If it is for him, then his aim should be to give direct and prompt expression to the dictates of his study and analysis, once they have led him to a basically sound conclusion.

The individual who is naturally conservative and calculating, will find a special blessing in recourse to the stop-loss order. By using this type of protection whenever he fears the upsetting of a conscientious and searching analysis, he may venture definite action on his conviction, with the serenity that comes from knowing exactly how much it is possible to lose in case the market does move unexpectedly in opposition to analytical conclusions.

We do not want to give the impression that the individual who cannot sincerely place himself in this class of conservative or cautious traders is doomed to failure in practical chart trading. Far from it. It merely happens that conservatism in moderate doses is a propitious characteristic for market success, but conservatism may be carried to profitless extremes just as easily as radicalism. A healthy mingling of decisiveness and conservatism is the ideal mixture for the successful trader, as for most other careers as well.

The Danger of Stubborness

The decisiveness which we have recommended to the too conservative trader as a desirable quality to cultivate should not, however, be carried to the extreme of over-confidence or stubborn persistence in a decision which has been contraverted by subsequent chart action. If the stock does not act according to one's primary analysis, then the market itself is trying to tell the trader to change that analysis.

One of the greatest fundamental mistakes which the chart trader can make is to assume that success or failure is the result entirely of his own analysis. This is perhaps true to a large degree but it is a dangerous attitude for it tends to make the trader feel that the market movement rests upon him, upon his analysis, upon his ideas of what should happen in the future, and thus it begets both over-confidence and stubbornness. The successful trader should realize that his analysis has nothing to do directly with market movement. It is not the trader telling the market what it must do, but rather the market telling the trader. The market speaks constantly, and through technical analysis the trader tries to interpret and understand the market's action and advice. But it is important always to realize that the market can change its tone of converse at any moment and that preconceived notions based upon previous technical whisperings are distinctly out of place.

> *Not the trader telling the market what it must do, but the market telling the trader.*

If the market action was the foundation of a technical forecast last week but has not acted in accordance with that forecast during the present week, then give technical action the right to change its mind and thus the trader's mind, and do not assume a stubborn attitude, of feeling that last week's analysis, however ideal and certain it seemed then, must endure indefinitely.

But Give the Market a Chance to Act

On the other hand, the technical chart trader must not lack in patience. Stubbornness and overconfidence are to be avoided, but so are impatience and over-eagerness for quick action. There is no necessity for changing last week's analysis simply because it has not worked out as quickly as was then indicated. There is no reason for changing one's mind or market position on a basis merely of delay, sluggishness or inactivity, but only on the basis of true and definite action in direct opposition to the previous analysis.

Review of our various chart examples cited in previous studies will serve to present myriad examples where the analysis was correct but where the indications came early in the technical formations and where considerable patience was needed to carry out successfully the initial forecast. If a commitment is justified at all by the chart action the fulfillment is worth waiting for patiently.

Weigh Risks in Advance

Another general principle, somewhat allied with all of the foregoing but especially with a healthy conservatism, is a rational weighing of the total risk involved in any commitment, in advance of making that commitment. This principle implies that before any individual stock is bought or sold, the trader will assume that his hopes, his expectations, his plans, his technical analysis, may all turn out to be just about 100% wrong. Postulating the action of the stock on that basis, he should consider what course he would pursue if such an unfortunate event should come to pass.

This may seem like an easy, logical and commonplace thing to do, but it is, in fact, extremely uncommon among the general run of traders. The truth is that the great majority of stock market losses would be completely avoided if such a mental process of looking ahead at both sides of the situation were indulged in. The average trader, even of fair experience and ability, is so prone to become wrapped up in his own analysis, his own expectations of what is going to happen to the commitment he is about to make, that he fails to give any thought whatever to the other side of the picture which may possibly develop after he has actually made his commitment.

If a trader is considering the purchase of a stock at around 45 he is naturally confident that it is going to advance and his mind is filled with the pleasant anticipation of selling out the stock later on at around 55, perhaps, or 60. His analysis may well be correct, but something may transpire to upset it entirely, and he is false to his own position if he fails to weigh the most serious consequences that may befall him in the, even remote, possibility of his judgment being wrong, or of the market's turning unexpectedly against him.

Helps to Avoid Over-trading

Such a mental weighing of all possibilities, including the worst, brings rewards either through cutting of losses, through freedom from over-worry or, more usually, through the guarantee of well-laid plans for any possible contingency. Consideration of every possibility brings a healthy conservatism, perhaps desertion of the anticipated commitment or, better still, either an actual or a mental stop-loss price at which the possible future loss will be limited.

It is likely also to result in scale trading, or at least in keeping down to conservative levels the units of trading. This latter point is an important one. Over-trading brings much greater loss, financial and psychological, than it does profit. That assertion can be guaranteed, purely from the wealth of his own experience, by any market analyst and adviser, before whose consideration pass many living examples of the failures that result originally, almost entirely and directly, from over-trading.

This fault was at the bottom of the majority of tremendous losses and even tragedies which followed the "new era" bull market of 1929. Profits seemed so certain that the average trader did not stop to think about losses. So long as he could borrow money he never stopped to consider how much he might possibly lose through his over-trading commitment if his judgment should be wrong. If he thought first of buying 20 shares of a certain stock he immediately calculated mentally the profit which a 10 point advance would bring him. But that was only $200. Not enough. Not fast enough. The simple way to increase profits faster was merely to increase his commitment, even on slender margin, to say 100 shares with a mental profit of $1,000, or to 1,000 shares, with a mental profit of $10,000.

But he forgot utterly about considering his potential and possible loss if the stock declined instead of advancing. He forgot entirely about the bleak prospects of long years of worry, struggle, despair which he might have to spend in paying off his loan, in recouping his capital, if, by some odd chance, things did not go just as he fondly imagined they must go.

Avoid over-trading, and decide before you go into the market how much of your total capital you should risk in your trading operations. Don't spread yourself out too thin; keep something always in reserve against the unexpected.

Don't Lean Too Heavily on Outside Advice

Finally, when all that we have learned from this course of study, from experience, from studious research, from all other channels, has been digested and made a part of our practical market knowledge, let us remember that we are our own masters in the matter of personal market actions. Let us remember that no one is infallible, any more than our charts are infallible, that no finite being has the ability to foresee exactly what any stock is going to do.

Let us remember then that, within reasonable boundaries, and still avoiding overconfidence and self-sufficiency, we have approximately an equal basis for analysis with most other traders; that the garnering of various rumors, opinions and news figments, is likely to distract our attention from a genuinely sound and scientific approach to our problem; and that if we are intent on analyzing pure technical action, we shall not need to clutter up our imaginations too much with outside facts. The market itself will evaluate all such data for us, together with much important inside information that we could not obtain for ourselves or from our most trusted authorities.

We need not shut our eyes to fundamentals, or close our minds to basic trends and figures, to earning reports, balance sheets, business prospects, public psychology and such elements of assistance. Our technical chart studies are merely supplemented by such aids when they are reliable, are properly evaluated and reasonably used. But we need pay scant attention, in our technical analysis, to ticker talk, to board-room gossip, to brokerage advice, rumor, uncon-firmed report and hearsay.

> *The garnering of various rumors, opinions and news figments, is likely to distract our attention.*

Let the Market Do its Own Forecasting

In short, we may let the market, and our proper analysis of its own technical action, be sufficient for our own personal guide as to what is going on inside the secret sanc-tums of the directors' meeting room, the corporation order books, the private con-ferences of professional operators and the other indefinite mediums of gossip and unfounded rumor.

We need not go near a brokerage office in person; we need certainly not hang over the ticker or devour the news releases as they come over the heated wires. Without ignoring other basic news and confirmed information, we may rather sit back in our own office or study, not secure in our own conceit, not smug with contented over-confidence, but assured none the less that if we have properly prepared ourselves, properly attuned our inner ear and eye, with study, with patience, with hard work, experience and understanding, then our most faithful friend in practical market operation is the market itself, as it outlines in the present its probable future course for those who can successfully read its signs and signals.

Judging Personal Aptitude for Chart Trading

By no means will every individual find himself eminently fitted for chart trading. For one thing, it requires time, interest and patience to a fairly high degree. Proba-bly the most important characteristics are a basic sincerity and a desire to learn, for practical experience is the fundamental key to success. And only actual trading or simulation of actual trading, will show the neophyte how well-fitted he is for suc-cessful and active trading.

It would be slightly foolhardy for an inexperienced student to plunge immediately into practical trading with cold, hard-earned cash, to test his mettle. Paper trading is the proper substitute and affords a pleasant, painless and comparatively simple means of testing groundwork, experience and practical ability in the market without the immediate risk of capital.

Paper trading requires no cash, no brokerage account, no rash plunge into the maelstrom of actual trading. It requires merely an adequate set of charts and a notebook. If the paper trader will study his charts, formulate his opinion of proper action, and enter his theoretical trades on paper for anywhere from a month to a year, and will follow this test with perseverance, with regularity, with close simulation of actual cash trading, and above all with conscientious honesty and sincerity to himself, he should discover very quickly whether or not it would be wise for him to continue his technical trading with the risk of actual cash capital.

Paper Trading

If paper profits do not work out successfully under the conditions of trading previously tested, the student need not lose hope, though he should assuredly refrain from entering the market until he has hit upon different methods which do yield a consistent profit. He may need to trade more actively, but more probably less actively. He may be better suited for long-swing trading, for cyclical investment or for commitment in only certain lines.

The worst that can happen, in any case, is a paper loss, and if the student is sincerely interested, then further testing, longer experience and healthy patience should lead him to discover ultimate success on such foundations as have tried to set forth in our study.

SUMMARY AND REVIEW

In the earlier chapters of our course we have attempted a fairly complete observation of the individual chart patterns which may prove of assistance in our general study of technical stock market action. In the later chapters we have attempted to co-ordinate this material into a comprehensive science from which the student may proceed to his own practice and experience in technical analysis.

As we come to the end of our Course, therefore, it should be helpful to devote a little time to a general summary. In reviewing our catalog of formations, for instance, there are certain chart patterns which generally suggest reversal of the previous price movement. Most of these are area formations of some sort, and are little more than varying pictures of a highly normal and natural rounding off process as the reverse technical strength increases, gradually overcomes the technical strength of the preceding movement, and brings about a reversal of price trend.

Reviewing the Reversal Family

Thus we have the Head and Shoulders formation, the Common Turn, the Multiple patterns, the Complex pictures with double heads and double shoulders, and the Broadening Top. The Triangles, we have seen, may lead to either reversal or continuation, but are probably to be found more frequently as continuation formations. In the minor area reversal group we have also the Wedge, the Rectangle and the Diamond. All of these reversal formations are simply the varying pictures which result from a straight price movement meeting technical strength in the opposite direction and being gradually overcome by it. More or less in a class by itself we have the Island Reversal.

Certain chart patterns generally suggest reversal of the previous price movment.

Many of these various formations, in actual chart observation, tend to verge from one picture into another, yet that need not bother us much because their indication is much more important than their specific pattern to which we can give one name or another, so long as in any case the indication is for reversal of the previous price movement. The critical lines – the lines whose breaking becomes the signal for action – are apt to be clearly defined regardless of the exact classification of the pattern, especially when the all-important volume indications are watched with care.

Reviewing the Continuation Family

In the classification of continuation patterns, the Symmetrical Triangle stands probably at the head of the list. Then we have the various other forms of Triangle, including the Ascending and the Descending types in which the hypotenuse indicates the direction of the ensuing move. Next we have the Rectangles and the less definite pattern to which we have given the name of Continuation Head and Shoulders. We have noted the Flags and Pennants as being especially reliable continuation formations. Then we have the price congestions with Drooping Bottoms and Accelerating Peaks, the Horns, and such minor indications as the Zig-zag formation, One Day Out-of-line Movements, Scallops, etc.

Other Special Figures and General Consideration

In addition to these specific chart pictures we have the additional helpful suggestions resulting from the application of other more general factors, such as resistance levels, support levels, the factor of sales volume taken in relation to the price movement, and the highly important influence of trend lines, single and parallel, fanning and flattening. And then, rather in a class by themselves, we have the entire family of Gaps, which add their suggestions to the general pattern. We have the Common Gap, the Continuation Gap, the Break-away Gap, and the Exhaustion Gap, as well as the measuring theories based on single and multiple Gaps for determining the possible extent of the ensuing move.

We would not for a moment have the student expect that he will make use of every one of the patterns, chart formations, rules, theories and hypotheses included in our study, in his every observation of practical chart action. We have tried to point out the more important points in our catalog but it must also be remembered that it is somewhat of a catalog none the less. We have attempted to present a complete study of all the chart forms and theories which have proved to have forecasting value and, for the sake of completeness, have included many points of minor character which the average reader will perhaps have comparatively few occasions to use in actual practice.

The Question of Too Much Theory

We are quite sensible, for instance, to the possible criticism that we have presented too much theory. The skeptical critic may perhaps remark that while any major price movement is reversing its previous direction the chart is almost bound to present some sort of a picture resembling one of our many reversal formations, and that when we add the warning that even such patterns may often be fallible and misleading, the entire framework of our science falls to pieces in one great shamble of truisms. Such a criticism is so patent a misunderstanding of all that chart theory claims and implies that it probably would never even occur to the average reader or the experienced student, but it is only fair to expose its fallacy to the possible few who have missed the fundamental point of our theoretical science and reasoning.

Have called attention to certain laws and rules which have been working from time immemorial but have never before been clearly defined.

The advocate of stock chart theory does not lay claim to having evolved any new principles of fundamental technical action but merely to have called attention to certain laws and rules which have been working from time immemorial but which have never before been clearly defined, definitely recognized or cataloged into any set routine of science. The very simplicity of the logic behind our various chart theories is not only the basis of such criticism as has been above proposed, but is its best answer as well.

Chart Science Chiefly a Cataloging of Experience

We can admit freely and frankly, for instance, that practically any process of technical market reversal will fall, naturally and logically, into some one of our many reversal patterns. But, after all, that is all that we claim, or need to claim, to prove the usefulness of such patterns. The various patterns are simply a practical aid in detecting the development of a price reversal. Our definition of all these patterns, our various technical names for them, are merely an aid to the study of the laws that have always existed. They are made much more simple, much more easily understandable, definite and practical by the process of their cataloging and definition.

The science of astronomy does not lay claim to having influenced the movement of planets in their orbit, but merely to have cataloged facts which have always existed, simply to make the study of those facts easier and thus to lead into the observation of additional facts and laws. So the science of technical chart reading lays no claim to influencing the market or to developing new laws by which the market must act, but rather only to the cataloging of facts, reactions, laws and theories which have always existed, in order to clarify the study of the market and make easier further additions to the knowledge which goes to make up our science.

Why Charts Are Not Infallible

Unfortunately, the stock market and our stock charts do not move in such fixed and exact natural cycles as the planets studied by astronomers. Consequently we have always the danger of false moves and other misleading phenomena in our study of technical market action. The elements of human fallibility, of unforeseeable news development, of sudden catastrophe, or sudden improvement and of consequent quick changes in popular psychology, all make our normal rules of technical chart action liable to error, to fallibility, to sudden change of forecast. But, in further defense of chart theories, it may merely be mentioned that in perhaps the majority of such cases, it is not the fundamental indication of the chart which has gone astray so much as the plans of the traders or investors whose operations were leading toward a definite major forecast and movement.

The average investor knows how often his attitude toward the market or a specific stock changes overnight, either because of some piece of news or merely because of a psychological reversal of heart. But only the insider knows how often professional operators are fooled in their carefully laid plans, how often they accumulate a stock and are just ready to put it up, with the chart already indicating that projected upward move, when the market grows too weak, when other factors intervene, when, for any number of reasons, it suddenly becomes impractical to carry out the original plans, and the stock is dumped overboard in a hurried scramble to unload, even with a heavy loss to the insiders. Such developments cannot be foreseen by the stock chart any more than by the operators whose trading influences the forecast of that chart.

Chart Deception Engineered by Operators

Insiders and professional traders are by no means unaware of the growing public interest and education in chart theories and patterns. In normal trading there are certainly not enough chart traders to make it worthwhile for the professionals to play against them instead of against the general public, but we have learned that the professionals must play against someone in order to make their money. It is quite conceivable, therefore, that the insiders might take a "crack" at chart traders now and then by manipulating false patterns in their campaign stocks, with the knowledge that, by arranging certain chart pictures, they could draw in a certain amount of buying or selling, as they chose, with a view to strengthening their own position.

This theory gives the professional credit for more power, perhaps, than he actually possesses, but it is merely a theory. The student's best defense, and his best policy in any case, is in keeping and watching a goodly number of individual charts. The professional can hardly swing more than a handful of his pet individual issues to suit himself, much less the market as a whole, and the misleading action of a few individual charts will often be adequately exposed by the contrary indications of a great many other ones.

And then, of course, there is always available the protection of the stop-loss order, deserting situations which do not work out properly, as well as the inevitable development of new technical indications which help the student to revise his forecast and market position. It is reasonably safe to say that even the most powerful and well-financed of operators cannot long prevent the chart's showing the true technical picture.

A PROGRAM FOR THE BEGINNER

Having completed this Course, the student is now ready to test himself and his newly acquired theoretical knowledge in actual market operations. If he was a trader of some experience to begin with he has, no doubt, already charted stocks and applied some of his technical theories to them, perhaps has even made a few trades on the basis of technical action. And the novice, in his quite natural impatience for action, has probably begun to keep at least a few charts and to try out thereon his new forecasting rules. Nevertheless, it should be helpful to both if we outline a reasonably complete program of action – the practical steps which the beginner should now take to put his studies into profitable use. In outlining this program we shall simply be bringing together, for the most part, the detailed suggestions as to procedure which have been made in various chapters of our Course, but assembling them into a definite working plan.

For the student who has already made some sort of start (which, as we have said in the foregoing, is certainly to be expected in the great majority of cases) this program will serve as a means of checking his technique, calling his attention perhaps to certain points which he may have overlooked or suggesting certain changes in his present procedure which he may find it profitable to try out at least. Our program, however, will be only suggestive; each trader, in the final analysis, will have to discover for himself the methods which are best adapted to his abilities and to the time and money he can safely devote to his trading operations.

1. Making Up the List

The logical first step in our program is the selection of the list of stocks to be charted with a view to trading in such of them as develop profitable opportunities from time to time. The more important points to be considered in making up this list were discussed in Studies I and XI. We may summarize them briefly as follows:

A. Number to Chart.
Time is the limiting factor here. The best results generally speaking, are obtained by charting as many individual stocks as one is able to maintain and study thoroughly every day. Fifty is a good number. Less than 25 will hardly provide the necessary background for comparison or a reliable reading of the general market trends. More than 50 is fine provided one has the time to both maintain and study them. The personal equation enters here. With a little practice, the entering of the data is simple and easy, but do not attempt to keep up more charts than you can or will find time to analyze and interpret. The more charts you keep, obviously the more good, clear opportunities for trading you will discover, but remember that you will have to discover them yourself, that the mere keeping of a large mass of undigested chart record will not automatically bring them to your attention. Finally, don't waste your time keeping charts of stocks in which you would not be willing to trade.

B. Diversification.
Because some industries prosper while others decline, because the stocks of certain groups are moving in the market while others are standing still, it is best to select a well-diversified list for charting. Include at least one or two good trading stocks from each important industrial group. Beyond that, your personal preferences may be allowed reasonable scope.

C. Price Level and Capitalization.

With certain exceptions, stocks in the middle price ranges are most satisfactory for technical study and trading. Avoid "cheap" stocks – those selling under 10, say – unless you have some very good personal reason for following one or two of them. Concentrate on stocks selling in the general 15 to 60 range. Select actively traded issues with a reasonably large number of shares outstanding, but here again the middle ground is best. Thin stocks with a very small floating supply are easily manipulated and are apt to move erratically without developing good chart patterns. Stocks of extremely large issue, on the other hand, are usually sluggish in their market action and offer limited trading profits except on a very long term basis. There are, of course, exceptions to both rules.

D. Swing Power.

This consideration in the selection of stocks for charting and trading purposes entails a study of the back history. If the back weekly or monthly charts, preferably the former for a period of years, are available for analysis they will show graphically which of two issues habitually moves in wider and, consequently, more profitable swings. If charts are not available, the percentage spread between the yearly high and low prices over several years as published in a great many statistical services and brokers bulletins will give a fair indication of swing habits.

E. Group and General Market Averages.

Our advice is not to bother with either. They are, as we have previously stated, likely to be more confusing than helpful to the average trader. However, if you feel that you want to watch them, general market average charts are published in many magazines and newspapers and may be followed therein. Group charts also are published in certain weekly and monthly magazines. If you wish to chart certain group averages for yourself a weekly record should suffice for all practical trading purposes.

F. Changes in the List.

This is a question which, naturally, will not come up until after you have kept charts for some little time. It is brought up here only to introduce the general advice not to drop a stock from your chart portfolio without good reason for doing so. A certain chart may present an uninteresting, even tiresome, picture of inactivity for months but that is no reason to discontinue it in favor of some other issue which may be attracting public attention at the time by its spectacular action. The chances are that the inactive stock will eventually have its turn and, when it comes, you will be glad you have the complete record and early, first-hand information of its movement.

2. Starting the Charts

Having selected the list of stocks which we are going to chart and study, the next step, naturally, is to start the charts. The matters of paper to use, time and price scale, sources of data, etc. were covered in detail in Study I (pages 14–21) and it is hardly necessary for us to review them here. Start keeping daily charts on the entire list at once, and weekly charts as the data accumulates and time permits.

There is, however, one important step in connection with the actual charting, which you should take at this time. Get or make up the weekly charts on your chosen stocks back at least to the beginning of the last completed cyclical trend. Analyze these back weekly charts carefully to determine the probable support or resistance levels that may appear in the current trend (see Study IX). Note these levels on the newly started current daily charts. Analyze also the nearby back history as depicted on the weekly charts to determine whether any trend lines developed on the weekly charts should be projected on the current daily charts.

This study of trends, besides enabling you to project what may appear to be important lines on our new charts, will determine in most cases the basic trends in which your stocks are moving. You will make use of this information in establishing your general trading policy later, following the rule of always trading, so far as possible, with the major trend.

3. Studying the Patterns

Having studied the back record and transferred to your new daily charts such information derived therefrom as lends itself to current interpretation, your next step should be to watch for and try to discover significant patterns or other price and volume action of forecasting value. You will hardly be able to do this with much confidence until you have posted at least a month of new daily record; begin then, however, to draw (in pencil, very lightly) all lines bounding the minor trends and areas of price congestions that may appear. It will develop very quickly that some of these lines have no continuing significance; they should be erased or at least disregarded. Other lines will have to be slightly re-drawn as the price action progresses. One point which the beginner frequently forgets is that trend lines and pattern boundaries are drawn across established reversal points. It takes at least two such points to determine a good chart line. Not until a price movement has actually been reversed is a reversal point established. The reversal need not be an important one in extent or duration; it may be a matter of only a minor fluctuation lasting two or three days and extending over a range of only two or three points, but it must have actually occurred, nevertheless, before its reversal point is known and can be used in technical analysis.

At the same time, follow the action of volume closely, watching particularly the action of prices when volume tends to decline and when it suddenly increases.

Compare the price levels at which patterns or congestions develop with the support and resistance levels suggested by the back history. Study the action of prices as these levels are approached and after they have been penetrated.

Compare the patterns formed simultaneously on different charts and make tentative forecasts of the relative possibilities for profit which they present, taking into account trend action, support and resistance levels and other measuring indications if any. (See Study X.) Check your forecasts by the subsequent price action.

4. Studying Price Movements

When a profitable price movement takes place, unexpectedly perhaps, look back to see from what patterns or foundation it proceeded and what break-out signal was given. If your daily chart does not show what appears to be an adequate foundation for the move, look back on the weekly chart to see if a forecasting pattern appeared there.

Watch for break-outs and study the extent of price movement and volume action attending them. Note the closing price levels. Study the action and reaction of prices following break-outs.

5. Trading on Paper

After you have charted your stocks for at least a couple of months and have learned by trial and error which pattern and trend lines are apt to be most reliable, and after you have made a number of tentative forecasts and checked them by subsequent events, start trading on paper.

Conduct your paper trading exactly as though you were managing a real trading account with actual cash capital. Keep an exact record of each buy and sell order, each stop-loss order, and the results of each trade, as well as brokers' commissions and taxes. Keep your commitments within the bounds of your assumed trading capital. Don't fool yourself by assuming that you had done something which it develops later you should have done but which you did not, in fact, do at the time. Second guesses don't count if you are sincerely desirous of perfecting your judgment and your technique.

Don't worry about the opportunities you may have missed because you didn't see them at the time or because your capital was already tied up in other situations. Study rather to recognize your mistakes and the reasons for them. Remember that your mistakes will be of greater value to you in your ultimate success than your correct forecasts. Learn to avoid the losses, and the gains will take care of themselves.

But remember also that there will always and inevitably be some losses, so don't let yourself be unduly upset by an occasional miscarriage of plans. Learn to use stop-loss orders correctly to cut your losses short when the unexpected happens.

6. The Final Test

After you have traded on paper for several months and have thoroughly demonstrated to your own complete satisfaction that your forecasts are working out profitably, then and not until then, take the final test. Put a part of your cash trading capital actually into the market. Now you may find that you are beset by an entirely new set of problems – worries, doubts and temptations which did not trouble you in your paper trading. Your first cash trades may not work out. But don't lose your confidence. Don't be stampeded into changing your tactics; don't listen to tips and rumors any more than you did before; follow the same methods which you followed in your successful trading on paper. Analyze your mistakes and study how to overcome the tendencies which prevented you from putting theory into successful practice. Go back to paper trading, perhaps, for another course of schooling and then try again.

INDEX OF FIGURES BY NUMBER

INDEX OF FIGURES BY SUBJECT

INDEX TO FIGURE REFERENCES

Pages in text on which references are made to figures

INDEX OF SUBJECTS

THE BEST
QUALITY
EDITIONS

of

THE BEST
FINANCIAL
BOOKS

CPSIA information can be obtained
at www.ICGtesting.com
Printed in the USA
JSHW040439190321
12714JS00003B/14

9 780857 199164